MW01222896

Nietzsche and the Necessity of Freedom

Nietzsche and the
Necessity of Freedom

JOHN MANDALIOS

LEXINGTON BOOKS

A division of
ROWMAN & LITTLEFIELD PUBLISHERS, INC.
Lanham • Boulder • New York • Toronto • Plymouth, UK

LEXINGTON BOOKS

A division of Rowman & Littlefield Publishers, Inc.
A wholly owned subsidiary of The Rowman & Littlefield Publishing Group, Inc.
4501 Forbes Boulevard, Suite 200
Lanham, MD 20706

Estover Road
Plymouth PL6 7PY
United Kingdom

British Library Cataloguing in Publication Information Available

Library of Congress Cataloging-in-Publication Data

Mandalios, John, 1958–
  Nietzsche and the necessity of freedom / John Mandalios.
     p. cm.
  Includes bibliographical references and index.
  ISBN-13: 978-0-7391-1004-1 (cloth : alk. paper)
  ISBN-10: 0-7391-1004-7 (cloth : alk. paper)
  1. Nietzsche, Friedrich Wilhelm, 1844–1900. 2. Liberty. I. Title.
  B3318.L43.M36 2008
  193—dc22   2007047762

Printed in the United States of America

♾™ The paper used in this publication meets the minimum requirements of American
National Standard for Information Sciences—Permanence of Paper for Printed Library
Materials, ANSI/NISO Z39.48–1992.

To Ελευθερία and Αλέχανδρος Mandalios
– for their vital Alexandrianism

Contents

Figures

Abbreviations of Nietzsche's Works

A   The Anti-Christ
BGE   Beyond Good and Evil
BT   Birth of Tragedy Out of the Spirit of Music
D   Daybreak: Thoughts on the Prejudices of Morality
EH   Ecce Homo
GM   On the Genealogy of Morality
GS   The Gay Science
HH   Human, All Too Human I
AOM   II: Assorted Opinions and Maxims
WS   II: The Wanderer and His Shadow
PP   The Pre-Platonic Philosophers
TI   Twilight of the Idols
UO   Unfashionable Observations
Z   Thus Spoke Zarathustra

. *For unpublished notes and notebooks*
WP   Will to Power (compilation by Elisabeth Nietzsche and Peter Gast)
UW   Unpublished Writings: from the period of Unfashionable Observations

Reference to Nietzsche's works and passages follow conventions of citation by abbreviated title section numbers rather than page numbers. Abbreviations of Nietzsche's published works translated into English refer to translations of Walter Kaufmann and Reginald J. Hollingdale except where otherwise indicated. References to *Twilight of the Idols* ('TI') refer to chapter and section number respectively; and '*P*' refers to the preface of the work cited. Limited use of Nietzsche's unpublished notes from his *Nachlass* reflects the philological point that notes are indicative, not final, statements of an author's thoughts and arguments. Notes consistent with (Nietzsche's) published material have been incorporated in the analysis.

Preface

As words and thoughts emerge of necessity out of affects and states of the soul, this project grew out of the struggle to understand the 'eminence of one's task' (EH Why am I so wise 4) from a perspective of therapeutic liberation. Nietzsche understood both his and our struggle for joy as the imperative, the necessity, to 'liberate the soul' from the victory of resentment as the 'first step toward recovery' (6). Yet recovery—from oneself, malaise, decline and sickness of soul—brings to the fore an inexorable impulse for freedom, for *becoming* recovered, vital and joyous, that is, *becoming* free. For Nietzsche 'freedom' was never a static concept or state. Nietzsche and life itself are both tough masters and my *logos* in the present work I sincerely hope reflects such a struggle. Through loss and gain, degeneration and growth, melancholy and joy, destiny and will, and rule and good conscience, one looks on the horizon beyond recovery. Necessity *and* freedom at some point in time became the evident horizon upon which the future lay ahead. For even the Wanderer has a future beyond simple 'recovery' and good health—Dionysus shows it. Nietzsche's tragic wisdom charges us to create a future *out of* freedom so that we may reign as free creative spirits.

Investigation of Nietzsche's corpus, following work pursued at Cambridge University and the British Library with the generous help and support of Bryan Turner—as well as leave taken from the Faculty of Arts of Griffith University (Australia)—lead inexorably to a puzzling question. If Nietzsche the philologist had encountered the limits of historicism and the aesthetic justification of life, what did he envisage as the possible future for the human being who had finally transvaluated decadence? What, in other words, follows on from our encounter with the Nothing and (cultural) decline. If it is neither scientific positivism nor idealist romanticism—and clearly not pessimism—what enables non-feeble human beings to draw on *and* inscribe beauty and meaning from earthly life? The question of freedom and its relation to 'necessity' revealed itself, forming the basis of a research paper which in time was presented at the Friedrich Nietzsche Society conference 'Nietzsche and Post-Analytic Philosophy' at the University of Southhampton (1999). Part of the discussion in Chapter One extends the analysis provided therein and formed the basis of an article submitted to the *Journal of Nietzsche Studies* (UK). I wish to express my sincere gratitude for the encouragement received from an anonymous reviewer of the JNS and for the permission granted by Sage Publications to use some material originally published in my 'Nietzsche, Freedom and Power', *European Journal of Social Theory* 6 (2) May, 2003: 191-208 in this chapter.

Throughout this period, a time of generation and cultivation, life continued to inevitably bring regular migraine headaches, deaths, growth and its concomitant responsibilities, ill-health, loss, and thus a need to continually affirm time. Beauty and unsightly existence intermingled dangerously. Preservation constantly needed overcoming by the pressing need to find freedom in that which presented itself through *ta mysteria* of life. It was necessary to find freedom in those responsibilities which had become definitive of living, dwelling, creating-laboring, and thinking. Without so many others (both present and past) this project would simply have remained 'bookish'—a mental labor. I therefore benefited enormously from this important sociality and suffering, making the pain and struggle of Nietzsche's enduring of isolation and perpetual wandering that bit more tangible. Without others, fellow human beings with whom to share one's 'wandering', we seem incapable of experiencing the 'good conscience' of responsibility and thus of realizing (real) freedom too. Nietzsche's 'free spirit' calls out to the presence of another and how beauty may be crafted from the art of living jointly in the cosmos—living as oneself, not atomistically, but in regular intercourse with human and extra-human forms of life.

Nietzsche conceived of new or different social forms being established and cultivated out of life's perennial 'recurrence of the same', transfiguring the merely 'human all too human' into a nobler piece of 'second nature' (GS 290). Here Apollonian beauty emerges out of the pathos of necessary freedom, to sculpt man (sic) into a *morphe* which is not only existing but is also something splendid to behold—a splendid *form*ation (i.e. joyful freedom). The process of becoming is therefore something not given over to an anonymous 'fate' or cycle of recurring sameness, since for Nietzsche it is important that 'man himself' is placed back in that space between the earth and the divine One (God) where freedom exists. Nietzsche's vertical pathos of distance may be summarized thus: first it was 'Thou Shalt' (obey), then 'I Will' (strive) and finally 'I Am'[1] (formed, freely). Here each moment of the present reflects each one of our past ethical orientations until we reach the 'I Am' of what Nietzsche called our 'second nature'.[2] Arguably, this more plastic nature of the willed creature lies between the Abyss and the Divine, just as the God-man (Christ) was a synthesis between immanence and transcendence as shown previously by Hegel (to Wagner and Nietzsche). It is not enough to claim the same recurs infinitely because *venir entre* (coming between) Abyssal void and Divine perfection is humankind's struggle to form itself *out of* a putrid indifferent matter.

Elements of Chapter Two derive from a paper first presented at Cambridge University for the Friedrich Nietzsche Society conference 'Nietzsche and Science' (2001), at which the late R. J. Hollingdale was present. A later version was subsequently presented at the Australasian Society of Continental Philosophy conference at the University of Melbourne (2002). Some of the discussion in Chapter Four was presented at the Australasian Association of Philosophy Conference (Canberra, 2006) thanks to the assistance of faculty support and leave. I also had the advantage of presenting elements of the present analysis at an international conference held in Sydney at the University of New

South Wales. Throughout this entire period, I received the kind support and encouragement of Wayne Hudson and Robin Small who were each most generous, supportive and most collegiate in company. I have learned from the astute work of Robin Small as I have also over the years from Maudemarie Clark, and corresponding with each of them has also proven valuable. No doubt over the years much inspiration has also been indirectly drawn from my Hegelian educators, both past and present—to acknowledge one's origins. These teachings have undoubtedly been borne out in my teaching of Nietzsche, Hegel and Heidegger in a regular seminar of delightful and engaging philosophy students over a period of ten or more years.

Finally, I wish to take this opportunity to thank Nicole and Michael for their joy, the constant help and back-up of Bianca, the friendship and encouragement of Johann Arnason, the efficient assistance provided by staff of the university library, and the helpful assistance provided by Patrick Dillon and others at Lexington Books. Above-all, for their audacious genealogy and exuberance of spirit I am forever in the debt of my beloved mother and father to whom this work is dedicated.

Notes

1. See Karl Löwith Nietzsche's *Philosophy of the Eternal Recurrence of the Same.* Trans. J. Harvey Lomax. Berkeley: University of California Press, 1997, 37.

2. 'Second nature' is examined in the present analysis of freedom and responsibility in terms of the 'historical becoming' of human subjects and by means of what the ancient Greeks called 'bios' as that form of life which exceeds simple being—'zoi'. The latter in particular leads the discussion on to a third critical aspect: temporality is always already marked by the *futural* moment when the promise of creativity and overcoming resist the recurrence of the same servitude.

CHAPTER ONE

Freedom, Will and Power: *Entretenir* Responsibility

How did my soul rise again out of such tombs? Indeed, in me there is something invulnerable and unburiable, something that explodes rock: that is *my
will.*[1]

A central motif of Nietzsche's *Lebensphilosophie* and its critical assessment of
modern society which remains to be systematically examined—perhaps because
of 'French' deconstructive maneuvers—is the question of freedom. In the following discussion, we will explore this key thematic underlying Nietzsche's
work from his early to later writings and find that it radically departs from conventional (modern) presuppositions and Kantian treatments of freedom. Against
radical denunciations of freedom proffered by Derrida and Deleuze—freedom as
essentially a bourgeois humanist illusion—we shall find Nietzsche offering an
alternative (post-liberal) conception of freedom which accords more closely to
the artist-scientist Johann Wolfgang von Goethe's life-work.[2] Additionally, a
corrective move to be confirmed here stands in relation to the distorted understanding of Nietzsche in Habermas' theory of modernity, primarily as that 'dark
figure' which propelled today's neo-Heideggerians into a totalizing critique of
modernity via a thorough-going disenchantment of the 'belief in truth'.[3] Rather
than eschewing freedom in reference to the modern world or even the state of
the human soul, Nietzsche can be understood, by contrast, as a serious thinker of
human freedom and its political moment *vis-à-vis* his complex conception of
will, power and freedom and their necessary entwinement ultimately with responsibility. From this complex constellation emerges all that which comprises
animations of the soul and the drive to affirm life: namely the constitution of
human subjectivity. Contrary to Habermas' account, we shall find Nietzsche not
to be a proto-postmodern figure of 'taste' but rather someone who affirms the
value of freedom in human existence. Moreover, we will find that Nietzsche's
affirmation does not rest, as Habermas maintains, on an aesthetic recuperation of
essentially outmoded archaic myth-content. Furthermore, this complex constellation holds some import for contemporary political and moral thought since
much of Nietzsche's work is oftentimes unnecessarily reduced to variants of the
'will to power' thesis either of the weak or strong type. Deleuze, for instance, in
a highly influential work written over three decades ago presented an anti-

Hegelian interpretation of Nietzsche which failed to accomplish this theoretical linkage between freedom, will and power; moreover, he committed Nietzsche to a double reduction. First, Nietzsche's philosophy of the overman being the theory of being and human culture par excellence is nothing but a 'genealogical philosophy' that remains untainted by any Platonic, Christian and Hegelian metaphysical baggage. This reduction to the genealogical is no less spurious than Heidegger's reduction of Nietzsche philosophical stance to the 'will to power', a position not too far from Deleuze's. Second, as the will to power is (considered) the central organizing concept underscoring all of Nietzsche's other philosophical postulates, it is understood incorrectly as exclusive of desire and aspiration; that is, the will to power is thought not to desire, seek, aspire nor even desire power itself because essentially it *gives* and is creative, argued Deleuze.[4]

Contrarily, it is possible to approach this complex question of freedom in a *demonstrable* fashion; namely, to undertake a hermeneutic interpretation that demonstrates how a quite different concept of freedom issues immanently from Nietzsche's critical valuation of will and power as commonly conceived. In particular, the study of forms of power, will, domination and moral valuations in the itinerary of the soul and its metaphysical correlates feature prominently in his work. This is almost always allied to the capacity for a critical discernment which itself gives evidence to a kind of quasi-transcendental intellectual and philological competence in drawing fundamental distinctions between mere manifestations of will or power and their actuality in historical life. Of considerable importance to Nietzsche's own work and, in particular, an understanding of his conception of freedom, is the fundamental distinction he drew between will (and its epiphenomena) and power. To discern properly what Nietzsche's concept of freedom entails it will be necessary first to outline what he conceived 'will' to be and then how it ought to be distinguished from power. Nietzsche linked his concept of freedom both to will and resistance, arguing that it always comes at a cost: freedom has a cost because it is part of a more general economy of forces and expenditures. Its purchase only comes with forms of resistance and the defeat of an other's resistance itself embodies a form of expenditure. To give over some thing necessitates power but it also requires a particular kind of expenditure. As we shall see, to will to be free, to be free *from* some constraint or limit is merely an illusion—a modern humanist misunderstanding of human existence and the operations of power quanta. Furthermore, rather than propounding some anarchical notion of freedom, Nietzsche seeks to expound a conception of freedom which entails responsibility. Eschewing any nihilistic sentiments of 'anything goes', the individual, according to Nietzsche, can either remain in the slavish morality of the herd—who level all values and thoughts to a common evaluative datum (i.e. relativism)—or instead choose to no longer deny the centrality of will to power in life and thus acquire freedom, that is, to possess it. But before we move on to the forementioned task of a hermeneutical demonstration of his idea of freedom and willed activity, we turn first to a highly influential interpretation of Nietzsche that took aim at debunking both the neo-conservativism of French neo-structuralism and the somber gloominess of

Adorno and Horkheimer's Nietzschean-like despair of the preponderance of domination in the age of (possible) nuclear annihilation.

Habermas and Nietzsche

Philosophical debate after the Second Word War was indelibly marked by the trenchant debates concerning the theoretical and moral status of a dialectic of enlightenment. Eschewing atomistic, juridical, functionalist, psychologistic and positivistic analytical approaches, Adorno and Horkheimer worked out a critical outlook onto the modern world which stemmed from their historico-immanent critique of western culture as a scientific-technologically oriented civilization. Their manifesto, *Dialectic of Enlightenment*, marveled many in its rich inter-weaving of grand theoretical perspectives and motifs, allowing individuals to understand the distant origins of their (and prior generations') forgetfulness of Being. A student of Theodore Adorno who later wrote on Friedrich Schelling's philosophy—Jürgen Habermas—would subsequently review this glorious truth. Habermas as a second generation critical theorist who was involved in the re-forms of the German University, could not accept the 'wisdom of the elders' as far as the evacuation of human emancipation was concerned. Arguably, most of what later was said against the idea and normativity of a coming postmodernity is bound with this intent to hold on to a dire need to struggle for freedom in human affairs—something which we shall see accords perfectly with Nietzsche. Rather than merely an abstract argument about the relative epistemological status of reason, Habermas essentially wants to defend modern philosophic thought from the onslaughts of pessimistic yet positivistically conceived radical critiques of social action and life-world presuppositions. To *re*-read the dialectic of enlightenment,[5] therefore, means to re-invest it with the possibility of over-coming constraint or unwarranted forms of distortion in social intercourse—a task that would seem to require salvaging the project of enlightenment from its too trenchant critics.

To this end, Habermas finds rather too uncomfortable the close affinity between Adorno and Horkheimer's pessimism and Nietzsche's despairing of modernity as the culmination of cultural nihilism. Compounding this was the added dilemma that his intellectual forebears—after the publication of *Knowledge and Human Interests*—were now considered by many in the new avant-garde to be close precursors to what Manfred Frank called, with Habermas following suit, a 'neo-structuralism' (c.f. Frank,1989). Hence Habermas set out explicitly to distance the essentially dialectical (Hegelian-Marxist) conception of concrete life of his Frankfurt colleagues from the structuralist-informed analyses of Foucault, Deleuze and Lyotard who liquidate the subject altogether. To perform this task, Habermas identifies Nietzsche as the linchpin in both cases because Nietzsche is considered to be the penultimate critic of both cultural modernity and the philosophy of the subject. However, I wish to argue that because Habermas fails to identify this important motif in Nietzsche's philosophy of life—freedom and responsibility—he unnecessarily overlooks the 'natural' affinity which exists between Nietzsche and Adorno and Horkheimer on this plane. This of course also overlooks another important distinction worth preserving: namely, that the neo-structuralists (including contemporary neo-Heideggerians) abandoned any understanding of Nietzsche as a serious thinker of freedom being a problem and task for future human beings. Thus we can say that although Adorno and Horkheimer similarly maintain a suspicion concerning the Kantian notion of the autonomous subject, they share *with* Nietzsche—but not his so-called heirs—a normative and intellectual commitment to the problem of freedom.[6]

In a seminal essay precisely on the question of how one might reaffirm the 'critical ability to take a 'yes' and 'no' stand, to be able to distinguish between what is valid and invalid', Habermas[7] takes aim at Nietzsche as the espouser of a cultural nihilism that is predicated on his view of Nietzsche as fundamentally a man of discrimination: namely, 'Taste'. Habermas finds Nietzsche to be a most compelling advocate of cultural criticism as self-criticism but charges him with an illusive form of self-referentiality. In the same way in which he later would accuse Foucault of this kind of self-exemption from historicist discourses of power, Habermas wonders if Nietzsche cannot in fact escape his own demystified logic. That is, whether Nietzsche simply repeated the failure: 'the revenge of the primordial powers upon those who tried to emancipate themselves and yet could not escape'.[8] Whilst the charge of mysticism is more strongly (and properly) leveled against Heidegger and his notion of the call of *Sein*, Habermas also sees Nietzsche as seeking to re*value* modern life through the primal originary force of Dionysus—a kind of pre-reflective instinct of life that ultimately transcends culturalistic limits upon life. Myth and enlightenment, as Nietzsche and later on Adorno and Horkheimer showed, are inextricably bound up with one another; validity must then find a way to escape the double bind of mythical powers on the one hand, and rationalized consciousness on the other. When Nietzsche is said to affirm values which might cut through the tenacious hold of nihilism—without a necessary *Aufhebung*, however—he is considered to be engaging in a philosophy of Taste or voluntaristic judgment. For instance, since Habermas takes his forebears' conclusion that Nietzsche's radical critique consumes its own critical impulse as a valid premise, his argument proceeds to the reductive view that for Nietzsche interpretation must go 'all the way down' and since all interpretations are valuations, then claims to truth are simply disguised preferences, i.e. *Wertschätzung*, value-estimations that give rise to 'Yes' and 'No', 'High' and 'Low' etc.

Habermas correctly understands that Nietzsche did not espouse a theory of modernity that simply propagated the call of '*wanting to be different*' but instead sought to *demonstrate*[9] how science and Christian or herd morality perversely dominate existence. However, since Habermas reduces Nietzsche's critique to a theory of power—a theory devoid of the validation of freedom as a meaningful ideal or (counter-)ideal of the future noble spirit—he sees no way out of this interminable cul-de-sac. So even though 'Nietzsche's theory of power is intended to provide a way out of this aporia', ultimately he proves unable to overcome the limits of his own philosophy of taste (normative valuations). Habermas pessimistically renders the task of unmasking pervasive ideologies as predicated,

in Nietzsche's final instance, only on the criterion of the palate: its discrimina-
tory 'Yes' and 'No' becomes (for Nietzsche) 'the sole organ of knowledge beyond Truth and Falsity, beyond Good and Evil'.[10] In more sublime language—
essentially that of Schopenhauer—the form of validation (*sic* evaluation) which
the judgment of taste provides is said to be 'merely an expression of the "ex-
citement of the will by the beautiful"'.[11] We know, however, that neither Kant's
notion of the beautiful nor Plato's *to agathon* are reducible to the dictates of the
palate. Moreover, as we shall see below Habermas misrepresents Nietzsche's
work by way of an unnecessary aestheticization of his oeuvre which fundamentally fails to take account of Nietzsche's own movement away from, as well as
disaffection with, Wagnerianism and Schopenhauerian and Romantic motifs
most evident in his early work.[12] What is lost sight of then is the important conception of an *en*-nobled spirit of modernity, one which no longer shuns suffering, struggle, willed action, resistance or loss through expenditure. Freedom is
not only worth fighting for, talking about and valorizing in a distinctly post-
nihilistic form, but it also remains an ongoing thematic of self-overcoming, including the overcoming of mythical illusions whereby the truth of errors is worthy of examination as is also the transvaluation of slavish morality. Neither the
first nor the second/third generation of critical German philosophy would wish
to disavow Nietzsche's insight into the formation of herd consciousness or his
proposal to transvaluate the banality of mass culture and modern patriotism. The
Nietzschean redemptive motif evident in Nietzsche's futural attempt to transfigure nihilistic decadence, is especially exemplary of his *nouveau idée* of freedom—one that embodies responsibility for what-is-to-come.

Beyond the forementioned beautiful value-criterion, we will find that
Nietzsche in certain respects goes even further than Adorno and Horkheimer
ever did in apprehending the necessary connection between historical culture,
freedom and *responsibility*. Responsibility—though central to Nietzsche's understanding of the noble spirit and a culture of health (well-being)—is largely
invisible in both the universal pragmatics of undistorted communication and in
moral discourses predicated on mutual recognition.[13] Needless to say, it is altogether omitted in Foucauldian theories of governmentality, power regimes and
disciplinary practices found in abundance in social science and liberal arts literature. The following section turns to an analysis of will or willing in respect to
Nietzsche's work on freedom and how his conception of it differed from idealist
precursors; this will be necessary as the will is ordinarily given inordinate value
in theories of morals that posit some notion of responsibility. Responsibility's
connection to freedom will emerge more immanently and become manifest in
the latter part of our discussion. I raise it now mainly because contemporary
analysis arguably is in need of such a concept of human action, especially insofar as the presence of the stranger-as-other in national states raises all kinds of
questions concerning 'my freedom' versus your right to cultural preservation.
And this takes on added salience due in part to the predominance of two species
of theoretical investigation which nevertheless fail to raise the question of responsibility: rights centered political philosophy and counter theories of authentic subjectivity. Regarding the latter, 'Dare to be honest' like the call 'Dare to

think for yourself' is the Nietzschean appeal to develop one's *own* (i.e. authentic) life—a distinctive *Dasein* cultivated in the midst of herd thinking and behavior. This relative freedom to think and act otherwise of necessity involves *willing* as was already well recognized by Nietzsche himself.

Will

Not unlike Heidegger's lamentation over the too readily used and diluted concept of being in philosophical discourse, Nietzsche lamented the over-extended use and hence encompassment of the word *will*. Philosophers have been prone both to over-extending the usage of this small word and, not unrelated, oversimplifying the concept despite its warranting extended philosophical elaboration. That there should be simply one word to express a number of human actions and conditions bewildered Nietzsche. Compounding this unhappy situation was the apparent fact that philosophers, to their discredit, historically presumed that we all somehow understand the will or at least what we mean by 'will' in our various utterances. Schopenhauer, as we see in *Beyond Good and Evil* (19), only took up what was in fact a 'popular prejudice and exaggerated it'. Through a whole series of false evaluations we have fabricated the belief that willing alone suffices for action which in turn produces the truth of its own false claim. While Nietzsche on numerous occasions makes it clear that he believed there exists no will as such, the will as the 'thing in itself', he quite unambiguously asserts the actuality of willing in civilized life. So while there is no transhistorical 'bad will' versus 'good will', or free will versus slavish will, he can discern forms of willing by means of examining—in historico-genealogical ways— forms of domination, conquest, elevation, aesthetic expression, intellectualization and cultural fecundity. The will to power both gives evidence to this and presupposes it simultaneously. Hence it is plausible to speak of life characterized by weak and strong wills (BGE 21), each referring us back to the fundamental life drive expressed as the will to power. Nietzsche determined there to be three essential aspects to willing, regardless of the type of will. First, the plurality of sensations: that is, the 'sensation of the condition we *leave,* the sensation of the condition towards which we *go,* the sensation of this "leaving" and "going" itself'(BGE 19). Second, just as a multitude of sensations belongs to the will so does thinking itself: 'in every act of will there is a commanding thought', in which the thought is entwined with will itself. Third, apart from will constituting a 'complex of feeling and thinking' it is 'above all an *affect*'—more precisely, the 'affect of command' as Nietzsche puts it. Here we see that there exists a 'commanding thought' and an 'affect of command'. By affect, we understand 'to act on', to disclose a sensation, to show an effect or to produce an effect or change in something. The term 'freedom of the will' denotes, more essentially, the 'affect of superiority in relation to him [or her] who must obey', giving rise not only to the obeying person but a consciousness within oneself that gives testimony to one's commanding position and its attendant sensations of effecting, transforming and instituting. Commanding and willing as a result entwine: ' "Freedom of will"—that is the expression for the complex state of delight of the person exercising volition, who commands and at the same time identifies himself with the executor of the order' (BGE 19). Contrary to what the synthetic concept 'I' connotes, we are always simultaneously *both* commanding and obeying subjects rather than exclusively one or the other. Overestimation of the will, however, leads us to the erroneous conclusion that any success of a commanding thought in soliciting obedience from an other, owes to the will itself and not 'the carrying out of the willing' (BGE 19). Overcoming various kinds of resistance in the act of instituting is thereby confused with the will itself—not its concept but its ontology—since the commander wrongly attributes the overcoming of resistances to the will.

Causality and Freedom

For Nietzsche, we err in mistaking the will as both cause *and* effect. Unlike the physicalists, he argued that will only operates on an other will (or set of wills), not upon matter. There is no 'free will' as previously thought; now that man has no such faculty as a will endowed from some higher order, the 'old word will only serves to designate a resultant, a kind of individual reaction which necessarily follows a host of partly contradictory, partly congruous stimuli' (A 14). As long as we believe in causality, we also as a matter of course believe in unfreedom. This is because we condition freedom to mean the freedom to perform a thought as an action, identifying ourselves as the cause, and, the effect as the success of the cause, conceiving of the whole as an act of will. As with modern physics, resistance is integral to the phenomenon (or appearance) of causation. Forms of resistance are only overcome by will and action combined: a commanding thought followed by an affect of command which itself requires strength of will. It is for these reasons that the weak-willed identify unfreedoms in every causal connection. Their continuance in this belief owes to their perception of freedom as a freedom to perform the original commanding thought; when they inevitably find resistances such individuals have the sense of being unfree because their will is not considered to be strong enough to produce the *affect* of command. Conversely, the sensation of power increases proportionate to the degree of resistances overcome, thereby elevating the feeling of freedom and the measure of freedom won. Of course, there is no doubting a thought is 'caused' in some way; if the ego does not 'cause' thoughts then how could one be *free* to perform them and consequently be responsible for them? Nevertheless, it is a mistake to believe that all this refers us inextricably to some kind of 'inner world', an inner abode where the will, ego and spirit reside.

   We seem to have generated an objective world based upon a constitutive world of causes—the world as will. However, the thing itself is a concept: the appearance of an effect merely reflects the belief in an ego, will or spirit as cause while the concept itself points to a symbol world ('inner facts'). This takes us back to the insights proffered by Kant's critical philosophy in which causality comes under scrutiny in the form of the operative antinomies underlying both understanding and cosmological ideas. Under the third antinomy, Kant (1933) had shown that contrary to Newtonian-like laws of nature, there also existed the possibility of conceiving of a spontaneous or 'original' causality of freedom, contiguous with its own concept which the symbol world of the faculty had instantiated. Maintenance of the 'thing itself', Nietzsche argued, only perpetuates the nonsense of acting *mythologically* (BGE 21). Once we recognize that both cause and effect are merely concepts of a fabricated symbol world, it becomes possible to discern that wherever effects are detected, will is operating on another will. In real as opposed to mythological life, there are, Nietzsche argued, only ever weak and strong wills. And in *The Will to Power*[14], he reduced the 'supposed instinct for causality' to only a 'fear of the unfamiliar and the attempt to discover something familiar in it' (551). This was, in the final analysis, Platonism's Achilles heel: the ineluctable need to render the void of chaos knowable should nothingness otherwise swamp άνθρωπος (mankind).

Freedom and Responsibility

Freedom for Nietzsche is understood in exactly those same terms as those of the 'strongest kind' of 'strong human beings': freedom is 'something one has or does *not* have, something one *wants*, something one *conquers*' (TI 38). Freedom we can see here is inseparable from ownership, desire and overcoming. However, this timely philosopher could be challenged on his perhaps untimely, unmodern reflection that 'our modern concept of freedom is one more proof of degeneration of instinct' (TI ix, 41) since our insatiable drive for all kinds of freedoms—civil, social, bio-physiological, sexual, religious and ethno-national—suggests to the contrary a vigorous instinct for overcoming servitude is alive and well. More effectual perhaps are Nietzsche's observations regarding the relation between freedom and responsibility. When he asks 'For what is freedom?' he replies: 'That one has the will to self-responsibility. That one preserves the distance which divides us. That one has become more indifferent to hardship, toil, privation, even to life' (TI ix, 38). Freedom can thus be measured by the 'resistance which has to be overcome, by the effort it costs to stay *aloft*.' The free man is a *warrior*, someone who also combats in psychological terms that 'which demands the maximum of authority and discipline towards oneself' (TI ix, 38). Hence Nietzsche denies us a human existence in which indulgence in unreasoned, undisciplined modes of being and pleasure predominate; rather than English happiness, the power of will, *and* therefore the will to power also, dictates a rigor of self-conduct and development: 'Blind indulgence of an affect, totally regardless of whether it be a generous and compassionate or a hostile affect, is the cause of greatest evils' (WP 928). To possess affects is human but certainly not merely human-all-too-human; to be possessed by the affects on the other hand is to be a slave, not a free spirit. A free subject is one whose spirit is free or 'higher' and this of necessity negates our servitude to the affects or other slavish morals, thus affirming mastery. In *The Will to Power* as indeed elsewhere we find perhaps unsurprisingly Nietzsche arguing: 'Greatness of character does not consist in not possessing these affects—on the contrary, one possesses them to the highest degree—but in having them *under control*' (928). More congruent with the vision of the aesthete, we can say the Apollonian spirit harnesses and directs Dionysian forces and impulses of life and growth. Obviating the need for a denial of the affects on the one hand, and transvaluating the naturalist's reduction of human 'being' to physio-organic drives of self-preservation. (In chapter two, this transvaluation is explored in some detail).

The higher spirit in this sense is one which is not marked either by hubris or renunciation but rather by the '*greatest responsibility*' endurable. The noble or free being is one who can bear the greatest responsibility and so not collapse under its onerous weight, as exemplified by a Caesar, Napoleon or Venetian aristocrat. Similarly, the philosophers of the future ought to be those who will take the greatest responsibilities instead of collapsing under their cognitive, moral and psychic weightiness. It is for this reason that Nietzsche conceives of the ripest form of *Wesen* as when the individual achieves the ripest perfection, namely *freedom*. Only with such a full perfection is the 'classic type of the *sovereign man* attained', according to his late notebooks (WP 770). There he also sees 'responsibility for the whole' training and permitting the individual to 'a broad view, a stern and terrible hand, a circumspection and coolness, a grandeur of bearing and gesture, which he would [otherwise] not permit himself on his own behalf' (WP 773). Similarly, when it comes to whole societies or species of peoples, the feebler they are or they become a corresponding weakness in responsibility and will can be evinced (898). Conversely, Nietzsche conceived as a main precondition for the transvaluation of nihilistic values and the cultivation of higher spirits an increase in 'the feeling of responsibility' as well as in courage, independence and insight (907). Flattened out social structures and moralities—those falsely founded on equality—only serve to diminish not only the most spiritual things of life but most importantly for us in this context, the 'will to self-responsibility' (936). The enoblement of man can therefore only occur with a counter-force or drive toward another more antithetical desire: that 'one instinctively seeks heavy responsibilities' in life rather than lighter ones or none at all as is the mark of decadence. Modernity is shot through with decadence when our lives are lived *irresponsibly*: 'One lives for today, one lives very fast…whenever the word 'authority' is so much as heard one believes oneself in danger of a new slavery' (TI 39). Mastery of the latent condition of nothingness, of cycles of meaninglessness in a world of symbolic sameness, also allows the free spirit to will to have responsibilities concomitant with its ability to see farther, that is, to look into the valleys of existence where more servile spirits envy the cold crisp air of strong blue skies which appear both translucid and transcendent of mundane life.

Will to Power

Valuing freedom over organic life and over happiness is a very important step on the way to power: 'What is happiness?' Nietzsche asked, 'The feeling that power increases—that a resistance is overcome' (A 2). There must be freedom, true freedom, in the will to power; in mythological existence by contrast, we are overwhelmed by our sense of an illusion of unfreedom [see Figure 1].

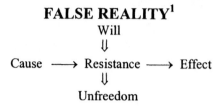

FALSE REALITY[1]

Figure 1

Recall Nietzsche's question 'For what is freedom?' elicited a threefold conception: 'That one has the will to self-responsibility. That one has become more indifferent to hardship, toil, privation; even to life. That one is ready to sacrifice men to one's cause, oneself not exempted.' Three prominent points are worthy of examination here: the will to self-responsibility, the willingness to sacrifice one's own life for power, and third, gaining mastery over the instincts.

We have already looked at Nietzsche's conception of responsibility and its relation to freedom. Turning to the willingness to sacrifice one's own life for power, Nietzsche's Zarathustra states:

> Indeed, the truth was not hit by him who shot at it with the word of the 'will to existence': that will does not exist. For, what does not exist cannot will; but what is in existence, how could that still want existence? Only where there is life is there also will: not will to life but—thus I teach you—will to power. There is much that life esteems more highly than life itself (Z, 'On Self-Overcoming').

In *The Gay Science* Nietzsche argued that the struggle for existence is only an exception, a temporary restriction of the will of life; and wherever there is a struggle there is struggle for power. Therefore, the will to exist is only in accordance with the will to power—to extension, formation and even overflow. To wish to preserve oneself is essentially the expression of a state of distress, a limitation of the actual basic drive of life—found here (see Figure 1) in the resistances.

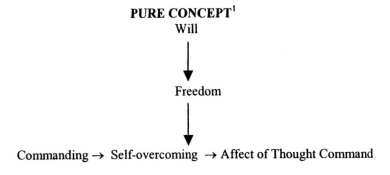

Figure 2

It is clear that for Nietzsche the 'basic drive of life' tends towards an extension of power rather than any obedience to a will to self-preservation, thus calling into question Darwinian presuppositions of self-preservation. I argued earlier that freedom promotes strength that also allows us to conquer resistances resulting in the sensation of power. This process is referred to, by Nietzsche, as 'self-overcoming'. Our previous concepts of self-responsibility and the capacity to regulate the drives are very much bound up with the idea of self-overcoming in Nietzsche's work. Life itself confided this secret to Zarathustra: 'behold, it said, I am that which must always overcome itself'. To overcome oneself means to move from a commanding thought by means of one's own resistances and weaknesses to the affect of command (see Figure 2 above). In the case of Figure 1, resistance is made into a material thing from the external world. By contrast, the will to power—as indicated by Figure 2—shows the resistance to be expressed as the overcoming of the self which is the ability to obey oneself. Zarathustra heard the speech on obedience; it read:

> Whatever lives, obeys. And this is the second point: he or she who cannot obey himself is commanded—that is the nature of living. This, however, is the third point that I heard: that commanding is harder than obeying; and not only because he who commands must carry the burden of all who obey, and because this burden may easily crush him. An experiment and hazard appeared to me to be in all commanding and whenever the living commands, it hazards itself. Indeed even when it commands itself it still must pay for its commanding. It must become the judge, the avenger, and the victim of its own law. How does this happen? What persuades the living to obey and command, and to practice obedience even when it commands...Where I found the living, there I found the will to power; and even in the will of those who serve I found the will to be master (Z, On Self-Overcoming).

In 'On the Way of the Creator' (Z) Nietzsche explicitly refers to the problem of the moral law, as Kant would call it:

> Free *from* what? As if that mattered to Zarathustra! But your eyes should tell
> me brightly: *free for* what? Can you give yourself your own evil and your own
> good and hang your own will over yourself as a law? Can you be your own
> judge and avenger of your law? Terrible it is to be alone with a judge and
> avenger of one's own law.

Thus, like a star we are thrown into the void to find the icy breath of the
ethical command. This requires great strength since the overcoming of oneself
takes us upon the path of affliction. Therefore, you could say that the will to
power is a way to affliction that remains inescapable for us. According to
Nietzsche, this process involves our striving for distinction or put differently, a
striving for dominion. We value this domination over ourselves and others so
much that even when it hurts us we can still sense happiness, because happiness
is the feeling that power increases, that a resistance is overcome. This is where
we find the martyr who feels the highest enjoyment by enduring *himself*. However, the martyr is a tragedy of a drive for distinction in which there is only one
character which burns and consumes oneself. So in both cases where one inflicts
one's will upon oneself and upon others there is an implicit happiness at the
sight of torment. Not dissimilar to the martyr Nietzsche refers to how self-
overcoming involves a defiance of oneself in which one tyrannizes over oneself
as does the martyr. He describes this in *Human All Too Human* as a mockery of
one's own nature:

> Thus a person climbs on dangerous paths into the highest mountains in order to
> laugh derisively at his fearfulness and his trembling knees...people have a
> genuine pleasure in violating themselves with excessive demands and then idol-
> izing this tyrannically demanding something in their souls afterward. In every
> ascetic morality people worship a part of themselves as god and therefore need
> to diabolize the remaining part (HH 137).

This diabolic self is interposed between the gods and the animal—that is its *fate*:
a tragic joyful wisdom.

The other part according to *Daybreak* can be glimpsed in relation to what
Nietzsche said about praise and blame:

> If a war proves unsuccessful one asks who was to 'blame' for the war, if it ends
> in victory one praises its instigator. Guilt is always sought whenever there is
> failure; for failure brings with it a depression of spirits against which the sole
> remedy is instinctively applied: a new excitation of the *feeling of power*—and
> this is to be discovered in the *condemnation* of the 'guilty' . . . . To condemn
> oneself can also be a means of restoring the feeling of strength after a defeat (D
> 140).

In relation to self-overcoming, if we refer to Figure 2 we can see that the resistances are resistances that we *ourselves* create. Moreover, these may take the
form of innumerable excuses for an unwillingness to take on self-responsibility
and the unforeseen consequences of our commanding thoughts and actions.
Hence, whereas Figure 1 emphasizes resistances from without, Figure 2 shows
these resistances to be inextricably bound up with the inner world that for
Nietzsche is explicitly linked to the symbol world of concepts. Nietzsche de-

scribed the person who has the fortitude to overcome oneself, embrace freedom and thus will to take on self-responsibility as the *Übermensch* (a type of 'overman'). It is the overman that is the type of species of mankind who we should be cultivating, promoting and willing to emerge out of the twilight. This valuable species of human subjects have hitherto been regarded as an exception, a lucky accident, not someone willed into existence. This exceptional great human being has, unsurprisingly, been feared, which is why also the mark of modernity is that of feebleness and decadence. This mighty exception is also the reason why the opposite has been realized in actuality, bred and willed—the animal man, the domestic happy creature, the herd, the Christian, and the juridical subject of rights. How has this come to be historically? Nietzsche states in *Beyond Good And Evil, Twilight of the Idols, The Anti-Christ,* and *On The Genealogy of Morals* that we owe this primarily to the decadent values of Christianity, democratic politics and Platonism. While we cannot explore the complex interrelations between each of these here, it can be said that for Nietzsche this is because virtues have been manipulated for the sake of power. Although this may appear *prima facie* counter-intuitive—since Nietzsche's discourse is commonly associated with the rhetorics of power—Nietzsche lamented the abuse rather than use of power for the vulgar pursuit of self-interest and self-aggrandizement. Both of which, he noted, were crudely on display with the crusades, the conquests of the high cultures of Peru and Mexico, the expulsion of the Jews and the burning of books. As is the case with the *tyrannos,* Nietzsche thought whoever possesses power over the ruling virtues that the masses generally abide by, has promoted those virtues that are harmful to the individuals' will to power. This is evident from his discourses in *Daybreak* in which we find a condemnation of the lust for power expressed as power for power's sake. That is to say, *machtpolitik*s is an illogical conclusion to the will to power. Being bereft of both the value of self-responsibility and the ripest form of freedom makes it the furthest thing from his specific conception of the power of willing and therefore the will to power.

Freedom's Higher Spirit

The importance of 'soulful activity' for an understanding of Nietzsche's conception of freedom as inclusive of an ethic of responsibility can not be underestimated. That is to say, the activity of the soul—including the 'spirituality' of our culture—is explicitly linked to the vitalism of the drives as well as the drive to labor over the soul's multiple constitutive forces. Analogous to Nietzsche's numerous denunciations of 'the will', his denunciations of the traditional 'soul-concept' of Platonized Christianity belie the otherwise paramount importance accorded to the moral and 'spiritual' status of the soul. The later Nietzsche, in particular, was most emphatic of the need to take account of the soul of the higher (and lowly) spirits when criticizing decadent civilizational forms or imagining how higher spirits could surpass prevailing forms of unfreedom. In fact, any disregard of soulful activity or labor which finds a person taking it upon himself or herself to not only acknowledge the operations of the soul but to, more specifically, recognize the need for one to continually labor over one's soul and its multifarious sentiments and states, runs the risk of lacking *insight* and a proper diagnosis of our times. Any physio-psychological diagnostic attitude toward self, world and morals—one that significantly is bound up with the Platonic thematic of well versus ill-being—would exemplify this; however, it always awaits our interpretation. Such interpretation beckons forth from the psycho-physician of the soul of Man—not simply the 'German' or 'French' or 'European' soul. Although Nietzsche goes to great lengths to dissect the body of ideas which form his 'soul superstition' hypothesis—especially in his *Beyond Good and Evil* and *On the Genealogy of Morals*—his diagnosis of European nihilism and herd thinking is most centrally concerned with the impoverishment of the human spirit or spirituality of an age and peoples (i.e. *Volkgeist*). The critical distinction falls back upon an intention to decisively steer clear of neo-Platonic and psychologistic hypostatizations of the soul that have promulgated a) egological doctrines of human nature/existence and b) superordinate beliefs in a disembodied, half-god being that remains wholly otherwise than instinctual.

Eschewing both of these problematic understandings of the soul, Nietzsche ventured the idea of a 'genuine spirituality' of the soul with all its attendant historical vicissitudes (BGE *P.*). True or 'genuine' conceptions of an epoch's spirit or, alternatively, a culture's spirit are inextricably linked to the primary quasi-idealist[15] metaphysics of being, that is, being well or being physio-psychologically *un*well, or, sickly decadent, i.e. nihilistic. Much earlier than *Beyond Good and Evil*, when Nietzsche most enthusiastically took to a close examination of modern chemistry and a distinctly Goethe-like study of the forms and shapes of nature's fecund living beings, we find the pronouncement (contra the English naturalists and physiologists): 'Even the determination of what is healthy for your *body* depends on your goal, your horizon, your energies, your impulses, your errors, and above all on the ideals and phantasms of your soul' (GS 120, emphasis added). Beyond any vulgar physicalism therefore lies a recognition of the efficacy of the *Seele* (soul) as a correlate of the human spirit: 'your virtue is the health of your soul' (GS 120). Hence the necessity or 'advantages' of psychological observation: 'reflection upon what is human, all too human…psychological observation—is among the means by which we can lighten the burden of life' (HH 35). Our depressively burdensome being of life owes to a particular kind of lack; namely, the 'art of psychological dissection and combination [which] is lacking in all ranks of society, where people speak about human beings, to be sure, but not at all *about humanity*' (HH 35). European decadence along with its nihilistic soul is both evidence of and cause for the prevalent absence of mature psychological dissection: 'Why do they no longer read the great masters of the psychological maxims?' asked Nietzsche when writing his book most attributed to his own corporeal sickness (HH 35). Unsurprisingly, this critical dimension of Nietzsche's thought is borne out once again when his personal physio-psychological suffering later in life produced a trenching critique of moral and epistemic idols developed from the point of view of not merely a hammering philosopher but a psychologist of leisure.[16] Moreover, it is in this latter work that Nietzsche the anti-moralist-educator-psychologist most explicitly refers to the importance of self-responsibility already discussed. Indeed, a commitment to self-responsibility can be seen to be a sign of a vigorous, taut and therefore healthy soul, i.e. an affirmative soul-structure, one that is both well structured and governed—a healthy body-politic of the soul.

The state of freedom, as contrasted with that of unfreedom, is one in which there is a lively *pathos of distance*, both in the social relations of individuals and of their drives. As distance signifies differentiation and multidimensionality, it also denotes a particular sense of vitalism. With each of the drives seeking to gain prominence and inexorably undergoing constant change in their order of rank within the soul, life is continually affirmed. Necessity not denial determines their forcefulness in life. However, as no particular priority or station is *a priori* accorded to these drives, their relative stability and therefore position is only determined by innumerable negations and 'spiritual' wars. Their effects are manifest in the morphologies of the soul, including the Christian conscience that for millennia was erroneously accorded spiritual qualities beyond Man (sic) and history. Instead, we can think of Nietzsche as closer to Hegel when he conceives of the spirit of the age and its concomitant form of the soul as the results of human historical making and hence self-legislation. Any operations of the psyche are, therefore, expressly human in that they correspond to the order of rank established historically by any individual self or society. When the psycho-physician of the soul pronounces the present age as sickly or decadent it frequently involves denunciations of poor 'spirituality'. Moreover, this of necessity is always expressed by placing spiritual(ity) within inverted commas, so as to distinguish this highly denoted ('Christian') word from its more vulgar Christian popularization of it. Overcoming the pitfalls associated with both the traditional soul-concept and 'free will' concept, however, does not preclude us from taking up the already stated 'microscopic psychology' that is integral to the 'art of transfiguration' known as 'philosophy' (GS 3). Higher spirits are not afforded the same delusions as the (common) people, that is, philosophers or artists 'are not free to divide body from soul as people do; we are even less free to divide the soul from spirit' (GS 3).

The 'art of transfiguration' as much as the transvaluation of all values is therefore especially marked by the reverberations of so many physio-psychological travails and metamorphoses undergone by means of diverse human experiences of life. The disciplining metamorphoses of the human spirit and hence soul can only be properly apprehended for Nietzsche by a *philosophical physician* who is able to grasp the fact that a 'philosopher who has traversed many kinds of health, and keeps traversing them, has passed through an equal number of philosophies: he simply *cannot* keep from transposing his states every time into the most spiritual form and distance' (GS 3). This imperative toward spirit-ual transfiguration, entwined with contingent corporeal worldly existence(s), is philosophizing itself: the movement, action and *techne* of philosophizing over the torments, joys and expenditures of *bios*, of *living*. Living self-responsibly is to have the freedom to transfigure one's life anew continuously; hence the 'ripest form of freedom' is that which faces up to Nietzsche's dare—the dare to be honest—by equally not foregoing the dare to be challenged by this brutal honesty of (philosophic) life, whether in sickness or in health or both. The 'consciousness of this rare freedom' otherwise referred to as a 'proud awareness of the extraordinary privilege of *responsibility*' posits the *'sovereign individual'* who 'has his own independent, protracted will and the *right to make promises*' since '[m]an himself must first of all have become *calculable, regular, necessary*, even in his own image of himself, if he is to be able to stand security for *his own future*, which is what one who promises does!' (GM II: 2). The 'emancipated individual' as Nietzsche himself described the ripest fruit of existence is therefore not one emancipated *from* responsibilities but rather from their evasion.

In the present discussion, it may be clear by now that variants of European philosophy once construed (incorrectly) as 'postmodern' or deconstructive—whether Foucaldian or Derridean—can be found wanting on both hermeneutical and normative grounds as a result of their misappropriation of Nietzsche. Fundamentally, a certain negative teleology—even if in the guise of an anti-teleology—pervades much of this type of theoretical work; a negativity which, unlike Hegel's, forgets that Nietzsche himself presented us with an alternate vista of the nihilistic cul-de-sac. Since freedom is eclipsed by the totalizing critiques of power and subjectivity offered to us by these eminently (French) negative thinkers, modern European thought in its (so-called) 'deconstructive' guise suffers from a tragic omission. By contrast, both first and second generation critical German philosophy comes closer to the spirit of Nietzsche when it maintains the necessity to constantly think through and, concomitantly, rethink the possibility of freedom *and* the conditions of its possibility in a decidedly post-Kantian fashion. Habermas is therefore right to pursue ideology-critique as *Selbstkritik* (self-criticism) and to seek to identify strategies that successfully problematize the 'frozen constellations of power' that impede any fundamental advancement in human emancipation. However, for him to be able to do so a particular corrective turn is required, one which does not, in the first instance, depict Nietzsche as simply a dark, irrational figure who eschews knowledge and the 'knower'.[17] In the second instance, it would need to realize that Nietzsche is an important part of the original and subsequent thesis of the dialectic of enlightenment; a realization which following the logic of *Selbstkritik* would give cause to reflect upon Habermas' interpretation of Nietzsche as itself being inexorably bound up with myth. That is to say, critical self-reflection would grasp the saliency of Nietzsche's idea of freedom and thus posit the possibility of rupturing the tenacious hold of nihilistic instincts currently all pervasive in the disenchanted West. Indeed, it further proffers a stronger thesis about an ethical substance which sadly was missing from Adorno and Horkheimer's critique of instrumental reason. Namely, that this so-called dark 'anarchistic' thinker encompassed a strong notion of responsibility within his analysis of the individual and its subjectivity of mourning the world-that-once-was through a lost Father—our 'killing' of God the Father. In a world where the gods have been dispelled and consciousness confronts its own limitations in and through the constructive quality of social phenomena, freedom appears to require an ethic of responsibility that will abate a collapsing in upon one's own experience of the world. To *re*-read, dialectically, the moment of enlightenment therefore means to critically re-evaluate the cognitivist-linguistic problematic formulation of the 'better' or 'freer' condition; it also means having to think through freedom onto a plane of action which no longer finds the drive to responsibility an onerous task, let alone an antithesis of freedom. It means, in particular, that post-metaphysical thinking of this discursive kind can no longer afford to make omissions of this type: beyond competent speech acts lies the capacity to be responsible for the spirit of 'man'. Even the Greeks after all well understood that mortals and deities alike held their own gods responsible. We turn now to Nietzsche's alternate analytic of responsibility, commencing with a schema of its distinctive conception.

Responsibility as 'Extra-Moral' Freedom

Nietzsche's abjuration of the 'free will' argument and its related causal theory of objective reality is of great import for how responsibility may be re-thought after Cartesianism apropos Kantian moral philosophies. While further exposition of the erroneous 'freedom of will' related to this central concept of free will—and its kin *causa sui* which moves the universe—will be provided in later chapters, we can begin to outline the architectonic logic of Nietzsche's extra-moral responsibility. What is meant by 'extra-moral' is discussed in detail in chapter four 'Freedom and Responsibility' so here we shall be simply concerned with Nietzsche's alternate conception of responsibility after it has eschewed a pernicious 'moralization' of human existence. This also entails a repudiation of the moralistic (conventional) predilection for 'responsibility' as an effect of duties which are categorical in nature (Kant).

Let us begin where Nietzsche begins: an historical perspective of the conscience. Contra *moderne* precepts, the individual who now forms the 'fount of law' has not always reigned sovereign either in affairs of the community or moral action. While many commentaries dwell on the historicality of Nietzsche's criticism of the 'bad conscience' in the *Genealogy*, fragment 117 of *Die fröhliche Wissenschaft* (1882) clearly states the 'anthropo-logic' of human doing. While not critical of the immanence of the spirit per se, Nietzsche sets out to identify the civilizational form of 'the good'—a move he makes against the transcendentalists. He observes: 'During the longest and most remote periods of the human past, the sting of conscience was not at all what it is now.' Its force today owes to a process of individuation which originated in older herds of tribes which emphasized the self-preservation of *the all* and its customary (moral) norms. The social idiom was such that egoism was experienced as 'something painful and as a real misery'. What is more, 'Today one feels responsible only for one's will and actions' whereas in other societies the human being was responsible for the maintenance of the herd, its tribe and appeasing numerous gods. The individuality of one's being was more akin to alone-ness, 'for being alone was associated with every misery and fear'. Consequently, 'in those days "free will" was very closely associated with a bad conscience' for to follow the herd instinct in an action made one feel more moral. Under Nietzsche's historicist precepts the individual conscience cannot therefore be presumed as the departure-point for a critique of morality and domination. What needs to immediately be grasped is the unreality or 'error' of aprioristic arguments that begin with an indisputable 'free will' in human nature.

Having rejected the ahistorical 'moral conscience' of modern liberalism, we now see Nietzsche re-conceptualizing responsibility in a wholly unorthodox manner. From the outset it is noteworthy that the herd instinct—customary morality of tribes—is not dispensed with in modernity because it is articulated or, more precisely, rearticulated in a different form. Because Nietzsche also maintained the history of past cultures passes through our souls, the 'bad conscience' of (former) herd instincts still has a hold on our conscience. Only now if the human being betrays the customs of his morality (system) his guilt-ridden conscience filters all that which Protestantism invented and imbued into the modern spirit. Individuated spirits now torment the soul, demanding that the person be dutiful with respect to the moral norms of its community while at the same time demanding recognition of the autonomous power of the conscience in the form of an active, powerful 'free will'. In sum, the individual human being must internalize into the rumblings of its own labyrinthine soul the (categorical) duties of an external moral system that sits transcendent above him or her, as an authority from without *and* from within. The command: follow the herd's commands but also follow the commands of your (inner) free will. This is the state of unfreedom: servitude plus feeble inaction due to an immanent contestation that wreaks havoc on him or her who is unprepared for the 'greatest responsibilities' of freedom. Lacking freedom (i.e. the freedom to exercise the will) these besieged souls are filled with resentment and the will to revenge those who are accountable for their suffering and injury (in chapter five we shall explore the twin deleterious forces of resentment and revenge). Nietzsche's idea of overcoming is aimed precisely at this complex: overcoming is not merely an overcoming of 'decadence' or nihilism in values—it is the regaining of strength and ethical fortitude so that any contestation both within and without the soul of man will be fought nobly, with self-regard and heightened autonomy ('sovereignty'). The languishing individual of 'modern society' shall be overcome as will the masses' herd-instinct of blindly obeying customary morals.

We can represent dichotomously the contrast between the conventional concept of responsibility—with its ahistorical roots and self-evident individual conscience—and Nietzsche's emancipated concept. The following diagram incorporates 'Figure 1'above and shows the problematic notion of 'responsibility' as it arises out of the conventional wisdom of free will and duty:

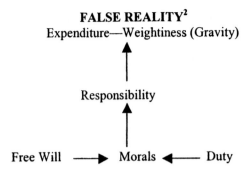

FALSE REALITY²
Expenditure—Weightiness (Gravity)

Responsibility

Free Will ⟶ Morals ⟵ Duty

Figure 3

Here morality in time is the twin effect of the Free Will and moral duty or imperative which sustains morals as a coherent system of customary norms of obligation and 'right-doing'. For Nietzsche, moralities emerge out of the becoming of herds, tribes, classes and 'slaves and masters': they are *in* and *of* time, forming a system which envelops the individual of 'necessity'. Against romanticism, the necessity of group morals—their necessary 'rank of order' of values—forms an objective historical 'fact'. We know this from Nietzsche's comparative historical sociology of civilizational forms as already alluded to above. In general, responsibility is inextricably linked to the formation of individuals, classes or 'herds' and the making of regular, measurable conscious human beings who eventually desire to transcend the *agro* (wild, untamed) culture of nature. It is thoroughly saturated with the edicts and symbolic codings of a particular community's instinct for self-preservation. What Figure 3 shows is the arrival of 'free will' in post-barbaric societies where morals are no longer simply an effect of some religious caste or master's measure of Justice and 'goodness'. Another way of expressing this important turning-point in becoming is: with the overcoming of tragic visions of the cosmos by 'moralistic' metaphysical systems—derived mostly from religious-occult world-views—the *dunamis* ('faculty') of free will begins to displace the older wisdom of αναγκη (necessity). A new sovereignty is inaugurated with the so-called moralization of the naturalistic world: now the conscience sustains both a sense of self and an irrefutable core to morality (a system of moral codes and ranking of 'the good' versus evil) that steers social intercourse along moral actions. Once the discovery was made, it became difficult to imagine an ethical life without the conscience—a point not too dissimilar to Emmanuel Levinas' rethinking of ethical responsibility.[18] On the other side, reciprocal moral duties embedded in the sense of identity of a given community encode the definition of 'ethicality' in morals and so ward off the nihilism of suffering life. The conscience internalizes the standard of moral precepts and poses strictures as well as demands on the exercising of one's free will vis-à-vis meeting obligations toward the common good.

Free will as a *dunamis* of human nature, in Figure 3, guides action toward the *Gemeinschaft's* 'table of values' while contrarily signaling to the self its right or power to instantiate 'right' and 'good' within the constellation of natu-ral-cultural life of the community. This unhappy existence between an autarchic will and demanding moral imperatives working from without exact an enormous affective toll on the economy of the drives of the human being and its spirit. Formal responsibilities as exemplified by Figure 3 make onerous demands on the self as it seeks to act in the world according to opposing laws of necessity: willing and conscience-norms. Due to the absence of the instincts/drives in this diagram, the 'law of gravity' is what comes to reign supremely in the soul of man. Already the inauguration of a Christian moral *Weltanschauung* has brought about a schism within the spirit of man, one which significantly is overlaid upon an already existing tension between Apollonian and Dionysian elements. With the Pauline individual will of conscience, the human being expends energy and affect in order to follow two (mostly) opposing laws: freedom of will and cus-tomary morality. What is most distinctive about this constellation is the simulta-neity of the sublimation of the instincts into holier actions on one hand and the declaration of such a condition as (universal) freedom on the other. The former demand results in a destructive 'unselfness' while the latter leads to what Nietzsche called a 'slave morality' of 'the herd'. It is no coincidence therefore that the *Geist* of 'modern man' is weighed *down*, is overawed by the weightiness of actuality (reality). Paradoxically, his mind thinks he is the agent of freedom and can set out to fulfill the demands of Kant's 'categorical imperative' even though his 'unselfness' nature is not ready, is ill-prepared, for the toughest re-sponsibilities that attend higher free spirits.

What Figure 3 shows is the heaviness or weightiness of an exacting respon-sibility which issues from the axis of truth shown on the bottom line: free will—morals—duty. Human beings who fall under the sway of this kind of 'responsi-bility' manifest the weightiness of gravity as they continually expend in order to fulfill formal moral imperatives that strictly prescribe obligations (external) and unegoism (internal). Lacking preparation and the fortitude to keep to one's word in contractual exchanges,[19] the dutiful self of moral responsibility is gradually overburdened and worn-down by onerous (moral) duties that the conscience endeavors to fulfill lest it be overrun by guilt-sensations. For Nietzsche, the con-science is ultimately perverted by an unwarranted 'bad conscience' that torments the soul of modern persons even while they hold onto the illusion of being 'free'. How can man be free if he is enchained by the gravity of 'bad con-science' and on the other side the demands of an illusory 'free will'? This is the metaphysical error and not the existence of God per se: the substitutive effect of the *causa sui* which grounds belief both in a free will and the verisimilitude of moral truths (and hence responsibility). To dispense with such metaphysical errors is not, to be sure, to do away with responsibility as such; the falsehood of conventional moral responsibility is revealed by the 'seeker of knowledge' whose 'gay science' admits of the necessary entwinement of truth and error. Nietzsche's truth claim here of an identifiable error—falsehood—is coupled to his notion of a higher, nobler freedom that is characterized by a *capacity* and preparedness for the greatest responsibilities (e.g. Napoleon).

We can represent his alternate conception of responsibility thus:

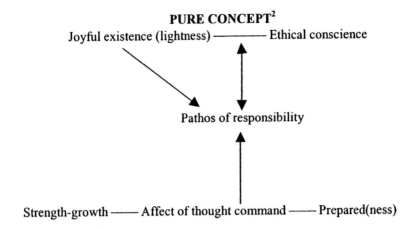

PURE CONCEPT²
Joyful existence (lightness) ———— Ethical conscience

Pathos of responsibility

Strength-growth ——— Affect of thought command ——— Prepared(ness)

Figure 4

Conversely, responsibility according to Nietzsche does *not* require a soul be weighed down by the weight of gravity (a declining spirit owing to the lawful necessity of abstract duties). Elevation is the mark of those souls that live life joyously, dancing to the gay science of existence which of necessity incorporates the (true) artist's plan of commanding and creating out of strength. Omitting 'free will', Nietzsche's pure concept entails the elements of 'commanding' and 'self-overcoming' (from Figure 2) within what he often calls 'strength'. The immanent fortitude of the self allows for overcoming, which, as we have already seen, is connected to the affect of thought command. The above figure (4) shows the twin supports of this Affect, with the preparedness of *Bildung* on one side and the vital drives of growth, extension and affirmation of suffering (pathos) complimenting the other side. Indeed, preparedness as the artwork of culture can be conceived in largely botanical terms as Nietzsche—who had contemplated gardening as a vacation—likened the processes of *becoming* to the cultivation, growth, extension, ripening and pruning of plants.²⁰ What achieves this, in part, is the 'culture complex' (WP 462) of *Bildung* and the fatality of one's own 'development' out of nature (in Greek, *zoi* within *bios*). 'Preparedness' then is cultivation, polishing the mirror, so that growth takes on a beautiful noble form, a form to behold within the chaos of human-all-too-human impoverishment. Gravity impoverishes while elevation (like organic plant life) enhances and reaps beautiful fruits of life. One of the 'fruits' of growth—extension, form, measure, becoming fulsome—is responsibility. From Nietzsche's later notebooks we find for instance a decidedly Goethean motif in Nietzsche's observation on this point: 'to what extent responsibility for the whole trains the individual to, and permits him, a broad view, a stern and terrible hand, a circumspection and coolness, a grandeur of bearing and gesture, which he would not permit himself on his own behalf' (WP 773). A light, bright ethical conscience is also added to the *morphe* of the noble soul in his published *Genealogy* since as Figure 4 shows, it stems from the 'pathos of responsibility' and indirectly, the 'affect of command' *and* 'strength-growth'.

Without each of these vital dimensions of subjectivity and objective life, an 'ethical conscience' would be dissociated from a 'joyful existence (lightness)'; and as we shall see in later chapters, our 'ethical conscience' is not synonymous with the standard 'moral conscience' (later promulgated by Luther). What proves decisive in Figure 4 as opposed to Figure 3 is the presence instead of the absence of 'pathos', 'affect', and strength—all elements of the vitalist, once Schopenhauerian 'honest naturalism', and Goethean nobility of spirit that is devoid of romanticism. It eschews the formal abstractions of idealism while simultaneously rejecting the romantic's *laisser aller* and affirming the noble value of responsibility in the formation of higher, free spirits. Why? As we saw from Pure Concept[1] commanding is an essential feature of Nietzsche's concept of freedom and therefore when a person has the ability to command, 'to legislate' according to their 'artist's plan', then he or she must also have the power to take responsibility for his promises and stated 'word' on matters. To shy away from important responsibilities is to take an industrial (i.e. modern plebian) view of things as if one can reduce life preoccupations to mere 'tasks' and jobs, that is labor. This thinking is the thinking—the mark—of a slave, an industrial slave who believes it is emancipated by the principle of equality. Being slavish to 'tasks' and 'jobs', they fail to rise to the heights of noble responsibilities because they are fearful of them; that is, they fear failure in themselves. It is logical that they would since they are ill-prepared: the culture-complex affords them belief in the metaphysics of free will while contrarily demanding conformity to norms and mores of the tradition (*Sitten*) that prescribe concrete obligations/duties. The unthinking masses are unfree because their affect-structure disallows the letting go of a faith in the belief of a supreme Free Will and its causal basis in actions (i.e. blame, guilt). The (industrial) slave's imprisonment is not merely external or political then, but fundamentally metaphysical-religious: faith, belief, and soul are inextricably bound up with each other, thereby making 'domination' intrinsically a matter of the spirit and not merely a question of the 'grand politics' of 'order of rank' (i.e. distance, power, hierarchy).[21]

By contrast, those of joyful spirits, whose nature is not weighed down by the pessimism of life or the resentment within reactive souls imprisoned by their own herd instinct (obeying), take delight in all that which life offers, seeing challenge and opportunity as a moment to grow, extend or command. They interpret every moment that demands a design, a height of viewpoints, and forthright valuation and decision an opportunity to weigh-up, measure and assume responsibility for any form-giving that occurs by the will of power. To this extent, the *form* of 'herd' or 'slave' of a particular society—the self-formation of other types under the principle of distance—is configured in relation to the distance and height of the 'commanding spirit'—the legislator or 'true philosopher' as Nietzsche calls them at times. As every type of human being in the social figuration of power and time embodies a quantum of will, of power, it is only relative or, as Aristotle would call it, 'proportionate' to the totality of the matrix and its 'order of rank' i.e. 'weak will' versus 'strong will'. The weakly or decadent 'type' of human being, as indicated above, cannot assume or desire the 'greatest responsibilities'; therefore it mistakes the superior willed for 'dominators' instead of 'rulers' since their relatively lower position—underprivileged task-laborer—must be *caused* by the autonomous 'free will' of the master. The master is held responsible for his subjugation, his suffering and his injury, since after all his master appears to possess the caliber, the mind and *Geist* for commanding. As legislator, his commanding will must have an object upon which to act upon just as force in physics acts upon a surface to *cause* movement. Thus subjugation, one's actual servitude, is intricately tied up with the myth of *causa efficiens*.[22] The modern industrial slave lacks cheerfulness we could say in part because his own (nihilistic) scientific civilization—his milieu—perpetuates the error of causation and this inexorably flows over into what Kant called 'practical reason'. Man reasons this way in various modalities, particularly in matters of moral action and social intercourse so much so that duties constitutive of one's "moral obligations" inevitably stem from the myth of "cause—effect" binaries. Later we shall see that the great moral 'falsehoods' of contemporary 'herd-morality' are further imbued with the mythical substance of the *causa sui*. At this point we note instead the distinct lack of joyful affirmation in the order of rank of the soul of an 'underprivileged' subject. The burden from without is now replicated from within, transforming the human animal soul into a burdened, camel-like creature who moans, complains and seeks revenge out of hostility for his onerous burdens. Yet this creature simultaneously subscribes to Christian precepts of unegoism and the moral virtues pertaining dutiful actions, making his burdens of the camel even more torturously painful. "Deny the ego-instincts even while you surrender more and more by your good deeds and intentions" is the catch-cry of the 'modern man'—a nihilist who avows the value of *this* life but celebrates the life *after*. The camel must carry the burden of life—the flesh and its weakness—in order to sanctify a dreaded existence and attain redemption from all human suffering. 'Height' here is transfigured—by Christian nihilists—into the Heaven of which all redeemed souls shall be 'lifted up' in the End. Noble free spirits who impose form onto the chaos of *this* world instead take delight in the cheerfulness of fulfilling their own responsibilities as part of realizing the promise of the earth.

We can now show the 'psycho-physician of the soul's' tableau of the 'free spirit' versus the slave-soul thus:

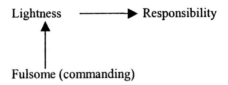

Figure 5

Against the conventional 'camel' *imago* of taking on moral responsibilities, Nietzsche's concept of responsibility by contrast shows lightness of spirit— complimented by depth and breadth of soul—to enable responsible acts. The joy of life seeks more than self-interested preservation, relying not upon formal abstract *dis*interested[23] duties, but staking a claim on the happiness and beauty which comes from esteeming one's worth in life, in nature. To *become* free is to see the joyful beauty of this life as unfolding, manifold life that is marked nobly by 'distances' and distinction rather than 'flatness' and uniformity. This vibrant, colored beauty of forms has a morphology which Goethe-the-botanist well understood as abounding in magnificent form; its 'lightness of feet' stems, like the plant-stem, from the 'soil' of immanent fulsomeness. Through becoming fulsome—manifold, measured, comprehensive, broader and deeper—the individual is not overcome by pessimism of spirit for she also marshals the instincts by her side. Being still part 'animal-soul', though transfigured, this most interesting animal discharges and recharges her instinctual energy—her *eros* of life, her *oreisis* (desire)—through her freedom to keep her word, be accountable for her commands and designs, while affirming creatively the wonder and splendor of all things necessary in life. Her own destruction-creation, good-evil, commanding-obeying, willing-resisting, destining-future making are part of the totality of necessities that constitute life (*bios* as against organic *zoi*). The wondrous beauty of affirmation in the midst of "misery" is what gives joy to the human being who might otherwise despair over the finitude of one's being. Joyfulness emanates out of the ugly despair, pain and injury that one tirelessly has to endure if there no longer is a "God" because once this pathos is wedded to the splendor of form (e.g. Wagner's operatic music) it is found in the overcoming man (sic). Dignified and esteemed by his own form-giving powers and "faculty", the fulsome form is capable at once of commanding (which also means obeying himself) and surety of light-footedness so that the 'dance of life' is now what denotes his Dionysian nature. The Dionysian union of impulse and sight lift the soul of man in defiance of gravity's 'pull'—a weightiness of resentful injury and pain owing to man's own self-torture (self-hatred and torment). Negatively, man knows joy at least because of joy he gains from tormenting his soul, his very being, by turning vengeful feelings against himself and later murdering "the Father", God. To have willed nothingness, the nihilist, Nietzsche argued, enjoys the reverberations of his own soul. If no Supreme Being or authority any longer exists then this 'willing' power resides in no other than yourself. "You must be responsible for that which you have taken charge of" is Nietzsche's retort to the pure nihilist and romantic idealist. In other words, you are "not a man if you hate yourself" and to love yourself as the gospel had commanded requires that you render yourself accountable to no other than man himself—thus says Nietzsche the 'immoralist', the advocate of an ethical conscience which demands a fulsome joyous nature. That is Nietzsche's decidedly non-bourgeois, "liberal" conception of freedom: free *to be* responsible as opposed to "free *from*".

The negative psychology (of will and cause) manifested by the feeble 'decadent' represents the latter kind—free *from*—even while his belief maintains an obligation toward formal "oughts" and "shall nots", i.e. formal moral duties. Contrary to many commentaries that are happy to stop at pointing out the indeterminate, battle-ridden contestation between drives of the soul, we find below the counter-schema to a noble soul, the slave-soul, as more than simply a moment of *agon*.

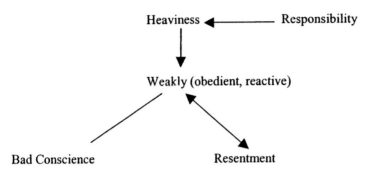

Figure 6

In other words, there are decisive processual differences in the operations and concatenations of the soul of higher type and lower type human beings (just as there are between human animals and non-human animals, according to the *Gay Science*). It is true that Nietzsche's language often suggests or implies a high degree of indeterminacy and essentially combative struggle. While that is not in itself particularly problematic it would however be quite erroneous to think that Nietzsche had leveled out the topological surface of man's *Seele* (soul). Types of 'man' and types of soul are intricately interwoven just as overcoming is tightly interwoven with social forms of mastery—slavery throughout epochs. We can, that is, identify a form that is superordinate—the ugly form of 'degeneration'—and a superordinate counter-type: the healthy, supple and sublime form. While these clearly undergo metamorphosis in time, owing to particular civilizational constellations and manifestations, they encapsulate the *Idée* of each quantum of force and will: the antipodes or *Gegensatz* of the eternal struggle. Nietzsche himself drew attention to his *Idée* of 'slave' and 'master' without necessarily explicating it thus, preferring instead to outline immanent characteristics (not 'virtues') of those a) dwelling in the valley of life and b) those in the mountain air as *Zarathustra* shows. Yet a 'true philosopher'—as against a pure genealogist, psychologist, artist, experimenter and perspective-interpreter—must have the astuteness of a 'seeker of knowledge' and the acumen to discern the truth of ascetic degeneration, nihilistic despair and weakness of instinct and soul. Like Plato—though not Socrates—his noble elevated vision grasps the forms which prove elusive to the *demos* of the *polis*. These two essential forms emerge out of a synoptic, comprehensive 'gay science'—as a following chapter shall demonstrate—which, following Goethe and Schopenhauer, aims at the totality of life. Forms while undoubtedly made evident by perspective—by the

eyes as Plato and Heraclitus said—transcend any one particular optic onto the
πραγματικòς.

The real philosopher as against mental laborers is untimely in his age partly
due to his cutting, incisive 'eye and ear' which overcomes all prevailing sense-
appearances. Hence the 'charm of the Platonic way of thinking, which was a
noble way of thinking, consisted precisely in *resistance* to obvious sense-
evidence', to resistance to mob senses and to sensibilities for theatrical *phantasia* (BGE 14). It is not surprising to find Nietzsche in the company of Plato if we
think of many types of Plato(nism) and how Nietzsche mostly sought to overcome dreary Christian, Augustinian neo-Platonism as well as the mob-ish 'So-
cratic-Plato' who was a mere dialectician. A noble Plato is one which stands
opposed to Christian resignation and pessimism. Thus the higher forms of each
of these 'ideas' of 'master and slaves souls' is unmistakable to Nietzsche the
critic of historicism and philology; he came to such a realization, as with each
new dawning, when he proclaimed in *Beyond Good and Evil* (260):

> Wandering through the many subtler and coarser moralities which have so far
> been prevalent on earth, or still are prevalent, I found that certain features re-
> curred regularly together and were closely associated—until I finally discov-
> ered two basic types and one basic difference.

The 'certain features' found to be recurring regularly in societies over time
are grasped conceptually by the discovery of 'two basic types': master morality
and slave morality. Similarly, the ascetic figure and his ideals can be readily
found when 'wandering through the many subtler and coarser moralities' of diverse civilizations since the religious ascetic too is another 'basic type' with its
own soul-morphology. Preferring to explicate the importance of *becoming* and
its attendant *amor fati*, Nietzsche did not venture so far as to expound on the
idea of master-slave types even though he continuously made reference to them,
particularly in the nomenclature of 'low' and 'high'. He did refer to both elements occurring 'at times' 'directly alongside each other' 'within a *single* soul'
(BGE 260). And yet the pure concepts outlined above transcend the particularity
of any single place, time and person. This has less to do with German Idealism
than an earnest attempt to challenge the limits of Greek philosophy via intense
challenges to different 'Platonisms'. Against Heidegger, we concur with Michel
Haar that Nietzsche's thought has greater affinities with Plato than is ordinarily
supposed by most twentieth century observers.[24] But it is only the more '*noble*
way of thinking' of Plato minus Socratism that is endurably compelling and
felicitous for Nietzsche's way of thinking. Both rejected historicism and mob
morality; and both found truth not in consciousness per se but in unfolding
forms of *becoming*. For present purposes though we are mainly concerned with
the distinct *morphe* of the 'master' soul and 'slave' soul and their distinction in
architectonic terms. This overcomes the limitation of imprecise, generalistic
depictions of soul-drives and their inner battles which are generally known to
plague civilized, tamed human beings. Nietzsche, in short, possessed not only
the 'idea' of eternal recurrence and self-overcoming but also the idea of the
dominated soul versus the responsibly free soul-structure in an extra-historical

sense. The affirmation of life, after all, requires a transcendence of historical subjects, historical consciousness and historic sociability.

The strength of this Pure Concept[1-2] approach affords Nietzsche a certain interpretive and normative perspicacity to identify various slaves, ascetics, nihilists and mediocre cultures throughout history while on the other hand not reducing the futurity of existence to the contingencies of 'men' (sic), society and national-linguistic chauvinisms. Specialists, mental laborers, state officials and the 'everyday man of the newspaper' may in fact show a predilection for such contingencies and chauvinisms, but not true philosophers and artists. Each of the latter can dance and compose forms with soul-structures (forms) depicted here in Figures 4 & 5; and because of their relatively extra-discerning 'eyes and ears' and preparation,[25] the *idea* of morbid, 'sickly' slave-souls is grasped. As healthy, joyful spirits, they are not weighed down by the weight of guilt, resentment and vengeance or even herd-consciousness (see Figure 6). Yet the converse 'seeing' does not apply: the herd slave-soul lacks the perspicacity of the 'true artist', the real philosopher or, in other words, the 'seeker of knowledge' with his 'gay science'. It is asymmetrical necessarily, as Plato well understood, because those who cannot command themselves are by definition ill-prepared for the great task, including the great task of 'legislating'—creating, evaluating, and inscribing the future onto the present. This great task of 'legislating' or commanding as Nietzsche often called it, of course cannot be performed without a decisive vigor of spirit that issues from having overcome oneself, that is, without having first commanded and obeyed oneself above all else. This strongly Platonic leitmotiv regarding what is required of the human being to perform the great task of commanding and legislating—experience of *kairos* (time) within a polis—is now coupled to the mob's (*demos*) inability to apprehend their task. Namely, that the 'common people could possibly understand anything of what is most remote from them' is what is doubted: viz, the 'great *passion* of the seeker after knowledge who lives and must live continually in the thundercloud of the *highest problems* and the *heaviest responsibilities*' (GS 351, emphasis added). Hence not the removed, otherworldly sage-like ascetic type who is an 'observer, outside, indifferent, secure and objective' but instead the lover of joyful wisdom who 'must live continually' in the heights of the 'highest problems' and 'heaviest responsibilities'. It is the peculiar task of he who exercises disciplined mastery through the right to take responsibility for that which comes under his powers, his "designs", and Nietzsche would say elliptically 'destiny'. Those not "destined"[26] for such great responsibilities are integral to the task of preparing and laboring for such purposes and goals—'distance' does not preclude them from this activity but merely differentiates them from the 'higher ones'. What is of utmost importance for a life lived continually in the *heights* of the 'highest problems' is that lightness of soul (figure 5) which feels free in its modality as opposed to that more dour, heavy spirit that yearns for brightness through release: philosophers and "free spirits" after nihilism shall feel 'At long last the horizon appears free to us again, *even if it should not be bright*' (GS 343, emphasis added).

Setting out upon new seas and horizons, with all the responsibility associated with the most commonplace dangers, these free spirits do not demand "brightness, optimism" as do, conversely, overburdened, severe and 'dance-less' spirits who too readily succumb to exhaustion owing to heavy moral imperatives. The former possess inner strength and independence of mind as well as vitality and the know-how and preparation to perform responsibilities under varying conditions—favorable, challenging, adverse, dangerous or uncertain. As they are not outwardly oriented (reactive), conditions from without neither deter them nor estrange them from their grand task; external conditions merely act as a form of resistance to be overcome when instituting a tableau of commanding values and "legislating" new ways of self-direction. Being capable of self-direction they are devoid of that acerbic resentfulness normally directed at the external world because their fulsome nature (figure 5) requires no hostility toward life, toward others. 'Self-direction' here refers to that fulsomeness of spirit which can realize greatness through steadfast overcoming; it is a decisive term Nietzsche used in a note subsequent to 'The Four Great Errors' of *Twilight of the Idols* in the *Nachlass* (705). In performing a reversal of the standard error of free will 'virtues' Nietzsche here explains: 'all fitness the result of fortunate organization, all freedom the result of fitness (—freedom here understood as facility in self-direction. Every artist will understand me)'. Fitness or robustness and healthiness of soul—represented above in figure 5 as 'fulsome'—is considered the 'result of fortunate organization' and this fully concurs with our foregoing analysis of soul morphologies through Pure Concepts, i.e. the *Idée* of 'slave' and 'free' human beings exemplified in history. Distinction in the spiritual arrangement or 'organization' of the human being is what ultimately proves determinative in the realization of both greatness and freedom, for English 'happiness' did not particularly concern Zarathustra. It is noteworthy that in this same passage freedom requires a certain 'fitness' or robustness for its realization which is precisely what figures 4-5 above illustrate. Without a careful cultivation of soul and spirit there can be no freedom; and without freedom there naturally can be no responsibility either. This in fact is what will necessarily entail 'greatness'—Nietzsche's most pronounced normative ideal, the enhancement of mankind through greatness. Like Wagner and Goethe, Nietzsche's philosophical preoccupation with enhancing 'man' is expressed through this fundamentally Greek valorization—greatness. We can see that in overcoming the nausea of Today, higher human beings and souls who aim at greatness do so not primarily in some aesthetic or moralistic sense; they rather seek to enhance human culture through manifoldness of soul and overcoming of False Reality[1-2]. Without each of these—manifoldness and overcoming slavish illusions—there can be no 'open seas' and no future horizons full of promise. In further discussion obstacles posed by the 'slave-soul' and Today's nauseating spirit of revenge shall be examined in later chapters via 'bad conscience', resentment and revenge-taking.

Notes

1. F. Nietzsche 'On Self-Overcoming', Second Part of *Thus Spoke Zarathustra* [Z] Translated by Walter Kaufmann. London: Penguin, 1978.

2. On problems with French deconstruction, see Jürgen Habermas *The Philosophical Discourse of Modernity*. Translated by Fredrich G. Lawrence. Cambridge, Mass.: MIT, 1987 and Maudemarie Clark *Nietzsche On Truth and Philosophy*. Melbourne: Cambridge University Press, 1990.

3. Habermas, *The Philosophical Discourse of Modernity*, 97.

4. G. Deleuze *Nietzsche and Philosophy*. Trans. Hugh Tomlinson. New York: Columbia University Press, 1983: 85.

5. J. Habermas 'The Entwinement of Myth and Enlightenment: Re-Reading the *Dialectic of Enlightenment*', *New German Critique*, 26, 1982: 13-30.

6. As Axel Honneth communicated in a conversation with me at the Johann Wolfgang von Goethe University, Frankfurt (February 2005), a deep ambivalence nevertheless presided over the minds of Adorno and Horkheimer with regard to the import of Nietzsche's philosophy.

7. Habermas, 'The Entwinement of Myth and Enlightenment', 18.

8. Habermas, 'The Entwinement of Myth and Enlightenment', 16.

9. This italicized word appears in the original essay by Habermas. The decidedly demonstrative nature of Nietzsche's working out of fundamental 'errors' and illusions is crucially apprehended here by Habermas ('The Entwinement of Myth and Enlightenment', 27).

10. Habermas, 'The Entwinement of Myth and Enlightenment', 25.

11. Habermas, 'The Entwinement of Myth and Enlightenment', 26.

12. See further Karin Bauer 'Nietzsche, Enlightenment, and the Incomplete Project of Modernity', *Habermas, Nietzsche, and Critical Theory*. Edited by Babette E. Babich. New York: Humanity Books, 2004.

13. A. Honneth *The Struggle For Recognition: The Moral Grammar Of Social Conflicts*. Translated by Joel Anderson. Cambridge, Mass.: Polity Press, 1995.

14. I have made only limited use of Nietzsche's posthumously published notebooks (i.e. WP) consistent with the vital distinction drawn by some contemporary Nietzsche scholars between published works and unpublished notes, for example Maudemarie Clark.

15. This argument, contrariwise to more recent materialist reinterpretations of Nietzsche's work, posits the centrality of Helleno-Germanic philosophic concerns with the fundamental orientation to the world we take up and not simply the 'mind of Man' as promulgated by some logico-analytic thinkers. Any proper physiologico-psychological physician, argued Nietzsche, takes care of both bodily and soulful symptoms, effects, forces and *morphe* in their diagnosis of individual and social forms of life.

16. *Twilight of the Idols* was originally titled *A Psychologist's Leisure or The Idle Hours of a Psychologist* before Nietzsche was persuaded to change it prior to its publication into its present form. In Nietzsche's revised notes to his much earlier work *Human, All Too Human I* he sets out the great importance of 'a microscopic psychology' as no less necessary than his much valorized 'historical perspectivist optics' in more recent literature (chapter 1, note 1).

17. See Richard Schacht's incisive treatment of Nietzsche as a thinker who is centrally concerned with forms of knowledge, types of 'knowers' and the virtue of experimental investigations, in *Making Sense of Nietzsche*, chapters 3 and 10.

18. See further Emmanuel Levinas *Totality and Infinity: An Essay on Exteriority.* Translated by Alphonso Lingis. Pittsburgh: Duquesne University Press, 1969. In Nietzschean terms, the invention of 'bad conscience' also harbored the good (bad) conscience beyond the naturalistic 'animalic' state of being human (i.e. pre-moral history).

19. This point concerning exchange relations and the contractual relationship is discussed at some length in a subsequent chapter (chapter 5 'Revenge of Modernity').

20. Moreover, the 'promise of the earth' and later on Heidegger's celebrated 'pathway' are related to the symbolic importance and axiological value of the earth's soil, the 'ground'. Noble spirits are likened to the greatest ripened fruits that result from so many nutrient, selective processes including birth, destruction, reproduction, seeding and root-fundaments. The implication is that the gardener, as the handmaiden of nature, is an artist of form.

21. Two notable treatments of Nietzsche's thought which appreciate and explicitly acknowledge this important added dimension of overcoming and the 'regime of the soul' are Alex McIntyre *The Sovereignty of Joy: Nietzsche's Vision of Grand Politics.* Toronto: University of Toronto Press, 1997 and Horst Hutter *Shaping the Future: Nietzsche's New Regime of the Soul and Its Ascetic Practices.* Lanham: Lexington Books, 2006. In his note of 1888 "Redemption from all guilt", Nietzsche sums up the psycho-politics of the social rank thus: 'Here the claim is made to judge history, to divest if of its fatality, to discover responsibility behind it, guilty men in it. For this is the rub: one needs guilty men' (WP 765). The intimate connection between guilt-responsibility-resentment (resistance) herein is consistent with the logic of Nietzsche's argument in published writings and therefore worth examination.

22. In a notebook entry of 1888 (WP 551) Nietzsche critiques the concept of 'cause' along lines described in our discussion and further adds that we combine our feeling of "freedom", will and responsibility 'into the concept "cause": *causa efficiens* and *causa finalis* are fundamentally one'.

23. In contradistinction to Kant's idea of 'imperative' Nietzsche posits the 'natures of Caesar and Napoleon' with their '"disinterested" work on their marble' whose future in essence entails 'to bear the *greatest responsibility* and *not* collapse under it'; these highest men possessed a 'faith in one's right and one's hand' (WP 975). Particularly noteworthy here is the requirement not to 'collapse' under the weight of the 'greatest responsibility'. Otherwise, how can one lay claim to individual sovereignty if one simply folds under the weight of some great burden—a project, goal, politics or task of self-enhancement?

24. Michel Haar *Nietzsche and Metaphysics.* Albany: State University of New York Press, 1996.

25. The question of preparation, training and the work of *Bildung* (of *bios*) is examined later in 'Freedom and Responsibility' (chapter four).

26. The vital instinctual-spiritual animal, the human being, is interpolated between striving (for self-directedness) and Greek fatalism. Complimentary rather than antithetical—or "tragic" instead of "optimistic"—these twin poles of existence push or direct this 'most interesting animal' along its temporal lines. Greek fatalism, joining up with Goethean naturalistic freedom, is properly captured by a passage from *The Antichrist* (57): 'Difficult tasks are a privilege to them; to play with burdens which crush others, a

recreation...They rule not because they want to but because they *are*; they are not free to be second'. One's form, the *morphe* of one's constitution in other words, is determinative rather than a supposed lust for power or status-dominion over others. One does not, contrary to 'modern ideas', merely *choose to* be free—that is mere "superficiality".

CHAPTER TWO

Being Human, Nature and the Possibility of Overcoming

What distinguishes the higher human beings from the lower is that the former see and hear immeasurably more, and see and hear thoughtfully—and precisely this distinguishes human beings from animals, and the higher animals from the lower (GS 301).

Foundations

Overcoming is the condition of overcoming blind necessity—this is a necessary truth of the condition of freedom. In this chapter 'necessity' will incorporate the dictates or limits of nature herself. To conceive of human freedom is, for Nietzsche, to therefore ponder the extent to which human beings negotiate the limits of their own 'nature' and conditions of existence while simultaneously acquiring varying degrees of self-mastery, or, more accurately, self-overcoming. Given Nietzsche's repudiation of romantic, humanistic ideals of self-*mastery* we can more accurately refer to his interpretive and normative stratagems as a philosophy of self-*overcoming*, including the overcoming of nature's blind limits (civilization, will to power). Because of Nietzsche's frequent denunciations of the soul-concept, Being and the (psychologist's) Ego, it is often overlooked whether his anti-metaphysical stance is girded by a certain philosophical anthropology of the human being, one that issues from his own frequent appeals to (pursue) a 'historical philosophy'. Without an historical philosophy of the human being and its natures, it arguably is very difficult to grasp the idea of freedom which permeates much of Nietzsche's oeuvre. This idea has eluded many serious commentaries on Nietzsche especially those which have read him in strictly anti-Hegelian terms—Deleuze, Derrida, Habermas—or which have summarily dismissed Nietzsche's intense dialogue with prominent figures of German and Greek philosophy including Kant, Schopenhauer, Wagner and the famous Tübingen group. By contrast others such as the prominent English translator of Nietzsche's corpus, Walter Kaufmann, correctly maintain the proximity that abides between Hegel's historical philosophy and Nietzsche's genealogy of moralities and forms of self-understanding. Similarly, the prominent Nietzsche scholar Richard Schacht has shown strong analytical affinities between the work of the spectacle lens grinder Baruch Spinoza and Nietzsche the boy of a near

absent Lutheran Father.[1] Both Maudemarie Clark and Brian Leiter[2] have further
extended the analysis of Nietzsche as a thinker who continues rather than abandons the examination of major philosophical motifs within the tradition of western philosophy. Consistent with this approach is the possibility of examining a
set of arguments and experimental descriptions—there are 'no explanations' as
such argued Nietzsche—which distinctly situate Nietzsche within the grand tradition of western philosophy, evincing a type of thinking which essentially in-
vokes a kind of philosophical anthropology of human nature(s). This distinctive
analytical method arguably has not been eclipsed either by linguistic-centered
approaches or by Heideggerian inspired treatments of Nietzsche, especially
where ironic play and style have loomed large. Indeed, contrary to Martin Heidegger's relegation of the study of beings in their concrete historical form to a
devalourized 'cultural anthropology'[3], our analytic concern places the fundamental drives and conditions of being human at the centre of Nietzsche's con-
certed effort to take *Bildung* beyond the present confines of modern humanism,
scientific rationalism and liberal nationalist politics. Nietzsche's concept of
Bildung (self-cultivation, education) will prove decisive later in our discussion
when we turn to Nietzsche's acclaimed naturalism, particularly as it shows him
diverging in significant ways from Lange's famous materialism, British physiology and the logic of the atomic physicists.

Nietzsche's philosophical anthropology instead will be linked more explicitly to the ancients' struggle to elevate man to a 'height' (the eagle) lesser than
the gods yet higher than that of creatures who lack βιος (life), i.e. captured by
bare ζωη (sentient life). Of necessity this will also entail the affirmative spirit in
which Nietzsche wrote and developed his critiques of European nihilism, registering the twin importance of self-creation and the process of becoming 'what
one is'—both critical facets of Nietzsche's conception of the tragic *sophos*.[4] The
spirit of this philosophical stance and its attendant creative drive captures the
saliency of the artist for Nietzsche who, as the heir of German (and French)
Romanticism, developed a philosophical anthropology of the human being that
recognizes the artist's work in the formative process of transvaluating nature
herself.[5] When Nietzsche spoke of the noble higher being, for instance, he envisaged one who 'calls his own nature *contemplative* and overlooks that he himself is really the poet who keeps creating this life'. 'As a poet, he certainly has
vis contemplativa and the ability to look back upon his work, but at the same
time also and above all *vis creativa* [creative power]' (GS 301). Two points can
therefore be made at this early stage: first, we know that this philosopher was
unwilling to place himself under the sway of a fully blown (material) naturalistic
outlook; second, it is an unmistakably universal (trans- perspectival) conception
that allows the possibility of a cheerful wisdom or 'gay science' to be realized.
Such a method (science) aims to overcome the antithesis between art and science, and the 'particular' and 'universal': 'Whether I contemplate men with be-
nevolence or with an evil eye, I always find them concerned with a single task,
all of them and every one of them in particular: to do what is good for the preservation of the human race' (GS 1). This broadly comprehensive observation
captures the essential universality of Nietzsche's conception of human endeav-

ors and predicaments whilst also showing human action to be goal directed even though history (like nature) lacks any purpose, i.e. Judaeo-Christian teleology. Further, it runs counter to the commonplace mistake that Nietzsche, following Spinoza, advocated a normative conception of philosophy based upon the principal of self-preservation. To concur fully with Clark (2000), it is possible to argue *against* the centrality of his claimed 'power ontology' and essential Darwinian notion of self-preservation while also on my account maintaining the paramount importance of 'becoming': becoming as self-cultivation involving the overcoming of Nature's cruel indifference. What raises us above *physis* (nature) therefore is *Bildung* understood as something essentially agonic and spiritual in nature. Freedom is thereby not associated with a determinism latent in a form of naturalism that is supposed to countervail the moralism of modern humanism. We shall see that Nietzsche's understanding of freedom presupposes a *potentiality* inherent within each horizon of the future and the kind of 'soul' mankind has developed historically.

The universality of arguments in Nietzsche's schema also appear when he cautions us against a simple divisibility with respect to our neighbors: namely of 'good-evil' and 'useful-harmful' instead of his preferred standpoint of a 'large-scale accounting' whereby reflecting 'on the whole a little longer' will work against a bleak myopia that obscures the totality of reality from our sights. Nietzsche goes on to say this about the species' primordial human nature: 'to do what is good for the preservation of the human race. Not from any feeling of love for the race, but merely because nothing in them is older, stronger, more inexorable and unconquerable than this instinct—because this instinct constitutes *the essence* of our species, our herd' (GS 1). To inject an 'anti-essentialist' argument at this juncture—as some French and American philosophers have— would be nonsensical because Nietzsche's conception of this supra-animal 'man' remains irreducible to any particular cultural particularism or perspectival value since this only further implicates us in the myopic mire which he set out to free us from. The great significance accorded to the instinctual powers of the human being owes after all to a philosophically derived image of the human being that is not in the least dismissive of the species' historical-empirical variations. Neither *der Herdentrieb* (herd instinct) nor *der Naturtrieb* (instinct) can by this account be easily reduced to the vicissitudes of sociological, political, linguistic or aesthetic values. Nietzsche the knower of tragic-wisdom well understood life as a work of art, and intellectual interrogation requires that we take a species-wide, comprehensive view of the predicament of *human* life. Stoic thinkers had previously understood the saliency of geocultural variation whilst simultaneously probing into fundamental 'predicamental' facets of living a human life. And after the Stoics, in the twentieth century, the work of Max Scheler returned to the question of 'the human', highlighting the importance of affect and concrete sensuous existence over and above abstract reifications similar to Kant's *a priori* and 'things in themselves' (noumena). His concept of *Sonderstellung* highlighted the significance accorded by Nietzsche to this most interesting animal 'man' (sic) consistent with the great leitmotiv of the ancient Greeks; namely of the exceptional position of man in the κοσμος (universe).

Although our analysis aims to establish the efficacy of understanding Nietzsche as a proponent of an unexplicated philosophical anthropology, it by no means postulates that other thematics concerned, for instance, with the order of the physical world are to be rendered subordinate. I maintain that a certain metaphysical background—a synthesis of Heraclitus' and Schopenhauer's philosophies—shadows his conception of Becoming and thus underscores much of Nietzsche's analyses of our worldly experiences despite his purportedly post-metaphysical stance. So rather than setting this analysis against other superordinate discourses which directly address this matter, I aim instead to draw out the deeply philosophico-anthropological dimensions of his thinking in order to better understand the possibility of freedom in human existence. For what reason? Its importance lies in reconnecting this much abused and oftentimes radicalized figure of philosophical investigation with interpretative questions left dormant in contemporary philosophy regarding the conditions of freedom experienced by human beings. Whilst others have transformed this question essentially into what it means to *be*—to exist, of Being or spatio-corporeal extension (*res extensio*)—the question of what kind of being is a human being is arguably determinative of Nietzsche's investigations of Becoming in terms of the processes of *Bildung* that can realize conditions of freedom. It is pertinent for us simply because he speaks to us on *this* basis rather than on the basis of a supposed deconstruction of western philosophy. Its recuperative effort can be gleaned by the sub-title assigned to one of Nietzsche's later texts, *Beyond Good and Evil*, viz 'Prelude to a Philosophy of the Future' (1886). Nietzsche understood the imperative to overcome present prejudice, myopia and nihilistic decadence as constitutive of his 'philosophy of the future'. By doing so he conceived of human drives and conflicts in history from the vantage-point of asking what comprises our distinctive human psychology and will to life. *Kultur* on the other hand is that which allows development or 'elevation', as he called it, of our individual and species efforts; it allows us to exceed our mere animalic nature, articulating a higher mode of being that is not contrary to our human, all-too-human nature. Since there is a diversity of beings in the cosmos, the human form is a kind of being or existent that is distinctive from other beings that appear decidedly non-human, i.e. plants, (most) animals and divinities. It is only in Parmenides' world of the One or in Friedrich Wilhelm Joseph von Schelling's natural philosophy of the Absolute that we encounter a possible counterfactual to this divisibility of beings in relation to an all encompassing unity. Otherwise, Nietzsche draws on a quasi-naturalistic 'materialist' philosophy to delineate the discernible forms in which man *qua* man expresses his will to life through a constant struggle to overcome servitude in the form of meaningless existence. A struggle (of pathos) which is not against φυσις (nature) itself and yet decisively is also a process which can elevate him above *der Herdentrieb* (the herd-instinct) existence of mere αγριο ζωη ('wild life'). Here we find Nietzsche to be closer to Plato in preferring to situate the project of life with βιος as against ζωη, implying a less organic form of life, of growth. Further evidence of Nietzsche's antipathy toward an unproblematized naturalism can be found in a work which succeeds his famous 'chemistry' empirical statements in *Die fröhliche Wissenschaft* (1882):

Beyond Good and Evil. In this work Nietzsche rallies against the British Darwinists, unsophisticated English physiology and the reductionism of atomic physicists. However, it is perhaps the criticisms he laid against the ancient Stoics that is most relevant here:

> "According to nature" you want to *live*? O you noble Stoics, what deceptive words these are! Imagine a being like nature, wasteful beyond measure, indifferent beyond measure, without purposes and consideration, without mercy and justice, fertile and desolate and uncertain at the same time; imagine indifference itself as a power—how *could* you live according to this indifference? Living— is that not precisely wanting to be other than this nature? (BGE 9).

We might say then the question for those beings who are co-determined by *nomos* and *physis*, and therefore language and consciousness is not one primarily of a basic ontology of existence—biological, psychological, sentient or cognitive—but one relating to the plethora of known human forms deriving from constitutive processes that encompass both pain and joy, knowing and enigma, fate and determination, cultivation and forgetfulness, and distance (height) and proximity (sociability). In this regard, what it means to be human in quite general terms will diverge from the kind of analysis proffered by John Richardson's[6] otherwise eloquent work on Nietzsche centered around his claimed 'power ontology'. It also diverges from the aestheticization of life found in Alexander Nehemas' reading of Nietzsche.[7] While it will aim at a truthfulness regarding Nietzsche's view of social relations and the world of experience, it does not approach truth in quite the same abstract way that scholars do when using traditional dualistic language derived essentially from Kant(ianism) regarding the 'things in themselves' versus the phenomenal world of 'appearances'. In believing he could uncover major 'errors' of understanding which also coexist with empirical truths, Nietzsche from his early to late writings conveys a certain truthfulness regarding his claims to the fundamental basis of human actions and normative value regimes as well as psychological states as originating sources and tragic tensions of the condition of human freedom. which we act and live according to within various classes, races and epochs. We gain some idea of the importance accorded to truthfulness when the penultimate exemplar of the seeker of knowledge, Zarathustra, declares:

> . . . what is more important is that Zarathustra is more truthful than any other thinker. His doctrine, and his doctrine alone, posits truthfulness as the highest virtue [EH: Why am I Destiny, 3].

Hence a better theoretical approach to the vexed question of 'truth' would be to examine arguments that appear quintessential with regards to the relative truthfulness of his claim to pierce through manifold falsehoods without necessarily being drawn into the strictures of Kant's dualist world of *noumenal* versus 'apparent phenomena' (i.e. fallible concepts). This renunciation of neo-Kantian explanations of Nietzsche's idea of truth owes in part to the incisive critique developed—in *Beyond Good and Evil*—of Kant's fundamental contradiction.

Namely, that the 'old man of Königsberg' commenced the German habit of scouring for 'faculties' of mind, intuition and so forth in order to explain how synthetic judgments are *a priori* possible. But in doing so he never 'discovered a new faculty in man' but rather merely begged the original question posed to found a sound basis for human understanding. Yet *niaiserie allemande* prevented Germans from comprehending that old Kant must have been dreaming because his purported resolution "By virtue of a faculty" was no answer or explanation at all but 'rather merely a repetition of the question' itself, argued Nietzsche (BGE 11). This does not mean that Nietzsche eschewed rationality and its concomitant *ratio*; he wanted rather to recognize its real force without having to impute a special ontological (categorical) status to that which allows human beings to give expression to their thoughts and perceptions. A similar strong argument is made by Richard Schacht when he defends, in a decidedly analytic fashion, the correct view that Nietzsche never intended to develop a relativistic perspectivism whereby all interpretations are considered of equal standing. Nor did Nietzsche restrict himself to the metaphysics of Kant's academic language but rather saw himself as a philosopher who could distinguish between more worthwhile and less worthwhile ways of living, between more and less advantageous arguments *for* the affirmation of life. Schacht (1995) refers to this trans-perspectivism as a kind of 'cheerful science': how to philosophize about life with all its Schopenhauerian pain and suffering, cheerfully. And he shows how this 'science' of knowing and understanding involves an examination of 'types of man' which the 'knower' or experimenter can discern in the long historical processes of recurrence and overcoming.

Such an observation is hardly incongruent with the richly interpretive treatment proffered by Nietzsche concerning the essential ambiguity of reality with all its tragic dimensions. Indeed, it arguably goes directly to Nietzsche's philosophical anthropology as it dispenses with spurious dichotomous categories such as realism-romanticism and reason-instincts. It entails the argument that man is neither necessarily rational nor instinctual in essence. A commonplace *prima facie* reading of Nietzsche often leads to the implausible yet popular conclusion that Nietzsche set out to negate rational inquiry due to his staunch advocacy for instinctual life. The proposition offered here—similarly explored by Schacht and Ludwig Feuerbach earlier on—is more subtle, complex and accommodating regarding 'human types' because it overcomes traditional dualisms such as reason versus instinct. It rather posits the fundamental contestation between different human drives or powers immanent within the human being, each vying for sovereign rule. To be sure human beings possess both the intellectual powers of *Nous* and Dionysian drives of creative *Trieb* (impulse), enabling thought and growth simultaneously; moreover, human natures are constituted by the lived *history* of this complex symbiosis as experienced in and through the ongoing contestations between competing human drives and wills.[8] Indeed this constitutes one of Nietzsche's fundamental commitments to truthfulness: to show human experience to be a wholly this-worldly affair, determined in part by historical destining (fate) and in part by human instigation (drive, willing) while at the same time underscored by humanity's will to knowledge—a derivative of the 'basic drives of man' (BGE 6). This includes the destining effect which errors have in history and not merely the drive of a will to truth that aims to know *a priori* the constitution of the genus *homo sapiens*.

Nietzsche 'the philosopher' like Zarathustra himself, increasingly valued the strength of incisive thinking because he understood its power to lift the veil of various myths, thus rendering inept the feeble servitude of moralists who are encaged by their own severe ascetic values. We can discern lesser and grander forms of understanding—about ourselves and historical reality—Nietzsche showed in the tale of that great riddle of history: the fearful encounter with the figure of the Sphinx. This most ancient, mythical and powerful figure who possessed more than one nature exposes us to a fundamental question: What is man or *anthropos*? We must remember that it was the Sophist Protagoras who expounded the argument that 'man is the measure of all things'; he impressed upon Nietzsche the idea that by virtue of the genus *anthropos*, every human being through its own immanent experiences has recourse to the intelligible. This point signifies a fundamental enigma which concerns not only the natural order but a particular opaqueness specific to the fundamental conditions of being *human*: what does it mean to say I am a being who understands itself to be a distinctly *human* being yet remains puzzled by this question? For instance, whilst apes may possess the former they are not necessarily overtaken by an *aporia* regarding their own ontology. Since every being lives or experiences its own *Wesen*, it is more definitive for human beings to inquire into the nature of their experience of life. That is to say, to turn their subjectivity into an object of intellectual inquiry and axiological reflection (i.e. value problematization). Rather than an opponent of critical self-understanding Nietzsche can be seen as a strong proponent of the human race turning its own endeavors into an object of investigation. When examining the 'moral imperative' of human natures in the historical process in *Beyond Good and Evil* (188) Nietzsche located it neither in formal categorical imperatives (Kant) nor in individuals but in 'peoples, races, ages, classes—but above all to the whole human animal, to *man*'. This is wholly consistent with our conception of man as the complex effect of life (bios) rather than organic nature (zoi). This is aptly demonstrated by the metaphoric illustration of the predicamental nature of human life in the story of the Sphinx given in this same work.

In Sophocles' tragic work Oedipus embarks on a journey of destiny which finds him grappling with Homeric divine forces. In confronting the fearful Sphinx the majority of mankind seem unable to comprehend the Sphinx's cunning question and consequently err in the face of death. Whilst life beckons, calling us to come forth from our everyday stupor, comfort is sought in the familiar, the common, the fraternal, the same and the certain. Ordinary existence encapsulates a true falsehood; it beguiles us into an ignorance of what we 'human-animals' are. We are thus strangers to ourselves, as Nietzsche argued in *On the Genealogy of Morals*, principally because we have not really sought to know ourselves. The obvious question therefore arises 'How can we attempt to answer this daunting Sphinx if we dare not ask ourselves its cognate, "What is man?"' The Riddle of history is therefore justly named; history becomes the just taskmaster as it also was for Hegel. The 'will to knowledge', as this context well demonstrates, cannot therefore be abjured since Nietzsche well recognized that we *do need* to respond to the Sphinx in order to have *life*—his penultimate value. Knowledge (of man) *eo ipso* is highly valuable but remains illusive, difficult and almost always veiled. Nietzsche used the elevated figure of Zarathustra in his previous work to signify not only the one who might correctly respond to the Sphinx but also the spiritual height of the real philosopher as it stands in relation to the valley-existence of 'the many', as Aristotle once called it. The valley is where men and women have sought shelter from Nature; yet the clue lies not in seeking refuge from life but instead in being willing to be exposed to the cold hardships of life where history blows furiously and sweeps away certitude. At this juncture of the argument, we may note briefly how this vision entails a large modicum of Roman courage and strength, virtues that are, to be sure, more present in the valiant civilizational norms of antiquity than in their Christian successors. Indeed given Nietzsche's remarks concerning the vigor of the Old Testament in contrast to the New (and concomitant literatures), Zoroaster can be likened to those grand stoic Prophets who marked history with their visionary life of transcending suffering, fear and repetitious banality. This is a far cry from the British thinkers of utility who reduced life to the maximization of ordinary happiness for the greatest mass thereby reducing the Sphinx's challenge to slothful mundane existence.

Returning to the theme of not knowing ourselves, philosophers paradoxically are not "men of knowledge" like Zarathustra is, consequently 'we *have* [had] to misunderstand ourselves' since 'we do not comprehend ourselves' at the level of the Sphinx's demand and the human species (GM, *P1*). To comprehend ourselves would require an historical philosophy that is able to apprehend things in a comprehensive way. To understand the world, that is, requires a particular Zarathustrian elevated 'height' from which to gain a synoptic perspective that transcends the limits of any single valley (parochial perspective). Although this is not the place to explore such a point, Nietzsche gained his insight concerning the efficacy of synoptic perspectivism from both Schopenhauer's philosophy and contemporaneous physicists. His philosophical anthropology therefore is inexorably bound up with such a worldview: the *logos* (language of, inquiry into) *anthropos* conceived in its broadest, comprehensive manner.

Natural Limits and Necessity of Meaning

Yet, as with most things Nietzsche attaches a cost, a form of expenditure to our purchase of a (more) comprehensive understanding of human nature. A comprehensive perspective is in fact—in life that is—something obtained by sacrifice: the fairest virtue of a 'man of knowledge' 'is the magnanimity with which' he 'offers himself and his life as a sacrifice' (D 459). Nietzsche as Zarathustra considered himself committed to just such a sacrifice. One must sacrifice, that is, one must surrender one's life to this task. And its takes discipline to be able to do this as both Zoroaster and Nietzsche the son of Christianity understood:

'the means through which the European spirit has been trained to strength, ruth-less curiosity, and subtle mobility' is located in the 'long unfreedom of the spirit...the discipline thinkers imposed on themselves to think within the direc-tions laid down by a church or court' (BGE 188). Freedom is thus associated with a discipline which—like incisive comprehensive thinking itself—involves the difficult work of long agonic struggle; a struggle against solitude versus friendship, joy versus melancholia and strength versus pious feebleness. The strength of this disciplining process in time makes for a certain elevation that produces an overcoming of the feeling of despair, fear, dread and *ressentiment* that arise out of our human-all-too-human nature. Agonic sufferance and over-coming, Nietzsche argued, develops a 'keen eye and nose' which allow us to discern and determine comprehensively 'the whole history of the soul *so far* and its as yet unexhausted possibilities' (BGE 45). This is an important facet of any inquiry into the nature of human beings: the development of intelligible senses and affects which enable comprehensive 'interpretations' and understand-ings regarding not only customary moral codes but also the 'whole history of the soul' to this point in time and, importantly, its unforeseen possibilities. Disci-plined strength of will and thought or freedom in this particular sense allows the unfolding of horizons of existence which have yet to be mapped or designed. Future individual soul types can therefore be discerned by these strong perspica-cious 'eyes' and 'ears' that long disciplining processes develop in historically fortified, disciplined members of the human race.[9] Morphologies of the soul remain an open-ended horizon in which the human-all-too-human dimension of man will recur alongside with new valuations of life and creative legislations that demand obedience, steadfastness and sharp eyes and ears with which to comprehend the totality of things. This is 'freedom' as such.

Hence, freedom is actually bound up with what Nietzsche conceived as the *great hunt* of modern human sciences, including the philosophic-anthropology of man's spirituality (i.e. the study of the history of the soul). However, it ap-pears just when the scientists should appear ready and useful for the 'great hunt' of history—the search for the beast (the itinerary of the soul)—they actually cease to be useful. Languishing in despair and scholastic battles over the enor-mity of their task, scholars falter just 'where the "great hunt", but also the great danger begins': namely, 'the human soul and its limits, the range of inner human experiences reached so far, the heights, depths, and distances of these experi-ences, the whole history of the soul *so far* and its as yet unexhausted possibili-ties' (BGE 45). Against this sad state of affairs in which one appears to fall dead at the feet of the Sphinx, the classical historian Thucydides qualifies as a vale-dictory 'hunter-scientist'; that is, Thucydides has sufficiently sharp eyes and ears to rank him even higher than Plato because he is able to capture the many-sidedness of this supra-animal, man, in all its life aspects. Contra Plato, Thucy-dides understood where the *great danger* begins; he thus took the 'most com-prehensive and impartial delight in all that is typical in men and events and be-lieve[d] that to each type there pertains a quantum of *good sense*' (D 168). Without any disparaging moralism, he could attribute a certain kind of rational-ity and value to different ways of being human in the world. By contrast, Plato is reckoned not to have understood human nature and consequently denigrated that which he rendered unacceptable. Like Sophocles, Thucydides possessed an uncommon sense for cunning, danger and power in human existence, giving him the certain advantage of a comprehensive, impartial perspective on man's mixed and vexed conditions of living on earth. To see the conditions under which humankind lives, both free and slavish, therefore requires thinkers who do not fear the kind of truthfulness Thucydides captured in his work. We can add here the allied virtue of honesty. Since truthfulness implies the intent to speak honestly about the truth (of the matter) by means of our aforementioned 'comprehensive understanding' of life—a certain 'tell it as it is' without any metaphysics—Nietzsche links the virtues of honesty, disciplined sacrifice and commitment to the total spectrum of human experiences and drives (knowing) with the 'great hunt' of knowledge that is the prerequisite to answering correctly the Sphinx's question. In one sense at least we might say then the journey which brings us before the gates of the city (Thebes)—at the behest of this dangerous half-beast (Sphinx)—metaphorically is the journey of the ψυχη (soul) in temporal space.

Following our exemplar Thucydides, knowing ourselves now requires that we understand what makes humans 'all too human' and yet more still: to avoid reducing humanity to its mortal finite limitations. "Dare to be honest" in regards to the human condition means shedding the illusions of metaphysical grandeur to perceive the anthropomorphic necessity of living, dwelling, thinking, doing, willing, growing and decaying. But as we are also the most interesting animal of history Nietzsche defies the blind faith of *Naturphilosophie* in sentient life, and affirms the necessity of imposing, or, as he says 'tyrannizing', Nature with meaning, direction, interpretation and the work of creative drives. After all is not living, he asks, 'precisely wanting to be other than this nature?': preferring, estimating, being limited, wanting to be different, employing the 'most spiritual will to power' (philosophy) in contrast to 'being like nature, wasteful beyond measure, indifferent beyond measure, without purposes and consideration, without mercy and justice, fertile and desolate and uncertain at the same time' (BGE 9). Owing to our historical trajectories, our purposive drives for direction in Time and willful imposition of meaning onto the void, *Mensch* cannot remain 'indifferent beyond measure' as Nature does. Human beings impose difference or inclination—Plato's desire for immortality as eloquently presented in the *Symposium*—onto their 'natures' and thus transform Nature's wastefulness a là a *lack* of mercy, justice and purposiveness. This is not to deny natural limits or morphological types—Lamarck being important in this regard—since Nietzsche's intent is to deny Romanticism's idealization of humanity in the form of so many accolades to man's moral development. Notably what logically proceeds from the end of speculative metaphysics is the question of the extent to which men and women can be situated in *physis* without tyrannizing the human being by means of reductive organicist presuppositions, i.e. spurious universal canons (laws) of nature. A philosophical anthropology of man therefore must be mindful of the 'human-all-too-human' tendency to project one's desire for canon-like knowledge of 'the natural' (i.e. positivism) lest we forget the above lesson of 'comprehensive understanding' which showed the human to be irreducible to organic determinism (i.e. *zoi*). As previously gleaned from the *Gay Science* (301) what 'distinguishes human beings from animals, and the higher animals from the lower' is the historicality of human striving and willing evident in how 'the former see and hear immeasurably more, and see and hear thoughtfully'. Thoughtfulness and comprehensive seeing is thus co-terminus with achieving human freedom.

This was in essence what *anthropology* originally constituted in both classical Greek and German before it assumed the more spurious empiricistic form of modern ethnography or natural anthropology. A philosophically construed *logos* of *anthropos* would be less concerned with the tired old age antithesis between nature and civilization or in classical terms *nomos* and *physis*. Contrary to Kant, Nietzsche's philosophical anthropological inquiries entail a transvaluation of opposites: 'The fundamental faith of the metaphysicians is *the faith in opposite values*' (BGE 2). By transvaluation we mean the overcoming of opposing values such as those accorded to 'consciousness' and the 'instincts' so that we find Nietzsche (BGE 3) arguing that '"being conscious" is not in any decisive sense the *opposite* of what is instinctive'; a proposition which signals a shift from his earlier (wholly skeptical) stance that rendered consciousness a là Gottfried Leibniz epiphenomenal to an ally of the drives. Once again, this is wholly consistent with the aforementioned thoughtfulness that characterizes the higher animalman: one considers the whole of phenomena, with the drives and conscious thought working in unison (and conflict as well). One can reason, that is, about the drives' interpretations and pulses, as well as objects in the world. Moreover, philosophizing itself is considered one of the strongest spiritual drives, even if it errs on occasions in glorifying Reason over and above everything else—something which neither Hobbes nor Spinoza bequeathed to modern philosophy. And since 'errors' are only the antithesis of truths Nietzsche expects such errors in philosophy to emerge just as Hegel had already shown *Dasein* to be inexorably defined by the *nihilo*.

This philosophical position led Nietzsche to renounce the age-old metaphysical supposition that life exists essentially because of our pneumatic being. That is to say, he repudiated the proposition that 'mere existence' itself, owing to the workings of the *pneumos*, provides a sufficient reason for life (or answer to the Sphinx). The will to life, in other words, fails the test of adequacy since Thebes (i.e. direction, objective) itself presupposes life; simple being thus cannot be the project of life but rather a noble free life. Here again, and consistent with Clarke's interpretation of Nietzsche's position, 'will to power' remains insufficient as the penultimate aim of life. While the metaphysics of nature may point us to fecundity, the *will to power* behind different modes of creation or 'interpretation' ought not to be confused as the *finalis* of his thinking *in toto*. This important qualification serves the purpose of distancing Nietzsche from a rather too narrow Darwinian[10] conception of his philosophy. In terms of the project of conscious instinctual life—the ability to get beyond the Sphinx's grueling test of 'what is man' and thus arrive at the City of man—a number of vital elements are necessary: sacrifice and expenditure, knowing oneself, honesty, courage and strength. In short, not merely 'consciousness' but a *developed* historical awareness of being distinctly human that is capable of attributing meaning to nature's tiresome indifference (as noted earlier). Nature wastes and furthermore knows no mercy or justice. Whereas *bios* in the Greek sense encapsulates a sense of *nomos* in the 'justice' or order of life which governs and 'tyrannizes' us. The point appears analogous to Schopenhauer's apparent shortcomings. While Schopenhauer could discern the *ugliness* of life, 'he lacked development: just as development is lacking in the domain of his ideas' (D 481); and therefore we too are required to take account of the *development* of the species in the most comprehensive terms. Hence the reason for his continuous antipathy towards British physiology, Darwinism and Stoicism—in short, specious naturalism. Hegel rather than Schopenhauer or Spencer now appears closer to Nietzsche's conception of the unfolding of the human in social-historical time, for Hegel too never accepted the naiveté of eternal opposites defining the *ousia* of the world. Heraclitus after all was always already there before Hegel, according to Hegel himself. Nietzsche on several occasions acknowledged the strong challenge which Hegel's historical philosophy represented, including in *The Gay Science* (357): it is 'the astonishing stroke of *Hegel*, who struck right through all our logical habits', including logical habits as positing ahistorical beings, eternal opposites and things-in-themselves. Hegel struck through such 'bad habits when he dared to teach that species concepts develop *out of each other*' rather than from absolute opposites (GS 357). Prudently eschewing Schopenhauer's envious and resentful attack on Hegel, Nietzsche discerned the great debt that even the British physicalists and materialists incurred from Hegelianism: 'for without Hegel there could have been no Darwin' (GS 357). We cannot be certain here but if Hegel had not been a dialectician—and *in fact* he was not—but was more consistently Heraclitean rather than Parmenidean, Nietzsche may have reconsidered this philosopher's conception of overcoming through *negation*.

The notion of a 'developing humanity'—integral to any non-relativized genealogy[11]—is very suggestive because it posits two crucial points: first, we cannot make statements about human nature in an ahistorical fashion; second, it builds upon the thesis that at birth human beings are essentially *unfinished creatures*. That is why life for us is inherently dangerous and why at the same time morals assume penultimate significance: we must preserve life both in its natural and symbolic forms but, in addition, we hope to fashion something beautiful out of the chaos of pain-joy oscillations. Even moral evaluations are attempts at creating the Good here on earth in the most beautiful way—a splendid noble vision of Plato's which allowed him to repudiate both dumb sensualism and decadent Socratism. Infinity has a purchase on us because our temporality is continuously imbued with a sense of our ontological make-up as incomplete creatures. With sharp eyes to pierce through the many layers of vain interpretations that have been scrawled over 'that eternal basic text of *homo natura*', the astute observer (for example Thucydides or Goethe) discerns that 'man is the *as yet undetermined animal*' (BGE 62). This lends a particular sense of openness to the formation of the self and the 'species as a whole' contrary to the over-inflated importance accorded to the logic of recurrence in Nietzsche's thinking by some interpreters.[12] Human freedom requires such openness even if defined to some degree by our enigmatic human nature, viz *homo natura*. This slate of nature, to be sure, is determinative even while it remains relatively open to human creative impulses and destructive forces, because the human being always *commences* its (unique) world as an unfinished creature. The 'savage' text of nature, we could say, pre-formats a civilizing process that asks of man what task he is to set himself, as a distinctly inquisitive cultivating (thoughtful) animal.

With time the processes of taming and domesticating this human-animal places a greater distance between our unfinished natures and our complex, socially formed natures; consequently we begin to 'forget' the distinctiveness of those drives, instincts and affects which still register an undomesticated nature that arises out of more primordial origins. A tragic irony emerges out of this: the dangers of a state of nature is surpassed now by the dangers of this kind of 'forgetfulness'. (This irony became a preoccupation of the once famous Catholic student of Theology, Martin Heidegger, who sought the restoration of the Call of Being). The comforts of civilized life, not to mention complacency in moralistic language, gradually came to reign over individuals' drive to embark upon more dangerous, painful and risky expeditions to Thebes. Rather than seeing this as a mere oversight or forgetfulness, it goes directly to the matter of knowledge itself as universal comprehension. Comparatively we now live 'in far too great security for us ever to acquire a sound knowledge of man', argued Nietzsche in *Daybreak* (460) and subsequent works until his death. Comprehensive eyes that can see all-around and thus produce noble forms of life are now more tamed; they have unlearned what was once demanded from life itself. It means that the genealogy of civility has obscured from our eyes a lucid appreciation of what we have become and hence what individual beings might otherwise become too. On this account, a historicity of regression makes opaque what a 'sound knowledge of man' would otherwise disclose because error is always instantiated in empirical life. Such opaqueness—and by implication, forgetfulness—shrouds the historical emergence of three important phenomena: man the most interesting free agent; idols; and the lofty investment in greater ontological security in the ideal 'real' world. Any undertaking to understand ourselves—a *logos* of *anthropos*—naturally then becomes entangled in the chimerical images of all pervasive idols such as unegoistic reasonable, passive and moralistic (democratic) citizens of the modern state who exude polite tolerance in the face of constant resentment and mediocrity. Ideals of the domestic yet unfree 'modern man' reign supreme while the values or estimations of those with wide comprehensive visions and souls are made subordinate to an all-pervasive subjective solipsism that denies a 'comprehensive understanding' of the human type in all its variations.

For this reason Nietzsche declared: 'One has deprived reality of its value, its meaning, its *truthfulness*, to precisely the extent to which one has mendaciously invented an ideal world' (EH, *P* 2; added emphasis). To overcome this decadent state of affairs requires a particular kind of human being, one capable of overcoming the mediocre *mentalite* and moralisms of bourgeois democratic ('feeble') man—the overman (*übermensch*). That is why the celebrated notion of *Becoming* may need to be tempered by a critical understanding of the forgetfulness prevalent in the modern human condition. The point is to acknowledge this as honesty would demand and that would mean internalizing it within our truth-fulness of whom and what we are: namely, as animal-beings that are susceptible to self-preservation and owing to civilizing processes a sublimation of the will to power already immanent within ζωη (natural life). In short, truthfulness can help overpower the Sphinx. As it entails embarking upon the 'great hunt' of self-knowledge which raises (potentially) the human race above lower forms of life as well as animals. Similar to Greek reasons of justification, this anthropomor-phic claim rests on the valid argument that lower animals (and historical socie-ties) lack just such 'comprehensibility' in their perception of the world.

Constituting Man As 'The Problem'

This means that if a sound knowledge of man is possible, a propos the overman, conceivably we possess the means by which a wider, more comprehensive view of our present conditions and ourselves can be ascertained. In the second essay of the 1887 publication *Zur Genealogie de Moral* Nietzsche asks: 'man has all too long had an "evil eye" for his natural inclinations, so that they have finally become inseparable for his "bad conscience". An attempt at the reverse would *in itself* be possible—but who is strong enough for it?' (GM II 24). Moreover, he goes on to add, rhetorically, yet also prefiguring the type who could answer the Sphinx's question: 'To whom should one turn today with *such* hopes and de-mands?' This is why freedom is difficult. It cannot simply be liberty—freedom 'from something'—but must also contain within its instinctive rational kernel the ethos required to undertake a Sophoclean tragic journey. Life itself is the great hunt and to remain confined to domesticated safe spaces where reflection is considered the pathway to truth is to deny reality of the great hunt that pro-duces vigorous natures, types of man, and the vigorous ethos required for self-understanding. Against the idols of the present, the work of thinking, of evaluat-ing and the great hunt of the human sciences underlying the 'civilizing' of natu-ral man entails a joyful science that embraces Sophoclean astuteness and drive. It overcomes our present experience of absent-mindedness in part because of the cheerful spirit of this worldly orientation: 'For cheerfulness—or in my own lan-guage *gay science*—is a reward: the reward of a long, brave, industrious, and subterranean seriousness, of which, to be sure, not everyone is capable' (GM *P* 7). This statement toward the end of Nietzsche's life pays testimony to the metaphor of the Sphinx as it affirms the historical and practical reality of human heterogeneity, in the form of 'pathos of distance' that defines humanity and its wondrous variability (BGE *passim)*. It refers to the empirico-psychological fact that not every human being is constituted alike and therefore only some are ca-pable of embarking upon this arduous and serious 'great hunt' undertaking that puts raw life at risk. However, in those types that do—Napoleon, Jesus and Goethe—we find the 'ripest fruits' of historical purposiveness and struggle; ex-emplars of resistance to herd-consciousness and noble free spirits who answer the Sphinx and then pose questions of their own. Thus they also reconstitute the meaning of human freedom by extension of our understanding of power, self and nature. Freedom that results from expenditure in the great hunt of life and not from constitutionally guaranteed rights.

For Nietzsche, modernity is bereft of a true understanding of the species and its human natures because contemporary nihilism erodes our fundamental relation to the human. What reigns is a 'fear of man' and consequently for Nietzsche we have 'lost our love of him, our reverence for him, our hopes for him, even the will to him' (GM I:12). This would appear inexplicable for anyone who would construe Nietzsche as an opponent of Greek humanism, yet he has often been interpreted as such and ironically, this further perpetuates the anti-human form of being that is the mark of today's ignoble morality. Rather than setting out to destroy man (sic), arguably, it remains the opposite case in Nietzsche's philosophy namely, how might we revere man, hope for him and even 'will him' again? This kind of alienation from ourselves, an alienation of love of self—a correlative of the value of unegoism—is the mark of a destructive nihilism which pervades the everyday existence of individuals. "Everything else but man" is the common concern of the inverted world in which truth has been stood on its head. This upside-world—although fashioned according to the ideal world of the 'thing-in-itself'—no longer knows how to be in awe of man because it has grown weary of him. Weariness and our distinctive lack of will of him go hand in hand; it forms and registers the empty void that is characteristic of the condition of nihilism. In his essay *"Good and Evil, Good and Bad"* (GM I:12) Nietzsche declares 'what is nihilism today if it is not *that*?' We have reached the point he says where even 'the sight of man now makes us weary'. Contrary to some fashionable continental interpretations, Nietzsche finds us to be actually weary *of* man rather than weary of scientific explanations. For cosmopolites, the diminution and leveling of 'European man' constitutes '*our* greatest danger'; and this is because today we are inclined towards the security of a good life that inexorably leads us to 'see nothing today that wants to grow greater, we suspect that things will continue to go down, down, to become thinner, more good-natured, more prudent, more comfortable, more mediocre, more indifferent' (GM I:12). Freedom properly defined therefore stands against the modern Golden Mean of safe but mediocre egalitarian life. Hence as man is no doubt 'getting "better" all the time', he paradoxically grows wearier and more fearful of himself, preferring to steer away from Socrates 'know thy self' and instead focus on *grammata* (language) or technological innovations of the *cogito* (empirical sciences). Comfortable mediocrity breeds this contempt for understanding man, ensuring the decline of a self-understanding built upon a tragic vision of life which nevertheless endorses comprehensibility of knowing and 'eyes and ears'. Therefore, he (or she) who has not grown weary and fearful *of* man is not heard or even understood. When Nietzsche asks: Am I understood? or states that perhaps only future philosophers will be able to listen to his words and understand the books he wrote so well[13], he alludes to the production of a weariness of sight (denigrated vision), smell and audibility characteristic of the nihilist who is a stranger to himself/herself. Once the senses of intelligent being become increasingly mute, the scientific method embeds itself further in the nihilistic age that eschews the problem 'What is man?' and thus perpetuates the present misrecognition of man's *bios*. I wish to call this Nietzsche's implicit concept of unfreedom—the condition of being unable to realize freedom in the technical sense defined in chapter one above.

Nietzsche did not conceive of this predicament in terms of some 'natural' tragedy befallen of man; he properly understood this to consist of a needless self-torture of kinds. When we moderns embodied this nihilistic pessimism, via *ressentiment* and a dilution of the noble strength found within the ancients' vigorous ethos, we invented man the 'deprived creature'—a fool who is dominated by a tenacious 'bad conscience':

> Hostility, cruelty, joy in persecuting, in attacking, in change, in destruction—all this turned against the possessors of such instincts: that is the origin of the "bad conscience" (GM II: 16).

Man in having become a fool filled with 'bad conscience' is similar to a deprived creature who turns in upon itself with rage as a result of having to domestic (tame) the instincts. In his analysis of the genealogy of guilt or bad conscience Nietzsche attributes its origin to 'the repressed cruelty of the animal-man made inward' due to the impulse to 'hurt himself after the *more natural* vent for his desire to hurt had been blocked' by the creation of a state-society (GM II: 22, original emphasis). This form of estrangement is one of the longest standing and cruelest forms of diminution (diminishing of the human-animal nature) known in world history; its origins stemming as far back as humankind's entry into political society. When human beings moved toward political organization, out of the cruelty and innocence of their natural primordiality, the 'old instincts of freedom' were set against the newly forming *zoon politikon* who brought upon himself the aforesaid joys of persecuting, attacking and hating as a result of a grand historic reversal: 'all those instincts of wild, free, prowling man turned *against man himself*' (GM II: 16). At this stage in the argument we may note the theoretical paradigm in which Nietzsche is working to delve into the condition of man vis-à-vis notions of *homo natura* (*zoi*). Namely an anti-metaphysical framework which takes the historical-anthropologic point of view as all important within a broader philosophical perspective that claims to have demythologized the world. By rendering the world comprehensible—as the Enlightenment indeed presupposed—Nietzsche could draw upon secular *gnosis* to declare man to be a member of the animal kingdom in the first instance and a member of civilized society in the second instance. Similar to Sigmund Freud and previous physicalists his model is one of the physio-energistic economy of drives (impulse, affect, willing) that both push and steer human life but also divide and conflict the human being. This reality—essentially Schopenhauerian if even veiled by many 'reversals'—appears to be premised on a naturalistic reduction: within the forces of nature there exists an imperative for competing organisms to maximize their extension of growth and strength in order to optimize the conditions of life (existence). 'Every animal...instinctively strives for an optimum of favorable conditions under which it can expend all its strength and achieve its maximal feeling of power'; and it instinctively abhors any obstruction to its 'path to the optimum', i.e. to action or 'the most powerful activity', not happiness (GM III: 7). The Greeks, Nietzsche believed, well understood '*the animal* in man' because they deified it whereas Christians centuries later lacerated the animal in man, causing it to 'rage against itself' (GM II: 23).

More importantly for the present discussion, Nietzsche argued in quite foundational terms that if these human-animal instinctual drives are prevented from their natural 'venting' then the dire consequences of a cruel self-torture (internalized rage) will bring about the deformation of humanity, i.e. the tame but feeble 'decadent' human being. Nietzsche's *telos*, even if a grand teleology is denied in his schema, is the realization or the actualization of the life-drive in reality. Accumulation or denial of drive energy thus explain the reasons for the torment or elevation of the human-animal. Thus, man most often or not remains unconscious of the directions of his own life for the reason that the economy of his (sic) own psychical powers destine him in ways which reason aims to apprehend post-hoc. Destiny or 'fate'—as captured by his phrase *amor fati*—therefore plays the same role which Necessity once did for both ancient and modern thinkers alike. And the sense of being determined is again found in the idea of types, types of nature or physio-psychological morphologies, which shape and fashion the individual's comportment in life and hence their relative strengths, weaknesses and inclinations.[14] In becoming 'who we are', we are therefore the objects not only of historical conditions but of individual willing and morphological inclinations. For example, a Nietzschean interpretation would have it that one may strive in becoming/being a great athlete but that this person would—according to the pathos of distance—already have a greater capacity (disposition) for physical endurance than others. While others may also similarly strive to achieve the same level of acumen, their specific 'nature' or type may work against their noble endeavor. However, regardless of one's specific nature-type humanity in general is marked but an internal *polemos* of the soul—civil war of the physiognomic self—as a consequence of the taming ('internalization') of her instincts. Whether the impulses (and affects) are sublimated or repressed we find Nietzsche's philosophical anthropology to posit the necessity of 'quanta of power' to be 'vented', to be *actual*-ized by way of a discharge. His metaphysics of force in nature suggest this: either allow their discharge or otherwise realize their necessary channeling in other forms, e.g. revenge and hatred toward others. Normatively, of course, Nietzsche sides with what he called the *vita creativa*, the creative impulse within every human being which Henri Bergson would later espouse as a penultimate force of the universe. This is Nietzsche the tragic-scientist: on one side we have knowledge of the natural conditions of life itself and on the other a tragedian who affirms life by overcoming (sickly) pessimism in and through the impulse to create, build, write and interpret. Such a conception remains interpretively useful not merely for an understanding of modernity but for an investigation of civilizational forms of the kind which Nietzsche himself undertook and embodied in his critique of European modernity. Thus we can say that metaphysics and civilizational-analysis are in fact kin rather than adversaries.

Having looked at the underlying premises of Nietzsche's philosophy we return to our discussion and find that instead of merely 'fearing man' we per-

petuate this condition of estrangement by our feebleness: our *un*willingness to
overcome today's negation of man himself. This amounts to an overcoming of
our hatred as well as fear of man; a condition which Nietzsche described as
'self-torture' and burdensome like the burden on a camel. It is no cognitive
oversight as rationalists would have it. Rather the want to *will* ourselves into this
unnecessary, destructive self-torture is what currently constitutes 'our greatest
danger'—the heart of 'European Nihilism'. The grand task before us therefore is
larger than any epistemological problem, i.e. how we ought to know this or that
about the world, because it involves the historical insight and human effort
(strong will) sufficient to stop the lacerating of ourselves, that is, to suspend
man's 'rage against itself!'(GM II: 23). Why we are strangers to ourselves can
now be seen to be symptomatic of this self-imposed estrangement from the human, from *Mensch* itself. Misunderstanding, incomprehension, hostility, attacking, *anomie*, and needless self-torture go hand-in-hand with the effort to Know
Thyself: error and truth abound in each other's unfoldings. A penultimate truth-
claim in Nietzsche's genealogy of the human race encompasses this dialectic of
error-truth as well as the foregoing proposition concerning a cataclysmic Fall in
the development of a civilized humanity. Nietzsche argued that in the absence of
a love for man, our reverence and will 'for him', a deep nausea overtakes our
capacity to redeem him thus leaving room for unhelpful ascetic ideals to plant
themselves in the soil of our nihilistic revulsion of man on earth. To redeem the
earth we must first redeem him—Man. The question is, as his father would have
recognized, one of atonement—"to atone" as the Hebrews used to say. Why is
this so? Because this reprehensible situation owes to a particular psychical cruelty, 'a madness of the will which is absolutely unexampled: the *will* of man to
find himself guilty and reprehensible to a degree that can never be atoned for'
(GM II:22). In light of his *Zarathustra* it remains an aporia in Nietzsche's philosophy why this impossibility should be affirmed with such certitude, particularly as it comes from an historical philosopher who emphasizes *overcoming* and
the freedom immanent in the promise of the earth. The origins of this monstrous
creature, what is called 'this insane, pathetic beast—man' erupted out of the
political circumstance in which man placed himself after having overcome the
constraints of organic being to then experience external (objective) constraint
(i.e. state-society). Again we find the same naturalistic reduction evident in his
explanation of this world-significant event: 'what *bestiality of thought* erupts as
soon as he is prevented just a little from being a *beast in deed*!' (GM II: 22).
Since state-society or political life (*civitatum*) prevents beastial deeds, the *eros*
of mankind is vented by way of savage thoughts as well as fine interpretative
works. In other words, processes of civilization pitch man against himself, *eis
heauton*, as the Greeks would say. In a salient passage which makes conspicuous
Nietzsche's philosophic-political anthropology of man as a tamed civilized animal, we see the effects of this kind of encagement:

> The man who, from lack of external enemies and resistances and forcibly con-
> fined to the oppressive narrowness and punctiliousness of custom, impatiently
> lacerated, persecuted, gnawed at, assaulted, and maltreated himself; this *animal*

that *rubbed itself raw against the bars of its cage as one tried to "tame" it . . .* (GM II:16, emphasis added).

became the ugly 'pathetic beast' that is divided by its own 'homesickness for the wild' on one hand and the guilt of bad conscience on the other. Due to its tormented state of self-estrangement this civilized creature of political organization, social order and ascetic moral virtue developed an interiority (*soul-hypothesis*) governed by bad feelings; that is, by guilt, envy, resentment, hatred and revenge. These are the characteristics of the Fall as I have described it here. Bad conscience overtook him and filled his heart, producing a madness of hostility and negativity towards its own life-circumstance. By inventing political life and the social contract of mutual utility through various forms of moral regulation, the inventor of the πσυχη imprisoned himself in a state of bad conscience that happens to also offer him the joys of security and diverse embellished pleasures of technological life. 'This fool, this yearning and desperate prisoner' is none other than the 'inventor of the bad conscience' (GM II: 16). Hence we can say that moral guilt complexes originate from the formation of civilizational norms or the 'civilizational realities' of the human-animal as he put it.

However, contrary to the pessimism that marks the life of this encaged feeble creature, Nietzsche posits the possibility of an other self-understanding, a 'type of man' that lies ahead in time. Within the negative moment of the guilt ridden consciousness historical fate delivers up to the inventor of the bad conscience a promise of the earth that is yet to be realized—an *adventure* held in the bosom of βιος. (It may be possible to conceive of man's atonement, his redemption, lying ahead in this adventure as well.) Although Nietzsche states we have yet to recover from this 'uncanniest illness' of man, the human being still holds out as a being 'who had to turn himself into an adventure' thus becoming the possibility immanent within time of overcoming—the overcoming of his foolish contradictory existence.[15] In the same passage of *"Guilt," "Bad Conscience" and the Like* Nietzsche reverts back to his first philosophical proposition regarding the truth of man: 'To breed an animal *with the right to make* promises—is not this the paradoxical task that nature has set itself in the case of man? Is it not the real problem regarding man?' (GM II:1). And is it not therefore of great importance to us too for understanding modern freedom, a freedom predicated on a capacity to make promises that in time may be fulfilled and owes to a life cultivated within political society? Consistent with Greek thinking Nietzsche finds *physis* to have given human beings the necessity to form political communities within which they develop the will to grow in their responsibilities because as moral human-animals they may ripen under such conditions. That is, as political and moral subjects they can become persons who are capable of committing themselves to promises that require some assuredness that they will in future be kept. This commitment stands in place over time due to the noble strength with which such subjects can fulfill their commitment (*praxis* in the Greek sense), and not because of some contractarian view that Nietzsche may be adopting. Human nature, neither fully animalic nor vegetative, provides the 'promissory paper' upon which man writes his and her promissory note of commitment to the other once having developed a political community—a *zoon politikon*. A commitment of this kind is not one of self-preservation or sweet nature nor can it be to a 'will to power'; rather, in Aristotle's language it is to a human *arête* in things noble, difficult and affirmative of life, i.e. that which affirms and expands the immanence of human experience against the servitude of the given ἀρχή (order/origin). Being in time, man becomes something he might not otherwise have been had he remained in the wild; a making which beholds a promise as forthcoming *in* time just as Husserl envisaged the human subject as constituted *in* time. In this respect, Nietzsche remains consistent with the central idea of absolute freedom espoused by Idealists such as Friedrich Schelling. Remaining close to their naturalistic concerns Nietzsche expressed this world-historical rupture in terms of the emergence of 'an animal soul' turning against itself, that is, 'taking sides against itself' and is *a fortiori* something 'unheard of, enigmatic, profound, contradictory, *and pregnant with a future*' (GM II:16). To any Hegelian this would make perfect sense. Its world-significance suggests an antithesis to Nietzsche's sometime (uneven) reductive tendency towards naturalistic explanations.[16]

The following passage however gives us a clue to his transvaluation of naturalism (i.e. fundamental drives of man) as a method of interpreting the world: the emergence of such a soul against itself meant that the 'aspect of the earth was essentially altered' (GM II: 16). Against plants and creatures, αγριο ζωη ('wild life'), the divided soul of *Mensch* alters the world inexorably because unlike these forms of life, mankind has altered the earth by the appearance of its own promise-making capacities. To be sure this appearance is attended by the profound, contradictory and futural nature of this divided 'animal soul' of man. Set against its twofold nature, its wont to set itself against itself, the human being remains an enigma—something 'unheard of' and 'so new'—because time holds the promise of this promise-making animal to become willfully responsible within its own freedom. Even contradictions themselves will prove useful rather than harmful for a soul that strives to transvaluate the limits of mere animalic existence. This important alteration first began with the ever new appearance of 'teachers of the purpose of existence'—those who inexorably changed human nature itself by daring to pose questions about the purpose and meaning of life (GS 1). Elsewhere in the same text Nietzsche referred to this penultimate transformation as a 'second nature', a nature that man artistically cultivates and acquires through *Bildung* just as a gardener who cultivates plants to refashion their form and shape. These educators and their educators as well grasp the *potentiality* of this 'second nature' with all its profundity and contradictions and turn the future of man into a promise—a becoming. Hence the face of the earth is transformed doubly: by the emergence of a conflicted 'animal soul' and then the breeding of a human-animal 'with the right to make promises' as the above states.

The third facet, Plato's *paideia*, harnesses each of these through the spiritualized drive of philosophy to know, to posit, to calculate, to propose, to divide, and to analyze (examine). Thus tutelage no longer leaves mankind where it was in simple organic life but rather shows that the future is pregnant with possibilities, with promises that bridge the human being over time. This includes the potentiality of the 'unheard of' individual, the new profound and perhaps enigmatic 'type of man' to emerge *in* time. Against romantic naturalism this holds that civilization—as an extension or 'second nature'—delivers up both errors and promises to the once happy 'animal soul' that had as yet not been caged and domesticated by civilized morality. It thus challenges the pre-political creature to become something other than what its *physis* has bestowed to it: to strive, to overcome, to enhance (the spirit of a people), to impose order and purpose on Nature, to create and divide, and to perform experiments through the will to truth. In sum, to interpret the world after the educators have already interpreted it and changed it thus; and to do so without fear of erring since error is no less valuable than 'truth'. That is Nietzsche's metaphysical truth of the Whole. Valuing the whole of life is what Nietzsche the philosophic-tragedian proposes. Although foolishness obviates a proper understanding of this threefold phenomenon and its world transforming power, we possess the capacity, that is potentiality in time to realize the necessity of our *'freedom above things'* that our ideals demand of us whenever we gain consciousness of this promise of man (GS 107). 'Above things' suggests a worldliness of a kind that is not necessarily reduced to the givenness of things as they are. Hence it infers an elevation, a height, which can be attained because one is not always and wholly bound by the moment (of Today). Freedom from "today" and its grand (state) politics, its mechanical industriousness and its serious scholarly laboring—all of which threaten the promise stored up in the future of mankind and not merely the individual[17]—is what such a 'freedom above things' encompasses. Such a freedom furthermore requires a lightness of joyful affirmation that exceeds the decadence of Today lest it lapse into a nihilistic pessimism: 'we must occasionally find pleasure in our folly [i.e. error], or we cannot continue to find pleasure in our wisdom'. And Nietzsche adds 'At times we need a rest from ourselves by looking upon, by looking *down* upon, ourselves and, from an artistic distance, laughing *over* ourselves or weeping *over* ourselves' (GS 107). Without laughing at life it seems we cannot hope to experience the 'freedom above things' which the promise of life holds out for us. The will to life realistically harbours the possibility that we will in fact err (e.g. forgetfulness) even while we are tutored and committed to the *promise* of freedom that lies within the potentiality of overcoming ourselves. This proposition obviates the attendant issue of whether or not Nietzsche in fact endorsed an unapologetic egoism in his treatment of human subjectivity (freedom). Our argument concerning freedom and responsibility suggests otherwise. It posits that freedom 'above things' also means above our own egoistic finitude (temporality) since *potentiality* as we have described it so far necessitates the transcendence of given limits. Always sympathetic of French aphorisms Nietzsche could easily invert the famous supposition 'l'homme propose et Dieu dispose'.[18] However, this is a decidedly different conception of the promise immanent in the potentiality of dwelling on earth than the more traditional *libera arbitria* (free choices/decisions) that has its roots in Thomist philosophy.

Seeing through the profusion of imagery and veiled masks that Nietzsche's writings intentionally evoke, the human being in the final analysis stands as a 'bridge' or 'a way, an episode' in life; that is, something yet to arrive, *to become*, to exist, and quite possibly something unique so that even the face of the earth shall be transformed by this enigmatic promise of man in time (including his errors). As both predicate and subject, he is promising, as the verb emphasizes. This potential to be something other than forgetful and Today's fool—to transcend various kinds of servitude—means that the Actual can always come under scrutiny and criticism because it too is susceptible to error, e.g. perceptual myopia and decadence, owing to our human-all-too-human nature. Like Zarathustra, it is possible to climb high above the busy turmoil of "Today" and see farther than the limited horizon of valley life where forgetfulness keeps the eyes fixed on the immediacy of things thus preventing a transvaluation of Today's mediocrity and an apprehension of life as a question of existence for our being. Such a height requires a tenacious strength to overcome the necessity of herd-like living and thinking; in other words it requires a distance between the ontology of herd morals of 'belonging' and the untimely 'dangerous one' who yearns to realize a promise in the future that remains distant yet possible despite all errors. *Physis*, like mountainous winds, can be challenging whilst valley civilizations soften and domestic this half-animal man so that its enfeebled nature demands security in the mass psychology of the herd rather than taking up time's promise of a 'bridge' across nature's abyss of nothingness (meaninglessness) understood as man becoming a free spirit. Holding the promise that our drive to knowledge may aide this process through 'teachers of the purpose of existence'—who assist in the task of harnessing the potential of this 'divided animal soul'—the καλον (beauty) of life is revealed by the power to will and create that which nature could not: culture, or, independent spirit of a people as crystallized in time through their particular mode of life. Some of the best 'high spirits' are those teachers of existence who have breached the abyss to found 'a way', a bridge to a distant future that will come one day, e.g. Napoleonic Europe. Freedom is thus dissociated from the necessities of today's imperatives—moral, political, cultural and cognitive—showing instead the human being to be a fulcrum of creative force and striving in a process of *becoming* simultaneously different and same. Again, the Whole must imply the confluence both of continuous and radically different elements of the cosmos.[19]

At this point, it may be useful to draw a distinction between two types of natures: one implicitly refers to an inner nature that pertains to the historical trajectory of this 'animal soul'. This concept of an inner nature—now constitutive of both modern psychoanalysis and neurobiology—becomes useful in the investigation of various phenomena pertaining to moral psychology such as guilt, envy, resentment, revenge, denial and sublimation. These are linked to the struggle with nature because a kind of civil war that is both intra-subjective and inter-subjective takes place once political man has arrived. It forms part of Nietzsche's vision of life as one fated to be (in part) *agonic* (painful and disappointing) because the soul undergoes a tensing of a kind that finds no apparent *cephalous* (sovereign) ruling over its competing agencies. In political terms, a conflictual polity governs the many tumultuous states of the human being who on one hand acts as a master over *Physis* and on the other hand is subject to masters within the social structure of the polis. Political in emphasis Nietzsche describes the primordial freedom of the human-animal soul as something existing before socialization into political society: the progenitor of 'bad conscience' came 'under the stress of the most fundamental change he ever experienced— that change which occurred when he found himself finally enclosed within the walls of society and of peace' (GM II: 16). This caging process delivered up ζωη to political organization and social domestication thereby curtailing the instincts of his 'animal soul'; made captive by their new environment these 'semi-animals' suddenly found themselves in the New World of the polis and intellectual reflection (i.e. civilization). Nietzsche's philosophic-anthropology posits that they 'felt unable to cope with the simplest of undertakings; in this new world they no longer possessed their former guides, their regulating, unconscious and infallible drives' (GM II: 16). His language suggests a diachronic shift since it is now their 'former' guides which prove inept, lost in a new foreign world of restraint and conscious mediation of immediate impulses just as former sea-creatures who had to abandon their former 'guides' in order to transit into terrestrial animals. In almost topographical language Nietzsche claims they were 'reduced to thinking, inferring, reckoning, co-coordinating cause and effect' and consciousness—that 'weakest and most fallible organ' (GM II: 16). Contra Kant this quasi-Darwinian, neo-Romantic interpretation performs something of an inversion of the Enlightenment edict concerning the supremacy of the human intellect. The cephalic *cogito* here no longer assumes epistemic or ontological priority over and above his preferred comprehensive synoptic view of the Whole (now cosmos and *bios*).

Following the work of Friedrich Lange, Roger Boscovich and African Spir as well as Charles Darwin and Wilhelm Rolph, Nietzsche eschewed the cunning word-games of the rationalists to expound a philosophical anthropology that places man in a variegated cosmos of inter-dependent life-forms. In that sense, man is not a teleological end within some divine purpose but a child similar to Heraclitus' 'great child' where the exciting 'lucky throws in the dice game' a là Heraclitean cosmic Justice is given equal determination (GM II: 16). This 'luck' as it were sundered man from his animal past, plunging him into radically 'new surroundings and conditions of existence' where his now tortured animal soul confronted the possibility of either self-annihilation or seeking and acquiring strength and joy in alternate 'subterranean gratifications' (GM II: 16). We ought to remember that this circumstance also presents man as if 'something were announcing and preparing itself', that is, as something more than tortured, caged and negated by the state. The project of humankind paradoxically is bound up with the domestication of this once animal soul: society giveth and taketh away just as nature does. To lean on one side or another is mere fantasy. By means of external constraints (institutions), the "soul" and man's inner nature more generally underwent a certain expansion and extension. Consciousness came to the fore, allowing the once 'animal soul' to 'acquire depth, breadth, and height, in the same measure as outward discharge was *inhibited*' (GM II: 16). Here we note an inverse relation existing between the inhibited discharge and acquired depth and breadth of soul: restraint gives rise to internalization and this allows the spirit of man to elaborate and extend upon nature's primordial *tabula*. Leaving aside the question of measure, our aforementioned 'right of promise' can now be discerned as constituted dually by objective constraint and luck on one hand, and agonic struggle and inner sublimations of impulses on the other. Our limited pre-social creature is overcome to become plausibly the most interesting human-animal on earth in part thanks to the those 'most dangerous priests' who made everything more dangerous including love, lust to rule, revenge, guilt, disease, revenge and *in toto* evil. Spiritual depth and psychical complexity arrive therefore not merely with political society but also with those noble 'decadents' who began to chastise and condemn all things sensual as 'evil'. These 'decadents' or moralists justified life on the basis of a concept of *soul*, a mere 'soul-hypothesis' which never the less transformed the whole of humanity, particularly through the birth of scientific thinking. With a growing consciousness of what ought to be renounced and abrogated by means of the ascetic ideal comes the development of man's 'spirit' or soul: objectification of God and moral codes as a form of externalization means that formerly discharged impulses 'turn inward—this what I call the *internalization* (*Verinnerlichung*) of man' (GM II:16). When Kant later spoke of a timeless subject, a subject of consciousness, he took this formed subject as given, thereby giving no account of the formative *processes* which lead to the development and growth of a spirit-substance—the conscious (human being) as moral agent. Only Kant's *a priori* reason attempts to look back in time to locate an unmistakable 'faculty of understanding' within the ontological order. Yet understanding in this form can never apprehend its own formation since it simply relies upon static and abstract postulates that lack any *logos* of *anthropos* in the fashion outlined here. In short, rational concepts are inseparable from historically shaped images of man.

Consonant with this argument, Nietzsche struggled with the pre-eminent ideas of his age including those of Darwin, atomic physicists and most of all Richard Wagner and Arthur Schopenhauer. Not unusually, he read sympathetically the works of controversial and insightful thinkers including scientists such as Friedrich Zöllner and Gustav Teichmüller, the author of *Die wirkliche und die scheinbare Welt*.[20] Nietzsche was deeply skeptical of Darwin's claim to a natural selection taking place within nature according to a logic of external constraint and species-adaptation. Because Nietzsche's interpretation of the inner workings of the organism owed much to the insights of Wilhelm Roux's *Der Kampf der Theile im Organismus*—a significant contribution to evolutionary theory according to Darwin himself—the argument concerning the constitution of this 'most interesting domestic animal' could not therefore depend upon external 'causes'. This meant that although human beings undergo a number of changes due to shifts in the balance of forces in their milieu, the so-called animal soul equally participates through its social milieu in the metamorphosis of the incomplete man-animal into a spirited conscious being who acts in accordance with its drives, thoughts, evaluations, resistances and will to legislate, grow, command, exceed 'given' truths/errors and dominate weaker types. This derives, to be sure, partly from Roux's conception of the organism and its multiple inner struggles, a counter-paradigm to Darwin's overly 'externalist' explanations of change in nature. Having undergone a number of transformations our former 'animal soul' begins in its new environment to experience a whole array of new experiences that emanate from its will to abandon Nothingness and institute interpretative schemas such as Good and Evil, Divine and mundane, that engage the soul of man and uphold the promise of joyful wisdom in time. These experiences we must emphasize reflect not only the vicissitudes of good-evil and noble-slave moralities but also the contradictory sense of our human, all too human struggle with these vicissitudes. Roux had formerly shown the multiple inner struggles which reverberate throughout a living organism; Nietzsche now similarly found *Mensch* riven with contradictions that arise out of multiple inner struggles within its 'soul' (now more than just a 'hypothesis'). For this reason he maintained the mind or *Cogito* cannot sufficiently grasp the origins of these necessary contestations and their attendant contradictions even if it attempts to resolve fundamentally non-cognitive problems by cognitive means. Thus with some degree of certainty, we can say that Nietzsche eschewed both polarities of exegesis: neither externalist determinations of being nor Idealist immanent accounts of being prove sufficient. The tension between these two unacceptable polarities of explanation opens up an interpretive space from which to view the earth's most interesting half-animal: 'man'. This soul-filled animal of the polis that is neither fully animal nor 'spirit' possesses the potentiality to stand resolutely before the Sphinx and give the answer 'It is Man'. As Nietzsche infers in the opening fragments of *Beyond Good and Evil* (1)

> Is it any wonder that we should finally become suspicious, lose patience, and turn away impatiently? that we should finally learn from this Sphinx to ask questions, too? *Who* is it really that puts questions to us here?

Since it is we who now pose such difficult questions, Nietzsche puts into question the taken for granted Homeric idea to ask: 'Who of us is Oedipus here? Who the Sphinx? It is a rendezvous of questions and question marks' (BGE 1). This is what the artist does according to his polemic against Wagner: the artist can redeem life by putting existence into question thus giving it value. The adventurous 'promise' of man holds for him a potentiality which owes to the distinctive operations of soul-contestations rather than merely the objective *Kräfte* (forces) of biological life, inner disputes which require interpretation (and not explanation). For man according to his philosophical anthropology is essentially an interpretive, *valuating animal*. Here in Nietzsche's words we can hear what he considered *Mensch* to be if not merely a biological creature: 'man designated himself as the creature that measures values, evaluates and measures, as the "valuating animal as such"' (GM II: 8). This is why in the preface to his earlier work he ties together the work of the spirit with the nature of this 'valuating animal': we still feel the 'whole need of the spirit and the whole tension of its bow', as well as the arrow and the task of aiming, even after the troublesome work of the 'soul-superstition' as he called it (BGE *P*). It should be evident then that Nietzsche contra naturalism and its undeveloped understanding of the possible tension within man (and his social relations), finds creative heightening[21] as the clue to man's moral, psychological and physiological constitution. For example, because of the workings of this spurious 'soul-hypothesis' of Christian civilization, Nietzsche correctly discerned the production of a 'magnificent tension of the spirit the like of which had never yet existed on earth'; a phenomenon that proves prospective for the once 'animal soul' of man because it is 'with so tense a bow we can now shoot for the most distant goals' (BGE *P*). In June 1885 Nietzsche envisaged those whom he called 'good Europeans' as capable of such a task as they would embody a noble spirit that is constituted precisely by this creative heightening (of the spirit). When Apollo's arrow shoots farther it is because of the tension within the soul of man; it shoots to a distance that is yet to arrive but will in the destiny of our promise. It is with these Good noble Europeans who have overcome ascetic morality and cultural mediocrity that 'the way', the 'promise of man' lies in the future; namely, with their fortified spirit and honest truthfulness that the transvaluation of modern decadence and forgetfulness, that is servitude, can be realized.

As part of the historical development of our *Auslegung* (understanding) and its socio-historical *Gegensätzlichkeit* (contradictoriness), the tension of the bow incorporates the important work performed by man's most spiritual drive—the will to know(ledge). Knowing as an interpretive activity is itself a form of spiritualizing the impulse *for* life. It forms a certain world-historical moment of distancing us from our once primal animal soul (ζωη) even though human beings can now shoot further into Time. The glance backwards we might say is the naturalist's glance; Nietzsche's glance on the other hand is on the achievable heights which may be obtained despite error and recurrence (of slavish types)— a forward glance with the benefit of comparative analysis. This spiritualized drive (of knowledge), captured by philosophy, can elude the 'faith of the metaphysicians'[22] by overcoming the opposition between Being-Becoming, consciousness-sense, Good-Evil, and beast-god, and thus enable the spirit of man to deepen and broaden itself. Freedom lies therein, in neither opposing Being nor in denying the primal soul's will to life. That is, freedom in part owes to overcoming unnecessary antitheses because as Hegel said they depend upon onesided accounts of *Dasein*. Perhaps it is for this reason that Nietzsche's view of humanity appears at times fundamentally contradictory precisely because it endeavors to reflect the contrariness of the human condition, including its concomitant *polemos* of soul. My argument here suggests that Nietzsche could indeed be so charged if he were a thorough going naturalist. But that would be implausible or in other words reductive since it ignores the important place which Nietzsche accords to the force of the 'soul-hypothesis' in history and its *sui generis* manifestation in the 'spirit of man' that shoots further into time by means of interpretations of the world. In normative terms Nietzsche objects with a decisive *Non* whenever we unduly restrict and diminish the vast array of experiences to a neat reassuring classificatory schema that pretends to be 'scientific'. Against the epistemologists therefore stands the itinerary of the soul with its own irreducible power that the materialism of either Darwin or ancient atomists cannot account for. This 'spirit of man' is not merely some epiphenomenal effect of a bygone religiosity; for Nietzsche maintained that the religious instinct in modern societies is increasing and will prove useful for certain cultivation purposes—something often overlooked when nihilism is inadequately conceptualized.[23] Moreover, it is associated with a rather more ancient development than modern civilization: the emergence of a will to negate nothingness. That is, with the will to overcome the 'meaninglessness of suffering, *not* suffering itself'—the curse over mankind—a spiritual will to overcome the void saved the will itself. The '*will itself was saved*' when this act of meaning-giving—the interpretation of the world as having value or purpose via metaphysics—rendered man itself as purposeful; it meant 'man was *saved* thereby, he possessed a meaning, he was henceforth no longer like a leaf in the wind, a plaything of nonsense…he could now *will* something' (GM III: 28). The anti-naturalist language is quite evident here when we see that whereas an object of nature (the leaf) is a plaything of the wind, man on the other hand construes 'sense' out of its own existence in the cosmos. Indeed, the human being *knows* fear while the leaf cannot.

Amplifying further the distinction between organic forms of life and the human conscious being, Nietzsche states in the *Gay Science* that not only the will to know is growing but so is the self-consciousness of man himself. To interpret the understanding of our fear of the wind is to exemplify this very self-consciousness which the leaf or beast cannot have. And this is where the priests and their ascetic ideal come in because they helped further propel our self-consciousness as *human* beings—a type of being who possess *conscience* and spirit and is not mere matter. The priests and teachers of meaning both assisted the 'will' in forming a *Geist* (conscious mental life) that sets a human being apart from a leaf or ant, and therefore apart from the indifference and arbitrariness of *physis*. The 'mind' or spirit of human beings would, for instance, understand the fear of being blown now-this-way and now-that-way. It is not force that is determinative here but rather the interiorization of once purely external phenomena into the soul of man as states. These states embattle the human being but are, importantly, amenable to interpretation, misunderstanding and error-making. A leaf cannot err; it simply knows no erring powers. What is more, once man developed a conscience, it set itself even further apart from the leaf: this in fact is Nietzsche's 'storm' in which volatile forces accumulating in the deepened soul of man produce the ripened fruit of the responsible self who is *over* himself (as we have already seen). Poetry and music most evidently demonstrate these strong stormy forces in the mind (culture) and soul (interiority) of man but so does the will to self-redemption in mankind's soul. The immensely significant role of the will to redeem man from nothingness—the Void—is most evident in religious life. Nietzsche links the religious 'hunt' for meaning with the formation of the self: 'one might ask—would man ever have learned without the benefit of such a religious training and prehistory to experience a hunger and thirst for *himself*, and to find satisfaction and fullness in *himself*?' (GS 300). Naturalism we might say only deepens our misunderstanding of the labyrinthine nature of the soul and its particular trajectory through innumerable arduous experiences in life. The redeeming of life cannot be answered organically or (merely) somatically. Similarly, on the cultural-political plane French culture is

valorized not for its naturalistic elements but for its vital, noble spirit (in contrast
to a largely languid German spirit).

As more developed interesting animals that possess 'spirit' and *bios*, humans can no longer return to some kind of primordial horde or blind organicism
which Romanticism attempts to recover from the ashes of civilization. Mere
animalic existence would deny man of its promise because a future of possibilities and noble horizons lie not within nature or Today's industriousness but in
the potentiality that is imminent to a life of the polis—a community where error,
herd-morality and security are extant realities that the *overman* knows and yet
transvaluates. That is, the free spirit is not bound by the limits of the cage that
first domesticated the primordial 'animal soul' of man but now is no longer immediate to his conscious life. In other words, Nietzsche agrees with Hegel that
becoming negates and overcomes 'simple being' thus transforming our experience of life inexorably. The sovereign individual—a human being who has
overcome both himself and the nausea associated with mob sentiments—cannot
in fact exist without a 'second nature' that specifically is the outgrowth of *bios*,
of cultivating, evaluating, measuring, redeeming, interpreting, legislating and
contracting promises with others. A political *koinonia* is a moral community;
nature however is bereft of both, or, as Nietzsche says, she is indifferent. How
can humankind have a future if it is beholden to indifference?

The other force that militates against nature's indifference is the so-called
drive of knowledge; a fallacy[24] to be sure but a most powerful drive that declares
the striving to know as immensely transformative insofar as it relentlessly torments man in its striving for mastery—a fact that further distances these moral-
political animals from their own 'animal soul'. In time, this striving itself takes
on a distinctive value in its own right because it salvages the will (from solipsism) and 'man himself' both at once. Hence it seems reasonable to say that although will to power is in evidence in nature, in human societies it becomes
'striving' to know: to ascertain goodness, to redeem, to extend self-
consciousness, and to act responsibly under conditions of freedom. Thus
whereas nature beholds 'excess' and fecundity, it cannot instantiate 'striving' as
a value let alone a value amongst an established rank of values. As purely 'animal soul', nature in other words cannot comprehend either nihilism or the promise of the future. Man bestows purpose whereas nature is bereft of it. The purpose of man is to realize a kind of freedom that is difficult, that is responsible.
Nature cannot be responsible because as we have already established she is indifferent and lacking of measure. Man's measure is different; it is the promise of
the earth after he has undergone the pangs of diremption, political sociability,
nihilistic nothingness, ascetic renunciation, logical positivism, and herd-
morality. The *agon* of existence gives measure to his freedom; yet pain itself
does not make us 'better': it simply makes us profound. In so doing it thereby
gives humanity *potentiality* since through its profundity and contradictory existence it possesses a potentiality to affirm life in its totality. That is, to ascribe
value to life and thus intervene in nature's wayward indifference by continually
fashioning 'something that had not been there before: the whole eternally growing world of valuations, colors, accents, perspectives, scales, affirmations, and

negations' (GS 301). In this paragraph written at the end of his life, Nietzsche once again reaffirms his longstanding objection to the naturalistic fallacy: 'nature is always value-less, but has been *given* value at some time, as a present—and it was *we* who gave and bestowed it' (GS 301). Freedom then does not exist 'in' nature but instead arises out of human struggle and its *vita creativa* to redeem the spirit of man from the faith of those 'materialistic natural scientists' who seek to divest life of its 'rich ambiguity' (GS 373).

Freedom in these terms takes on a certain substantive rather than formal form. What Nietzsche stressed was the importance of inner contestations that amplified the range of human experiences, including the intermingling of thoughts and emotions. Those who can 'think and feel at the same time' and who possess an intellectual conscience are best able to affect the transformative power of two powers: *vita contemplativa* and *vita creativa*. Intellectual conscience is what Nietzsche found wanting in the majority of people, almost to his astonishment. Having continuously to resist denial of this fact, Nietzsche lamented the prevailing herd mentality: 'I keep having the same experience and keep resisting it every time....it has often seemed to me as if anyone calling for an intellectual conscience were as lonely in the most densely populated cities as if he were in a desert' (GS 2). Those in possession of an intellectual conscience by contrast can 'think and feel at the same time', employing more finely tuned 'eyes and ears' within a more perspicacious synoptic perspective of life: they seek after the Whole rather than take comfort in Today's reality. Being so constituted a certain distance between competing conscious-affect states finds the spiritual life of individuals is headed by fundamental concerns which the Many (as Aristotle called them) wish to overlook. Namely, the most fundamental concern that 'separates the higher human beings from the lower': whether one accounts '*the desire for certainty* as his inmost craving and deepest distress' (GS 2). Yet our civilizational reality is distinctive insofar as it is capable of making human beings entertain larger questions and tasks that were too vast for previous civilizations: 'it is for precisely this reason that individuals and generations can now fix their eyes on tasks of a vastness that would to earlier ages have seemed madness and a trifling with Heaven and Hell' (D 501). This development in part owes to the operations of the 'soul-hypothesis' in terms both of modern soul-atomism and aesthetic-cognitive sensibilities of the spirit of humankind. If this were not the case then how could Nietzsche claim the pronouncement of the death of God as a timely one—one brewing over a millennium or so but never the less a development specific to a particular kind of self-conscious skepticism. Provided Europe did not succumb to the seductions of socialism and Chinese Buddhism—herd thinking and asceticism—the ground was ready for planting new forms of life. Neither inevitable nor predictable, this untimely thinker sees the possibility of a certain potentiality coming into realization in the West's[25] horizon of becoming.

Perspicacious eyes and ears no doubt see more, hear more, discern more and evaluate more autonomously even in the existence 'errors'. When Nietzsche wondered who read and understood his books, it was a quandary about whether or not the *demos* had achieved sufficient self-consciousness of its *potentiality* to digest his eminently difficult ideas. In short, the species develops but it develops unevenly both vertically and horizontally. The world is composed by degrees of difference between individuals, groups, religions, and temporal modes of existence. On the horizontal plane, homo sapiens are not of equal standing in their abilities or cultural prowess and cultivation since the will to strive—to transform oneself and one's world—is distributed unevenly. The 'pathos of distance' as Nietzsche calls it on various occasions leaves its mark on humanity as much as it does on nature, hence the reason for an undeniable unevenness in the physio-psychological and 'spiritual' make-up of individuals and collective groups. Yet it is precisely this distance between ourselves (and one's competing inner drives) which for Nietzsche defines the space in which subjectivity and spiritual elevation is developed in diverse indeterminate ways. His 'pathos of distance' points us to two salient aspects of being human: firstly, pathos itself refers to the impermanent, transitory nature of lived experience where only time releases us from its tenacious grip; secondly, distance represents differentiation in both the psychological and sociological senses wherein higher—more 'comprehensive', remote, rarer and 'further-stretching'—states of being are distinguished according to the principle of the 'enhancement of the type "man"' (BGE 257). This foundational principle is drawn from a somewhat remote source though it will also appear in Greek tragedy: the ancient pre-Platonic philosopher of fire and justice, Heraclitus, who also conceived of δικη (justice) in the cosmos in terms of Necessity and its differentiated distribution. It is in Heraclitus, not Parmenides or Socrates, that Nietzsche found the attractive concept of Becoming (as opposed to Being) sufficiently justified and defendable. Although this is plainly evident in his *Philosophy in the Tragic Age of the Greeks,* it was preceded by earlier writings on pre-Platonic Ionian and Eleatic philosophers of ancient Greece[26] that were based on his lectures delivered at the university.

Heraclitus provided the necessary departure point from which Nietzsche could simultaneously endorse the concept of *Becoming* and, secondly, what he named the *instinct for freedom* (cf. GM). Beyond the material reality of a mechanical world where utility and English longings for happiness prevail, an altogether different, more sublime order of things exists wherein individuals, like particles, cannot be defined in terms of either their *ousia* (substance, in Latin *esse*). The latter points to the need for a single 'One' as Parmenides and the neo-Platonists had it, but for Nietzsche who eschewed the metaphysical idea of Being, Will and Atom, it was most important to look underneath the veil of appearance to find formative processes within nature's chaos. Things or beings become what they are as a result of multiple processes of formation rather than Force or causation. Since history flows like a river and all its tributaries, we find man to be analogous to those processes of Becoming which only came to the fore once Thomson and Faraday had overcome the twin masters of modern science, Newton and Leibniz. Therefore, in a sense Heraclitus, although lacking a concept of the drives, antedates or anticipates what the twentieth century will come to understand in terms of a post-mechanical universe. He attributed to ἀρχή (principle/origin), in opposition to Anaximander, all predicates and qualities since the 'One' of Parmenides evidences itself in all of them. Consonant with the precept of πάντα ρει ("all things flow"), Becoming and Passing Away are conjoined in this principle. Nietzsche argues: 'Becoming never ceases at the indefinitely small. Yet at the greatest [level] nothing absolutely unalterable exists'. '[T]hat which becomes is one thing in eternal transformation, and the law of this eternal transformation, the Logos in all things, is precisely this One, fire (το πυρ)' (PP: 62). Thus, the forces of death and life, wakefulness and somnolence, and composition and decomposition are intertwined like a knot, with each antithetical force being present in every predicate. So the human subject is likened to a knot; its Logos being man inexorably entwined in processes of formation and *transformations* that 'stretch' the human between the small and the great, the high and the low, the general and the individual element. Where to start, one asks? Well, there is no equivalent mathematical Archimedean point here, so Becoming renders man an unfinished *zoon Logoistikon* ('Logos animal') who similar to the Sphinx does not entirely belong to any one world. We have finally arrived at the central proposition underwriting Nietzsche's philosophical anthropology; namely, since there are απειροι κοσμοι (countless worlds), man's γιγνομενον (coming to be) within the Indefinite (το απειρον) is fundamentally effected by countless shifting and mostly competing constitutive forces. Human nature is ambiguous it seems because it is rendered unstable while enmeshed in multiple, interrelated processes of Becoming. Even so as we have already seen this never prevented Nietzsche from developing a conception of the human being (and humanity) based upon an implicit philosophical anthropology. In this regard, I am in full agreement with Richard Schacht's analysis of Nietzsche's thinking as grounded in a form of philosophical anthropology.[27] However, our analysis by comparison does not maintain that it accords with a (fuller) version of experimentalism; experiments are valid but they do not found his idea of Becoming or equally importantly the uniquely human divided soul that trajects itself into time with an 'arrow'.

Leaving to one side observations to be explored further regarding noble spirits and responsibility, I wish briefly to focus on a discernible if subtle shift in Nietzsche's conception of the human. It relates to a corrective shift in Nietzsche's initially enthusiastic encounter with modern sciences from the period of *Human All Too Human* to the commencement of his *Zarathustra* book. Since Nietzsche wrote with a heightened sense of his *bios* informing his world-outlook, it would be logically consistent therefore to look out for conceptual 'overcomings' in his own writing. Here is not the place to enumerate or identify his various self-overcomings. Nevertheless, it appears the case—consistent with Clark's[28] rejection of an underlying biologism in Nietzsche's philosophy—that the Becoming human is *seen* in more syn*optic* terms in his later writings. The foregoing discussion of comprehensive, perspicacious eyes and ears that distinguish the human soul from its simple 'animal-soul' gives reason to lay emphasis on this perspectival shift *upwards* (Nietzsche never shied away from the language of 'superior' (higher)and 'inferior' (lower) which is more self-evident in French and Italian than in English). Higher synoptical apprehension of how this being becomes 'human' refers us to the *sui generis* logic of 'the human type', a type and form that has departed from lesser beings who had no capacity to answer the Sphinx, or, alternatively to take on those vast oceans of sea-wandering in self-understanding which earlier types of man were incapable of. Resisting any Kantian conception of the self-evident dignity of persons as moral agents and, on the other hand, the abstract *cogito* of Descartes that thinks itself into existence, Nietzsche sought to demarcate a new 'space' for thinking man's radical freedom in time. That is, by incorporating an historical philosophy of the animal-soul of man into an account that duly acknowledges the force of man's own exegesis (will to truth) as transformative, Nietzsche was able to transfigure both idealism and realism in his new image of radical freedom. It is, however, a depth-hermeneutical enterprise that clearly relates to man's 'spiritual' drive to know, a venting or discharge of *willing* power toward its object: man himself and hence in his γνωθι σαυτον (Know Thyself) as originally stated by Thales. With an animated soul that finds expression in its own particular *belebende Kraft* (invigorating force), the task of knowing oneself, of inquiring into the constitution of both outer and inner nature, is vigorously taken up by philosophers in their desire to give meaning to the world. When writing the second preface to his *Gay Science* later in his life, Nietzsche captured the essence to this spiritual drive and yearning when he depicted the core of philosophy thus: 'he simply *cannot* keep from transposing his states every time into the most spiritual form and distance: this art of transfiguration *is* philosophy' (GS *P* 3). The art of philosophizing we note is distinct from the being who had not yet entered into socialized, political communities; who had not yet learned the arts of *necessity* (*ananke*) because the free immediate spontaneity of being had not as yet known the necessity to *discover* meaning beyond organic sufficiency. *Ipso facto* it did not know innovation because its 'simple being' had yet to be sundered from its animalic origins. Cultivation is social; spiritual cultivation as expansion of the 'spirit of man' on the other hand is both immanent and transcendent of social (historical) forms, suggesting that it cannot be caged by the state or buffoonery of the masses (for very long at least).

Towards the close of his life Nietzsche expressed it this way in his unpublished notebooks (WP 616): 'That the value of the world lies in our interpretation...that every elevation of man brings with it the overcoming of narrower interpretations; that every strengthening and increase of power opens up new perspectives and means believing in new horizons—this idea permeates my writing'. That the organic too 'constantly presupposes interpretations' is shown later in his assertion 'there must be present something that wants to grow and interprets the value of whatever else wants to grow. Equal *in that*—in fact, interpretation is itself a means of becoming master of something' (WP 643). Mankind therefore interprets itself, its world, in *extra*-zoological ways in order to intervene in Nature's indifference by symbolizing value in human *ergon, praxis, exegesis, euzōia* (work, activity, interpretation, well-living). This is the reason why the Greeks correctly understood cultivation in cultural terms as an important impetus for striving, growing and willing including the will to transcend despair and egoistic docility. And language, as the lover of words well understood, was an important means for its transvaluation of organic-animalic life and all its limitations. Although there is a constant struggle between the commanding and obeying powers of both organic impulses and human interpretations, Nietzsche identified a uniquely *extra*-nutrient επιθυμια (inner desire) at work in the human sciences and arts of exegesis. Where bio-chemistry might reveal something similar in the life of the organism, Nietzsche's joyful wisdom apprehends the particular desire of the human to impute meaning to a painful agonic life: to know oneself and not simply 'be' like a leaf which swings in the wind in any direction; and to evaluate life according to anthropic values that are purposefully imposed onto an otherwise indifferent, arbitrary nature.

Since the human itself requires instantiation, individuals feel the want to impute meaning, establish values and hypotheses, and experiment with truth-schemas so as to develop themselves. This is the work of willing (verb): 'man would rather will *nothingness* than *not* will' (GM III: 28). And it does not particularly matter what he posits or willed into existence but rather that this 'bravest of animals' repudiated organic necessity in place of man himself. The cage—civilized society—gave it purpose. By establishing the soul-concept through a priestly ideal of renunciation and the *ergon* of truth-telling man at least saved himself. Once again we see the will revivified:

> man was *saved* thereby, he possessed a meaning, he was henceforth no longer like a leaf in the wind, a plaything of nonsense...no matter at first to what end, why, with what he willed: *the will itself was saved* (GM III: 28).

Against a senseless existence of being flung here and there by nature's forces, the willing human-animal extends its horizon by means of so many political, aesthetic, spiritual and legislative elaborations of the experience of βιος (always in tension with ζωη). Secondly, a stronger argument is put forward in terms of its inner dwelling desire, one that stems from Nietzsche's depth-psychological reading of human nature. Namely, that such interpretations aim at securing a kind of certainty with respect to human ontology. In *The Gay Science* (2) Nietzsche discerned this as a facet of superior life-forms: 'that which separates the higher human beings from the lower' is the capacity to recognize one's '*desire for certainty* as the inmost craving and deepest distress'. Certitude then is a part of this inner desire and force of growth which the 'leaves swaying in the wind' by contrast cannot know. By instigating and demanding a judgment such as "Yes, I am worthy of living!" man thereby distinguishes himself from other animals and becomes something more than dangerous or courageous: the human now becomes 'a fantastic animal that has to fulfill one more condition of existence than any other animal: man *has* to believe, to know, from time to time *why* he exists' (GS 1). Owing to its particular morphology, the human being who is possessed of *pneuvma* (air or spirit) requires *aitia* (reason/cause) to have a life that is worthy of living—as the neo-Platonists had maintained. This *aitia* mode demands explanations that will sustain the belief in life, something that reaches far beyond the limits of Darwin's organic instinct for self-preservation. This explains why Nietzsche could charge Darwin with having forgotten the Mind in his account of transformation.

The emphases that Nietzsche laid on the value of the *necessity* of knowing and believing (i.e. faith) in reasons for life indicates the power of επιθυμια for man. The world takes on a certain anthropic dimension in which truth and error, and trust and despair oscillate within processes of Becoming. Leaves which sway quite senselessly do not by contrast demand reasons let alone faith in reasons for life. Humanity in contradistinction 'cannot flourish without a periodic trust in life' (GS 1). What is this trust, we may ask? Nietzsche replies: 'without faith in *reason in life*' man cannot call itself human. What then does Nietzsche's philosophy propose in terms of our discussion of 'what is man' and the problem of freedom? We can summarize it this way perhaps:

1. Becoming is most significant for understanding humanity and *Dasein*, not the void of a metaphysical Abyss.

2. Teachers of meaning of existence ineradicably alter the human being.

3. Freedom is difficult because of its demands for responsibility.

4. *Ad et credum*; only faith and trust in life, by the *duree* of time, sustains the value of *Dasein*.

5. Soul-hypothesis deepens and intensifies the 'spirit of man', thus making this half-animal more dangerous and interesting by knowing love, hate, guilt, resentment, sacrifice, redemption and so forth.

6. Promise of the future holds out the prospect for radical freedom, not the repetition of archaic events in a recurring cycle.

7. Synoptic comprehensive knowing allows a discernment of the Whole of life from distant continents of seeing more historically and comparatively.

8. Human beings' contradictory 'animal-soul' transforms life with the emergence of political subjects in civilized communities (*Bios*). *Zoi* is rendered more remote and lacking an 'itinerary of the soul' (history) by *Bios*.

9. Ontology of desire to obtain certainty in the midst of fear of Nothingness. Immanent to the vital human being, the will to ascribe meaning to life *saves man* himself.

10. Elevated height of noble individuals who transcend herd-morality and mass politics hold the potentiality of freedom in the 'promise' without any teleology.

11. Specific to human beings is the rank of values established by commanding-obeying individuals in (state) society; plants and animals have no such predicament.

These points suggest that Nietzsche's thinking cannot be properly encapsulated within the limits of 'eternal recurrence', nihilism or the naturalistic critique of morality. They point to something else which often goes unexplored. Nietzsche did indeed have a sense of what would follow on from his critique of modernity and European nihilism. His philosophical anthropology of Becoming and its potentiality *in* time point to a form of freedom which encapsulates responsibility and overcoming oneself. This actually refines the original Heraclitean idea of the human order with lessons taken from modernity that man is 'a bridge' across time, holding out the promise of becoming something finer, stronger, nobler, honest, unrevengeful, insightful, joyous, responsible and thus freer. The 'psychology' (broadly defined) was missing from Heraclitus' somewhat austere account of Justice in the cosmos. Of course, these are not understood as virtues but rather as states of the human condition that have undergone radical alteration.

Hence Heraclitus' *Logos* in the universe becomes for Nietzsche's philosophical anthropology a kind of *fröhliche Wissenschaft*: that which affirms life as a peculiarly this-worldly affair because it can also affirm the affinity between faith and reason, evaluation and psychology, spirit and body, and *physis* and *nomos*. Faith in life possessing reasons *for* man is therefore crucial for a sense of trust in knowing life has meaning (purpose). That is, in declaring 'Yes, I am worthy of living' the human being found that 'Life and I and you and all of us became *interesting* to ourselves once again for a little while' (GS 1). Thus the experiment of life goes on, with new interpretations and meanings for why life is intoxicatingly interesting and enjoyable regardless of its tedious disappointments and sufferings emerging in time. For the 'knower' the experiment of life throws up a vast array of enigmatic experiences which makes her ponder, scrutinize and evaluate them. On the other hand, the investigations and evaluations themselves are deepened and stretched by the establishment (institutionalization) of a class of teachers of meaning as we discussed earlier. Even the Greek tragedians that so influenced Nietzsche 'the philologist' acted as educators of tragic life in promoting the interests of the human species by declaring "Life is worth living" (GS 1). Freedom we might say requires the *paidagōgoi* (teachers) because they open up new spaces in which to think, evaluate, feel and live. The priests did this as much as the natural philosophers and 'decadent' moralists. We need this statement in case we mistakenly assume that only music and poetic sensibility underscore the transformative impulse of the overcoming individual, something inexcusable even for the early Wagnerian Nietzsche. Going with and against Aeschylus' 'eternal comedy of existence', the ongoing regeneration of 'teachers of the purpose of existence' has fundamentally altered the condition of humanity. Human nature underwent particular transformations with the emergence of a class of sage-priestly types of man whose theologico-philosophical teachings of purpose gradually took on an independent power of their own. Their task was to turn life into a problem. They had to investigate the *meta*-physical dimension to life. With the rise of this autonomous class of contemplators the purposefulness of life assumed a greater hold over human beings than was justifiable. In other words, our examination into life itself—its enigmatic and diverse experiences— becomes integral to our own self-understanding that humans are more than simply ζωη.

It is important at this stage to reflect upon another conceptual advance which oftentimes goes amiss. We noted earlier an influence certain strands of modern physics had on Nietzsche's understanding of force positions, relations and dynamics. Such empirico-theoretical ideas rejected any unilinear, casual images of processes of change in the natural world. Eschewing simple notions of progress and scientific advancement, Nietzsche understood that the *nomoi* (laws) of αναγκη (necessity) nevertheless do not preclude any metamorphosis. Eternal recurrence, in other words, need not necessarily imply *stasis*—the eternal cycle of sameness. If it did, that is if it inferred repetition of the same, there could in fact be no 'philosophy of the future' or any going beyond nihilistic values. Noble values, similarly, could not have metamorphosed out of decadent slavish values without such a transformation. In turn, this would endanger any idea of a noble free spirit transcending the normative strictures of any given political or moral community. Mutations and vicissitudes are in fact possible within a theory of the Indefinite and a genealogically informed philosophical anthropology that preserves the Schopenhauerian insight that events and forces often recur in the cycles of our cosmos. A species can expect to undergo both novel (innovative) *and* repetitive types of experience; change and recurrence are not as is commonly supposed antithetical to each other. Freedom does not imply an ahistorical existence. We are reminded, for instance, of the challenge which that 'Platonic way of thinking, which was a noble *way* of thinking' consisted of in resisting 'obvious sense-evidence'; and how the 'tough' work of today's 'bridge-building' machinists will mean the transvaluation of British empiricism once their task has been completed and the drive to spiritualize being will once again prove indispensable (BGE 14). A further illustration of the need to apprehend freedom emerging out of historical recurrence is the comparative thrust of Nietzsche's historical philosophy (and sociology): modernity is placed within a horizon of difference whereby ancient Greece serves an instructive critical dimension to modern mediocrity even though its civilizational reality is unrecoverable—the world of tragic Greece cannot be repeated in the present. This impossibility marks a moment of possibility, of creating something out of the extant as a distinct *potentiality*; the impossible hence makes real the freedom that lies in the future of possible 'presents'. Thus we can posit that civilizational forms are co-dependent upon generative and degenerative processes, or, put another way on freedom *and* necessity. It is 'necessary' that Greek forms remain distant to us even while we get on with life believing—as Winkelman and his heirs did in Germany—that we are the natural modern outgrowth of Greek fire and *sophia*.

However the thesis that change and recurrence are interlocked in the projection of human life has an added dimension. The necessity of recurrence—though not repetition—is founded in another aspect of the nature of the human being. It is the human being's desire for predictable, languid and placid existence that stultifies the new and innovative from emerging. Nietzsche states the lack of any trembling craving for questioning and the rapture hereof 'this whole marvelous uncertainty and rich ambiguity of existence' elicits a certain contemptible feeling, one that 'every human being has...simply because he is human' (GS 2). Human nature inexorably is defined by this want to evade the scrutiny of life because philosophical examination appears to threaten the cozy facticity of a pleasurable life. Yet without questioning there is no danger and life without danger appears to Nietzsche, *inter alios,* not worth living; after all, it is only the feeble ones who decadently seek an *un*dangerous existence. Undangerous and undeveloped go hand in hand. The priests, philosophers and seekers of *episteme* however, have permanently changed life; life now demands meaning, direction, interpretation, power, contestation and study. The 'danger' of life now includes knowing the general contempt for investigation and resisting it, as all untimely humans know all too well. In this sense the Greeks turn to a *bios theoretikos* was not so much foolish as dangerous; they made life more dangerous by presuming the task of unmasking the inner secrets of *physis* was ordained for them. Once one begins to conceive of life as an 'experiment of the seeker for knowledge' rather than a calamity or duty, it becomes 'truer, more desirable and mysterious every year' (GS 324). Of course, this is linked to our previous observation that with respect to other animals man (sic) is the more 'interesting', 'fantastic' animal because of its spiritualized drive to disclose the concealed truths of world and nature, and hence experiences of its inherent mysteriousness. The *pedagogoi* as much as the priests perpetuate this dangerous curiosity in the guise of important civilizational forms, i.e. writing, tutelage, oration, procedural rules, ascetic training, higher values, meditation and reflection, discourse, self-discipline, otherworldly dispositions, brotherhoods, ritualized practices, and universes of discourse which create new possible worlds unavailable to the sheep, goats and dogs of this world. That is to say, they take freedom as *necessitās* because the Greeks must experiment with necessity (law, lawfulness) in order to found freedom out of self-transformation. Once having 'discovered' the soul, priests and artists have ultimately broken with the primordial blind alley of zoological existence. Their spirit, in other words, prevents them from any penultimate return to a simple organic being.

Do we have a metaphor that perhaps captures this nuanced argument? I think it to be that of Nietzsche's dance: the musicality of his Dionysian 'gay science' is one that enjoins knowledge and joy with an Heraclitean sense of successive moments of change turning our object-world into a constant rhythmic movement between wonderment and ecstatic intelligible forms of Becoming. This means joyfulness of the kind associated with curiosity of knowing the world, and the structure of music as first conceived by mathematical philosophers, are now brought into closer proximity, into a productive union. The untimely philosopher (Nietzsche) represents this important amalgam; on the other hand, herd-thinking prevents the Many to break out of such false dichotomies. The truth of error we can now argue is to think the converse: that joyfulness is dissociated from (and by) knowledge and, secondly, that our object world can simply be grasped by static, abstract concepts which the philosopher projects onto the world and subsequently fails to *see* movement in time and space.[29] Both in Plato's *Symposium* and *Phaedo* the inter-play of opposites in processes of Becoming and transformation are evident; and we also know that Heraclitus' *Logos* greatly influenced Plato's appropriation of pre-Socratic thinking. Both Nietzsche and Plato realize that it is not necessarily contradictory to assert the co-existence of opponent pairs (e.g. warm-cold, day-night) in the process of things becoming what they are *and* to assert that errors are indeed knowable. Finally, they each maintained this position whilst adhering to the possibility—

first sustained by Anaxagoras—that the boundless *cosmos* is replete with beauty, a contrary notion to the Eleatic's view of the sky as being black.[30]

What is then novel as a world-historical phenomenon is the decisive intervention which interpretive-psychological forces make in these Heraclitean-like processes of formation and flux. The dual historical determinants entwined in the emergence of the drive to give meaning and purpose to dumb existence—to interpret the world rather than merely breathe its air—and on the other hand, the formation of a group of master teachers of evaluation and epistemic disclosure are pivotal. Life becomes an experiment for those seekers of knowledge who through enquiry and error and illusion, amplify human experience many times over thus transforming life into something more *dangerous* and more *interesting*. This insight can be paralleled to extensions of the botanical-physiological kind which so keenly exercised Nietzsche's mind from a quite young age. The metaphors of growth, formation and cultivation—all key facets of human culture—were in some respects kin concepts to those dynamic processes mentioned in the context of Heraclitus and the physics of nature. It is this dimension of his thinking which arguably works against any notions of an elitist valorization of masterly virtues and any Homeric valor expressed in a rhetoric of power commonplace in Wilhelmian Germany. Notably, Nietzsche enjoyed nurturing plants and at one time in his life seriously considered becoming a gardener—a *philos* of *terra* and its plant life.[31] Perhaps this is the reason why Zarathustra stands as an emblem not only of self-disciplined autonomy but of that noble kind of human who knows nature and enjoys her attendant dangers, pinnacles, troughs and ridges. Against the void, Zarathustra (man) forms a bridge across nature's abyss and with dangerous delight, edifies his world by making his existence within, yet beyond nature's laws. *Against* organicism and physiological determinism this 'type of man' finds the task of bridge-building compelling—an imperative to overcome the natural limits of his existence (i.e. the abyss underlying the bridge to his Future). So although Zarathustra must stand afar from civilization's marketplace—in order to 'see' it properly—he also is the *beyond-animal* that cannot return to mere organic life. Potentiality, as introduced earlier, necessarily looks forward like Apollo's Arrow—it cannot be retrogressive. Hence the reason why Nietzsche's philosophy is neither conservative nor elitist[32], or even naturalistic.[33] Returning to the metaphor of the Gardener, life like the old Judaic idea of the tree grows (upwards) and extends out into multiple directions, seeking to enhance its presence and hold on life. Stunted growth, shallow roots, poor nutrients and pernicious lesions to stems consequently stood opposed to Nietzsche's vitalistic sensibilities. When Nietzsche spoke of decline and sheer blind destructibility he often attributed this to a lack of those nurturing life enhancing (socio-cultural) nutrients that enable personal and social cultivation. *Kultur* is what Idealists named it though this problematic concept tends to privilege the Mind, the ideational and the Spirit (*Geist*). By contrast, civilization signifies a certain deferment from the immediacy of nature: myth, faith and language (concept)—as Hegel had similarly pointed out—estrange the human being from its primordial nature thus laying the ground simultaneously for its own self-cultivation and extension. Being-in-time, that is, interrupts the order of *physis*. Certainly the human needs *physis* as its task-master and yet it always wants to transvaluate her, to transgress her 'laws' of repetition and thus exceed her bounds—nature's limits. This exceeding or 'extension' is particularly acute in art, science and tragic literature because here we are most forcefully reminded of the pull-push polarity of existence and the tension it produces *in* man. The will to spiritualize this immanent tension acts as a father impetus to human-kind's aesthetic and axiological extension, causing this fundamentally incom-plete and dirempted creature to constantly search for its potentiality in other possible worlds. It approximates the vivid image portrayed by Aristophanes' speech (in Plato's *Symposium*) where the incomplete gendered being goes on its perennial global search for the other half that will complete it and thus provide happiness.

If conceived through the eyes of a Persian Zoroaster, the fantastic animal who is the more courageous and interesting of nature's creatures relates to its own nature not as an enemy but as an ally. The corporeal or psycho-physiology of man is an integral part of his conception of how cultivation and potentiality arise out of certain force-points and force-relations that form states or configura-tions of power-discharge in the world (*cosmos*—the natural and social worlds). Therefore, it is doubtful that Nietzsche would countenance a mis-reading of his philosophy as one essentially and reductively founded on the will to power and its claimed justification for dominating nature through the instrumentalization of Greek *techne* (Heidegger's error). We have returned therefore to the foregoing idea of the bow and its productive tension, where the human being is like an arrow that can shoot further thanks to these dual polarities of *physis* and *nomos* (or cultivated humanity). In other words, Nietzsche is wholly consistent with the main font of Western metaphysics—Greek philosophy. Indeed, it can be ar-gued—against Alain Badiou—that Nietzsche's thinking is more Platonic and consistent with the idea of *paideia* than he himself appeared to have realized.[34]

Philosophy of Overcoming, or, Transcendence

It is clear from the foregoing discussion that philosophical activity serves also to raise the human above its mere bestial form—an observation wholly consistent with Greek philosophy and Roman Stoicism. What differentiates man from other animals is precisely its unwillingness to accept simple being as given to him by nature—a *Was-sein* (whatness) that is accepted without questioning. Essential to its species-being it seems is the argument that 'man has to believe, to know, from time to time why he exists' (GS 1). Nietzsche does not say it is by happenstance that man seeks to know or that he simply considers it desirable to do so. The point is that *we have to know* and *have to believe* because as a race we 'cannot flourish without a periodic trust in life'. Other animals do not require *faith* or *belief* in order to 'be', to experience their inner and outer natures. *Fide*, in other words, remains significant even after God is proclaimed dead only now it is invested and directed towards life itself, particularly through the immanence of being human. Nature has cycles and processes but only the human being acquires faith *in* life, in the purposive meaning accorded to it and therefore in the self-acknowledgement that this determination (along with 'the teachers') helps maintain a certain 'pathos of distance' between the human and the organicity of ζωή. Furthermore, the argument retains its saliency even once it is conceded that illusion and mystification are a part of this reality. Why? Because as we have already seen error is a part of truth and therefore imaginary realities cannot a priori be excluded from the moment of 'Nietzsche's dance'. There is one further level of argumentation concerning the property of distance; namely, that humanity as a species or race cannot flourish properly 'without faith in reason in life' (GS 1). Unifying Jacobi's faith concept with Kant's concept of reason, Nietzsche shifts the essence across to the futural power of *Bildung* as the creative, disciplined process of *bios* so that belief is now invested in the rationality or reasons given to life itself. Intelligible cultivated life—the Greek idea of *bios*—now substitutes for a deity that is simply a reification of human consciousness. The Gardener to return to our previous allegory invests *reasons* into nature's forms of life, into the activity of cultivating plant-growth, e.g. pruning, sculpturing, enriching and eliminating; but the plant itself has no 'reason', its *Ansichsein* (Being-in-itself) does not entail the *giving* of reasons, of meanings. This is not a point about a lack of self-consciousness regarding the plant's in-itselfness; rather it concerns the need for the human to posit, form and project reasons and desires to understand *why* life is a problem *for* him/her; and to continue doing so continually throughout life. Here we note three important analytic registers: time, willful purposive activity and thought. It is no coincidence then that the human requires *paideia* for its own *bios* as a being-in-time—training, education and ethos through learned acculturation—to refine its grasp on the potentiality of being human. This is precisely why Nietzsche declared man to be an unfinished animal: nature delivers up the human, yet only historical transvaluation through valuation and individual striving through willing can accomplish the remaining. No teleology is implied here so there is no deterministic outcome or Divine plan as Hegel may have thought. To attempt constantly to complete the project of man in time, that is, through a kind of 'development' which incorporates arduous struggle and tragic chance and the will to capture sight of the beautiful is to value *potentiality* itself. As Nietzsche's 'eternal recurrence' does not in fact mean that everything stays exactly the same, this project of self-overcoming via potentiality—'development' in time—requires a constant regeneration of a class of educators and thinkers: It now has one additional need—the need for the ever new appearance of such teachers and teachings of a "purpose" (GS 1).

The twin phenomena of belief in and reasons for life can now be linked to Zeus like strikes which deliver Daedalian knowledge and arts to mankind. The sociological (classes) and philosophical (reasons) converge at this point both to mutually reinforce one another and to transform the species' self-understanding in terms of its transvaluation of man's originary 'animal-soul'. The task of this class of teachers is to propagate the know-how, the techniques and ethos necessary for fecundity: the 'ability to control one's Pro and Con and to dispose of them, so that one knows how to employ a variety of perspectives and affective interpretations in the service of knowledge' (GM III:12). In the service of knowledge Apollo and Daedalus work in conjunction endowing man with the arts and sciences necessary to furnish a *deeper* and *wider* inner and social nature whilst at the same time imbuing it with a strong sense of measured judgment—'comprehensive synoptical perspective' one could say. These masters of interpretation, of authoritative exegesis, all too readily understand the importance of exercising measured judgment in the *will* of intellectual cultivation: to 'eliminate the will *altogether*, to suspend each and every affect, *supposing* we were capable of this—what would that mean but to castrate the intellect?' (GM III: 12 emphasis added). Contrary to an anti-epistemological reading of him, Nietzsche pushes the imperative of intellectual cultivation in the direction of 'speaking more and more precisely, demanding greater and great precision' (GM, *P* 2). And this is the latter Nietzsche rather than the young disciple of Schopenhauer. Indeed, the mature Nietzsche goes a step further to attach an important valuation to this kind of necessary activity of the human: 'It should now be considered the decisive sign of great culture when someone possesses enough strength and flexibility to be just as clear and rigorous in acquiring knowledge as he is capable of at other moments of letting poetry, religion, and metaphysics get a hundred feet ahead of him, as it were, and still appreciating their power and beauty' (HH 278). It accords with our argument thus far that a synoptical grasp of the Whole encompasses 'precision' and on the other hand religion and metaphysics which get a hundred feet ahead of oneself but nevertheless possess a certain 'power and beauty'.

Nietzsche's philosophical anthropology we can see then is not particularly averse to epistemology per se or the need for ever more precise articulations of thought and perspectivism. Rather it is the unnecessary hatred and revenge that is leveled against different and mostly irksome facets of life—the *whole* of human nature—that appeared ugly to Nietzsche. The point is more direct and fundamental: recognize what the (dynamic) powers of intellect and instinct can produce in the world *and* accord value to each of them in order to see the beauty specific to each. According to this logic, even the metaphysical enterprise from Parmenides to Schopenhauer has helped to edify man because if one looks down into its depths, its beauty is revealed.[35] The Truth adventure is worthy therefore because it has extended the human, the spirit of man. It has given humanity reason to investigate and *eo ipso* allowed us to extend the reach of human powers, its intellect and spirit so as to become *potentially* free and noble spirited. By contrast, a plant can not see itself as noble; it has no freedom to gain a perspective on itself. Yet the human is similar to the plant not merely because of its similar hydro-nutrient systems but because both genera embody processes (within time) of composition, metamorphosis, decomposition and extinguishment. The pursuance of knowledge for itself by classes of teachers nonetheless leads to another divergence: Nietzsche sees the achievement of a high culture entails transforming existence according to the 'idea that life could be an experiment of the seeker for knowledge' (GS 324). Plants and ants by contrast cannot transform life into an experiment; they exist not as experimental seekers of knowledge but rather as organisms of geo-physical atrophy which at best mu-

tate inter-generationally in nature's accidental 'experiment'. More phenome-
nologically speaking, the human turns his or her own civilized, moral-aesthetic
life into a worthy object of experimentation. To turn one's life into an experiment is to necessarily engage in hypothesizing, surmising, formulating, measuring, theorizing, studying, classifying, observing, and drawing conclusions and
results from diverse experiences. It means to *en*danger life by means of hypothesizing, a setting forth of a futural moment against a dominant present. It is human to do this, human-all-too-human but still more argues Nietzsche. The philosopher Thales, for instance, looks at nature to find a single principle regulating
all matter (water as his name signifies) and by doing so transforms simple life
into a 'problem', a question of what constitutes life itself and thereby giving
ground to the peculiar activity of speculating, hypothesizing, positing, deducing
reasons and finding an *archē* (origin) of the universe. This experimental attitude
to life is unique to this kind of species: *homo sapiens sapiens*. Against all declarations of an all pervasive chaos or fated existence commonly found in various
accounts[36] of Nietzsche's claimed 'naturalistic' outlook, Nietzsche explicitly
shows his unambiguous anthropology of human ontology in the following vital
passage:

> For man is more sick, uncertain, *changeable, indeterminate than any other*
> *animal*, there is no doubt of that…Certainly he has also *dared more*, done more
> new things, *braved more* and *challenged fate more* than all the *other animals*
> *put together*: he, the *great experimenter with himself*, discontented and insatia-
> ble, *wrestling with animals, nature, and gods* for ultimate dominion—he, still
> unvanquished, *eternally directed toward the future*, whose own restless ener-
> gies never leave him in peace, so that his future digs like a spur into the flesh of
> the present (GM III:13 emphasis added).

What therefore sets mankind apart from other kinds of *zoi*—sentient life—is
its ability and desire to challenge fate, to push against animals and nature in order to create a future that nature could not have designed for it. Being a 'change-
able' and 'indeterminate' animal, one that continually dares, does, invents new
things and bravely takes on a world which is 'eternally directed toward the future' leaves us with a non-fatalist vision of human existence. This *imago*, which
is not subservient to a destined fate, a blind kind of destiny whereby the 'great
experimenter with himself' would be impossible, instead leaves us with a strong
sense of how life ought to be experimented by the Yes-saying scholar, the one
who knows the *gay science* of the Whole of life—both its upside and its down-
side, that is, its creative *and* necessary dimensions. No other animal of Darwin's
animal world could achieve this feat; and for our purposes we can say that it is
due to this particular ontology that man's 'being' is distinctly different from the
plant and goat (despite their shared organic biological constitutive universals).
Through culture, that is educative cultivation, the species known as 'man' finds
that its essential 'insatiability' and discontentment regarding its power, joy and
desire in the world come to define its own ontology (ontology as 'there is', a
human). If other ontologies also exist, they are unlike man's since his is
uniquely directed to the future—a future that eventuates out of the challenges

which human beings lay against fate, as the above quoted passage also indicates. This is not merely a scientific attitude: it is an ennobling activity, a freedom of sorts and most importantly an expression of the Beautiful. Beauty or the beauty of freedom is found in that spirit of legislating one's human concerns and interpretations upon nature's declared blind 'indifference'. (This is what prevents us from accepting a naturalistic interpretation of Nietzsche's oeuvre.)

Like Plato we can see that Nietzsche was clearly an exponent, from beginning to end, of the beauty of agonic willing and free air. This form of life is both extra-animalic and extra-botanical for one other important reason. For Nietzsche, the freedom to find or create beauty is inconceivable without the totality of life: the range of experiences and elevated capacities and spirits of the historically formed human being that allow it to exercise measured judgment in the process of legislating values upon the world. Thus a noble form of life—one marked by an experimental attitude to truth/life—should be marked by ironic laughter at the errors of man even whilst it embarks on the Great Hunt of knowledge with its accordant values of 'more precise' and 'comprehensive' eyes and ears of discernment. Here the unity of Aeschylus and Goethe (as scientist) refers us to the necessarily life-affirming tension (bow) that is produced by the tragedic sense of joy and, on the other hand, the amoral experimental apprehension of living things as found in Goethe. In *Beyond Good and Evil* Nietzsche discerned the bankruptcy of such false oppositions—cheerfulness v realism—to expound a philosophy of the human that embraces the beautiful without eschewing the 'brutal hard facts' of Schopenhauerian suffering and organic atrophy. Because genealogy, as both an historical process and interpretation, shows the force of educators such as Plato and Thucydides in the development of contrary valuations, we need the educator[37] precisely because the beautiful still requires their skilful exegesis on the Why of life. Regarding beauty, the σοφος ('the wise') etymologically is linked to the ancient *sapio*, 'to taste', and sapiens to 'one who tastes'. Moreover, as Nietzsche notes in his pre-Platonics book (PP :8) the taste of the arts extended further to 'of sharp taste' and thus 'a sharp knowledge' without any connotation of "faculty". As sapiens then, in contradistinction to plants or charged sub-atomic particles, we learn (with no certainty or inevitability) to see more clearly and precisely—'more comprehensively' as per the noble Thucydides—the false one-sidedness of abstract schemas that juxtapose instinct —reason, joy—wisdom and *bios*—*physis*. This overcoming of false oppositions as part of the sapiens 'sharp taste' for self-knowledge, is an achievement specific to grand cultures and therefore unobtainable to mere organic entities. Seeing and hearing more deeply and widely—and not merely possessing consciousness itself as Gottfried Leibniz had already demonstrated—thus distances us from other life forms. It is further extended and reinforced by the formation of classes of 'knowers' and thinkers (or priests) once the philosopher steps out of the shadows of the priest. A philosopher is

> a human being who constantly experiences, sees, hears, suspects, hopes, and dreams extraordinary things; who is struck by his own thoughts as from outside as from above and below, as by *his* type of experiences and lightning bolts (BGE 292).

The philosopher's extraordinary experiences strike like lightning bolts from outside, making her both fatal and potential: there are 'constant rumblings and growlings' around this fatal human being 'who is perhaps himself a storm pregnant with new lightnings' (BGE 292). This is why it is possible to differentiate between the *development* of organic and transorganic natures. The experiential reservoir of the latter constantly produces these rumblings and growlings as *energeia* in the human; neither electrons nor biochemical elements by contrast constitute such powerful immanent storms (that are abundant with striking bolts of dangerous experimental theorems). Moreover, the potent force of these rumblings and experiential bolts recur again and again, partly because of the unique nature of this 'type of man' (*philosophos*) and partly due to the institutionalization of this phenomenon in the Educator *par excellence*. Hence future possibilities are carried within moments of experience, including the instance of forgetfulness, in which the (real) philosopher appears as a legislator—a creative, demanding authorial spirit of interrogation who commands what shall be so on the earth, in the City, in the mob and in his inner nature. The moral law, as Kant would put it, is put into existence by him or her and thus becomes a kind of order of (en)valuation and morality by which he affirms life. The legislator or commander wills life into a desired form of being thereby fusing power, will, comprehension, logos and responsibility into his *bios*—which not even the cultivated healthy plant can achieve. This is the 'height' of comprehensive understanding as exhibited by a free (educated) spirit. Although man does not choose a difficult freedom, he is afforded freedom only in and through an economy of error-making and agonic struggle against his human-all-too-human limits—through self-overcoming in other words. Beauty of freedom, that is to say, comes at a great cost. When Nietzsche declared, in an Odyssean fashion, man to be a 'manifold, mendacious, artificial, and opaque animal' he forgot to say that it is because of its distinctive beauty of freedom in self-overcoming that made man '*uncanny* to the *other animals*' (BGE 291). We might end our discussion of Nietzsche's philosophical anthropology on this note: above all, the value of beauty in the moment of instituting freedom within (our) becoming cannot be known to other lesser animals. Whilst they truly know eternal recurrence, the human being by contrast always remains challenged by a 'future [which] digs like a spur into the flesh of the present' (GM III:13).

Notes

1. For Walter Kaufmann, cf *Nietzsche: Philosopher, Psychologist, Anti-Christ.* Fourth Ed. Princeton: Princeton University Press, 1974; and Richard Schacht, c.f. *Making Sense of Nietzsche: Reflections Timely and Untimely.* Urbana: University of Illinois Press, 1995, ch. 9.

2. See Maudemarie Clark *Nietzsche on Truth and Philosophy.* Cambridge: Cambridge University Press, 1990 and Brian Leiter *Nietzsche On Morality.* London: Routledge, 2002.

3. Marin Heidegger 'The End of Philosophy and the Task of Thinking', *Basic Writings*. Ed. David F. Krell. London: Routledge, 1993, 434.

4. On the importance of the ancient (pre-Platonic) Greek *sophos* and its relation to the originary movement of φιλοσοφια, see F. Nietzsche *The Pre-Platonic Philosophers*. Trans. By Greg Whitlock. Urbana: University of Illinois Press, 2001, Ch 2. Hereafter designated as 'PP '.

5. See Richard Schacht *Making Sense of Nietzsche: Reflections Timely and Untimely*. Urbana: University of Illinois Press, 1995, ch. 8.

6. See John Richardson *Nietzsche's System*. Oxford: Oxford University Press, 1996.

7. See Alexander Nehamas *Nietzsche: Life as Literature*. Cambridge, Mass.: Harvard University Press, 1985.

8. Drives notably are always peculiarly human drives and although Nietzsche was influenced both by Darwin and Lamarck, he always correctly discerned a difference between drives more generally and those belonging to developed natures, i.e. of beings subject to historical development. No conflation between drives and animalic instincts is therefore necessary or implied as valid.

9. For an account of the impact which diverse disciplining processes had on the development of a modern 'tame' human being, see further my *Civilization and the Human Subject*, Lanham/Oxford: Rowman and Littlefield, 1999.

10. On Nietzsche's claimed indebtedness to Darwinian thought, see Daniel Dennett *Darwin's Dangerous Idea: Evolution and the Meanings of Life*, Ringwood: Penguin Books, 1995. However, against the naturalists Nietzsche importantly eschewed the argument that the sense-organs can be our departure point for deciphering reality (cf. Clarke and Dudrick 'Nietzsche's Post-positivism', *European Journal of Philosophy* 12: 3, 2004: 369-385.

11. On genealogy, see Richard Schacht (ed.) *Nietzsche, Genealogy, Morality: Essays on Nietzsche's* On the Genealogy of Morals. Berkeley: University of California Press, 1994.

12. For example, Gilles Deleuze *Nietzsche and Philosophy*. Translated by Hugh Tomlinson. New York: Columbia University Press, 1983.

13. In his biography, Nietzsche very suggestively inverted Schopenhauer's triumph, stating '*non legor, non legar*' whilst also maintaining 'Why I Write Such Good Books' (*Ecce Homo*: 'Why I Write Such Good Books': 1).

14. Although Larmarck influenced Nietzsche in this respect, the influence of Schopenhauer and Wagner on Nietzsche's way of thinking on constitutive matters must also be recognized. On fatalism Brian Leiter has usefully drawn attention to Nietzsche's claimed 'fatalism' in 'The Paradox of Fatalism and Self-Creation in Nietzsche', *Nietzsche*. Edited by John Richardson and Brian Leiter. Oxford: Oxford University Press, 2001.

15. This works against Nietzsche's problematical latent Lamarckianism with its emphasis on inherited traits and limits on one's 'type' through ancestral lineages. I follow Schacht (1983:335) in the interpretation of 'breeding', if properly construed, to mean intergenerational 'constitutional alterations to be achievable' even whilst some continuity is maintained amongst the different sorts of things that emerge in the process. Notable here is the repudiation of a teleology in human history as well as a strict version of the recurrence of the same (repetition) thesis.

16. For an eloquent defence of naturalism in Nietzsche's thought which avoids the reductive pitfalls of empiricism and biologism, see Richard Schacht *Nietzsche*. London:

Routledge, 1983. A later though limited defence of his claimed naturalism can be found in Maudemarie Clark and Brian Leiter's 'Introduction', *Daybreak: Thoughts on the Prejudices of Morality*. Edited by Maudemarie Clark and Brian Leiter. Translated by R.J. Hollingdale. Cambridge: Cambridge University Press, 1997. However, the present discussion is rather more consistent with the position more clearly defined by Maudemarie Clark and David Dudrick in 'Nietzsche's Post-positivism', *European Journal of Philosophy* 12: 3, 2004: 369-385.

17. Referring to the vital interpretive work performed by ancient tragedians, Nietzsche states in *GS* (1) 'It is obvious that these tragedians, too, promote the interests of the *species*... They, too, promote the life of the species *by promoting the faith in life*'.

18. 'Man proposes, God disposes'.

19. Nietzsche's idea of recurrence does not suggest an eternal repetition of things where only *stasis* prevails. This earlier misunderstanding has been properly rectified by Nietzsche scholars, i.e. see Clark 1990.

20. See Robin Small *Nietzsche in Context*. Aldershot: Ashgate, 2001, Chs. 3, 4.

21. Heightening is the word most often used by Nietzsche even though he did also acknowledge the saliency of Hegel and Darwin's idea of 'development'. Evolution would also be misleading in the Anglo-Saxon context because of its teleological implications. Therefore 'heightening' should convey a sense of noble development as well as *superior* valuations in the French sense, e.g. 'higher' learning.

22. BGE 2. This point was already argued by Georg Wilhelm Hegel who put into question Kant's predilection for opposites, maintaining the primacy of contradictions (like Nietzsche himself) and supersession within the manifoldness of the Absolute.

23. Gilles Deleuze *Nietzsche and Philosophy*. Translated by Hugh Tomlinson. New York: Columbia University Press, 1983. An otherwise lucid and cogent discussion of nihilism is provided in Bernard Reginster's *The Affirmation of Life: Nietzsche on Overcoming Nihilism*. Cambridge, Mass.: Harvard University Press, 2006.

24. It is rather curious that Nietzsche (*Daybreak* 45) should claim 'the problem of the extent to which mankind can as a whole take steps towards the advancement of knowledge has never yet been posed'. Though the statement at least exhibits an interest in forms of advancement and universality.

25. Nietzsche thought the impetus for greatness could most likely emanate out of Russia because of its strong will and resistance to decadent morals. 'West' here denotes this easterly region of the Euro-Asian complex.

26. See note 4 above.

27. Richard Schacht 'Philosophical Anthropology: What, Why and How', *Philosophy and Phenomenological Research*, Vol. 1 Supplement, Fall (50), 1990:155-176.

28. Maudemarie Clark 'Nietzsche's Doctrine of the Will to Power: Neither Ontological Nor Biological', *International Studies in Philosophy*, 32 (3) 2000:119-135.

29. Numerous errors have clearly been identified by Nietzsche. These include: the 'soul-superstition'; cause-effect; Absolute Knowing; pure being; thing-in-itself; the One and the All; absolute opposites; no 'eternally enduring substances' including matter (GS 109); no (free-unfree) Will; no Nothingness; and no blissful Nirvana. *Pace* in Nietzsche's work is the additional refutation of the idea of an asensual human being—a cogito that *purely* thinks itself.

30. F. Nietzsche 'The Struggle Between Science and Nature', *Philosophy and Truth: Selections from Nietzsche's Notebooks of the Early 1870s*. Translated and edited by Daniel Breazeale. New Jersey/London: Humanities Press, 1990.

31. Once Nietzsche overcame the spell of Wagnerian romanticism, he seriously took to the study of chemistry and to some extent, botany. As a child of German *Naturphilosophie* (and Goethe's naturalism) it is no surprise that this intellectual Wanderer found solace in the woods and mountains rather than the crass mayhem of the marketplace. Subsequently, Martin Heidegger would come to embody this liking for the soil and mountain Path in actuality.

32. See, for example, Ruth Abbey *Nietzsche's Middle Period.* Oxford; New York: Oxford University Press, 2000.

33. See Brian Leiter's otherwise astute account in *Nietzsche On Morality.* London: Routledge, 2002.

34. For Alain Badiou's views on Nietzsche vis-à-vis Plato, see *Manifestations of Philosophy* Ch 10 (Albany: State University of New York, 1999). Werner Jaeger's excellent three-volume work on the Greeks, *Paideia*, makes an exemplary case for this Platonic argument.

35. Beauty as such does not necessarily entail an argument about the necessity of eliminating all errors. Error formation, we might say, is part of the human-all-too-human aspect of being alive and knowing the phenomenal world. Since God 'introduced' error in order to reclaim Creation, it perhaps remains constitutive of noumenal things whether mortal or otherwise.

36. The criticism of determinist readings of Nietzsche whether of the fatalist kind or cosmological variants of determinism is also proffered by Richard Brown in 'Nietzsche and the *Bhagavad Gita*: elective or ironic affinities', *Nietzsche and the Divine.* Edited by Jim Urpeth and John Lippitt. Manchester: Clinamen Press, 2000.

37. In the following chapter we shall see how Nietzsche associates three fundamental tasks with the educator: to help us to see, to think, and how to speak and write. Without true educators and their attendant *finesse* the super-animal man consequently will be without *noble* culture, i.e. a creature driven by the immediacy of passions and prejudices.

CHAPTER THREE

Nietzsche's Analytic of Civilization as Historical Becoming

All great spiritual powers exert a repressive as well as a liberating influence;
but admittedly, it makes a difference whether Homer or the Bible or science
tyrannizes human beings (HH 262).

Friedrich Nietzsche's work is often associated with adventures into nihilistic deconstruction, usually with the effect of precluding discussion of determinate civilizational realities. Contrariwise to Derrida's undecidable reading of Nietzsche-as-stylist and Gilles Deleuze's flawed anti-Hegelian rendering, one can readily identify discernable axial themes that clearly fit within the tradition of civilizational analysis proffered by figures such as Sigmund Freud, Johann Goethe and Jacob Burkhardt. Indeed, Nietzsche's engagement with *Naturphilosophie* and natural science lends his philologico-philosophical work a certain affinity with the grand tradition of philosophical analysis, a point frequently acknowledged by contemporary analytic philosophers such as Clark, Schacht and Leiter. In this light and contrary to the once commonplace view of Nietzsche as an anarchistic, aphoristic writer, it is possible to view Nietzsche's critical thinking as consonant with the major concerns of civilizational analysis: how to develop a critique of European decadence on the one hand and an analytic for the 'condition(s) of man' on the other. These conditions are, importantly, irreducible to nature's dictates and instead act as vital catalysts for the extension of human powers, both imaginative and normative.

In the following discussion, I will argue that Nietzsche can be understood as a philosopher who sought the most comprehensive understanding of this most 'interesting animal', Man, and its historical-social conditions of formation. Viewed as a civilization-analyst, Nietzsche appears as someone who neither wholly accepted naturalism nor the Idealist strictures of metaphysical thinking. Therefore, beyond Natural Man and, conversely, the concept of Being, Nietzsche developed the tragic-poet's sense of joyful wisdom by delineating the manifoldness of life, of the individual living in a world of possibility *and* arduous necessity. This delineation importantly turns upon a world of *entwinement* rather than upon dualities. That is, the interdependency between 'good' and 'evil', truth and error, and *physis* and *nomos* as the underlying constant in his philosophical analysis. This means that we cannot understand him either as a Romantic or as an empiricist nor reduce him to a mere cultural stylist. Rather, he conducts an inquiry along the lines of an historical philosophy that incorporates a kind of historical sociology of morals and evaluations to explain why 'good' and 'bad' have a particularly normative hold on us. We shall consider this as the nucleus of Nietzsche's civilization-analytic: a realism of the interdependency of fundamental phenomena in the world and a historical philosophy that understands the *movement* behind social and cultural forms encompassed by different civilizational realities.

As a thinker who notably repudiated both Idealism and romanticism, Nietzsche can therefore be understood to be centrally engaged in a type of civilizational-analysis that is informed by these fundamental questions regarding the human condition: is our sense of 'what is man' overlaid (by necessity) with prejudices and truth figurations which are the result of long processes of taming and domesticating the creature-animal *Mensch*? I refer to this as Nietzsche's central *civilization-analytic*[1]; and its task is to demystify the voluptuous unfolding of human natures in the complex plenitude of the world ('earth'). Not unlike Goethe and his intellectual protégé—Arthur Schopenhauer—Nietzsche sought to look behind the multiplicity of manifestations of the human to disclose the *anthropos* that becomes enveloped by civilization. And this incisive disclosure, we must acknowledge, is not a dreary description of reality but rather a joyous embrace of the quasi-tragic sense in which the creations of this increasingly domesticated 'tame' animal, man (sic), sets itself above other forms of organic life through diverse civilizing processes. Eschewing both romantic and naturalistic suppositions, Nietzsche must therefore be considered as more than simply a critic of modern civilization(s).

I

Nietzsche the 'good European', as he called himself, found no solace in the nation. *Deutschland* for him, like nationalistic politics, was simply distasteful. What interested him instead was the impact which civilizational genealogies and potentialities had on modern humanity; in part because of his historical-philosophy and in part because of the great importance of the *élan* of human endeavour and its enormous transformative power in history expressed as 'self-overcoming' (both exoteric and esoteric). To refer to his 'historical philosophy' here is to distinguish it from other accounts of Nietzsche's thought that are naturalistic[2] in orientation. This is significant because following insights gained from both Renaissance humanism and Enlightenment scientific reason, Nietzsche decidedly made *Mensch* his datum-point for an analysis of this de-deified world—a world of Becoming in which the cold cruel world of Democritus' κοσμος (order) requires human *poiesis*: the will to transfigure *physis*.

For this reason we can see socio-cultural figurations (civilizational forms) working as a bulwark against the vicious circle of revenge and vindictive cruelty that is characteristic of *natura*, including human 'nature'. On the other hand, such figurations also work as effective power containers of *Bildung*. *Bildung* (immanent to civilization) acts as a dynamic force that is itself two-sided: one dimension of its force relates to the intensive elevation stemming from cultivation and wilful overcoming; and the other side to its *long duree* of taming and domesticating man via multitudinous moral codes and internalizations of the 'good' and 'virtuous'. In *The Anti-Christ* man is properly placed 'back among the animals' as any good anti-metaphysical naturalist thinker would; however then we find Nietzsche transcending the bounds of naturalism by raising the fundamental question *par excellence*: 'what type of human being one ought to *breed*, ought to *will*, as more valuable, more worthy of life, more certain of the future' (3). Nature, as Nietzsche repeatedly points out, can not give man its value and nor can it command, that is, it can not assume the position of commander over human life and its futural event of being 'more certain of the future'. He reached this philosophical stance via his critique of positivist science and its limits in determining what *axia* (worth) meaning and creation have *for* human beings. Normativity is not derivative of organic life. That is why the question of what type of human being we wish to will into the future is not attended by any naturalistic justification of the end of man: 'the human being is an *end*' (A 3 original italics). This comes rather close to Aristotle even if there is no teleology underlying its conceptual basis.

Therefore, while the human-type of being is clearly an end that can be valued and evaluated, and conceived and willed into existence, there is no fixed point from which it commences onto its horizonal journey. Rather like the Sphinx, our lack of a singular human nature makes us both 'fascinating creatures' and yet also cruel, violent and ultimately incomplete beings: a type *of* nature and civilization that Nietzsche consistently refers to as the 'human all too human' aspect. Returning to the question of interpretive method we can now say that the civilization-analytic therefore inquires into the conditions of the human being as composed by the vicissitudes of its immanent (incomplete) nature and the complex figurations of *nomos—physis* that give definition to the first. We may refer to this *schema* as a 'constellation': a constellation of forces, willing, power-quanta, *Erkenntnis* (knowledge/cognition), *Erfahrung* (experience) and moments of time which apprehend the incomplete yet interesting animal—*Mensch*—toward the abovementioned end which Man can realize. This is also the task of the philosophers of the future: to transvaluate existing forms of morality (moral natures) in order to achieve an end *for* (not *in*) Man. While this constellation of life forces and experiences conveys a realism of life's complexity and manifold experiences—good and bad together—it further encompasses the dance of necessity and chance as captured by Nietzsche's favoured idea, *amor fati. Amor fati* as love of life in all its fateful dimensions neither abandons the force of willing nor succumbs entirely to the forces of fate. It is, however, the fulcrum of that non-feeble being that Nietzsche described as the noble spirit—the one who denies the might of herd thinking. Civilizational analysis in this sense concerns itself with neither patriotic mass identification, subjectivist values nor aprioristic concepts of the *atomon;* it rather aims to penetrate in to the 'phenomenology' of this constellation by understanding life as essentially a process of becoming—an unfinished human type entwined by destiny and willing simultaneously. Such an understanding, which is the essential object of the philosopher, requires simultaneously the truth of power and the power of truth, Zarathustra's will testifies to it thus: 'verily, my will to power walks also on the heels of your will to truth' (Z III:12). While this wisdom escapes most of those living in the valleys of life, the overman Zarathustra embraces it as his creed. That is to say, in Nietzsche's version of civilizational analysis there is no antipathy between truth—power or between *fati*—wilful creation *cum* commanding. This is what the Idealists (or theologico-philosophers) of Tübingen never quite grasped: the hard reality of Thucydides' account of life.

Ennobled analysis of cultural-spiritual forms therefore aims at life itself, in all its totality, not simply concepts which tamed contemplators entertain whilst writing formal treatises on consciousness, Being and Truth. Why then is becoming significant for civilizational analysis? Because, firstly, *homo sapiens* arrive in the world essentially incomplete or unfinished. More than any other member of the animal kingdom man comes into society essentially dependent upon others, others who similarly belong to nature but who also bear the weight and potentialities of various 'civilizing' processes. Thus *Kultur* for Nietzsche helps to complete (and divide) the human being through historically significant struggles, pain and creations which the human being undergoes in becoming a social and therefore moral (civilized) animal. As a result of its 'completion' of nature's unfinished work, culture as dynamic processes of becoming incorporates the essential tension that arises out of the inner depths of the human 'soul', leaving Nietzsche to transvaluate the Romantics' infamous dichotomy of *physis-nomos*. An acutely honed axiological point underscores this quasi-naturalistic stance: namely the requirement that we discover the obtainable nobility to which *Menschen* (humanity) is 'promised' despite, or rather because of, its half-divine, half-creature nature. Against modern positivism, Nietzsche's analytic is steeped in normativity; *Werden* or becoming has a noble end even whilst it lacks any teleology or evolutionism a la Aristotle and Herbert Spencer. The 'promise' immanent yet unrealized (oftentimes) in culture is captured by the tragic wisdom developed by Aeschylus and Sophocles, and deployed further by Nietzsche, to illustrate a tension between the fallen state (of man) and the willing force of human beings. The overriding concern within Nietzsche's civilizational analysis regarding man's fallen state—for us 'European Nihilism'—is expressed succinctly towards the end of Nietzsche's life in Book V of *The Gay Science:* 'There is a human being who has turned out badly' (359). Tragic fate points to this reality in human history; that is to say, how predominant civilizational forms have delivered up a type of human nature that is again ignoble. Nevertheless, there is a notable difference: whereas the *morphe* of earlier ignoble, 'badly' formed human beings consisted of an existence ignorant of knowledge and therefore the capacity to legislate (values), modern decadents by contrast appear to possess the latter only to succumb to the detriment of collective herd thinking. Although Nietzsche was highly critical of modernity and its massified egalitarianism, he similarly repudiated those who urged for a 'return to Nature' as the Stoics did. For instance the high (elevated) figure of Zarathustra who dwells in the cold crisp air of Goethe's 'high mountains' is one who embodies the antithesis of British physiologists: namely, the learned, self-disciplined overman who is destined to deliver his message to those living herd-like in the valleys of civilizations.[3] This achievement, this type of human 'nature', is properly described in the forward to his *Anti-Christ*: 'And the will to economy in the grand style: to keep one's energy, one's *enthusiasm* in bounds....Reverence for oneself; love for oneself; unconditional freedom with respect to oneself...' Against naturalism, the achieved height of this free figure demonstrates the necessity of transcending the bounds of *physis*: Nature we find in *Beyond Good and Evil* is found wanting because she is 'wasteful beyond measure, indifferent beyond measure, without purposes and consideration, without mercy and justice', hence the demand to transcend her and be different: 'Living—is that not precisely wanting to be other than this nature? Is not living—estimating, preferring, being unjust, being limited, wanting to be different?' (9). Thus, we can propose that simultaneously there is an imperative to leave the decadence of the Valley and to return to its people living *down* in the valley where the human all too human presides. Zarathustra, because he also embodies willing, is strengthened by nature without being reduced to her dictates; and since *bios* is not synonymous with *zoi* (biological life) civilizational existence incorporates vital aspects such as 'preferring', estimating moral worth, valuations, 'love for oneself', purpose in 'knowing', and perhaps above all commanding and tyrannizing oneself (and others within the valley too).

To maintain his realist grasp of *bios* as a complex amalgam of affect-drive-valuations, Nietzsche the physio-psychologist reminds us of the necessity to place man back in nature lest we forget how morality is normally anti-nature. This positing however is discordant with the British physiologists' will to place the 'instinct of self-preservation as the cardinal instinct of an organic being' (BGE 13). As neither moralist nor naturalist, Nietzsche conceived of the human being as sphinx-like: half-animal, half-man with a severe strength to ask penetrating questions. Like one of the observers he admired most, Thucydides, Nietzsche claims the ground of the tragic-poet—a kind of joyous realism. Realistic apprehension hence demonstrates how nature artistically considered

is no model. It exaggerates, it distorts, it leaves gaps. Nature is chance. To study 'from nature' seems to me a bad sign . . . (TI ix 7).

Why? Because seeing '*what is*' is far more important; equally important in this noble realism is the imperative of self-knowledge, that is, 'One has to know *who* one is' (TI ix 7). Man's organic or animalic condition does not suffice in and of itself; it requires the human being to comprehend his (sic) manifold, complex historical world. The only justification Nietzsche gives for man's existence is this: 'What justifies man is his reality—it will justify him eternally' (32). And this reality of his transforms nature into a civilized nature; his own nature subsequently is also transformed, becoming complex and multidimensional as it grows out of its own inorganic *bios* which is itself part of a larger order-chaos constellation of forces. However, Nietzsche was most infatuated with how complex forms of social and artistic life also give impetus to man's growth as when for instance plants grow when cultivated by the would-be gardener Nietzsche (in his earlier years). Hence contra naturalistic arguments that posit natural man against moral man, Nietzsche's noble realism harbours the value of the tension produced by the 'conditions of man' within a Schopenhauerian world of nature;

and, on the other hand, the perennial striving expressed as commanding, willing, educating, and cultivating of value-forms toward heights which no plant can ever reach because it lacks both 'educators' and the historical contestation over millennia between two opposing classes of rulers, i.e. noble and slave.

Becoming therefore sets the human being apart from *natura* and in so doing, it similarly sets him apart from himself and from other human beings who occupy a common national or civilizational heritage. This is because 'development' or historical *poiesis* is spurred on by contestation, struggle and 'will to power' in the historical unfolding of different individual *and* social natures (*eidos*) throughout epochs of becoming, including the becoming of lower and higher types of human beings. There is an important physio-psychological point to Nietzsche's philosophical anthropology that must be acknowledged at this point. That is, since civilized life tends toward collective measures of utility and self-preservation, i.e., comfortable convenience, equal measure and functional industriousness, a certain dependency on valley-life becomes the Achilles-heel of man. A kind of collective stupor gains hold of his otherwise creative, striving and commanding impulses, which if better harnessed would see the development of more Napoleons, Caesars and Goethes. This culture of dependency is what perpetually encircles man in the logic of the same: conformity to 'herd morality'. Thus those who are seen to stand out of the crowd paradoxically are applauded as 'brave souls' or heroes but then on the other side are condemned by the envy and resentment stored up in souls characterized by 'herd' consciousness. The message is clear: "be like us, but please be unlike us so that we may have an idol to worship, to look *up* to".

II

Like Hegel, Nietzsche sought to undertake a long-term historical perspective on the development (as vicissitudes) of the human race in its actuality and, concomitantly, its different orders of power and forms of *Dasein*. Hence, one can readily discern a decidedly active historical sociology in Nietzsche's genealogical account of the vicissitudes of master-slave moralities. Contrary to most philosophers, Nietzsche challenged the common predilection for ahistorical, decontextualized thinking that largely attended much philosophical and philological work. He not only employed the ad hominem principle in criticizing this mode of analysis but also in step with his time attempted to found a mode of analyzing valuations and moralities on the basis of historically formed and self-conscious classes (or nations) of people who were in perpetual struggles with each other. Although missing the drive for recognition in Hegel's subtle 'master-slave dialectic' his explanatory account nevertheless implies recognition while explicitly identifying the logic of struggle for domination and usurpation as central to the formation of moral and decadent orders. While otherness was crucial to Hegel's developmental schema, it is the pathos of distance that proves supremely valuable to Nietzsche's idea of undulating movement and 'striving' as intimated earlier. But while the former proposed a certain teleology and *Geist* still lay behind the world, a world animated by Spirit, Nietzsche instead examined the coming into being of diverse civilizational forms—moralities, metaphysical ideas of Being, valuations, strivings for strength over others—that rendered opaque the morphology of human beings. Oftentimes this is assumed to be a naturalistic turn or perhaps even a quasi-Darwinian retort to Richard Wagner's Hegelian aesthetics of artistic production. However as stated above, this interpretive move is a problematic one. We have already seen the way in which Nietzsche aims instead to grasp—via a depth-historical civilizational optic of human reality—the 'what is' in all its many-sidedness. In other words, a noble realism is vouched for in order that we may recognize the eternally recurring moments of life within the 'human all too human' horizon while simultaneously also finding beauty in our transvaluations of its necessity. Why 'necessity'? Because Nietzsche's noble realism, as I have called it, is underscored by a philosophical anthropology that is grounded in the principles of *gai saber*[4]. This method, as he preferred to call it, is inclined toward affirmation rather than resignation, toward overcoming rather than admission to recurrence in life.

Thus our undeniable 'human all too human' nature does not in fact foreclose the potentiality of overcoming its own tyranny; we can always grow beyond the necessity of mere envying or self-denial because of the vital fecundity of the basic drives of man—Plato's Eros. He refers to this simply as 'striving', which on occasions is also referred to as will to power. Will to power while constituting a central political and social force in his work however does not adequately capture his real architectonic logic and philosophical spirit. Maudemarie Clark[5] has convincingly made this point. The point at which overcoming the tyranny of historical ἀνάγκη emerges is where Nietzsche could admire the noble vision of Plato's un-Socratic world, a world that is charged by the excess and energy of the Cosmos, of homoerotic love of wisdom. Yet one must remain vigilant at all times not to forget that for Nietzsche the human being is constituted much like a variegated plant (*zoi*): while some grow others remain stunted; while some are four sided others are three-sided; while some wither under arduous physical conditions, others use the occasion to extend and grow. Just as Goethe before him was compelled to explain the directionality of plants in his *The Metamorphosis of Plants*, so too Nietzsche feels compelled to take account of divergent human directionalities. Moreover, clearly for him, the stunted 'feeble' man of modernity is that type of human who seeks refuge in the Valley of life and with conviction humbles his being so that egoism is expunged from his daily modus. This is the 'dry soul' of modern individuals who are descendents of ascetic ideals—a spiritual state that lacks moist powers of vital growth and extension so that its drive to spiritualize life (philosophy itself) is held back because it has denied itself the essential nutrients of growth. *Bildung* we must remember is what declaredly modern Deutschland lacks owing to the state of its [then] present institutions; hence, education is only serving the perfunctory needs of a modern mass industrial society where the catchword "Utility" reigns supreme in most matters of state and education.

This has particular implications for his civilization-analytics in the mode of a 'joyous science'. The interpretive role of civilizational-analysis is now centred on properly situating thought (understanding) outside the bounds of existing temporal horizons; that is, outside restrictive 'timely' frameworks which are promulgated by predominant forms of value and ranks of order. It is for this reason that Nietzsche's exegesis of the formation and transformation of human sensibilities and values is heavily underscored by an acute awareness of the historicality of 'types of Man' and the spirit of cultures that give rise to them. Of equal importance is the observation that as our historical vicissitudes and conditions of (moral-aesthetic) existence transforms our understanding of the cosmos, so too our intellectual and axiological inquiries must also become comparative and perspectival in nature. Therefore, when Nietzsche says misleadingly 'life is perspectivism' he does not mean individual perceptions of reality or cultural world-pictures are paramount. Rather, the animal—or more still the half-animal Man—undergoes a metamorphosis of sorts by historically acquiring more comprehensive "eyes" that see more sides, angles and dimensions than the naïve eye. This countervails the other seemingly simplistic notion given expression to in the *Anti-Christ* (14): 'Man is not the crown of creation: every creature stands beside him at the same stage of perfection'. Here Nietzsche is criticizing British physiologists and in particular Darwin[6] and the Darwinians. The statement does not place man merely alongside the ant; that would be to commit a *reductio ad absurdum*. After all, knowing and the arts of *Bildung*, if not the will to power in striving itself, alter the creature as well as the animal in man (i.e. no eradication notably is implied in either case).

Nietzsche's normative critique of modernity assumes then the advantages of perspectivism on life that highlights difference through the adoption of comparative analysis. That is to say, the best angle on the essence of modernity is from without, from the vantage-point of comparative civilizational-analysis whereby the order or rank of morals and values in ancient Greece or Rome offer us an alternate vista of reality, of the human being in particular. Moreover, although he states on numerous occasions that the Greeks are too strange for us moderns, he constantly refers back to the noble figures and tragic vision of these great ancients in order to highlight the lack (feebleness or softness) of modern 'democrats'. The scorn with which he often describes the masses of today's democracies and their essentially Christian moralistic views owes to the strength of contrast that he is able to marshal as a result of his aesthetic historical comparative sociology of civilizational complexes. This often goes by the name of genealogy, particularly in commentaries on Nietzsche's work, but his analyses of the rise and fall of diverse master-slave figurations in his two later works (BGE & GM) can quite comfortably fit into this schema. It arguably would need to be complimented by a certain (non-empiricistic) moral psychology that understands the forces of resentment and envy (and malice) in the making and shaping of different politico-moral constellations. The 'genealogy of morals', as the title of one of his books published after *Beyond Good and Evil* suggests, can be seen as a work of this combinative kind where it conjoins historical comparative sociology and moral psychology through a kind of 'historicized' philological investigation. When we refer to a civilization in terms of a 'complex' it is the complexity of phenomena that this abovesaid method (gay science) aims to interpret and analyze—philosophy in itself, fails the task. Nietzsche the polymath philosopher knew this all too well; between philology and philosophy stood reality itself yet science appears unable to secure a proper account of such phenomena precisely for the same reason as Darwin: the mind. Then on the other side, analytical logical philosophy—where mental labourers of the bookish world reign—will also not suffice for completing the task. This is clearly evident from the first chapter (and its title heading) of *Beyond Good and Evil* where it is argued that Philosophy too has lapsed into a fallen state due to its bookish 'mental labourers'. From hereon, true philosophers of the future will understand the need to think *historically*, as first promulgated by that other genius Hegel. Thanks to him (Hegel) all Germans now think through the idea of development and contradiction and so facticity is no longer god in these matters. We see Nietzsche incisively cutting through his master's (Schopenhauer) malicious envy and resentment in various comments made in *The Gay Science* and in *Beyond Good and Evil* (204), where he rebukes Schopenhauer for his 'unintelligent wrath against Hegel' and calls him 'poor, unreceptive' in respect to the historical sense of German sensibilities.

The need to dispense with absolute ideal notions such as Being and Will was in Nietzsche's case inextricably linked to this historical sense, a sensibility towards concepts and objects that prizes the *formative* nature of phenomena. Becoming and formation are therefore sister method-concepts. Contrary to Hegel's *Geist* and Heidegger's *Sein* Nietzsche's preferred concept of *Werden* (Becoming) more aptly captures the historically constitutive nature of moral valuations and psychological affects such as envy and resentment. Using this vital 'dynamic' method in most interesting experimental ways, Nietzsche sought deep insights into why *Sitten* and *Moralität* were embedded in particular social relations of power; that is, in concrete social-symbolic matrices of power, authority and status that defined the normative meaning of Good, Evil, noble, slave and thus 'virtues' and vices. What was just or 'good' and 'bad' or 'evil' were dependent upon the civilizational pattern of reality that reigned at any particular time. As opposed to today, cruelty was formerly valorised even though it now appears repulsive to us. Axioms of truth in this context proved wanting because the ground from which they sprang constantly shifted. Against ontology, his method of historico-comparative analysis of words, things and morals sought to expound a more ripened synoptic of the human condition with the aid of philosophy in the service of a type of 'civilization-analytics'. After all as most philosophers need to bear in mind, Zarathustra and Dionysus are derived from premodern civilizational realities for precisely this reason—to show the shortcomings of contemporary national ideologies and the malaise of modern European nihilism. As a relatively young professor of Philology at Basel, Nietzsche in April 1878 declared:

> There are great advantages if at some point we estrange ourselves to a great extent from our age and are, as it were, driven from its shore back into the ocean of archaic worldviews. Gazing from there toward the coast, we survey its entire shape for the first time and have the advantage, when we approach it once again, of understanding it better as a whole than do those who never left it (HH 616).

Then in 1886, after having completed his *Prelude to a Philosophy of the Future* from sunny Nice, he laid out the demands placed on more free noble spirits: to have mastery of oneself and one's virtues, to apprehend the '*necessary* injustice in every For, every Against' and life itself which is '*conditioned* by perspective and its injustice' (HH1: *P*6). Of special note here is the double-proposition: perspective is a *conditio sine qua non* while simultaneously being partial, that is limited and therefore unjust. Why does it harbour injustice? (We shall look at injustice further on in our discussion). For two reasons: first, it is not the Horizon or the 'higher aim' of the free thinker. Second, due to its limitations, its 'condition', it requires the kind of comprehensiveness that is called for in the abovestated sea-metaphor. And it is so important to the higher task of 'rank orderings' that Nietzsche places 'comprehensiveness of perspective' only alongside power and right in growing toward the height of this goal: namely, the aim of affirming life with values that accept tragic (re)occurrence and joyful striving to create life anew. Knowledge becomes important then because it helps to achieve this essential comprehensiveness of 'seeing', of comprehending. In this sense, Nietzsche's civilization-analytic has a firm epistemological foundation which rather than eschewing knowledge per se aims to extend the analysis beyond 'merely knowing' (horizons). Besides this no experimental method would wish logically to eschew knowing and its strivings as virtuous goals. In the same 1886 passage (4)—the rewritten Preface to *Human All Too Human*— the free spirit is said to have the 'dangerous privilege of living *for experiments*'—a life of experimentation which can, if pursued arduously, disclose greater *comprehensiveness* in understanding life's diverse forces and experiences.

My argument here is that a comparative historical philologico-sociology of axiological orders heightens and expands the experimentalist's demand for comprehensiveness. Ancient Hellas and its Empedocles, Heraclitus and Anaxagoras help us to understand better our civilizational reality in all its pathos and tensions. We must move afar therefore in order to see more clearly the reality which otherwise remains too close to our being, to our prejudices, obscuring that which a comprehensive understanding may appreciate. We need to, as he says here, 'estrange ourselves' (almost as Hegel had said earlier) by driving ourselves afar off the shore of our present continent of consciousness back 'into the ocean of archaic worldviews'. 'Gazing from there', that is, from ancient Greece, Persia and Rome we more realistically apprehend 'the entire shape for the first time', understanding 'it *better* as a *whole* than do those who *never left it*' (see note above, emphasis added). Contrary therefore to any crude genealogical or anti-epistemic arguments we see a defence of the proposition that not all perspectives are equally grounded or valued. Moreover, to reiterate the earlier point, it bodes better for analytical purposes if we remember the status of perspectivism in his oeuvre as a whole: it is essential while not constituting the *higher aim* as such. Gaining the vantage-point on reality itself, a civilizational reality that is essentially enigmatic, is rather the superior noble aim (and claim). In 1881, consequently we find Nietzsche giving expression to his self-awareness of the force of this distancing, of this un*timely* comparison. 'Does the good historian not, at bottom, *constantly* contradict' insofar as she is out of step with those who never left their own continent of consciousness? For the comparative analyst's 'precise history of an origination' tends to sound 'paradoxical and wantonly offensive' to our feelings (D 1). Nietzsche's method of surveying the entirety of the contemporary landscape points to the saliency of a *comprehensive* understanding, one built upon what he called (as early as *Human All Too Human*) the necessity of a 'historical philosophy'. This kind of philosophizing—an anti-metaphysical kind—affords us a more realistic knowledge of our present age and thus gives the civilizational scholar a particular 'advantage' because he or she achieves a *better* understanding of the whole. This point is often overlooked in analyses of Nietzsche's thought due in part to the misconception of him as a relativist in epistemological matters. Even the adducing of arguments to establish his essentially naturalistic standpoint overlook the point with what Nietzsche himself castigated Darwin: Darwin forgot the mind (TI ix: 14). The whole perspective is 'better' Nietzsche argued because it no longer is tied down to constraints arising from the experiential dimension of existence but instead is historically formed by explanatory accounts of how the human is formed by so many constitutive forces. This allows him to claim a certain truthfulness regarding his incisive historical-philosophical interpretation: in *Genealogy of Morals*, he states rhetorically, 'You will have guessed *what* has really happened here, *beneath* all this' when outlining reasons for the 'psychical cruelty' that attends the 'bestiality of thought' of the man of 'bad conscience' (II: 22). In other words, there are intelligible realities for why things are the way they are and how they came to be so, and these can be accessed by interpretation. Nietzsche was no sceptic but a philosopher par excellence.

If it has been established that forms of knowing are central to Nietzsche's civilization-analytic we can also identify as indispensable the analysis of values, moralities from a psychological perspective and the exegesis of diverse civilizational realities according to the fundamental tension of Apollonian-Dionysian states. *Contra* the young philologist, Nietzsche the philosopher who overcame Schopenhauer's aesthetic romanticism well understood the necessity to overcome the artist's (e.g. Wagner's) intoxication with aesthetic value, especially after he had studied some chemistry and Boscovich and Spir[7] (HH1:1). In doing so Nietzsche began to strongly distance himself from that peculiarly 'Germanic impulse' to over-aestheticize reality, adopting an ever greater interest in the hypothetico-experimental attitude of modern science while nevertheless remaining sceptical of its positivistic logic. In *Human, All Too Human* (1:1) he argued: 'All that we need, and what can be given to us only now, at the present level of the individual sciences, is a *chemistry* of the moral, religious, aesthetic representations and sensations, likewise of all those stimuli that we experience within ourselves...' Tempering his initial enthusiasm for such individual sciences he progressed into his more mature accounts of civilizational forms, a healthy inquisitive outlook onto the world was vied for consistently in terms of experiments that notably do not adopt the reductionist platitudes of logical-empirical sciences. Logic after all is only the rational symptom of a sublimated inclination

(*Instinkt*) he claimed—an optimistic instinct for life expressed as the 'will to knowledge'. Logical thought is therefore to be neither negated nor valorised. Any 'gay science' would find this proposition palatable. What Nietzsche argued was necessary was to conceive of even scientific methods as always historical developments. That is, cognition alone will not suffice because its spider-like *cogito* spinning are mere illusion. Nor would crude experimentalism in the form of ant-type (vulgar empiricism) accumulation be much use as Francis Bacon had already declared in his famous *Novum Organon*. Instead of Aristotle's bee, Nietzsche proposed that the power-quanta of force fields and the essential dynamic interactivity of so many divisible forces that do not necessarily imply either a centre or a reductive logic propel human beings, along with other living organisms, into various constitutive processes. This suggests that Nietzsche's version of civilizational-analysis abjures both empiricism and rationalism while also putting into question both naturalism (e.g. Darwinianism) and Idealism (Kantianism).

We return now to the question of what therefore allows the perspicacious knower to 'see' his continent of being from afar more clearly, thus resulting in a 'better understanding'? I have suggested so far that it is the historico-comparative philosopher who thinks through the Actual via the social and moral relations of sensuous human beings. However, we must also add a further constitutive dimension to his interpretive schema, one that returns us to a paradigmatic tension lying within every civilizational complex. Namely, the abovementioned Apollonian-Dionysian tension that is wrought by every reality that pertains to the condition of taming the wildness of man and turning his instincts to those more subtle drives that find their expression in political life and artistic *poiesis*. In *Twilight of the Idols* (ix: 10) we find that Apollonian intoxication 'alerts above all the eyes, so that it acquires power of vision'. This power of the eye is for instance what engenders a more comprehensive vision of one's own continent of being. The Dionysian state on the other hand shows that the 'entire emotional system is alerted and intensified: so that it discharges all its powers of representation, imitation, transfiguration, transmutation...conjointly'. In their intercourse, the most important thing of all is achieved: 'facility of the metamorphosis'. Consequently, we see that no signal from the emotions is ignored while at the same time the individual (human or cultural constellation) 'possesses to the highest degree the instinct for understanding and divining' (TI ix:10). What oftentimes is overlooked in this context about the productive tension held in the Apollonian-Dionysian axes of life is what I would identify—in Nietzsche's own words—as *freedom of soul* (GM II: 23). This is brought out best once again through the comparative historical prism in order to show what lay behind the Judaeo-Christian veil of the 'holy God'. Namely, a type of willing that gave form to the Greek gods which by contrast to nihilistic moderns was not overrun by 'bad conscience' and its attendant vengefulness but instead was the result of 'reflections of noble and aristocratic men in whom *the animal* in man felt deified and did *not* lacerate itself, did *not* rage against itself!' (23). Hence, we see the Greeks succeeded in warding off bad conscience by creating a vital world of the gods 'so as to be able to rejoice in their *freedom of soul*' (23, emphasis added). Thus it can be argued that the spirit of any single soul or culture can obtain this condition of freedom once it has properly harnessed this productive tension (of Apollonian-Dionysian states), therewith hitting upon the most distant goals. For 'with so tense a bow'—Apollo's bow of antithetical forces—'we can now shoot for the most distant goals' as free spirits do (BGE, *P*).

III

The other dimension central to Nietzsche's philosophy of civilizational forms is the normative critical dimension: what is valuable, valued or devalued? And what is higher and lower in normative terms? As Nietzsche was no positivist and generally known for his strong evaluative pronouncements this aspect of his thinking regarding civilizational realities and demands becomes quite critical. Before moving on to his depiction of civilized life in terms of two predominant classes in history we should first consider how Nietzsche's work as a whole is marked by a particular realism with respect to the apparent ontology of injustice in all human and natural orders. To return to the most ancient 'pagan' sense of (in)justice we find that *dike* as opposed to right is considered pivotal to understanding constitutive processes in the Cosmos. In *Human All Too Human* (*P6*) Nietzsche draws our attention to the ineluctable persistence and ubiquity of injustice in the world: 'You must learn to grasp the necessary injustice in every For and Against'. A normative appeal not only to the ineluctable facticity of *adikia* but also to its embodiment in human interpretation, adding 'life itself as *conditioned* by perspective and its injustice' (HH1:1). Beyond any simple empirical observation, Nietzsche incorporated a deep philosophical appreciation for the necessity of human discernment into his otherwise sympathetic interpretation of rigorous scientific understanding. That is to say, we can but only interpret the world through feeble finite conceptual lenses; however once we 'dare to be honest' with ourselves we should admit the relative injustice which every act of interpretation involves whether tacitly or formally. By doing so, what does humankind gain? His answer conforms to the virtuous grandeur of a Napoleonic or Goethean deed: namely, rather than resisting asking questions such as why this hardship? Why hatred for my own virtues, the nobler, more inquisitive spirit dares to ask it aloud and even replies: "You must become master of yourself and masters of your own virtues as well" (HH *P* 6). Hence, it is possible to conclude that critique affords Nietzsche a complementary power to that of scientific authority; the latter serving a limited purpose but beyond this lays the efficacy of determining what ideals and moral-aesthetic valuations should direct human life. Neither physiology (naturalism) nor atomic causality (positivism) can actually accomplish this essential task of thinking and living: the development of an axiology. *What* to become is a question modern science cannot answer—an observation which Schopenhauer had previously made.[8]

This question is dealt with according to the pathos with which contesting collectivities of human beings have sought to impose their moral and hence axiological vision on earth. Historically, the vicissitudes of will to power and, concomitantly, master-slave contestations has produced a plethora of *Sittlich-keit*—moral communities in temporal existence. Thus unlike Spinoza and Pascal, morals are made independent of the omniscient One and rendered susceptible to the instincts of historical subjects who seek to impose their image partly through forms of domination and also partly through realizing their own ideals of 'virtue'. Accordingly, all types of civilized life exhibit features of these vicissitudes: different grades of domination, commanding, usurpation, envaluation and envy and resentment. Nietzsche in contrast to other thinkers linked normative orders to the strivings, ideals, ascetic values, and agonic willing of concrete historical groups (and individuals). The earth as opposed to the world of Homeric gods or the Buddha becomes the profane ground upon which the battle over 'good' and 'bad' takes place. And from the moment human beings left behind their naturalistic existence by adopting different masks of morality, their instinctual life has metamorphosed into numerous spiritual drives to negate the nothingness of mortal life. As Nietzsche exclaimed in somewhat metaphysical language: in history it is apparent that the 'basic fact of the human will' is that '*it needs a goal*' because of its *horror vacui* and therefore 'it will rather will *nothingness* [into existence] than *not* will' (GM III: 1). Hence we find that since willing (verb) empirically occurs then the vital powers of *Mensch* in strivings of diverse kinds suggests the necessity of understanding human beings as goal-making and goal-seeking animals. For this is what makes the human an 'interesting animal' even if there is no eternal self or 'being'; man becomes more than what he once was—a recurring feeble 'human-all-too-human' type.[9] By wearing so many masks—nihilist, anti-nihilist, priest, tragedian, moralist, and scientist—the human being has transformed itself into something *more* than just a stupefied creature of nature (as argued earlier above). Nietzsche conceived of moralities as the outcome of diverse competing forces embodied in distinct groups or classes of individuals: priests, warriors, believers, peasants, aristocrats, statesmen, artists, poets, and philosophers. The object of Nietzsche's type of civilizational theory is to link these classes to forms of willing that are associated with the struggle toward two purposive aims: firstly, the aim of achieving predominance in the social world; and secondly the aim of negating nothingness by the will itself. Traditional civilizational theory has to its detriment focused on the former, delving mostly into the social-political dynamics of struggle for power and status.[10] I propose to extend the analytic of civilizational forms by drawing out the saliency of the latter, a vista within Nietzsche's synoptic vision that grasps the fundamental importance of willing as an *energeia* that transforms and overcomes *stasis* in this world. This offers civilizational analysis an important dynamic image of human beings in intercourse with each other in nature and time and space as they seek to optimize their relative power over things and others. Notably such a vista is established without necessarily introducing spurious concepts such as Schopenhauer's 'the Will' and Kant's autonomy of the will. And rather than having anonymous invisible agents driving history—abstract 'doers' as is often the case in functionalist-utility schemas—we have here a concrete sense of *who* was doing *what* in attempting to achieve (what Nietzsche called) the 'promise of the earth'—the will to overcome nothingness itself instituted the will to overcome ourselves (the will must even overcome itself in the end, Nietzsche demanded).

Therefore, the above-stated question *'What* to become when shooting for distant goals'? returns because we can now link normativity (value creation and re-evaluation) with the historicity of struggles which evidence contestable 'ideals' of the human being and its grand legislating power, i.e. grand politics. The force behind the Olympiad's *agon* to excel and outdo one's opponent undergirds Nietzsche's conception of the contestation between master and slave in history—a central defining moment in the formation of civilized, moral creatures for every civilizational reality. This means the measure of 'the good' person or deed and therefore by necessity the considered *worth* of persons and their moral virtues (i.e. axiology) is bound up with the ad hominem principle; namely, *who* is doing the measuring, the willing, the contesting and the legislating (commanding) in particular civilizational realities. Unlike much contemporary analytic philosophy, Nietzsche not only practiced a form of historical philosophy but also coupled valuations and moralities to living, struggling human beings who occupy real concrete positions in social reality. The result is a philosophy that is critical of ahistorical propositions about morality and action. Moreover there emerges an incisive critique of certain givens in modern moral philosophy, including the notion that 'bad' or 'good' inhere in the objects of (moral) thought themselves. Underlying presuppositions therefore pass by largely unnoticed because the underlying basis of modernity is essentially not questioned. When 'good' appears almost synonymous with achieving democratic 'spread' (i.e. sameness) or benevolent sympathy for the suffering masses, from a different comparative perspective it appears as the elevation (to supremacy) of only one prior type of evaluating, that is, of one method of measuring the worth of a particular 'virtue'. Measures of the relative worth of a deed or moral precept depend, in other words, on recurring oscillations in the usurpation of dominance over other classes of people within a particular constellation of civilizational forces, or perhaps even across civilizational formations. With the founding of Constantinople—neo-Platonic Christianity—and mass republican industrial societies, a certain myopia set in with respect to the triumphant usurpation of the nobles by the lowly 'slaves' of these societies. Nietzsche exhorts philosophers therefore to think like Hegel—historically that is—in order to understand the *development* of a peculiarly 'flattened' moral outlook; to see how the vertical variegation expressed in nature's 'pathos of distance' was overcome and tyrannized by the asceticism of nascent warriors of democratic mediocrity (GS 357).

To this end, Nietzsche attempted to bring to light the hidden working presuppositions that govern modern moral and scientific discourses. In particular, to reveal the inverted world of modernity whereby 'bad conscience' and revengeful cruelty against man himself characterize the condition of 'European nihilism'. Within such a world, the slavish masses—the *demos* in Plato's language—are the legislators. Once slaves, they resented the rule of their masters and exercised envy in regards to their master's superior will; a more powerful will with which to rule others. Through sharp-cutting *ressentiment,* they negate noble values in

order to usurp the position of Commander. Inevitably they command top position only to announce the virtues of 'happiness for the many' and a comfortable
life in the valley where the cold crisp air of nature's high mountains do not
blow. Consequently, the measure of utility, common standards of evaluations in
moral matters, and unegoism are found to reign supremely; and to resist this by
seeking to reverse *their* inversion of the world would only bring on the wrath of
slavish revenge and envy and resentment against those who seek to depart from
the straight-line of herd-consciousness. The mark of modernity, and modern
philosophy by implication, is a mass intoxication in thinking oriented toward the
present; that is, in an unswerving docility in which herd-consciousness and herd-
morality reduce thinking *down* toward a blind pursuance of 'idols' expressed
mostly in the form of false ideals. Nietzsche's hammer set out to smash such
idols and this principally meant the idol of impartial objectivity in matters of a
moral judgement. It would also smash, under the heightened perspicacious insight of Zoroaster, the idols of massified societies and mass politics that degrade
the spirit of its peoples by transvaluating value with the common good, mass
happiness and democratized commerce thus leaving modern individuals bereft
of real intellectuality (i.e. teachers of value and *pathos*). By expelling hardship,
adventure and enduring kinds of challenge modern democratic societies have
brought about an inversion in both the structure of the soul and the city that has
had deleterious affects on the morphology of 'spirits of culture' and individual
souls. Although this is clearly stated in *The Gay Science* it is assiduously argued
in his most trenchant critique of modernity, *Beyond Good and Evil*, where the
ground is laid for a 'prelude' to a 'philosophy of the future' (its own subtitle).
This work looks forward to and therefore anticipates what *On the Genealogy of
Morals* will elaborate in more detail than any other work Nietzsche had published heretofore. Namely, that which all philosophers hitherto failed to recognize owing to their decidedly *a*historical analysis of forms of value, that is, *of*
valuations. (Hegel's thinking of *Sitten* in historical perspective, and the primordial status of the master-slave struggle, being possible exceptions to the rule.)
This is the important formative roles which masterly noble types play in antagonism with their counterparts—the 'slave' or herd type. As we shall see this perennial struggle ordinarily occurs between two classes in any civilized community. Notably however the logic is operative on a number of levels of social
intercourse and moral evaluation. Firstly, in relation to national figurations and
how they bear their particular spirit upon a whole civilizational constellation we
may note the following observation:

> European *noblesse*—of feeling, of taste, of manners, taking the word, in short,
> in every higher sense—is the work and invention of *France*; European vulgar-
> ity, the plebeianism of modern ideas, that of *England* (BGE 253).

Indeed, as a 'good European' Nietzsche lamented seeing European culture become infused with the Anglo mania for 'modern ideas', industriousness and
Lockean precepts of proprietary obligations. By contrast, his earnest comments
in *Beyond Good and Evil* about the strongest and substantive civilization of

(contemporary) Europe—the Jewish people—show grounds for Nietzsche's revulsion toward his sister's (and her husband's) fervent anti-Semitism. Lastly, the fortitude of the Russian peoples also convinced Nietzsche that Europe's next vigorous spirit of challenge would arise out of Europe's 'East'—ironically the holy abode of Eastern Christendom. Transcending this level is the logic of inter-civilizational conflicts and fusions which occasionally appear in his writings when for instance Moorish dominance in Iberian Europe and the Viking barbarian invasions are celebrated for their notable vigorous and rich complexity of spirit of soul—the antithesis of Christian humility and feebleness.

IV

Owing to his origins in classical studies and in particular philology, Nietzsche claims in *Beyond Good and Evil* to have discovered three fundamental classes of human beings who arrested the meaning of 'good' and 'bad': the noble, the herd, and an intermediary class. These fundamental orders of socio-cultural organization contain the dynamic force and valuation of measure: the according of worth and language concepts denoting 'bad', 'good', evil, high, low, decadent, noble by those who gain ascendancy through a struggle that is fundamentally a 'will to power'. Deploying a form of historical sociology that is well developed in *On the Genealogy of Morals* Nietzsche shows how notions of 'good' and 'bad' are in fact the effects of power and cultural pre-eminence of those in ascendant (or descendent) ruling positions, e.g. Florentine aristocracy versus feudal serfs, high priests of ancient Judaism versus faithful masses. In language reminiscent of a form of Lamarckism, Nietzsche points to a constitutive logic underlying their emergence: 'A *species* comes to be, a type becomes fixed and strong, through the long fight with essentially constant *unfavourable* conditions' (262). Historically, slavish or barbarous peoples who overcome ardous physical conditions and usurp the power of a reified authority—lord, master or priestly caste—eventually emerge triumphantly as the more vigorous and 'worthy' ones. As such they also become the rulers, that is, moral legislators who declare 'the good is that which does not profit a man' or 'to deny one's interest in gratification is to perform a good'. Ascendant classes, once having gained lordship over those who put themselves under their command, their superior knowhow or 'life-will', establish themselves as the legislators and defenders of the good—good manners, good ideals and standards of moral goodness. This assumes the form of 'good' contra 'bad', noble contra ignoble persons, and virtuous contra decadent values. It is necessary to note at this point the decisive role which so-called 'barbarous' peoples play in the formation of more vigorous and vital socio-cultural forms; namely, that of disturbing the linguine ethos of a civilized community. Invasions, interdictions, war and revenge are realities in the formation of new drive-economies and instinct-polities which Nietzsche considered important to understanding the morphology of 'spirits of culture' and human beings, particularly since modern liberal democracy shies away from admitting this reality even whilst contributing to its perpetuation. The stagnant waters of civilization, in other words, require unsettling 'agitation' by those more 'natural', *un*tamed human-animals that have yet to come under the sway of severe ascetic constraint—the constellation of civilizing forces found in long-established civilized societies that have contained the unruly instincts of natural man by so many forms of morality and bad conscience. The savage barbarian then serves as a reminder of life before it came under the spell of what Nietzsche called the 'priestly caste': life without the pessimism of moralistic religious precepts that are keenly suspicious of human instincts. The light glistens for a short time until formation has become consolidation of established measures of value and worth, i.e. creation and generation lead necessarily to petrifaction and the taming of once fiery instincts and drives. Undeniably, the benefit in the long term is the acquisition of teachers of meaning who embody *Bildung's* dynamic spirit of growth and cultivation; in this respect, Nietzsche's philosophical outlook was wholly Goethean no less than that of the gardener.

In the natural history of moralities (*Moralen*) formerly slavish types importantly also act as nihilists: that is, as agents who nullify the established virtues of their masters and hence help bring about an overturning of the moral and 'spiritual' order. This experience is initially felt as a kind of 'theft of enjoyment', a deprivation of normality, a kind of castration of one's organ of governance (mastery) and hence a feeling of aimlessness. These formerly 'lowly' types, therefore, act as a significant evolutionary impetus to the development of another formation—a post-nihilist class of moral (and characterological) legislators who wish to institute a noble order akin to those philosophers who possess a tenacious sharpness, 'hardness' and critical discipline that is fitting for Commanders. Reminiscent of Hegel's image of the slave's usurpation of his master, Nietzsche's historical sociology of divergent classes of slaves who once represented 'the common' and 'the feeble' types shows in *processual* terms the metamorphosis of once-held absolute value-standards. This perennial struggle for dominance *and* the establishment of firm, seemingly fixed value orientations points to the unassailable oscillations between commanders and subjects, between superior 'higher' ones and lowly obedient followers, and between the *aristos* (best) and the herd (commonly) in history. Yet individuals, lacking an historical consciousness of these determinants of power, come under the sway of an illusion that their particular regime of morality and value-criteria is the hiatus of human history; this illusion appears to them as a Truth, a permanency and certainty with respect to their efficacious moral worldview, e.g. modesty, self-denial, unegoism, disinterestedness and pity. This propensity to consider one's own historically formed moral life as more worthy or valid than other kinds is not only problematical for the historian but also for the philological philosopher who can identify a decidedly upside down world. Which is to say, simply because the Many have come to power and brought with them their (once) drab and slovenly manners or instincts does not necessarily mean that such virtues as modesty, humility and 'average everydayness' (as Heidegger called it[11]) signify a definite advancement of the species. Against high-modernism's self-confident attitude, Nietzsche's civilizational analysis shows a possible regression in humanity's condition if, for instance, honour is inverted to reflect the triumph of weak or 'incontinent' wills. That is, when modern society accords honour to those who lack a rigorous sense of control over oneself; whereas Roman heroic honour by comparison prized that masterly spirit which edifies its rulership not merely by mastery over others but also over oneself—their body, mind and spirit.[12]

One of the reasons why there occurs a 'slave rebellion in morals', as Nietzsche outlines in *Beyond Good and Evil* and *On the Genealogy of Morals*, is because envy once sublimated finds expression in the universality of herd values: the Jewish high priests' 'slave revolt' replaced intolerance with pity, courage with fear, noble with 'bad', hardness with tenderness, nature with 'God' and instinct with Law. The rise of a priestly caste therefore represents for Nietzsche a radical break from pre-history, perhaps analogous to the moment of emergence of the State—that most artificial construct.[13] It inaugurates, for Nietzsche, the preponderance of a deified world which in evaluative terms stands as a decline brought about by the slave revolt's rebellious overturning of once noble 'strong wills' by the instituting of the 'soul-superstition' and unegoistic ascetic standards of existence. Whether it is the metaphysics of Christianity, Judaism or Buddhism, this deified world saturates everyday life, infusing it with the untruths of a stultifying other-worldliness that denies the joyous moment of living in the present. The rise of an ascetic caste of individuals therefore finds noble virtues and vital instincts overthrown, replaced instead by ascetic valuations such as pity, humility, self-abnegation, modesty of manners, justice as righteousness, love as grace, and atonement for one's nature as a guilt-laden 'bad conscience'. Civilizational development thus depicted shows a co-extensive validation of equality and transcendental thinking: all are considered equal before the altar, and by faith in a transcendent being find certainty in an otherwise meaningless world. Ancient Buddhism and European modernity in this respect are not very different. Hence the equality revolution actually antedates democratic mob politics, giving impetus to an important historical co-dependency between *demos*-values and theocentric values. This particular entwinement of the secular and the divine is what consolidates the strength of 'herd morality' today, with transcendentalism sanctioning both 'mob' politics and an over-abiding preoccupation with the world thereafter. Because this cultural milieu eclipses 'natural man'—the human animal *before* it experiences ethical demands—Nietzsche prescribes a critical enlightenment of this highly problematic civilizational reality. Yet, it is important to note that such slaves of *ressentiment*—today's rulers—paradoxically prove beneficial for mankind by originally concerning themselves with the *soul* of human beings; as spiritual directors they invented the spurious concept of the 'soul' which concomitantly developed the adventures on to new seas of consciousness—of Becoming (that which you can be). Through various spiritual exercises and orders of self-discipline, they inaugurated a type of human being who now experiences the reverberations of bad conscience, guilt and envy. Notably, at this point Nietzsche's much claimed naturalistic account of moral man diverges both from Darwinian and Lamarckian precepts. This is because, *ceteris paribus*, the formation of a religious spirit is a definite intervention in the natural order therefore making the task of knowledge of one's 'true' ontological nature ever more enigmatic since *immediate* access to it is now obscured by the itinerary of the soul (if not of the mind as well). Quite spectacularly the priestly caste has handed down to prosperity the wider, deepened soul with all its strata of wilful drives which the figure of Zoroaster will later work further and thus elevate the general condition of *Mensch*.

Having completed his trenchant critique of modernity as essentially one pervaded by the condition of nihilism in 1886, Nietzsche sets out in his historico-philosophical analysis of morals and *Sittlichkeit* (customary morality) reasons for there being a 'positive' dimension to this otherwise nihilistic transvaluation of noble values. Extending his analysis in *Beyond Good and Evil* he observed: 'it is only fair to add that it was on the soil of this *essentially dangerous* form of human existence, the priestly form, that man first became *an interesting animal...*' (GM I: 6). Exceeding the limitations of Darwin's evolved animal, this interesting human animal is considered more developed, complex and supple due to the fact that 'only here did the human soul in a higher sense acquire *depth* and *evil*'—that latter of course being an important adjunct to the will since it suggests a conscience that knows guilt and the yoke of suffering. Evil in human 'nature' therefore partly owes to this radical historical moral innovation: 'For with the priests *everything* becomes more dangerous, not only the cures and remedies, but also arrogance, revenge, acuteness, profligacy, love, lust to rule, virtue, disease' (GM I: 6). This prized elaboration and extension of nature, of one's *human* 'nature' one might say, was much valorised by this grand civilization-analyst who never disavowed the reality of the essential dangerousness of life, a life of undulations and oscillations between the 'good' and the 'bad', life and death, harm and goodness. What is more, Judaeo-Greek-Christian civilization had further promulgated an ethics of the self over and above that of the herd; individual ethics of responsibility supplant the tribal morality that was once so indicative of herd life. Paradoxically enough the priestly form—and its type of rule—helped to instantiate the quasi-ascetic, quiet, self-disciplined spirit of Zarathustra—a sovereign individual who possesses a post-religious understanding of the world capable of transcending herds and their tribal consciousness. In sum, Nietzsche advances a form of civilizational analysis that ostensibly is predicated on the creative god Dionysus; yet his unexplicated moral philosophy suggests that since moral agents now believe they possess a soul that gives depth to the question of meaning in civilized life they ought to *embody* also the responsibility that attends it. Every civilization has made demands on the archaic man of nature only to then endow him with rich offerings of individual development and cultivation that it would be foolish to eschew. As much as errors exist, civilized persons may nevertheless acquire the authorial voice of a sovereign legislator who turns existence into an object of analysis, a work of art, and yet only Time will indicate to whom this call resounds aloud. In the end, Nietzsche's *Lebensphilosophie* turns upon that Greek metaphysic which understands the grandiosity of Necessity in the life of all living things: 'there is, of course, something unteachable, some granite of spiritual *fatum* [fate], of predetermined decision and answer to predetermined selected questions' (BGE 231).

Notes

1. For an extensive elaboration of this concept, c.f. my *Civilization and the Human Subject*. Lanham/Oxford: Rowman & Littlefied, 1999.

2. See Brian Leiter *Nietzsche On Morality*. London: Routledge, 2002, for such an account of Nietzsche.

3. Not only the Persian Zoroaster, but also the strong figures and imagery of the Old Testament are continually held in high esteem throughout Nietzsche's writings. The transcendence of height and its inert anti-gravitational force, as with also the pancosmic perspective gained from the mountaintop, relates to Moses' position on the Mount as further implied in the 'tablets' of Zarathustra metaphor utilized in *Thus Spoke Zarathustra.*

4. BGE 251. Otherwise known as his own *la gaya scienza*, the title of his famous joyful work translated in English as *The Gay Science.*

5. See Clark's 'Nietzsche's Doctrine of the Will to Power: Neither Ontological Nor Biological', *International Studies in Philosophy* 32:3, 2000.

6. Darwin, he reminds us, 'forgot the mind' (TI ix: 14). What is more, Darwin inverted the world: the small and many govern nature thus keeping down the best that could otherwise rise up.

7. See Small's useful account in *Nietzsche in Context*. Aldershot/Sydney: Ashgate, 2001.

8. Due to the '*barbarizing* effects of science', science in the modern age proves inept in determining value; hence, it 'is not a question of annihilating science' argued Nietzsche in 1872 but rather one 'of controlling it' ('The Philosopher', 28-29 in *Philosophy and Truth: Selections from Nietzsche's Notebooks of the Early 1870s*. Edited and translated by Daniel Breazeale. Humanities Press: New Jersey/London: 1990).

9. This is not to suggest the extinction of the 'feeble type' but rather that even in the figure of the nihilist (the decadent or ignoble individual) there is movement, there is willing that transforms the once mythical 'state of nature'. The priestly caste, for instance, helped to inject a vital dynamic in the constitution of spiritual drives and social orders simply by creating ascetic ideals and the 'soul-hypothesis'. This is another reason to eschew a reductionist reading of Nietzsche as a naturalist in the final instance (i.e. in epistemological terms).

10. C.f. Norbert Elias *The Court Society* and Shmuel Eisenstandt *European Civilization in a Comparative Perspective*. Oslo: Norwegian University Press, 1987.

11. Martin Heidegger *Being and Time*. Translated by John Macquaries and Edward Robinson. Oxford: Blackwell Publishers, 1962.

12. Nietzsche refers throughout his writings to the drives being in contestation with each other for supreme authority. A polity (of the soul) is depicted as analogous with conflicting tribes or herds within the polis who struggle to gain the commanding position (of the *tyrannos*; c.f. opening quote of this chapter). To be sure, *Bildung* enhances the human being's capacity to marshal these different competing forces within herself.

13. For a Nietzschean account of the development of the state and the individual, c.f. Norbert Elias *The Civilizing Process*. 2 Vols. Translated by Edmund Jephcott. Oxford: Basil Blackwell: 1982.

CHAPTER FOUR

Freedom and Responsibility

If Nietzsche reproved the American notion of liberty, we might ask whether his idea of freedom was more than simply the transvaluation of European nihilism. For once nihilistic values are supplanted by higher or nobler valuations, what would ensue for the human being? What condition, in other words, will characterize the life of more free noble spirits? Contrary to most continental interpretations, the ripe 'sovereign individual' is what Nietzsche conceived as a 'free spirit'. Moreover, naturalistic 'physicalist' reasoning similarly overlooks how Nietzsche vouched for this type of human being to transvaluate modern 'slave' values. Might we simply reply to this question: an absence of envy, resentment and revenge is part of the achievement of 'getting over oneself'? Of course, our argument thus far entails that becoming does indeed refer us to an idea of freedom that is irreducible to social-historical particularities. Looking *down* from an elevated height means that social and juridical particularity endangers human freedom as a potentiality in time. However, this does not suppose a so-called 'innocence of becoming' as the axiom upon which other measures fall or rise. The Lithuanian Jewish philosopher Emmanuel Levinas similarly eschewed the delimitations of the social-historical moment only to erect a 'slavish' alternative. Levinas maintained against Fichte and Heidegger that responsibility was superordinate to freedom: 'The responsibility for another, an unlimited responsibility which the strict book-keeping of the free and non-free does not measure, requires subjectivity as an irreplaceable hostage'.[1] Before finite freedom, there is always the *face* of the other before our recognition of its particularity (identity). Levinas ontologizes what was once Cartesian infinity: the infinite becomes absolutized asymmetry. In contrast, Nietzsche's conception of becoming and potentiality keeps the horizon fundamentally open without positing a structural (predetermined) relation, i.e. the passive self held continually hostage to the 'other'. His philosophical perspective is critical of any apriori surrendering to the other because essentially one must (first) *become* open to and responsible toward others. Otherwise, the human being endangers life with both a fixing of the inter-human moment and a slave-master relation that takes on robes that are more holy.

This often leads to the misapprehension that Nietzsche was never concerned with responsibility let alone desiring to associate it with conditions of freedom. In other words, does not the idea of 'hostage' render the other non-responsible and therefore unfree? For Nietzsche, to know freedom is to be capable of responsibility. However, if only I am responsible then what of the other's condition? And how do I nourish and care for the vulnerable other if I do not know freedom myself? The point is not to eschew responsibility, to exclude it from the process of becoming self or other, but rather to entwine it into conditions of becoming *other* or nobler and therefore freer than both the nihilist and 'hostage'. Levinas' transcendent 'pre-originary susceptiveness' is doubted no less than Martin Heidegger's *Sein* concept. While it may incorrectly be claimed that power serves the same metatheoretical role as these spurious concepts, we instead read Nietzsche as positing a fundamental shortfall in our understanding of worldly things because reality underneath is a host of processes of *becoming*. At this point, I shall argue that responsibility is part of this becoming without having to transcendentalize the priority of the other (*l'autre*) or Other (God). This is a positive step in clarifying the agonic—joyous condition of being human. Neither the self nor the other is acceptable as reified instantiations.

Because there are various 'other' individuals that confront and conflict with ourselves, Nietzsche wishes to maintain a critical distance to allow not so much an ethic as a *dynamic* tension to unfold, one that fires the soul into greater depths and breadths. A 'hostage' is given over to the structured asymmetry that is given holy resonance by Levinas' mystical thought; whereas Nietzsche's soul-experiment points to a rich plethora of growth and challenge in currents of life which stream through the human spirit's formation. Life must have its verve and we may respond to it in a number of ways, including by becoming more trustworthy and willfully accountable. Whereas the sign of a nihilist is one who abjures self-discipline, modesty and 'great responsibilities'. Nietzsche's clarion call is to find responsibility in *human* freedom, or, alternatively stated to find responsibility *in* becoming free. There is no Levinasian prioritizing of the other or of susceptibility here. If there were one would then become subjugate to the service of an abstract other. The decisive axial point is to be found elsewhere; somewhere neither Levinas nor Heidegger wished to go owing to the Husserlian dislike for psychology and 'anthropology'. Namely, to the question we examined in an earlier chapter regarding Nietzsche's method and philosophical anthropology. This concerns the problem of the two-sided inner nature of *Mensch* (humankind) illustrated in his *Gay Science* (110) thus: '...eventually knowledge collided with those primeval basic errors: two lives, two powers, both in the same human being'. Like the divided 'animal-soul', we witness a particular twofold morphology emerging out of the throes of becoming human in time. This two-sidedness, although productive for affecting a tension in the bow that shoots man into a future, is what necessitates responsibility. Otherwise, the potentiality for freedom in the 'future to come' may be subverted. Nietzsche recognizes in Christ, Caesar, Napoleon and Goethe evidence of a very identifiable tension. However, he sees in each of these great innovators the strength and know-how of how to marshal and indeed measure these 'two lives, two powers' to overcome history. To overcome rather than be overcome is the crucial difference. In order to be *for* an other—as Martin Buber once vouched—one must first have overcome a tyranny. It is the tyranny of this highly volatile two-nature morphology that stands as a dangerous challenge to a person becoming responsible. Lest one retreat into a passivity of susceptibility or a fearfulness of power because of this inexorable bi-cameral condition, one must exercise—through strong will—a mastery of the tension produced by these twin dimensions of being human. Although Nietzsche failed to make explicit the link between responsibility and self-overcoming it is discernible once we look at the implications of his line of argument. It can be discerned because he cannot posit a non-Kantian conception of freedom without simultaneously suggesting a) man has to contend with two-powers, two-lives while b) making necessary that the human cultivation of independence not be beholden to any inner schisms and fissures resulting from his peculiar morphology. The former holds to a will to be honest while the latter holds to 'the strength for the highest autonomy' (GS 21) which is reiterated once again in his *On the Genealogy of Morals.* We have a responsibility to be honest to ourselves about our fundamental twofold nature while at the same consciously not submitting to the one-sided (instinctive) dictates of our twofold nature. 'Overcoming' as both inner and outer cultivation aids in performing this task of difficult freedom.

In an earlier discussion, we examined Nietzsche's argument for the necessity of overcoming via a critique of naturalism. To be capable of being responsible means therefore grasping the reigns of our two-powers, two-lives with honesty at hand, and directing ourselves by means of cultivation and self-problematization to new horizons of measuring, valuing, commanding, ordering and expressions of spirit. Transvaluation is what Nietzsche calls it, a transvaluation of vulgar 'naturalism' (Darwin and Spencer) and historicism and their particular teleologies. If Nature has value it is because we had projected it on to organic life where even his much celebrated 'forces' are understood to require an interpretive tableau to render them real. The joyous moment of 'Nietzsche's dance' emerges out of this transvaluation of (both) natural and historical forms. It negates the notion of being 'hostage' to others because as we saw in a previous chapter Nietzsche abjured the idea of being hostage even to oneself, i.e. getting over oneself. Importantly, joyfulness associated with overcoming and transvaluation is thoroughly saturated with a desire and capacity for responsibility. Joy does not preclude the highest responsibility; instead, life is enhanced and made more attractive—more challenging and worthy of struggle—since one is given over to willing responsibility in a world that is replete with promises that are rarely fulfilled. Weak souls or spirits are defined by this failure to commitment oneself to the fulfillment of such promises. Once again to remind ourselves of the flaws of positivist reductionism: it cannot be due to one's weak 'blood' or genes that this failure occurs in individuals since Nietzsche well understood the 'herd' nature of this problem, i.e. abrogation of promises made cuts across individual and physiological differences.[2] To harness and reign in the constant antagonisms between our 'two lives'—Aristotle's and Marx's *praxis*—becomes productive *for* responsibility. Without a self-knowledge and incorporation of our twofold powers there would be no Napoleon or Zarathustra—higher noble men who were drawn to the power of greater responsibilities. Indeed, Caesar and Napoleon defined their freedom by the degree to which they could institute new responsibilities for themselves. Only the feeble or 'decadent' kind shy away from hard responsibilities. If there are only strong *or* weak wills as opposed to a *Wille* in the universe, then responsibility requires the cultivation of a kind of will that can withstand onerous demands placed upon its subject. Willing, as we saw in chapter one, is connected to freedom without having to posit a metaphysical Will. Duty is also repudiated and substituted for a willful freedom to act responsibly, leaving Kant and Levinas equally repudiated. (Duties will be examined further on in our discussion.)

Bios and Hard Work

The impetus to realize responsibility in one's mode of being is centrally concerned with the human being's development; a development through sociability that finds the original animal-soul undergoes a metamorphosis *in* time. Eschewing natural repetitions Nietzsche claims 'that everyone who wishes to become free must become free through his own endeavor, and that freedom does not fall into any man's lap as a miraculous gift' (GS 99). However, this process of *becoming* free and responsible is linked inexorably to the animal-spirit (twofold) nature that our *bios* and *Bildung* of existence remakes, forms, extends and examines in time through its manifest contradictions and vicissitudes. The Greek idea of *paideia* resonating throughout the modern German concept of *Bildung* also signifies a characteristic of art, of creativity; namely, the sculpturing of the human substance into something fine or something elegant and perhaps even beautiful. The 'good' comes out of such creative shaping and learning. Thus against modern nihilism Nietzsche prescribed a pathos (and ethos) of self-cultivation that enables something pleasing—adding 'style' to one's character is his Renaissance expression—to come *forth* out of the chaos of the *human-all-too-human*. Responsibly we recognize this chaos, what some even call 'evil' or 'bad', but do not bow down to it or its limits. What is this coming forth however? Indirectly it appears under the aegis of Zarathustra's renunciation of valley herd-morality and existence, in preference for the meditative solitude of high mountain existence. More analytically perhaps Nietzsche explains it in the *Gay Science* in the following way. For those who 'think *and* feel' the art of reconfiguration consists of surveying 'all the strengths and weaknesses of their nature' to 'fit them into an artistic plan until every one of them appears' (290). What this yields is 'a large mass of second nature'. This is very important for our argument against naturalism (fatalism[3]): instead of resignation to the forces of Fate and Luck, we find a large expanse of *second nature* emerging out of historical civilizing processes. He adds 'there a piece of original nature has been removed—both times through long practice and daily work at it' (290). The arduous work of self-cultivation performed within any political community (hence *bios*) can transform parts of our 'original nature' so that even if 'the ugly...could not be removed [it] is concealed'. He continues otherwise, 'it has been reinterpreted and made sublime'. This hard and long work on ourselves is the crucible of 'civilization', understood as both pain and joy in sublimation. Transformation is indeed possible but not as the socialists and liberals held: by revolution and constitutionalism. Nor is transformation as the Romantics had conceived it since going with Nature failed to understand that our 'artistic plan' is fundamentally anthropomorphic—an effect of *vita creativa* and physics but not pure idyllic *natura*. The role of culture, the spirit of a people or group as well as the singular person, can effect a transformative change on an ugly component of the original nature which itself was defined by our aforesaid 'two-powers, two-lives'.

As one would expect of an historical philologist and philosopher this renders the original nature malleable, for even when the ugly cannot be removed (by creative invention) it nonetheless is concealed, waiting to be exploited by long 'daily work' for distant, vague and perhaps immeasurable views. This 'growing power' associated with knowledge and self-formation intensifies the tension it has with 'primeval impulses and errors' thus standing as the penultimate mark of human life: 'Compared to the significance of this fight, everything else is a matter of indifference' (GS 110). One fights with oneself, with one's world before coming into responsibility proper. Just as Kant had claimed, it was more advantageous to think of enlightenment as a process of *becoming* enlightened, so too with responsibility—it is a process and requires time. Potentiality always infers it but never assures it. Why it requires time is because the unfinished or incomplete human-animal cannot possibly begin life responsibly. In reply to Levinas or rather Buber, Rosenzweig and Hegel, only the One (God) can know responsibility from the outset of *ov* (Being). Finitude prevents us from having any primordial intuition or access to responsibility. In becoming capable of rendering ourselves accountable for our deeds and character, we work—slowly and hard—towards freedom. This is quite dissimilar to the sacral order where the powers of the One or the Absolute can immediately put responsibility into operation because the One is simultaneously absolute freedom. Human beings by contrast are highly dependent, herd-animals who mostly get overwhelmed by the world they first encounter as evidenced by their original sensorial puzzlement. Being vulnerable at first means, we cannot be held accountable for someone else's vulnerability. Nietzsche's call is to take hold of our very own natural incompleteness and render it beautifully noble and free, forming another 'second nature' capable thus forth of shooting into distant futures thanks to its vigorous 'tension of the bow'. Who can be responsible is therefore never predetermined or known; it remains open to the horizon of becoming with all its attendant interpretations, eliminations, evaluations, concealments, measurings and will to knowledge. Contrary to fatalistic interpretations, human beings are characterized by their relative indeterminate malleable natures unfolding over time. Some 'types of man', as Schacht[4] has correctly pointed out, do emerge out of history according to their psycho-physiology morphology but certainly not because of any biological determinant of life. The historicality of Greek *bios* keeps relatively open the *potentiality* for a responsibility that is founded in freedom, but as no teleological logic is harbored by Nietzsche's schema, it means some will inevitably not accomplish the difficult task, thus giving history a certain uneven, contingent quality. This undulating facet of human existence is far more significant for Nietzsche—as it also was for Schopenhauer—than any biological organicism commonly attributed to him. Pleasure, work, and even boredom will oftentimes characterize the lives of 'the Many' as Aristotle called them. It meant for Nietzsche that mundane existence is not necessarily marked by a peculiarly responsible freedom, for the *demos* would more readily subscribe to Epicureanism. Against liberal philosophy this finds 'choosing' hardly a real option since the unconscious mostly overdetermines the range or viability of so-called 'choices', a range which is always already historically circumscribed. The road in-between is where Nietzsche treads: between objective fatalism and solipsistic choosing.

Responsibility as an important element of freedom requires the ability to read common subjective statements and sentiments as the effect of a) master-slave relations and b) the predominate morality within a given civilizational reality. If nihilistic nothingness lays the highest value on transitory, ethereal things then the relative truth of any single subjective judgment would similarly reflect its own conditions (of existence). Hence merely subjective 'truths' cannot prove any more efficacious than objective epistemic truths. Potentiality—understood as possibilities for founding freedom and responsibility through the ardor of labor and pathos in time—becomes manifest at the interstices of these polarities, including the interstices of Good and Evil, and truth and error. Why so? Because only those 'comprehensive eyes and ears' that aim at the Whole of life can tread the path in-between the seductions of both solipsistic and objectivistic truths while also abiding to the commitment of freedom *in* time. A connection exists here between responsibility and 'truth' (as the in-between of all false dualities): to be responsible about one's life, one's potential future is to aim at the Whole while recognizing the limits of false dualities. That is to say, responsibility is intricately interwoven with understanding that neither Fate nor choice (decisionism in modern parlance) is the primary dictate of life. Fatalism and modern decisionistic 'freedom' are retrogressive upon the essential unfolding of becoming human *in* time. We are required to be neither fated nor solipsistic about the potentiality of becoming free sufficiently enough to take on the great responsibilities. If it were a case merely of deciding upon such things then, Nietzsche asks, would it not be true that the majority of 'the people' would evade heavy burdensome tasks of responsibility. After all, republican liberty emphasizes liberty against state tyranny while French revolutionary politics hardly emblemizes responsibility. The masses as an effect of modern 'grand politics' may be more engrossed in their particular (or personal) rights and liberties than in large, grand responsibilities which can frequently overwhelm the comfortable (tame) self. Subjective expression can therefore only give vent to modern predilections for, say, security, ease of living, private values and herd-feelings of 'the good'. Perhaps it is 'untimely' to admit into philosophy that freedom presupposes a form of willing responsibility into operation over one's life while on the other hand denouncing the twin traditional 'errors' of solipsistic voluntarism and naturalistic fatalism. Because Nietzsche found Kant self-contradictory, he could not countenance the Will being given privileged authority in discourses on moral action and the life of the person. We have already discussed the reasons for this and can simply add that Nietzsche interrogated the silly practice of searching for 'faculties' in man pursued by various idealist philosophers. Because there is willing it does not necessarily follow that there *must* be a Will behind it. No 'faculty of will' is prerequisite to understanding the *long duree* of becoming and its potentiality of freedom in time.

The Greek concept of necessity—'Ανάγκη φύσιος—best captures what we want to convey here in terms of the compatibility between potential overcoming and compulsion (necessity). In ancient Greek, it did not imply determinism or causal overdetermination. Rather its meaning is 'the compulsion in the way things grow', carrying a more subtle meaning than its contemporary analogue 'necessity'. It simultaneously conveys the sense that things do *grow*, the world does not in fact recur and thus stay the same (fateful repetition). Nietzsche we know was a gardener-philosopher who conceived of human cultivation[5] in terms of the art of growing and temporality on earth. Growth, implying extension and height (away from the ground/gravity), becomes possible because of the fecund combinational elements and conditions prevailing in a particular milieu. If fatalism was Nietzsche's overriding catch cry as Leiter[6] claims then the 'height' of growth—expressed as the potentiality of overcoming servitude (nihilism, morality and so forth)—would simply be reduced to the 'gravity' of 'things as they are'. Presentism is what would ensue from an otherwise rich Nietzschean notion of *amor fati*. Cultivation-as-growth is *of necessity* part of the 'comprehensive view of life' previously outlined in foregoing chapters. Nietzsche well understood the logic of finite recurrence and that was precisely why his fundamentally Greek notion of becoming in and through time as extension surpasses *stasis* to become *Überwindung* (overcoming). For man in his present and previous forms is something that should be overcome as is proposed by the message of *Zarathustra* and *Beyond Good and Evil*'s account of modernity. Within the sinews of present society there lay the elementary nutrients to allow others to grow to become our 'future philosophers'. These are the *overman* type, the Napoleons, Goethes, and Jacob Burkhardts of the world. Fatalism hence fails to explain the emergence and saliency of these vital overmen, the 'ripest fruits' that botanically once again we know are the outgrowth of 'Ανάγκη φύσιος. To deny the compulsion is what is erroneous for Nietzsche. Romanticism and Idealism are under attack in this regard, because his realism wishes to acknowledge the human-all-too-human limit without necessarily having to succumb to it—to become subjugated by it and thus a *slave* to present time. Against fatalist resignation that things simply recur and stay the same—'I am simply that which I am'—Nietzsche inserts the tragico-philosophical idea that one should will joyously what *Chronos* brings forth and make the eternal wheel your own. He called this the *legislator*: the one who takes ownership of their life and puts into law, into actuality, those values and artistic plans covering our 'original-second' natures in *time*.

Yet we are also compelled to understand that human natures vary greatly in the degree to which they are malleable: masterly types possess greater degrees of relative openness while slavish characters will better exemplify the tragic vision of an 'unteachable' granite 'very deep down' in our own 'spiritual *fatum*' (BGE 231). In the same work it is linked to the extra-moral *legislator* who engages in a kind of *praxis* that extends (possibly) the 'growth in profundity';

namely, a 'self-examination of man' that heralds the 'threshold of a period' to be designated as *extra-moral* (BGE 32). Thus, when we spoke of the *necessity of overcoming* in an earlier chapter it becomes evident that it implies an undulation in both the human species and its history. It suggests that overcoming is arduous—and perhaps 'tragic' as well—because the datum-point of all (historical) development is this very deep down 'granite' of spiritual fate or destiny that can thwart learning—self-knowledge. In this same passage Nietzsche remains loyal to his commitment to the analysis of the Whole (of life) by stating that the task of self-examination is almost an 'insane task' because it involves mastery 'over the many vain and overly enthusiastic interpretations and connotations that have so far been scrawled and painted over that eternal basic text of *homo natura*' (BGE 230). We have already encountered this most primeval double-nature. However, the seemingly 'insane task' of inscribing onto Nature what it leaves fundamentally incomplete here is called *learning* (knowledge). 'Learning changes us; it does what all nourishment does which also does not merely "preserve"'; that is, we are more than what the Darwinian naturalists held or the British physiologists claimed (BGE 231). The necessity of overcoming we can now see inexorably involves learning, self-examination and therefore degrees of self-knowledge, but it is fundamentally uneven throughout time, the human race and its classes or tribes. The point is not to celebrate Difference a là Deleuze and Levinas but rather to note how difficult freedom *and* responsibility are coterminous in human existence—a human-all-too-human existence. Nietzsche is not interested in difference or repetition per se but rather in Goethean self-cultivation and extension; that is, *potentiality* for autonomy and responsibility becoming realized despite recurring hindrances and limits. What we add here is the insight (already observed in a previous chapter) that this necessarily involves the adventure or 'hunt' for a freedom on earth that no longer abrogates the 'greatest responsibilities' of an independent life. Self-knowledge alone and certainly no positivistic knowledge of reality will suffice. Self-examination is a necessary but insufficient condition of overcoming *stasis*. To shoot Apollo's arrow (time) on the other hand, requires a kind of self-knowledge that acknowledges the seemingly stubborn, unteachable part lodged deep down within our spiritual *fatum* or destiny. This is the type of work where 'choice' clearly fails us. Our rejoinder to fatalism however equally disputes the liberal decisionism that today slays itself on the rocks of subjected-centered foundationalism. The *agon* (in the original Greek sense) of overcoming is far more complex than either of these positions allow. Yet it does not retreat into a comfortable relativism or fatalist determination of (one's) destiny. Responsibility rather sublates variations in humankind and asks if the *agonic* struggle to welcome responsibilities is too much of a deterrent for those who would prefer instead to reap the pleasures and comforts of civilized society (the theme of 'civilization' is explored separately in another chapter).

But why is learning and development possible if human beings can tend to shy away from the agonic effort, retreating into one's complacent 'unteachable' haven? A retreat that costs dearly because it leaves 'the ugly' part (of the original) intact and thus immune from examination and interpretation, i.e. inscription and 'reading'. Such a retreat finds comfort in belonging to a herd of some kind and its concomitant 'herd morality'. The answer otherwise lies with the afore-mentioned 'artistic plan' of the legislator who commands a will on the earth and the question of his or her constitution being a two-sided phenomenon. Here the already mentioned 'two-powers, two-lives' copula takes on another hue or, rather, optical angle. It relates directly to the 'artistic plan' with which a human being develops and cultivates its 'second nature'. In a passage on the great bene-fit of suffering for the enhancement of man—that 'tension of the soul'—Nietzsche refers to man as both 'creature and creator': 'in man there is material, fragment, excess, clay, dirt, nonsense, chaos; but in man there is also creator, form-giver, hammer hardness, spectator divinity, and seventh day: do you un-derstand this contrast?' (BGE 225). As creator the human being gives form via her 'artistic plan' to shape, reshape and produce a kind of being who is pleasing to the eye, ear, heart and mind—something to behold in all its splendor. It comes out of the chaos, the clay fragment and Dionysian excess that is vital for some-thing to *be*, to come into form and thus gain value (i.e. color, shape, beauty, con-tours and purpose) through interpretation. This 'interpretation' is an inscription, an intervention, upon nature's indifference.[7] As creature though a human being remains to be completed; that is, remains to be *given* form, ends, goals, tastes, *persona* and that which may overcome chaos. Since the cosmos is constituted primarily as 'chaos' and not those micro-particles which the atomists of the day had claimed, mankind hangs like a rope over the Abyss. The danger of life is what the creator in him understands but also simultaneously deploys for the pur-pose of forming a more interesting, cultivated and nobler life, one characterized by an authentically free spirit which flies high above the Abyss and its deep void. Chaos is no foe for him but rather something to be admitted into the knowledge schema whereby the will to self-knowledge opens up the 'creature' to the demands placed upon it by political society.

To overcome shear chaos is to grapple with humanity's angst and dread of chaos through both creation and learning. It entails learning to negate the con-comitant revenge against man himself that stems from its sundering from an unbounded 'animal soul' (the pre-political original nature that remains creatural or animalic). This overcoming of chaos, self-revenge and Nature's stinginess requires what is aptly captured in the title of Book V of the same work: *We Fearless Ones* who understand that 'At long last the horizon appears free to us again, even if it should not be bright...our ships may venture out again, venture out to face any danger...*our* sea, lies open again' (343). The open horizon like that of Apollo above the Aegean sea stands for a potentiality to found new tables of the good on a distant shoreline. This is what the Fearless creators set out to accomplish, the *'creation of our own new tables of what is good'* (GS 335, original italics). Why fearless ones necessarily? Because they are not afraid of the tension within themselves, knowing that it will allow them to shoot farther into a distance where new tables of the valuable, the good, can be created. What is more, the fearless ones are those who can embrace becoming that which they are, notably sailors on the sea of 'becoming'—something 'new, unique, incom-parable' because they 'give themselves laws', 'create themselves' and above all embrace necessity (as defined above; GS 335). It is here that our aforementioned synoptic 'knower' makes an appearance and grounds the heroism of the 'sailor' of new seas and continents. Nietzsche says: 'To that end we must become the best learners and discoverers of everything that is lawful and necessary in the world: we must become *physicists* [as opposed to metaphysicians] in order to be able to be *creators* in this sense' (GS 335). Sailors or creators generally cannot do without a *physio-logos* if they are to venture the new seas and give form to new 'tables of what is good'. Here the adventurer and artisan possess *techne* (know-how, skilful knowledge) because they examine the 'lawful and neces-sary' aspects of the world—the forces and configured processes of formation amidst nature's chaos. This kind of naturalism concurs fully with Clark's[8] view of Nietzsche's position, particularly his 'naturalizing of morals'.

The question then becomes what is responsibility once we acknowledge the persistence of 'the necessary' and its concomitant knowledge (*technē*) which enables 'tables of what is good' to be created in different forms? From the be-ginning we notice that taking responsibility immediately involves knowledge and, in particular, knowledge of Greek 'necessity'. This means to be responsible requires a know-how of how the world works, its 'physics', says Nietzsche, be-cause the gardener must know the elements of the earth before it can *cultivate* the good, beautiful garden of plants. As with Machiavelli and Spinoza, one does not start out with theistic ethics or metaphysics but rather one must 'naturalize' the problem of world-forming and world-making. We have already seen how Nietzsche repudiates naturalism because of its numerous flaws. However, in a similar vein to Spinoza's[9] attempt to think of the world without a dependence on God or the presence of God, Nietzsche wants to secure a vitalist conception of freedom that embodies the power of the greatest responsibilities and its pathos. In the correct language of the overcoming man, such a pathos is part of the *en-hancement* of man and its condition on earth. This enhancement is required in order for humankind to overcome nihilism and its pernicious value of medioc-rity. Why? Because responsibility itself has prerequisites, spiritual *factum* that derive from the potentiality of overcoming Today, and its spiritual malaise. They are inscribed upon a pathos which symbolizes 'the craving for a new widening of distances *within the soul* itself, the development of ever higher, rarer, more remote, further-stretching, more *comprehensive* states' (BGE 257, emphasis added). Akin to semi-barbarian natures, a pathos of this kind represents the for-mation of 'more *whole* human beings' who are stronger not in physical terms but 'in strength of the soul'—their predominance owing not to might but 'develop-ment'. Whole human beings seek comprehensive knowledge, as we have already seen, and they do so in company with the affects—the soul's reverberations of the Real. The self-overcoming man thinks *and* feels simultaneously, his (sic) 'more comprehensive states' allow him to associate existence with the Whole of life, in part because of his acquired historical knowledge. Knowledge therefore is not antithetical to the strength of the soul since the 'knower' cannot be re-duced to the mindless laboring of today's positivists.

Moreover, whole human beings with wide comprehensive 'eyes and ears' (to use Heraclitus' words), in possession of a pathos where the soul embodies a further stretching, deepening and elevation, do not merely *agree* to a duty or imperative. For deeds count more than words and thoughts as was argued earlier in *Daybreak*. Instead of commencing with Descartes' *cogito* or the *ratio* (Aquinas) which exercises willful thought, 'I will to obey the imperative' or 'I will to do my duty', here there must be something more than *scepsis*, more than Aristotelian *Nous* mediated by so many scholastic logical reductions. Before its reduction, the Whole encompassed the soul's pathos and what inner 'strength of the soul' existed, if at all, to take on the task of responsibility in this human, sometimes all-too-human world. Development as defined in the present work, gives us the crucial clue: 'The conditions that one would have partly to create and partly to exploit for their genesis; the probable ways and tests that enable *a soul to grow* to such a height and force that it *feel the compulsion for such tasks*' (BGE 203, emphasis added). Being responsible clearly concerns 'a task' and thereof its sense; and such a task it seems requires 'compulsion'. Yet as we have already stated, thinking alone is insufficient. The human being must also 'feel' the compulsion—a compulsion to perform such a task. Moreover, they must grow so that the height and force of the soul reflects those conditions that it has *both* created and exploited as a 'creator-creature'. It will be recalled that the object is for new tables of the good to be created and formed (hammered), allowing Nietzsche to add in the same passage: 'a revaluation of values under whose new pressure and hammer a conscience would be steeled, a heart turned to bronze, *in order* to *endure* the *weight of such responsibility*' (BGE 203). One's self feels it, feels the weight of an otherwise onerous responsibility which nevertheless endures its exacting demands by forging a heart of bronze and a conscience steeled by its new formation. Something so onerous cannot, properly speaking, be imposed on the 'incomplete creature' that the human being is without *historie* forging this kind of formation of conscience and heart—it would simply tyrannize the 'animal-man'. Arguably, this cuts against reductive readings of Nietzsche's naturalism as it undermines the point that the savage state of the instincts is what subsequently determines the conditions of man in complex societies. The *historie* of forms of life draws essentially on a pre-Christian (i.e. pagan) cosmogony that establishes a 'supra-moral' image of the human by means of an extra-natural, sociocultural vision of humanity's formation. Mankind, the species at large, and not the individual is the fulcrum point of Nietzsche's analysis. Neither surrendering to the dictates of the law of the Other or the law of the instincts, Nietzsche proposes an alternative vision that incorporates the pathos of tragedy, the becoming of *historie* and the intelligence of Greek Fire in a joyful science that overcomes the stagnancy of nihilism.

This 'science' we can say also envisages a struggle of the human to become free, to attain a mode of being which is incorporative of responsibility. Since it rejects the existence of an 'unfree will' as much as it does the 'freedom of the will', our proposition is not predicated on any originary will. Nietzsche's joyful science does not begin with the Will a là Augustinian theology or Thomist philosophy. Rejecting Kant's idea of the Will means also to reject his Christianizing of Aristotle's virtue ethics. Before the Gospels of the New Testament, where Paul begins the discourse on the will, human beings and their motivations were understood in terms other than those of a will residing within human consciousness. Achilles took on Hector through the compulsion of his 'strong will' not because the Will autonomously acted upon its own decision to 'will it'. The Will as abstract object precedes becoming; whereas in the former case force stands in with 'strong will' and feebleness with 'weak will'. One has to feel the compulsion of the task to take on Hector—it cannot be simply a decisionistic preparedness. Both Hector—noble prince of Troy—and Achilles (one favored by the gods) possess a will to power similar to that found in other living things: an excess to realize the full force of their potential growth. Their nobility was, to reiterate an earlier point, in the strength of their spirit and not their physical strength. Nietzsche, in other words, insists that a human being cannot will something into being: actuality, as Hegel had also shown, cannot simply be determined by either will or reason. One must be made ready for responsibility. Otherwise we lapse into the myth of the *causa sui*. Causa sui is the hidden God problem, that is, it refers to something that is its own cause. The Will has fallen under the shadow of this causa sui and consequently human beings see their own conduct in terms of its invisible force: 'the desire to bear the entire and ultimate responsibility for one's actions oneself, and to absolve God, the world, ancestors, chance, and society involves nothing less than to be precisely this *causa sui*' (BGE 21). That is to say, individuals 'forgot' the world, their ancestors, chance, society and even God in their assigning of cause (blame) to their own individual will. As if the world is moved by a single will—the world is already objectified and operates according to the physics of 'the necessary' as already noted. Yet the human being wants to believe that it is entirely his or her own doing, their willing. That would, of course, suppose the existence of an Absolute self and this for Nietzsche is an absurdity of modern thinking. Causa sui in the form of either a metaphysical will or atomic self is a myth. Therefore, it follows that pronouncements of the 'absolute accountability' kind are also mythical—devoid of reality—because they stem from the fallacious notion of a will that is its own cause. In morality, as with all moral thought after Augustinian neo-Platonism, the Will has been rendered as a kind of *causa prima*—a 'first cause' of and behind every conceivable human action which stands in place for the grand metaphysical riddle: the Hidden God problem. To lift the veil in order to find the *causa prima* of all moral and extra-moral phenomena has been mankind's longstanding error.

In truth, we understand the vanity of such intellectual pursuits and begin to become responsible for ourselves as elevated human-animals: the 'eternal joy of becoming', that is, requires such a truth-insight if it is to *overcome* a certain malaise: the faith in a metaphysical Will expressed as the *causa prima*. To apotheosize an otherwise 'strong or weak will' is to render something merely human into something *extra*-human, elevating it to the rank of God. Is this not blasphemous, asks Nietzsche? To assume that we could, firstly, 'kill God' and subsequently raise something ethereal equal to that of the Creator. This would assume equivalence with the single Whole, a position only occupied by that that is responsible for the world as a Whole. Hence, we need to abolish this will to apotheosize because once the Real world was abolished (by Christianity's nihilism) so too was the Apparent world (TI 4, 6). The apparent-real world, that is to say, is mythical. Hence, our modern precept that we ought to be held responsible for all our actions is similarly an 'error' and unnecessary illusion. Intentionality and conscious will are, according to the argument, excessive aggrandized words for what the limited animal-human does in this earthly world. Overcoming men and women, that is, noble free spirits are not seduced by the tyranny of such ugly forms of self-aggrandizement. To eschew the (Buddhist-Christian) 'unegoistic self' is not necessarily to advocate what a spiritualized drive to philosophize seeks to establish: an objective 'moral will'. Intentional egoism, on the other hand, also proves insufficient because it fails to accommodate the necessary realism required in the 'decisions' and so-called 'choices' of individuals who espouse such erroneous views. Responsibility exceeds the drive for self-preservation but not because of the individual's innate 'moral reason' or Will as Kant had it. Nietzsche's view of the human being proposes instead that the egoism of the individual not be negated only so it can later be transfigured by new value estimations arising from overcoming the *I*. In short, the moment of responsibility is neither a priori nor an effect of a 'moral will' entity. Rather it owes to overcoming the limits of brute egoism by achieving an elevated, enhanced perspective of the type of 'man' because it no longer holds man in contempt. As with Zarathustra, those capable of achieving responsibilities must be steeled by a *preparedness* that is both hard and skilful.

Contrary to the standards of mass education (including universities), such preparedness would require vigorous, skilful and astute education (*Bildung*) in the substantive forms of learning: literacy, logic and spiritual extensions. Nietzsche's critique of modernity in *Twilight of the Idols* suggests that the condition of decadence itself is based on and yet perpetuates the problem of an adequate regime of proper preparedness. Modernity is kept alive by 'idols' which are erected on the false basis that a moral Will moves 'behind' each and every human action—'the conscience' confirms this, i.e. guilt as objective phenomenon. To rid humankind of this mythic illusion is to at the same time shatter the 'error' that everyone a priori is responsible for their own actions. Modern human beings evade charges of irresponsibility precisely because they at the same time unconsciously fear that the overbearing weight of 'great responsibilities' may be too much for them. A formal duty, a formalistic categorical imperative for instance, would only highlight the propensity for guilt-feelings once the value Standard has not been met. Here Nietzsche is espousing more than simple honesty; he wants to defuse the vengefulness of such tyrannical *formal* concepts of the good. Given his extensive writings on the finiteness of being human—the *human-all-too-human*—Nietzsche gives the realist rejoinder that human beings need *preparation* as much as they need completion. In fact for the unfinished human being to be 'completed' the promise of potentiality (futural overcoming) necessitates such a steeled, disciplined preparation; a preparation that proper education and cultivation (*Bildung*) can provide for a *bios* which can enhance man's spirit by means of various responsibilities. Animals know life as *zoi* but not necessarily as *bios* because the political, civilized state of human life necessarily transforms the 'animal-soul' into something in excess of what Nature had bequeathed it. Knowing contradiction, evaluation and (creative) form-giving, it can overcome the limit boundaries of its once animal-soul to realize a responsibility for its own unfolding in time—its own *cosmos*, or, constellation of necessity and freedom in the will to life.[10] Higher souls and true artists thrive in this constellation because they have abandoned the notion of the *causa prima* and incorporated necessity itself within freedom: 'that necessity and "freedom of the will" become one in them' (BGE 213). The much celebrated antithesis (e.g. German idealism) of necessity—freedom is overcome *and* incorporated into their nature. 'Higher' now referring to this development after it first shrugged off one's dependency on an abstract faculty called the Will.

To return to the question of the will and responsibility we can ask once more of what import 'preparedness' has? We have already established the necessity or compulsion of the task of responsibility, a 'compulsion' as opposed to a formal duty to act in this or that way. It is impossible hence to know responsibility without becoming, without the will to life being marshaled and cultivated in ways that produce an individual capable of noble tasks of *taking* responsibility. Higher souls understand the difference between 'improvement' as the 'taming of the animal' for domestication purposes and the actualization of potentiality in their noble task of taking responsibility. To be sure, Nietzsche's idea of higher noble souls does infer an improvement of sorts but not in its usual problematic teleological, i.e. modern herd valuations of 'better'. Higher as 'elevated' also refers us to the transcendence of mundane existents which lack growth, that is, stunted moralistic persons who evade the task of preparing for responsibility. The actualization of *dunamai*—'to be able, strong enough to do', in Latin *potentia*—is the marshalling and cultivating of the 'will to life' that can lead higher souls to the transfiguration of Today's freedom. Today's freedom is what Nietzsche explicitly renounced most clearly in *Twilight of the Idols*. Two dimensions to his critique of modern liberal freedom bear heavily on this discussion (of preparedness). Firstly, since Nietzsche thinks of responsibility as derived from *compulsion*, from the task of *dunamai*, the pain involved in overcoming complacent servitude must be acknowledged. The *affects*, in other words, register the compulsion and reality of the task; its possibility is bound up with those drive-affects which liberal institutions remain skeptical about. Modern liberal institutions harbor a perverse kind of psychology with respect to their valorized sovereignty of the will and hence individual action. Consequently, Nietzsche set out to disclose the perversity of its underlying psychology: 'Here I simply supply the psychology of all "making responsible"' (TI 6, 7). What is disclosed here? 'Wherever responsibilities are sought, it is usually the instinct of wanting to judge and punish which is at work'. Mankind's cruelty is evident here in a will that develops the 'bad conscience' and its attendant instincts of wanting to judge others and measure conduct according to the bad conscience. These themes are taken up more fully in his *Genealogy of Morals* but for present purposes, it is sufficient if we note the interconnection between this cruel psychology and the foundational status of 'free will'. The illusion of the latter justifies and confirms the reality of needing to 'judge and punish' those deemed irresponsible. People who fall outside the domain of Right have not respected the moral duty to obey the *rule* of law.

Yet before the 'rule', before any formal duty to follow something, there always already is becoming: 'Becoming has been deprived of its innocence when any being-such-and-such is traced back to will, to purposes, to acts of responsibility' (TI 6, 7). Acts of responsibility 'in their sense' are fallacious because they must of necessity regress back to an origin, an originary Will that is non-existent. As with Spinoza's denial of teleology and 'purpose' so too with the modern misconception of an objectively existing Will. Willing, Nietzsche argued, does not require a metaphysical Will nor therefore does it need a 'psychology of will'—a mere reification of the priestly order. The entire 'old psychology, the psychology of will, was conditioned by the fact that its originators, the priests at the head of ancient communities, wanted to create for themselves the right to punish—or wanted to create this right for God' (TI 6, 7). Modern morality, including contemporary notions of responsibility 'in this sense' can therefore be said to be religious in inception. Nietzsche's aim quite clearly is to peer through the veil first laid down by the ancient priests. His claim to truth becomes evident at this point: the concept of 'free will' 'we know only too well what it really is—the foulest of all theologians' artifices, aimed at making mankind "responsible" in their sense' (TI 6, 7). A specific conceptual disentanglement is demanded here because of the tyranny of this conceptual archaism. To advance self-overcoming 'future philosophers' will have to discern and disentangle the archaic 'psychology of will' and its guilt-complex from their (new) sense of willing responsibility in a new form of freedom. Not freedom *from* but freedom *to* know one's responsibilities and their compulsion. Instead of *feeling* guilty for one's own inadequacy or shortfall, a future understanding of responsibility will signify the degree to which the *duamai* of life has been incorporated and expressed through its affect of becoming. The right to punish is substituted for the affects of the pathos of one's responsibilities that are incorporated into his or her self-image as unique, single, hard, and nuanced by the subtleties of privilege. Unmasking their error and finding truth in a certain preparedness for taking on responsibilities appropriate to one's strength, know-how (*technē*) and compulsion-drive is Nietzsche's innovation.

The second aspect to the importance of affect in an individual's capacity for responsibility is the relative political economy of the drives. Contrary to superficial readings of Nietzsche 'the immoralist', there is an injunction placed on the self-indulgence of spontaneous impulses being given free reign. Nietzsche argues the reason for a prevailing malaise and cultural decadence in modernity is because their (too) liberal institutions fail 'the people', the herd-demos. Modernity's institutions not only propagate the falsehood that equality must be the Good but also fail to condition or *prune*, as he calls it, the drives. Drive-affects are combative; they are structured around an Olympian-like *agon*, i.e. 'contest'. Consequently for our form-giving 'creator' (rather than creature) to be herself formed, conditioned and shaped by time, it means that 'man' must first be made *possible*. Nietzsche calls it 'possible' because the human is no mere accident or effect of τύχη (Luck). The will to life is better harnessed by a form-giver who *becomes* possible in history—a value-measurer in the midst of the nothing—standing as an individuated being who lives in the configured Whole.[11]

The Whole makes her possible instead of our acclaimed innate 'moral will', as causalists maintain. Central to a person's formation (and humankind more comprehensively) is the realization of this possibility in the manifoldness of becoming. For this purpose, it is necessary that all 'growth' be cultivated, that is, 'pruned' rather than naively let go of. 'In times like these, abandonment to one's instincts is one calamity more', Nietzsche argued (TI 9, 41). Why so? 'Our instincts contradict, disturb, destroy each other' and thus if left to their own devices bring about a state which he describes as the 'degeneration of the instincts' (TI 9, 41). What is needed to countervail a state of degeneration or chaos is for the individual 'to be made possible by being pruned'; in education, rationality 'would require that under iron pressure at least one of these instinct systems be paralyzed to permit another to gain in power, to become strong, to become master' (TI 9, 41). *Agon* once again informs Nietzsche's understanding of the turmoil inherent in the instinctual economy of the living human. Cultivation-as-form-giving means directing 'growth' by allowing certain drive-impulses ascendancy while others are to descend in their order of significance, i.e. 'order of rank' as frequently stated. But the 'reverse is what happens' in *modern* valuations of freedom: 'the claim of independence, for free development, for *laisser aller* is pressed most hotly by the very people for whom no reins would be too strict' (TI 9, 41). Unsurprisingly, as a symptom of decadence 'our modern conception of "freedom" is one more proof of the degeneration of the instincts' (TI 9, 41). Vigorous self-discipline and training, and cultivation in the pre-modern sense of *Bildung* are what enables proper 'pruning' of the combative instincts. To *overcome*, in the sense of our present discussion, therefore means overcoming the perennial turmoil of states in our mode of being. If not, then the 'whole' cannot be embraced by our *amor fati* nor will institutions of learning secure rigorous acculturation in bios. In part, this is due to Nietzsche's anti-naturalist stance. When advocating that the artist 'must know *who* one is' he warns against using Nature as a model: 'It exaggerates, it distorts, it leaves gaps. Nature is *chance*. To study "from nature" seems to me to be a bad sign' (TI 9, 7). What is more, it is also 'unworthy of the *whole* artist' who is, as we have said, a form-giving creator. Nietzsche's point, and it is relevant to any discussion of freedom, is that the good artist possesses an awareness of her states and economy of drives—*who* she is becoming. Paralyzing or holding sway over an instinct is what the true artist has mastered within herself, though self-mastery as such remains elusive.

The second dimension to Nietzsche's critique of liberal "freedom" involves a demolishment of the confidence in modern democratic institutions. Essentially, it is due to a lack of spirit that institutions are failing us, or rather, we failing them as it turns out. This is in evidence particularly in the West where 'One lives for the day, one lives very fast, one lives *very irresponsibly*: precisely this is called "freedom"' (TI 9, 39). We prefer what disintegrates because that which makes an institution 'is despised, hated, and repudiated: one fears the danger of a new slavery the moment the word "authority" is even spoken out loud' (TI 9,

39). Leveling in grand politics has de-spirited institutions thus undercutting the spirit 'out of which a *future* grows' (TI 9, 39). Modernity's self-contradiction now becomes apparent: on one hand, it promotes the 'psychology of will' as the fulcrum for all moral actions while on the other hand it grows weary of what makes selves and institutions strong and enduring over time. The clamor for so-called independence produces a perverse form of freedom that is parasitic upon the illusion of an existing Will in all human affairs. People live 'very irresponsibly' while also being imbued with guilt that derives from the false concept of 'freedom of the will'. The value-order says 'You are morally accountable' while on the other side institutions rob you of a proper sense of the *future*, of possible responsibility in the future. By contrast, the 'human being who has *become free*...spits on the contemptible type of well-being dreamed of by shopkeepers...and other democrats' (TI 9, 38). They espouse another type of freedom, one that defines responsibility not by a formal duty (rule) or illusory 'moral will' nor by means of an instinct to punish, judge or render guilty other persons. These actions are the actions of a feeble nature; ignoble in nature they nevertheless appear noble in civil society. What is truly noble is to grasp the insight that responsibility is part of the Whole. The 'innocence of becoming' is trans*formed*, that is, shaped, conditioned and rendered 'possible' in time by means of its Whole. Will and choice are subsumed by it so they cannot precede it—the configured world. Instead, higher souls and 'whole artists' (form-givers) understand freedom not in terms of 'that which one attains by it, but in what one pays for it—what it costs us' (TI 9, 38). This point has already been discussed in chapter two. Expenditure is the key to understanding one's becoming, one's self-formative process and its attendant capacity to assume responsibility. In the same passage of *Twilight* Nietzsche asks directly 'For what is freedom?' He replies 'That one becomes more indifferent to difficulties, hardships, privation, even to life itself' (38). Possessing strength, being 'prepared', means not being averse to the 'hardships' and 'privations' of a responsible life. One is equipped by training, education, agonic struggle (i.e. 'war'), solitude, learning (consequently, by 'teachers of meaning' as well) and 'pruning'.

The aforementioned stinginess of Nature precludes us from being *naturally* responsible. Cultivation then can make the spirit become free, overcoming the instinct for 'pleasure' which is more lowly, thereby allowing the instinct for victory or dominance to gain ascendancy. This somewhat challenging process points to what might be called enablement, to use an old gymnastic notion. The enabling of a form of 'man' that is prepared for the hardships and grand rewards of great responsibilities. The key propositional statement in this passage is:

> For what is freedom? That one *has* the *will to assume responsibility* for oneself.
> That one maintains the distance which separates us (TI 9, 38; emphasis added).

Herein the 'will' does not refer to the conventional concept of an autonomous Will 'in their sense' but, to be sure, in Nietzsche's sense. His sense of the will is inextricably bound with the preparation, 'enablement' and affect of 'compulsion'. That is, it lacks a formal status of the kind warranted by Kant's categorical imperative; similarly, it lacks a metaphysical grounding of the subject, of the

Cartesian thinking *I*. Hence, Nietzsche's concept of 'will to assume' is not predicated on the Cartesian *cogito* or, equally problematic, an Augustinian *will* in human beings. Nietzsche rather conceived of willing against the more common hypostasized *Wille* concept as a dynamic force and facet of becoming human that is much closer to Schopenhauer's thinking than any previous philosopher. It is associated with the force and power within Nature to generate and degenerate living things, to expressed drives to come into being and then fall away into decay. However, the notable difference here is that the organic plant cannot be imbued with a *willing*ness to take on difficult tasks and render them great responsibilities, just as it cannot realize nobility in its will to life. Secondly, it posits a capacity to assume responsibility for *oneself*: that one is more than an animal-soul and more than a creature possessed of combative, excessive drives that sway the individual in every direction. Because as we have already seen pruning aids human cultivation and such a cultivation is the work of a form-giving creator who is responsible also for his or her own 'form'. One's life—at least for the artist of the Whole—is formable and because it can be given more beautiful or uglier forms, the will to assume responsibility becomes an important part of forming a healthy, vital individual who refuses nihilistic pessimism. To master and work with human substances is what the Dionysian spirit aims to do; an activity that is the unity of so-called Apollonian and Dionysian elements.[12]

This important (quoted) passage above also draws our attention to another dimension of *dunamai* conceived as creative form-giving, one that we yet have not highlighted in our discussion. Namely, that this *oneself* is neither one-dimensional nor reducible to the Kantian presupposition of *spontaneity* of thought. Rather than commencing with Idealist notions such as 'immediacy' and 'spontaneity' with respect to our self-relation, Nietzsche adopts a more Platonic image of *psuchê* (soul) that ennobles the half-animal man because of its multiple-layered soul. Distance is what marks this important facet of being human: Plato never made reason transcendent of life or mortality. Due to this commitment Plato properly understood that *anthropos* is characterized by the *agon* (contest) of different states both within and without the human soul. For Nietzsche, the 'distance which separates us' is at first immanent. The soul is structured by a principle of distance between contending drives and states which produces a breadth and depth that eventually comes to characterize the spirit of that most 'interesting animal' known as 'man' (GM I: 6). To collapse the distance between unconscious drives and conscious states is to endanger that most productive tension which sustains and invigorates 'higher souls', allowing them to shoot at more distant goals. Free spirits, those 'good Europeans' who eschew nationalism, mob-rule and Jesuitism, 'still feel it, the whole need of the spirit and the whole tension of its bow' (BGE P). In part this is thanks to Platonized Christianity and its so-called 'soul superstition'. It has bestowed to Europe 'a magnificent tension of the spirit the like of which had *never yet existed on earth*'; consequently those who are properly prepared and educated (psychically equipped) for it will be *able* to 'shoot for the most distant goals' with 'so tense a bow' (BGE P, emphasis added). This means that responsibility in a phase of nihilism entails having the wherewithal to overcome fear of such a tension thereby transforming that most magnificent tension of the spirit into a creative vital impulse for a new kind of freedom. Responsibility, we can deduce from this, represents a willingness to affirm and sustain this productive tension, an affirmation based upon a polity of the soul that valorizes distance over and above a flattened world of sameness. To level the 'social structure of the soul' is to threaten the *potentiality* of a future yet to come. Hence, this form of responsibility is arguably transcendent of temporal consciousness because of its commitment to a beauty of freedom that glistens on our horizon of existence.

To overcome decadence Nietzsche envisages a transcendence of temporal understandings of 'freedom' as delimited by an erroneous 'psychology of will' and *causa sui* on one hand, and a juridical interest in punishment that promulgates a bad conscience in humankind on the other hand. Thus, responsibility here refers to a strong willingness to reject these illusory realities and at the same time maintain the distance between various states that define everyday experience. Potentiality—as discussed earlier under the heading of overcoming—and responsibility are intertwined: to be responsible in the world means to abide by an unseen potentiality for human freedom in the present. Living for the present, for Today, for my pleasure by contrast is characteristic of feeble behavior, whereas the values of the aforementioned 'whole artist' are focused on a design that incorporates a wider comprehensive horizon of temporal existence. The Whole is what the 'free spirit', true artist and experimenter of knowledge each apprehend and discern about life—the transcendence of the visible presence for the invisible 'possible' man. The possible is a reference to the creation of something untimely or out-of-step with the present. The possible noble individual is forged necessarily out of the Is and Was; they 'have at their disposal the preliminary labor of all philosophical laborers, all who have *overcome the past*. With a creative hand they *reach* for the *future*, and all that *is and has been* becomes a means for them, an instrument, a hammer' (BGE 211, emphasis added). To forge another type of human being requires a vigorous overcoming of the present within oneself; it is the task of the Philosopher (and not a mental laborer) to hammer something new out of the old. The philosopher out of necessity is 'a man of tomorrow and the day after tomorrow' someone therefore in 'contradiction to his today'—an untimely individual (BGE 212).

But what do they forge these untimely ones? He says two things: 'to know of a *new* greatness of man, of a new untrodden way to his enhancement'; and to find the 'concept of "greatness" precisely in his range and multiplicity, in his wholeness in manifoldness' (BGE 212). Two key words emerge here: untrodden and wholeness. Each of these words adds credibility to the importance of the present argument: novelty, not repetition, is the mark of overcoming while wholeness encompasses our manifold states and experiential content. If the world was thought to simply recur eternally owing to a purported naturalistic fatalism, then why would Nietzsche declare in his rewritten preface to the *Gay Science* (4): 'one returns *newborn*, having shed one's skin...with a more delicate taste for joy, with a tenderer tongue for all good things...with a second dangerous innocence in joy, more childlike and yet a hundred times subtler than one has ever been before'. A 'second dangerous innocence in joy' is what a transcendent responsibility of freedom can fashion out of time. But owing to the absence of any teleology in Nietzsche's philosophy, there is no guarantee of this. Dangers and pain are what free spirits are *prepared* for instead of mere comfort and security. Whereas to live decadently in the present entails a pressure to alleviate pain and danger from one's existence yet these are the very birth pangs of a new 'second' beginning. Endurance of arduous conditions, including contesting the certainty of the absolute Will, prepares the human being for distant goals in the future that belie consciousness of being-in-the-world. Having been prepared and steeled for the task—enablement as opposed to duty-ridden fear— responsible overcoming men and women experience life with the gaiety of dance and play. They remain joyful in a life marked by dangers, errors and revengefulness against untimely ones since their 'knowing is creating' and their 'will to truth' is the experimental impulse to understand the world anew (BGE 211). Is this affirmation possible because they essentially scoff at reality? No, it is rather because a will to power is found in a certain transcendent responsibility that stems from the hard, disciplined preparedness that has forged such individuals.

Hence, we know from his account of responsibility that Nietzsche envisages a transformation of the morphology of the modern human being. The modern individual of necessity cannot meet this exacting task if left *ex natura* to pull himself up out of an illusory moral will or, perhaps worse, a pernicious bad conscience. Preparation for a 'greatness' still to come would by contrast enable this half-animal soul to tackle the main task at hand often mentioned in Nietzsche's later work: the creation of new values. When we connect this transformative, creative task with our two earlier points—a new untrodden way to his enhancement and greatness in his range and multiplicity—we gain a synoptic comprehension of *the task* and the aporia of (naturalistic) fatalism. Between teleology and fatalist predeterminism, Nietzsche inserts this *potentiality* of becoming free in time. The horizon remains open even if we declare Today decadent and mediocre; and a transcendent responsibility holds in good stead the promise of the future within the present. It abides by the strengthened willingness to become free even if we are living within a slavish herd-morality. This steeled and prepared human being, in contradistinction to neo-Kantians and liberals, is not fearful of the task of overcoming 'their sense of freedom' because the tension of the bow (a spirit) has not been eliminated. We now arrive at that moment when the following statement can be properly apprehended: 'He would even determine value and rank in accordance with how much and how many things one could bear and take upon oneself, how *far* one could extend his responsibility' (BGE 212). This is one of Nietzsche's clearest statements concerning the inadequacy of formal moral duty and, by contrast, the realist sufficiency of having human beings *become* prepared and capable of responsibilities corresponding to their particular psycho-physiological spiritual make-up. To do otherwise is to apply an *imperium* upon moral-psychical affairs of humanity almost synonymous with *Reich* politics. That is, any imperative that is categorical and formally given would be the most illiberal kind of morality while pretending to be sanctified and virtuous. Oppression rather than freedom is what would ensue and Nietzsche connects responsibility to becoming free. This is another way of saying, somewhat indirectly, that the man from Königsberg was acting irresponsibly to imagine that the *imperium* of universal obligations could bring about autonomy and enlightenment in civil life.

However, Nietzsche equally does not turn to 'the particular' as situationists and relativists might, nor to Epicurean pleasure to render this 'modern' kind of freedom deplorable. On the other hand, the anarcho-libertarian and modern hedonist would also come under criticism for evading the difficult task of becoming responsible in order to realize (proper) freedom. Freedom *from* and *in* are their holy idols; freedom to invent and generate grand responsibilities is inconceivable within their doctrinal horizons. What is more, fatalism would similarly fail the test because there would simply be no 'task', no 'to become free' in the midst of nihilistic despair because one would simply be fated to such a life. The 'future philosophers' would also have no *raison d'être* since if we are only destined a là some poor-man's version of *amor fati* (love of fate) then the following would also make no sense: 'that may be a strange and insane task, but it is a task—who would deny that?...Everybody will ask us that. And we, pressed this way, we have put the same question to ourselves a hundred times' (BGE 230). In fact, destination or determination in the case of our 'future philosophers' would ruin the subtle imagery of potentiality and 'danger' in which untimely figures emerge and take on the task of overcoming. They cannot simply be fated as per the fatalist doctrine; in fact, they must confront a reality of daunting odds because the exceptional ones (who know of a different greatness) have a much higher probability of not surviving owing to conditions more conducive for the proliferation of feeble mediocre characters. The life of the latter is easier than the hardship of the former in part because they are strongly integrated into the 'we'.

Responsibility and Capacities

Hence, the logic that finds the former having to be steeled by preparation and cultivation so that the weight of responsibility is not too onerous to bear is essentially realist thinking. It understands that *Dasein*—being there in the world of experience—underlies all moral claims and even the claim to being responsible for oneself that is inextricably bound up with life's conditions and the aforementioned 'tension' of the will to life. One must possess a capacity for transcendent responsibility rather than being compelled by juridical moral codes built upon guilt and the will to revenge (punishment) which is how modern liberalism now administers the 'moral will'. If you like, it is a substantivist-realist argument instead of a formalistic-idealist argument. Formal universalism would lose sight of the conditions of *Dasein* and the contextual limits of any *Bildung* or *bios* in which arise the vital nutrients for human cultivation. The penultimate end of the knowledgeable creator—the creation of new tables of the good (values)—is in fact made subject to this realist psycho-philosophical analysis. Note very closely the language used in the following (quoted) passage:

> He would even *determine* value and rank in accordance with *how much* and *how many* things one *could bear* and *take upon* himself, how *far* one *could extend* his responsibility (BGE 212, emphasis added).

New valuations and their relative position or status in a structure is made dependent upon 'how much' a human being can endure in this world, in their capacity to act upon the world in a particular way. This 'way' of acting or particular mode of existence within his *bios* is what 'his responsibility' entails. To 'legislate' upon Nature's animal-soul and to give himself goals that will realize (a different) greatness is Nietzsche's idea of the freedom *to be* responsible for yourself, for your relative 'servitude' (obedience) or 'mastery' (commanding freedom). There is, formally speaking, no absolute *a priori* freedom to meet—the Standard is an illusion of something mysterious called the *faculty* of reason.[13] One can *become* free; and one must become capable of incorporating responsibility in their cultivation of a noble spirit, a spirit that maintains a tension within itself. Without Being (*Sein*), we find the open-ended process of *Becoming* instead creating orders of value and freedom. The 'heaviest responsibilities' associated with this formation are described in the latest book of the *Gay Science* (351) as looming high above 'the people's' everydayness like a rumbling 'thundercloud'. The weight of such (tablets of) responsibilities is not given from on high by a Moses or God but rather by the necessity of overcoming the limits of formal moral obligations and their attendant psychology of 'bad conscience' (the law, mass politics, moral edifications). Weightiness, therefore, is not an outcome of abstract cognitive determinations of 'the good'; it is distinctly phenomenological, that is, a function of *Dasein* and its affects, drives, willing, thinking, creating, commanding and, finally, legislating power. Because traditional philosophers adopt an ahistorical view of responsibility they place the Will ahead of the concrete human being, forgetting that experiences of being human on earth is the sine qua non of responsibility in reality.

Weakness is a kind of pessimistic fatalism then because it limits the bounds of such experiences of life; they cannot endure these 'heaviest responsibilities' because they lack the necessary wherewithal, the wherewithal of 'affect of command' (see chapter one). To assimilate them into their very being they first would require 'growth', strength and height—all horticultural metaphors which Nietzsche's often happily deployed, particularly against the 'decadents' of Today. Once again, we see that 'becoming' can accommodate such a possibility, a possible development provided that is if the guilt-feelings of the bad conscience (psychology of will) are not too onerous to bear. Since there is no Will behind the willing expressed in 'how far one could extend' their responsibility, the *dunamai* behind one's *willing*ness to take on the heaviest responsibilities is more important. In moral terms: it is unfair to ask those who are 'unable' and unprepared to carry the weight of moral indebtedness that exceeds their being. Fairness in the democratic sense was not really Nietzsche's concern, but proportion or ratio of relative power, strength and psychological will certainly was. Why? Because like Hegel, Nietzsche placed the master-slave matrix at the centre of his thinking, a type of thinking that is thoroughly infused with the historicality and temporality of 'there-being' (*Dasein*) in the world. In which case, any imputation of a common identity to all human beings would be a denial of reality, unless one was to restrict the claim to a philosophical anthropology of the species man. Through time, humanity has differentiated itself in complex ways, but the class or type of 'masters' and 'slaves' has further stretched the distance between more feeble and more nobly strong human beings. This is also why Nietzsche worked so much against Kant and Idealism more generally; he repudiated Kant's attempt to give Christianity's universalistic ideals a rational, secular shell while seducing logicians and epistemologists at the same time. Earthly life is deeply variegated and the only singularity which obtains is that of the Whole, the whole of reality which encapsulates the *fatum* of individual human beings, their 'thunderclouds' and their 'two-powers, two-lives'. In archaic Greek terms—not in naturalistic fatalist terms—the Injustice of the cosmos conditions every struggle to become free (or merely happy), a moral-political point already raised in the Preface to *Human All Too Human* (6). The many-sided Whole that Nietzsche speaks of here is decisive for the making of noble free spirits, a type of individual who has extended its capacity for great responsibilities. Contrary to a peculiarly existential interpretation,[14] the art of self-making is contingent upon this Whole as a semblance of Time. In *Twilight of the Idols,* Nietzsche discusses the 'self' in terms of the overdetermination of the Whole even whilst urging us to think of goals of self-cultivation. These polarities define his metaphysics of being human: agency as cultivation and reality in its totality are interdependent polarities of the determinate. This would explain Nietzsche's penchant for language which seems to decentre the human being: 'no one *gives* man his qualities—neither God, nor society, nor his parents and ancestors, nor he himself...No one is responsible for man's being there at all, for his being such-and-such, or for his being in these circumstances or in his environment' (TI 9, 8).

So what is responsible for man's qualities? It is a *non sequitur* because responsibility cannot precede time; it cannot pre-empt becoming since it arises out of a *process* of form-making forces. Man's self-forming activity is itself one formative aspect of a complex configuration of forces shaping and forming the actual. The next passage confirms this interdependence: 'The fatality of his essence is not to be disentangled from the fatality of all that has been and will be' (TI 9, 8). Note here the temporality of *has been* and *will be*. That is to say, there is no imaginary prime mover or Designer 'behind' becoming as it unfolds in time. Denying both teleology and *causa prima*, Nietzsche conceives of the human-animal as without any 'special purpose, of a will, and end' and thus states 'one belongs to the whole, one is in the whole' and to that extent 'One is necessary' as a 'piece of the fatefulness' of the whole because 'there is nothing besides the whole' (TI 9, 8). Yet this whole lacks a semblance of unity, which both Kant and Hegel had claimed existed (as Spirit). The liberation from Today's 'bad conscience' then begins from this metaphysical liberation: 'That nobody is held responsible any longer, that the mode of being may not be traced back to a *causa prima*, that the world does not form a unity either as a sensorium or as "spirit" . . . with this alone is the innocence of becoming restored' (TI 9, 8). Responsibility obtains then not before Time but in the *hic et nunc* (here and now) of becoming responsible. We are 'free' because there is no mystical force that has destined us according to some grand design, purpose, biological end or metaphysical ideal of 'improving' mankind. This *hic et nunc* leaves us responsible *in* the whole, which in a sense makes the task even more complex because our doing—a praxeological 'forming and valuing'—is configured by a web of complex interdependent forces and relations. Nietzsche says we redeem the world by understanding it this way: to stop the pretension that a 'God' or absolute Spirit moves behind everything and face up to the challenge of the task of the future is to inaugurate the 'supermoral' individual capable of promising himself a future (GM I: 2). This redemption of the world happens primarily by way of a form of self-cultivation that incorporates 'a true consciousness of power and freedom', one that is fashioned around the human being 'who is *permitted to promise*' (GM I: 2). Nietzsche's explanation of the origin of responsibility (in his particular sense) is bound up with the preparatory, conditional basis of one's being as something 'calculable, regular, necessary' and therefore full of promise—a promise of the future. As a 'supermoral' philosopher Nietzsche's philosophical-anthropological psychology demands that the animal-human be bred according to 'condition and preparation' to enable it to make promises after it was possible to make 'man to a certain degree necessary, uniform, like among like, regular, and accordingly predictable' (GM I: 2). That is, a certain structured nature[15] which 'man' achieves above the animal is predicated on a development in time and this human development, importantly, requires a self-image that vouches 'for [man] himself *as future*' (GM I: 1). A self-image formed on a spirit of affirmation that sees man as unfolding *in* time, within the whole of becoming. Part of this whole therefore is the capacity to make promises because one's temporal experience in the world (*Dasein*) possesses a futurity that now is integral to one's self-image.

This is a pre-condition for those who can become responsible: a futural sense of our 'here and now' equips us rightly to make promises. Nietzsche rejects shallow promise-makers, that is, those who rhetorically can commit to a promise but are not capable of fulfilling their promise. They lack depth, lack preparatory breeding ('making') and therefore of necessity have only a capricious grasp of what promise-making entails. Capricious because they are unable to fulfill the ends of any promise given to an other. Why make promises if you cannot follow through with your commitments? The question gains saliency if we also foolishly endanger the trustworthiness normally associated with such promises of commitment. Those whose trustworthiness goes unquestioned on the other hand are in fact able, capable free spirits who possess the strength, pride and confidence to maintain responsibilities—they "realize" their commitments. It is a substantivist realist critique of formalistic external imperatives to 'act responsibly' that Nietzsche's instigates. No doubt, this owes to his strength in depth-psychology and his 'immoralist' critical perspective against *Sittlichkeit*—customary morality. Since the latter in reality weakens the will of most moderns, it leaves modern individuals ill prepared for the 'highest responsibilities' which attend the will to freedom. Instead of English happiness being pursued, Nietzsche's call is to resist customary morality—and the 'psychology of will' that underscores it—and instead seek after long distant goals (such as freedom) which turn you into an 'untimely' figure. This requires that responsibility must therefore grow out of a more fertile soil if it is to be cultivated by human beings who are capable of marshalling (in productive ways) their own contesting drives, desires or strivings. It is, otherwise, something too precious to be wasted in futile,[16] guilt-ridden, customary morals that build up 'bad conscience' in those souls who must carry the dead weight of formal, universal moral imperatives. The 'promise of the future' indeed lies within this very *Sittlichkeit*: to overcome is to hold out a promise of a *supramoral* existence in the moment, the now, as was exemplified by Johann Goethe's naturalistic, tragic artistic appreciation. Thus while decadence may predominate in today's nihilistic culture it does not necessarily preclude a resistance and noble struggle of which a strong will is capable. Perhaps Nietzsche here is all too alert to the animalic nature of human desires and instincts that sway individuals either into herd-behavior or general conformity in the form of 'English happiness'. That is to say, a noble transcendent responsibility may be rather too difficult to pursue when the tangible, empirical stimuli of life point in the opposite direction: presence is privileged over and above becoming (futurity) as is submission (to coded meanings of 'good') over and above overcoming because the latter requires a self-disciplined soul. Here the 'inner' and 'outer' conditions come into proximity: objective social conditions weigh heavily on the soul and thus necessitate an overcoming of a spiritual kind as well. To overcome a 'bad conscience' of the soul is the proper necessary work of a noble spirit that is driven by a strong will to legislate its own will and authority upon the world. However, the sentiments of guilt, *ressentiment* and fear all too often impede a large number of individuals taking up this worthy struggle and resistance. To relieve the dead weight of such sentiments, particularly if they arise out of imposing grand imperatives, ordinary souls ordinarily take flight in the desire to obtain happiness and pleasure in a world of the finite. At this point, the guilt-burdened citizen who 'falls short' of the mark of responsibility must have sufficiently Apollonian eyes to see farther on the horizon.

Nietzsche had such eyes: he declared the future philosophers were coming over the horizon even if they had yet to be announced. To know is to know what has been will recur, and what will come as a result of our self-overcoming. It is made evident in his conception of philosophy as a process of self-transfiguration[17]—philosophy being the spiritualized drive for self-transfiguration. But like Plato, Nietzsche understood that not all 'men' or persons are philosophical in this particular sense; some are ill-suited to attain such 'eyes' since their 'natures'—desires, pleasures, affects, impulses and soul—work better within the parameters of Today and its culture. Some are, for instance, busy machinists building bridges for an industrious age of machinists where even the Protestant Sabbath has been transformed into a work ethic to service the "workshop of the world"—England.[18] Others may be better suited to pursue chemistry and understand life 'organically' as processes of interaction and alchemical transformation. Instead of interpreting this through the usual (democratic) lens of inequality between persons, Nietzsche prefers to grasp the particular instance as part of the greater Whole, thus maintaining his all important distance between types and preserving the distinctiveness of each particular 'perspective', i.e. the chemical, mechanical, artistic, religious and philosophical. It appears therefore that no 'type' of person is *a priori* excluded from the potentiality (in time) of overcoming—there is no formal exclusion in his realm of freedom. Distinction—that quality that prevents industrial leveling from flattening everything—is recognized because the Whole cannot be constituted by a singular *ousia* or substance. Since history shows the variegation of humankind, Nietzsche as a realist Thucydidean-like philosopher wished to avoid romantic illusions of everyone having the wherewithal to accomplish great responsibilities *without having first been prepared*. Understanding the ancients so well and in particular the Greek's athletic Olympian struggle to achieve physical and 'soulful' extension and refinement, he used psychologico-analytical methods to evaluate the reality of *all* kinds of moral agents being prepared to question and challenge their own, customary reality. After all, in German *Sittlichkeit* better conveys the way in which 'moral life' and customary conventions are intertwined in one's life. It suggests that whilst human beings may find their *forte* in different approaches to and perspectives on life, it does not necessarily follow that all are *willing* to behave like salmon—many simply want to enjoy the 'flow' of life through custom, convention, security and predictable norms belonging to life in a village (valley and not mountaintop). Any reigning in of vast differences would also diminish the distance between historically and genealogically differentiated persons, persons whose very embodiment is inscribed with these distinctive qualities, capacities and, most importantly, limits. No human being, according to his philosophical anthropology, is devoid of these three definitive dimensions of life: qualities, capacities and limits. Their souls are archeologically stratified as a result; no individual soul in a sense is identical to another, no matter what British sociology claimed to the contrary. And this is wholly consistent with what we said earlier about Nietzsche's understanding of Greek *ananke*: of necessity, our individual morphology is part of the Whole and this means we can possess lesser or greater degrees of strength, will power, drive, wisdom and self-discipline—in sum, varying capabilities.

It is now possible to draw out another implicit thread in Nietzsche's moral theory regarding responsibility. The idea that one's morphology is linked inexorably to a person's capacity to fulfill their commitments in promises made to an *other* is particularly interesting. It is partly because it runs counter to most kinds of modern social contractarian, constructivist, and utopian liberal or socialist philosophies that take their departure, to varying degrees, from the revolutionary ideals of Jean Jacques Rousseau. Furthermore, since it is highly problematic to conceive of self-overcoming as derived somehow from a Darwinian naturalistic principle, Nietzsche's idea of being prepared and capable of great responsibilities is one that more closely approximates Goethe's artistic-scientific sensibility. For Nietzsche never really departed from his bicameral conception of reality, first promulgated in *Human All Too Human* (251), as the 'two compartments of the brain'—science and non-science. And this is what Goethe's achievement was from the perspective of high culture: it substituted *either/or* for *and/with* in respect of two modes of apprehending life in its entirety—the artistic and the scientific understanding combined. So while it is true to say that Nietzsche like Spinoza beforehand dispensed with the hidden God problem, he nevertheless resisted both wholly naturalistic and voluntaristic ideas of becoming free and promise-worthy. Between 'self-mastery' and, on the other hand, fated destiny according to one's inherited psychophysiology, there lies deep fertile soil for cultivating more free, disciplined and ripe individuals who are capable of upholding promises in the future. Deploying the 'two compartments of the brain'—science and art—to unmask 'that freedom from all partiality in relation to the total problem of life', Nietzsche sought an alternative path to natural determinism (Darwinism) and ascetic-idealist self-mastery. One's nature, one's character, style and spiritual fortitude in other words is neither entirely accidental nor environmental nor even wholly due to one's efforts. And although Nietzsche's (E II: 9) porous self-understanding points to an unwitting accidental ripening—'one day all my capacities, suddenly ripe, *leaped forth* in their ultimate perfection'—it by no means discounts the general thesis of human beings *becoming* ripened through time by processes of self-cultivation (and degeneration). Rather as a philosopher of the power of unconscious instincts as against surface-level consciousness, he sought to show that neither 'free will' nor conscious ideal strivings are responsible for who is and who is not responsible in the end. The philosophers as much as the 'improvers of mankind' have erred in wrongly attributing outcomes to the purposive aims, ideals, strivings and willing of conscious rational animals. As Aristotle once said about happiness, Nietzsche too declares that we only properly grasp our nature's unfolding form in time retrospectively: it suddenly appears in the course of life what this interesting animal has become in respect of both ascent (growth) and descent (decadence). 'I never even suspected what was growing in me' claimed Nietzsche, as his capacities were the result of so many gradual developments of instinct and thought which underlay the 'whole surface of consciousness':

> the organizing "idea" that is destined to rule keeps growing deep down—it begins to command; slowly it leads us *back* from side roads and wrong roads; it prepares *single* qualities and fitnesses that will one day prove to be indispensable as means toward a whole—one by one, it trains all *subservient* capacities before giving any hint of the dominant task, "goal", "aim", or "meaning" (E II: 9).

Nietzsche's self-understanding of his own capacities points to the centrality of the 'long, secret work and artistry of my instinct' which consciousness only much later grapples with and adduces: 'I cannot remember that I ever tried hard—no trace of struggle can be demonstrated in my life' (E II: 9). These less than convincing observations of his own life-course do not necessarily constitute the totality of the event of becoming. His point rather is to demystify the intentionality and ideal-purposiveness of 'freedom of the will' as represented in the minds of modern decadents and thinkers. Nietzsche's self-reflections follow on from his ruminations about the priority of not knowing what one will become: 'To become what one is, one must not have the faintest notion what one is' (E II: 9). This is of some importance to his philosophical anthropology of our nature's unfolding: 'So many dangers that the instinct comes too soon to "understand itself"' with the use of prose about 'purpose' and 'imperatives' (E II: 9). The abovementioned 'organizing idea' must be allowed to do its work in due time and if consciousness should prematurely intercede because it behaves according to some (external) imperative then it thwarts the development of individual capacities. In this same passage, Nietzsche raises the penultimate task of a 're-valuation of all values' in which 'more capacities may have been needed than have ever dwelt together in a single individual' whereby an 'order of rank among these capacities' is similarly developed (E II: 9). Hence, to hurry up the process of growth and development will unduly weaken the possibility of a proper ripening of the requisite capacities for such a grand task. What is required? He says, 'An order of rank among these capacities; distance; the art of separating without setting against one another; to mix nothing, to "reconcile" nothing; a tremendous variety that is nevertheless the opposite of chaos' (E II: 9). One cannot simply decide rationally 'this or that' about things because these capacities grow very slowly and do so in response to various stimuli which register beneath the surface of consciousness. The Will as conscious agent comes in rather late if it wants to act as the *causa prima* of my capacities and the task of my overcoming. Decoupling the Wille from my condition of freedom does not imply irresponsibility but rather liberation from the illusion ('psychology of will') that a reified force drives my everyday conduct and judgments. What is of greater importance in this quoted passage is the world-disclosing claim that more capacities may be needed than have ever dwelt together 'in a single individual'. That is, Nietzsche inflects futurity back into the formation of individuals as historically formed and cultivated (educated) beings.

'Genealogy', for instance, implies that the capacities of human beings have hitherto been temporally limited; the scope of these capacities within modernity proves insufficient for the task at hand. Nietzsche appears to have reached the conclusion that past overcomings and responsible promise-making had derived from capacities that proved efficacious at the time, i.e. Napoleonic Europe. As the 'last man' of European nihilism appears at the *dawn* of a new age, thinkers and evaluators with more extensive and subtle capacities will be required. The question for us moderns is whether or not we are 'ahead' or behind Goethe, Spinoza, Hegel, Newton, Da Vinci and Beethoven in our intellectual and soul-capacities. Is, in other words, human cultivation and education at present on the wane or inclining toward new heights? Kant is predisposed toward the latter judgment while Nietzsche most definitely sides with the former in both *Beyond Good and Evil* and *Twilight of the Idols*. Degeneracy has of course predominated in other ages and civilizations as has also generation and innovation. Hence Nietzsche's Schopenhauerian conception of becoming informs his understanding of the *Zeitgeist* as reflective of recurring oscillations between high-low, noble-degenerate, creative-stagnate and free-slavish forces. This has the effect of relativizing the present crisis in nihilistic values thus reducing its calamitous appearance and thereby giving impetus to a *faith* in the potentiality of generative forces to come forth as more extensive capacities (in the ripest of fruits, i.e. sovereign individuals). The *anti-Christ* Nietzsche, to be sure, is not altogether bereft of faith-concepts even if it entails imagery of an 'immoralist'. Zarathustra, that is, cannot entirely escape the *eschaton*[19] of the future since this untimely figure embodies the point at which 'time crosses into eternity'. However at this point we cannot stop to ponder the exact mytho-religious dimensions of Nietzsche's harbinger of the future to come. Our concern here is more precisely that of the preparation of individuals whose capacities would not simply mirror those of other times but represent a new vigor and rigorousness.

Once again, against the claimed thesis of becoming as an unchanging repetition in time Nietzsche we can see here demands that a new configuration for the soul (spirit) will be required. Contrary to cultural pessimism, he asserted in *Beyond Good and Evil* more clearly than elsewhere the promise of futurity in 'man':

> anyone who has the rare eye for the over-all danger that "man" himself *degenerates*...With a single glance he sees what, given a favorable accumulation and increase of forces and tasks, might yet *be made of man*; he knows with all the knowledge of his conscience how man is still unexhausted for the greatest possibilities and how often the type "man" has already confronted enigmatic decisions and new paths (203).

Of particular significance here is the claim 'might yet be made of man' because the 'greatest possibilities' for man have yet to be exhausted. Provided the interpreter has sufficiently perspicacious eyes to discern how 'a favorable accumulation and increase of forces and tasks' can yield the 'greatest possibilities' for self-responsibility apropos self-cultivation (*not* self-mastery though). This futurity, with its *potentiality* for overcoming servitude, can be recognized in the fact that the human being 'has already confronted enigmatic decisions and new paths' along the way of its becoming. Embarking upon the road of self-responsibility is of course fraught with dangers and degeneracy is a very real possibility given the penchant for communal security in the human-animal. Yet adaptation does not always impede innovation even if it might stifle growth and creative regeneration. Nietzsche's pseudo-Darwinian ideas do not prevent him from making the argument that human beings, unlike plants, can come under the sway of symbolic-political 'abundance', luxury and security. Civilization or political civilized communities may in other words foster petrifaction of the vital drives because customary ways (morality) take a hold of existence—*gesicherte Existenz* (secure existence). When the means of life become superabundant then 'the tremendous tension decreases' both within and outside the individual, hence the danger of cultural stagnation. Yet at the same time it is infused with possibilities, including the possibility that such conditions are conducive for variation and so allowing different 'types' to emerge—'the individual', as he calls it, emerges and thus too the commander: the one who is 'obliged to give himself laws and to develop his own arts and wiles for self-preservation, self-enhancement, self-redemption' (BGE 262). (Once again, *contra* naturalism organic life cannot know or experience self-redemption, namely that which is 'of spirit'.)

What is clear thus far is that Nietzsche's idea of becoming encompasses cultivation, preparation and the possibility of self-responsibility while simultaneously holding on to the inherent risks and dangers of life. He fashions a promise of the future for the human which remains decidedly non-deterministic and yet also affirmative in spirit. Instead of focusing on 'freedom from' (stagnation), he outlines a 'freedom to' in terms of the inherent futurity in every *Dasein* or *Wesen*, even if it is an existence fraught with limitations. This stance of his *gaya scienza*—to affirm life yet to acknowledge its two-sidedness—obviates the problem of 'Schopenhauerian pessimism' while retaining the ethic of (self) responsibility which Nietzsche took to be the mark of a noble outlook on life. What I mean here by 'responsibility' is that Nietzsche committed himself to the value of the 'highest responsibility' by expounding a realist philosophy of life that simultaneously acknowledged 'the dangers' (of error and decline) and the possibilities (growth, expansion, promises). His idea of *becoming* rested therefore not on naturalistic fatalist principles but on the tragic artist's knowledge of the *tension* in man, his social structure (*bios*) and quanta of power in general. Those who evade responsibilities because they fear the weight of them are feeble or weak-willed persons who find the 'tension of the bow' threatening—they cannot bear the struggle in other words. And we have already seen the great importance of 'pathos' in Nietzsche's tragic realist conception of life: the struggle, the affects and impulses of sentiments which feed the spirit of a human being or culture. Struggle, including internal contestation (*polemos*), is necessary for the expansion of capacities that may realize 'the possibility' of overcoming unfreedom (e.g. herd-morality) at any given moment. Yet the 'civilizing processes' of established political societies can incline individuals to a softening, luxuriant contentment in the herd's mode of living and thinking—that is 'the danger'. Hence Nietzsche's derision of democracy: in mass society the dangerous error of dissipating the spiritual drive to struggle and strive ('willing') works against the emergence of real thinkers, noble individuals and a hard disciplined self-responsibility. In particular, mass values or herd-thinking tend to thwart 'the individual'—a phenomenon of distinction or variation or 'autonomy', hence the heavy tones of *un*democratic criticism in his work. To be sure, Nietzsche's 'pathos of distance' does not discriminate on the basis of social categories per se: race, class, sex or faith. Distinction instead turns upon the master-slave dyad that is historically specific rather than ontologically grounded in a single group.

It is worth mentioning at this point not least for the reason that possible overcomings of spurious values are not a priori the preserve of any one class of people. Sovereign individuals, his 'ripest fruits' in human cultivation, as he called them in *Genealogy of Morals* in fact are irreducible to any single privileged 'herd' or group of society. We must remember his previous sanction against the simple claim that socialization brings about 'this or that' type of person. Observe the irony of the charge of aristocratism: although Nietzsche despised herd thinking and valuations, the misreading of him (as politically aristocratic) falls back upon the primacy of a class or group constituting such 'sovereign individuals'. Yet we find quite to the contrary that his analysis of master-slave relations in *Beyond Good and Evil* (260-61) points to: a) throughout history in all 'dependent social strata' the common man '*was* only what he was *considered*' by others and nothing else; b) in all higher cultures an interpenetration occurs between the morality of the 'ruling group' and that of subordinate groups; c) in the beginning, the noble class 'was always the barbarian caste', not the established ruling class; d) and their nobility was not defined by physical strength but instead 'strength of the soul'. Overall, the main marker for noble commanding is whether or not persons are 'more *whole* human beings'; restrictive, partial, small one-sidedness is perhaps the key signifier of slavish predispositions—not class, race, sex or physiology. The implication for our theory of responsibility which is necessarily extracted from Nietzsche's undeveloped philosophy of freedom is that *capacities* and *preparedness* are not social determined per se. Historical conditions certainly influence them, but otherwise no single social status or category grouping has priority in the elevation of man through extended capacities. Capacities, that is, which are developed through cultivation, struggle and *paideia*, as the Greeks had known it or in German *Bildung*. This open-ended process of historical becoming requires no privileged subject; it keeps the question of 'elevation' or spiritual enhancement suspended in the promise of the future that mankind itself represents. 'We have a different faith', Nietzsche declared, one that looks 'toward spirits strong and original enough to provide the stimuli for opposite valuations and to revalue and invert "eternal values"'—who are these original spirits? They are forerunners, 'men of the future who in the present tie the knot and constraint that forces the will of millennia upon *new tracks*' (BGE 203). Note the specifically strong language used to describe the necessities of overcoming: an Alexandrian-like will to tie the knot with powers of constraint (discipline) to reign in the 'will of millennia' instead of merely centuries for directing along 'new tracks'.

This finally explains why Nietzsche determined it necessary that new expansive capacities in individuals—eventually also classes—be cultivated for the *promise* (of the future) to be realized. Might and not merely struggle will be necessary in the morphology of those 'strong and original spirits' who will be the forerunners of a new age, a new table of values. The 'last man' of modern English happiness will not prove adept for the task it seems; the task is quite grand just as the goals of futurity are about 'greatness'. Hence, the charge of aristocratism comes unstuck at this point since noble (empirical) men and women are by no means resiliently robust—toughness is not the preserve of any one class unless of course we return to Homer's heroic warriors. *Prima facie* there is no case to be made that human beings are 'predestined' for such toughness or robust overcoming; yet the concept of *amor fati* (love of fate) ambiguously[20] suggests some human natures will inevitably be less or more predisposed toward such tough tasks. Variations in capacities will make some less and others more capable of embarking upon 'new tracks' after having successfully mastered the 'will of millennia' for this purpose. Denying the idea of a Designer (God) or absolute Spirit (Hegel) being responsible for such predestinations,

Nietzsche appeared to similarly eschew the logic of 'British physiologists' and Stoics who looked to nature. Are 'free spirits' in any way fated to take on grueling grand tasks of transformation? They cannot be because Nietzsche constantly reminds us of the tragic risk recurring in every society—'the accidental' in the 'law of absurdity'—as part of the 'whole economy of mankind': the higher type of human being will most likely not turn out well (BGE 62). Against Darwin, Nietzsche always maintained that the lowly type usually predominates in its environment while the exceptional higher spirits have to fight the probability of elimination. If it was their naturalistic fate to be 'higher' (nobler) then why in actuality do they not prevail? This is an important question because it acts as a significant counter-point to the claim that 'philosophers of the future' were somehow predestined. Between the opposite poles of a fated destiny on one hand and complete self-mastery on the other, stands the problem of what to do with 'man'—'the problem of man' *par excellence*. What I wish to raise to self-awareness here is that which Nietzsche himself subtly felt regarding the *tension* in every estimation and decipherment: between the absurd *reductio ad absurdum* of sensualism (how can organs determine the object-world) and idealism (faculties finding reason in nature) arises the question of how to place our awareness of 'the problem' (man) within our very own estimation of him? Why the human has now become a question *for* itself owes in part to the transfiguration of Homeric fatefulness by numerous pursuits of the 'seekers of knowledge' who finally arrive at the doorstep of life to ask continually questions.

In 1887 Nietzsche states in his most joyful work *The Gay Science*, that after the end of the 'pre-moral' naturalistic existence a new profundity painfully emerges, one that owes to the willing power of persons/groups. The will to truth henceforth transforms the earth and manifests itself in the will to question life itself:

> The trust in life is gone: life itself has become a *problem*...The attraction of everything problematic, the delight in x, however, is so great in such more spiritual, more spiritualized men that this delight flares up again and again like a bright blaze over all the distress of what is problematic, over all the danger of uncertainty...We know a new happiness (GS *P*3).

From this perspective, a pure fatefulness is no longer feasible, no longer acceptable. We are too serious, too profound not only to dispel the magic of Homeric gods but also to see life merely as it is. Problematization—the act of disclosure, measurement, evaluation, naming, separating, foresight and reflection—transforms the 'once natural' condition of human-animal. With the emergence of 'morality of custom' (*Daybreak*), 'philosophy' as an art of spiritual transfiguration radically alters the configuration of subjective life. Such a transfiguration—borne of the pain and 'errors' of religious morals—engenders 'long and dangerous exercises of self-mastery [where] one emerges as a different person, with a few more question marks—above all with the *will* henceforth to question further, more deeply, severely, harshly, evilly and quietly than one had questioned heretofore' (GS *P*3). Hence contingent conditions, circumstances, fortuitous and accidental events, and indeterminate decisions all now occur within the broader milieu of no longer trusting life but questioning it continuously. Hence Nietzsche himself cannot but question his own views both of 'love of fate' and on the other hand, artistic self-mastery in the art of living nobly. He was all too aware that his own problematization of freedom-destiny was already enormously affected by this 'itinerary of the animal-human soul' and how it in turn was transformed by the experimenters' will to knowledge. That is to say, the enigma underlying self-knowledge cannot be simply resolved by recourse to old-fashioned fatalist principles. This is what I referred to as 'necessity' earlier in the discussion: Nietzsche understood the *necessity* of rejecting both fatalist and self-mastery propositions whilst also finding it 'necessary' himself to identify shifts in modalities of being that suggest *greater* or *lesser* responsibility and freedom. He was being responsible by acknowledging the limits of both *amor fati* and creative self-mastery: science—non-science are thus brought into a productive relation to culminate in a kind of *Aufhebung* (a higher level of synthetic interpretation).

We can summarize this productive tension—a tension rather than a standard duality—in the form of two archetypes of man (human natures): *homo creativa* and *homo natura*. The former points to vital forces of self-forming while the latter suggests a relatively fixed disposition, a kind of characterological profile signified by an invisible strata of something 'unteachable, some granite of spiritual *fatum*' (BGE 231). This identity structure is represented by a form of 'this is I' in response to life's problems; moreover when solutions to problems inspire faith in ourselves it indicates how problems are essentially 'settled in him'—a basic structure of character that 'very deep down' appears unchangeable. In which case whenever Nietzsche speaks of the dice of τύχη (chance, luck) in Heraclitus' writing, it suggests this special convergence of forces, relations and individual will power that operates in time in the body of this particular 'this is I'. Clearly, it suggests that positivistic 'determinism' is flawed; and that we are, on the other hand, too profound to accept the Fate of the Gods. Yet life is ever so fragmentary and contingent, partly because of the flight of knowledge and its concomitant questioning of life, and partly because of the relatively indeterminate nature of challenge-response matrices of persons with differing quanta of *will* (will power). Nietzsche's supermoral ethics hence suggest that no universal imperative or 'measure' is supple enough for 'the sovereign individual' and its particular will to responsibility insofar as it embodies individual capacities for the 'weightiest responsibilities'. Violence is done wherever uniformity is allowed to reign over differentiated human beings; and since capacities are dependent upon forces in time as well as self-forming process, including modern institutions, large variations 'grow' out of our efforts to cultivate and educate human spirits. Engineering variations down to a mean average would only endanger the very *tension* that drives creative, innovative 'education'—cultivation becomes stunted. Stunted individuals rarely are prepared to welcome the greatest responsibilities that time throws up to one's *Dasein*. They mostly fear and at least struggle with such responsibilities, remaining incapable of welcoming the highest responsibilities. To 'be ready' is not to suggest nobility of birth, social class or physiology but rather a supple, vigorous morphology of the soul. Why?

Because Nietzsche had no faith in static categories or objects: historical philosophy, he argued, had to think Being as becoming; therefore no single object (or
class) could qualify as a privileged agent if the 'promise of the future' is to reside within becoming's potentiality.[21]

In synoptic 'comprehensive' terms, this potentiality is open-ended rather
than closed (teleological). But we must acknowledge at the same the order of
limits that Nietzsche places at the *microscopic* level: individuated beings. For at
the singular level of existence human beings do experience degrees of limitation
or constraint. Other than political-social relations of domination there are *limited
capacities* in individuals themselves and these impede the realization of potentialities that lie prospectively in the 'future to come'. In effect, this places a limit
on the 'creator' in us; we create in time while we ourselves are also shaped by
time. To overemphasize the creative drive, as self-mastery does, would be symptomatic of our will to deceive (ourselves)—deception being integral to
Nietzsche's understanding of human nature. Deception is related to this willful
overestimation of a mastery creative will: 'a shutting of one's window, an internal No to this or that thing, a refusal to let things approach, a kind of state of
defense against much that is knowable, a satisfaction with the dark, with the
limiting horizon ...all of which is necessary in proportion to a spirit's power to
appropriate, its "digestive capacity"' (BGE 230). Under conditions of self-
deception, it therefore becomes more complex as to what limit an individual can
work to with respect to difficult, demanding responsibilities. The resistful element here is not 'fate' per se but rather the constitutive nature of our 'digestive
capacity' which though a product of time cannot be wholly assailed by the force
of overcoming. In a rare passage on personal genealogy or lineage Nietzsche
makes reference to the role of heredity in explaining inferences which might be
drawn from 'breeding' (rearing): 'If one knows something about the parents, an
inference about the child is permissible: any disgusting incontinence, any nook
envy, a clumsy insistence that one is always right' (BGE 264). This comment is
preceded by a more macroscopic claim to limits (resistance to overcoming) in
the same passage: 'One cannot erase from the soul of a human being what his
ancestors liked most to do and did most constantly...It is simply not possible
that a human being should *not* have the qualities and preferences of his parents
and ancestors in his body, whatever appearances may suggest to the contrary'.
Rather than worrying about the sometime Lamarckian heredity overtones of
such passages—legitimately raised and scrutinized by Walter Kaufmann some
decades ago[22]—we focus instead on what this 'good European' did with genealogy to explain limitations *in time*, and not 'recurrence' as Gilles Deleuze preferred. This passage shows that instead of a repetition of the same or the past,
individuals are plunged into the potentiality of time's promise with particular
sensibilities rather than merely as *tabula rasa*.

It is in essence a kind of historical sociology of morphologies of the soul and
body that does not 'naturalize' one's capacities for freedom and responsibility.
Education within acculturation is what these formative characteristics and
'ways' of existing denote; they appear to lay the ground for any social learning
and historical transformation that may occur owing to the work of cultivation,

'growing' and finally self-overcoming. Without it, there would in fact be no overcoming because there would no existing ways and thinking to be 'overcome'. To overcome is to overcome the fear of exceeding one's given limits and known parameters of capabilities. Hence, Nietzsche's invitation to realize a form of freedom that includes responsibilities requires, to say it again, preparation and enablement. Such a preparatory disciplined kind of education would acknowledge rather than disavow this aforesaid 'digestive capacity' principally because hard responsibility requires the virtue of 'dare to be honest' with yourself. Facticity, through the eyes of honesty, would in fact aide the task of knowing *what* to overcome—freedom is an ability 'to' rather than 'from' something. Namely, to a) acknowledge what is your own intestinal fortitude while b) striving to overcome and extend this fortitude into a new *forte* is the art of a comprehensive creator—the artist who knows the limit and yet challenges it continuously. Therefore Nietzsche is no simple fatalist or naturalist but rather an affirmative thinker of the *possibility* of (self) overcoming in a realist mode (akin to the spirit of Thucydides). Only a realist would similarly demand that responsibility attend human freedom; realism dictates knowing what is genealogical only strengthens one's capacity to exceed the given limit, the given *arche* (order) of *Wesen*. Nietzsche's idea of freedom encompasses this call to rupture the *arche* of thought that we each encounter in existence and yet are not necessarily always faithful to.

Hence our argument thus far suggests that Nietzsche has no faith in the heredity of things per se, but rather posits that human beings all too readily resort to these inherited characteristics to explain away their reluctance to engage responsibilities and freedom more generally. In other words, a historical 'limit' becomes an excuse for feebleness; and plebeians of the spirit are spiritually feeble rather than noble. Nietzsche's hard realism points to the reality that what often equips us for life is in fact some kind of impediment to freedom or joy; hence what heredity gives us is not pure restraint but instead the challenging impetus to overcome resistance and inertia. Otherwise, we face what Nietzsche found most appreciable in the writings of Plato: general conformity arising out of a happy slave mentality. 'We, however, want to become those we are—human beings who are new, unique, and incomparable, who give themselves laws, who create themselves' said Nietzsche in his most 'scientific' phase (GS 335). Does this constitute a contradiction of what has been said so far? Are we incomparable 'unique' persons because we create ourselves? To speak of 'new' and of those who 'create themselves' may appear to contradict the proposition that our heritage conditions our being in this world. Arguably, these two propositions may conflict with each other if it were not for the kind of realism that Nietzsche maintains in his joyful science—a science of that which is 'necessary' in things (as per the Greek concept) as we become those which we are. This embrace of necessity in its broader sense ought not to be confused with a blind determinism since Nietzsche abjured all forms of positivist thinking, especially teleological forms of determinism.[23] The complex perspective we elaborated in a previous chapter under the aegis of Nietzsche's liking for a more 'comprehensive viewpoint' demonstrates that necessity plays a pivotal role in the ancient

Greek sense of this word. This is captured in the following passage of the *Gay Science* (335), the famous 'long live physics' passage: 'To that end we must become the best learners and discoverers of everything that is lawful and necessary in the world: we must become physicists in order to be able to be creators in this sense'.

The necessity to create, to overcome through creativity, is itself part of the operation of 'Ανάγκη φύσιος in this world—hence these dimensions of becoming human (as an unfolding process) are not antithetical to each other. Self-creation and overcoming, that is, are not disposed against what is 'necessary' in this world. If they were then we would simply relapse into the pitfalls of Idealism and its metaphysics, wishing to pitch 'freedom—determinism' against each other as the 'old Kant' was wont to do. In contradistinction to idealist thinking, Nietzsche posits what Da Vinci, Raphel and Thucydides well understood: the virtue of excellent craftwork requires knowledge of a specific terrain and its workable materials, in short 'physics'. Physics, broadly understood, enables one to operate in this world effectively, enhancing our capacity to create anew out of so many transformations (i.e. perspectival truths) which nature could never replicate, thus overturning and overcoming what went before as lawful truth. One then takes on responsibilities because excuses and 'ignorance' are ignoble in the eyes and ears of 'comprehensive ones'. Noble eyes and ears that are in pursuit of knowledge do not tolerate such excuse-makings; ignorance of the art or 'science' of being is an insufficient cause for being slavish, for being unable to create and thus become a 'creator' of value.

Yet this is what the majority offer up when resistance is first encountered; challenges further exaggerate a dependency on excuses (i.e. heredity of 'digestive capacities') and feeble ignorance. To learn physics for instance is to learn how the de-deified world of existence works and this is useful for all prospective *creators* who find necessity not to be an evil but an operative mode that may be deployed for *their* purposes. Against (most variants of) naturalism Nietzsche maintained that Nature has no purpose, no purposive underlying logic to it; therefore, it is incumbent upon us as creators to give purpose to (human) nature, to give it value and measure from the perspective of what he called the comprehensive artist—the real artist who harnesses nature's 'necessity' and thus overcomes present limits. Of course, this is all summarized in the concept of 'becoming': closure and openness unravel, ravel and then intertwine continuously so that the complex process of becoming that which you are can no longer be usefully understood within static oppositional terms. To delude ourselves that the world simply is or that accident and chance decide what happens in time would be simple-minded naiveté. Whereas a philosophy of becoming in its profundity understands that phenomena are subject to mobile (quanta of) forces that hold sway over them for particular reasons. Heredity is one such example and it denies that the world is constituted simply by accident, fate or chance. Instead of finding physics threatening or all determining, the creator marshals its insights to achieve what it wills over brute nature. Life as exploitation, *zoi*, now means the exploitation of natural philosophy (physics) for the purposes of new goals, evaluations and 'tables of the good'. This is freedom in essence; not a freedom 'from' but a willing, creative rendering that establishes a 'promise' in time's becoming (one's future) owing to the power of one to assume responsibility for one's life and acquired duties (i.e. 'fate'). It is linked to our discussion of Free Will in a previous chapter which demonstrated that freedom, for Nietzsche, was not a liberation 'from' something' but rather the command-will *to* overcome resistance to freedom. Such freedom does not pretend to have any inevitability or certitude about it, but is instead a facet of tragic wisdom in its broad sense, a will to life that embraces both destiny and self-overcoming. For this reason it is more prudent to speak of self-overcoming rather than self-*mastery*, the latter denotative of a problematic voluntarism that threatens to engulf life. Conjoining freedom to the kind of tragic wisdom, which Nietzsche advocated against pessimism and the naiveté of 'free will', renders freedom stronger and more resilient to errors within humanism and ascetic-naturalistic forms of self-mastery.[24] This is necessary, as the reason why 'I am a Destiny'—why a human being is shaped by time, its limits and the individual's artistic plan—is because no single human being can wholly master the forces of history, its *bios* and the future that is promised but as yet not realized.

The Task of Responsibility Beyond Destiny

A complex notion of responsibility thus ensues from this more nuanced understanding of (so-called) Destiny. We now need to consider the autonomy of what Nietzsche conceived as the 'sovereign individual', a human being who is well prepared, grown, cultivated, 'pruned' by education, and of noble strength in spirit. To be sure, these individuals cannot be manufactured by the brutal industrialism of today's industrious laborers. Responsibility therefore is not amenable to engineering by any ruler or herd or politic: it is an effect of human struggle, achievement and what he called 'nobility' (as opposed to Virtue). And we have said that this owes to a certain preparedness and readiness so that such a human being feels the *compulsion* of the task to be completed. Additionally, the openness of becoming and its concomitant promises of the future preclude us from asserting that we are simply fated to be responsible. Here are several reasons that further negate this simplistic proposition. Firstly, we noted how those with perspicacious eyes discern a certain incompleteness in the 'human' animal: what still might '*be made of man*' for he knows 'how man is still unexhausted for the greatest responsibilities' (BGE 203). Beyond heredity and the biologic-organic nature of his *zoi*, there lies this unique supramoral question. Time offers the human being the possibility not of more pleasure or leisure as a technological machinist of the age would think but a horizon of greatness in which profound responsibilities are found in the very make-up of sovereign free spirits. Such a horizon is decidedly marked by the knowledge that man will continuously confront 'enigmatic decisions and new paths', including the 'danger' of turning toward the degenerative path (BGE 203). Hence our first point obviates the classical 'fate-freedom' dichotomy—what the philologist would call a false logical copula—because it suggests that beyond determinants and willful choices lie the difficult tasks of promises and cultivated forms of freedom which may easily be usurped by those 'wretched things' that have so often 'broken a being of the highest rank' (BGE 203). If, to say it again, the highest noble ones were predestined to become free and noble (i.e. fated, 'destined') then why is life so fragile and history so thoroughly punctuated by usurpative successes? Nietzsche's freedom is realized when becoming is not overrun by decadent 'wretched things', i.e. degeneration. For this reason, *overcoming* resists degeneration by resisting the main doctrine of liberal philosophy: 'the greatest happiness for the greatest number'. Happiness and responsibility are not equal partners. But autonomy (as Nietzsche defined it) and responsibility on the other hand make a good couple.

Secondly, and against Darwinian logic, human beings possess the capacity to resist historical determinants and organic forces as exemplified by the promise held out to them by the range and manifoldness of their soul—a soul that has 'wholeness in [its] manifoldness' (BGE 212). This attribute (wholeness) is linked in the same passage to the 'abundance of creative power and masterfulness' in the 'higher soul' who does not shy away from neither 'the higher duty nor the higher responsibility'. For otherwise how could the artistic plan of the human being who aims at knowledge of the Whole of life—through the multifarious Wholeness of its soul—disavow ownership of its own 'plan' or commanding will upon the real? To be a form-giver and therefore capable of 'pruning' the combative states of the affects and impulses means that one's 'masterfulness' commits oneself to its attendant set of higher duties and responsibilities. To be sure, not because of a purported psychology of 'freedom of the will' which finds its natural heir in modern egoistic decisionism, as has already been shown. Autonomy thus conceived is no longer bereft of responsibility, of duty, but rather is defined by a willful consideration of the limit, *the potential* in its Whole soul: 'how *far* one could extend his responsibility' becomes the mark of the plastic human being (BGE 212). Within this unfolding potentiality of responsible freedom dissolves the unnecessary (classical) antagonism: 'in short, that necessity and "freedom of the will" then becomes one in them' (BGE 213).

Thirdly, because *zoi* is supervened by *bios* in the process, institutions emerge to organize forms of learning, including what might be called the development of normative structures (i.e. civilization). In socializing the individual human being, the now civilized human-animal with an interesting nature is herded into morals that are of a collective nature—herd morality. Herd morality is antithetical to autonomy but what helps entrench it in modern societies? Social and political institutions organize the management of such morals, norms, usually in a systematic or orderly fashion. Duties as a result are similarly fashioned—normative structures will delineate the manner in which 'higher duties' and 'higher responsibilities' are distributed and controlled. In short, the art of management usurps the responsibility over oneself, over one's independent existence and ethos of life. We are 'thrown-in' to a mass collective that can hardly be seen or known—a reified abstract collective. This converse form of will to power prevails as the will to organize and dominate, i.e. the State, bureaucracy. Mass will as a form of organizing the 'tables of good' and its propagation is what Nietzsche found predominate in modernity. In other words, the expropriation of the means of self-responsibility from the individual to the anonymous apparatuses of large modern institutions. In *Beyond Good and Evil*—a book most explicitly devoted to a critique of modernity and modern nihilism—we find a short aphorism which most aptly captures the 'untimely' thinker that Nietzsche was in this respect: 'Signs of nobility: never thinking of degrading our duties into duties for everybody; not wanting to delegate, to share, one's own responsibility' (BGE 272). Bureaucratic institutions detract from our ability and preparedness to tackle the task of self-responsibility because institutions will mostly foster a *management* of moral questions, predicaments that arise in life dealt with by norms that endorse universal duties as imperatives. Inversely, one's responsibility is usurped by duties that gain validity through normative structures that legitimate the relegation of one's responsibilities to 'delegation'—organized management. To usurp is to transform a responsibility into a duty, yet duty itself is transformed into a collective form of obedience even whilst it is depersonalized.

To obey the rule that duties are now delegated is, in other words, to lie at the feet of the master who is in reality feeble, i.e. the weak slave. Yet the slave now rules and his rule is predicated partly on the myth of the 'unfree will' and, conversely, partly predicated on the illusory 'psychology of will' which Nietzsche named a 'cruel psychology' that has become predominant. Its predominance in modern institutions is grounded in the metaphysical fable of a causa sui operating in the social world (as we noted above). At this juncture, we may further note a correlation between a ubiquitous imperative of dutifulness emanating from such modern institutions and the individual's subjective Will. By extension, it is plausible to claim here that Nietzsche unhappily found the modern individual interpolated between these two illusory forces. On one hand, the moral agent forgoes its ineluctable commitment to responsibilities to a higher abstract entity; for example, Luther's critique of Catholicism based on the hypostasized body or 'office' of the Pope. Individual faith and grace is surrendered to the central figure of the pope even while it remains ever so distant from the common German peasant. By surrendering one's responsibility to an official, impersonal authority the institution usurps the capacity of authorial right and thus declares to the world 'This is Good and you ought to follow this rule/imperative'. The 'voice', moreover, takes on the appearance of causa sui and moves about like the brooding spirit of God over the waters (in Genesis 1.). On the other hand, the moral agent now divested of its discrete moral judgment is also sanctioned with the power of a 'moral will', often called the conscience, which makes her or him believe in a definite *subject*—a subject of consciousness who possesses will and therefore a *conscience*.

Thus, we see in this line of argumentation that Nietzsche connects the weakly individual of 'bad conscience' with the metaphysics of modern institutions and their concomitant *banality* of formal duties. Why banality? Because empty formal duties imposed 'from above' have no semblance to real, substantive responsibilities particularly as they assume a false universality that their metaphysics prescribe. Ruling in this scenario appropriates the appearance of equality since all are asked to both obey and relinquish their power of self-responsibility to a higher reified authority (which in reality is only an interpretation, a concept). Two reified concepts—free will and causa sui—we find mutually reinforce one another. However, they do so in a fashion that, most importantly, detracts from the *preparedness* and *enablement* of human beings to welcome the hardest tasks of the 'greatest responsibilities'. Furthermore, it negates the force of the aforementioned imperative to examine how 'far' one's responsibilities can extend since it gathers and centralizes the quantum-force of the willing power of life—in this case, sociocultural life. Unsurprisingly for Nietzsche it in turn appeases the drives and states of the human being that would otherwise contest reality—norms, duties, forms of dominance—thus making the animal-human soul more placid, comforted and finally caged by today's order of morals. As Schacht points out 'morality' on closer examination is a set of morals ordered by particular conditions and forces that later appear as norms of a given society: *Sittlichkeit* (customary morality). If we look more closely, we can perhaps see in evidence Nietzsche's master-slave relation at work as it reveals a depleted yet conscience-ridden moral agent of meaningless duties. Subjugated and 'emptied-out' the modern human being is nevertheless made to feel happy by an illusory equality; and furthermore the universality of normative duties only further reinforces the essential equality of all those subject to the law of 'Thou Shalt'. Thou shalt stands now in place of 'I will' to acknowledge the task of my responsibilities. Consequently, a cultivating education (*Bildung*) is barely alive, leaving individuals yet still more vulnerable to moral malaise and inertia in the face of large institutional forces of normative regulation. A Dutch scholar influenced by Nietzsche's thought once gave an account of institutional forces of civility over the individual and called it *The Civilizing Process*. Too much civility or 'morality' as Nietzsche would put it, stifles the drives and states which compel one to grow and challenge the limit of one's responsibilities. In other words, unfreedom as moral constraint stultifies the power of one to *become* responsible; it alienates the vital drives and requisite pathos of freedom to assume 'the greatest responsibilities' to liberal institutions that transform responsibility into 'duty' (or rule). For this reason, Nietzsche found Kant responsible for the (rational) Christianization of modern values and, concomitantly, Europe. The 'old Kant' succeeded in legitimizing the 'plebeian' values of Christianity through a false universalism: duties 'from above' that are rationally justified are fundamentally theologically derived. That is to say, the great idol of German philosophy had not yet naturalized morals. For us however, Nietzsche overcame naturalism's limitations via a long circuitous route of exploration from the ancient Greeks, Ree and Lange to Wagner and Goethe.

Fourthly, having demonstrated that the weakness of oppositional thinking dissuaded Nietzsche from adopting a fully blow fatalist or naturalist outlook, it becomes apparent responsibility is inextricably woven into the formation of a free 'higher soul', a formation that is highly singular yet simultaneously the effect of 'all that which has gone before'. There is an analogue here in the way Nietzsche conceived of the soul and city of man: both the individual soul and 'city of man' are like fountains since both are constituted by that which flows (from before) through them. We are individual 'forms' of that which moves about (flows) in the cosmos, not merely some kind of self-preserving organism that is subjected to a ubiquitous will to power. Against Darwin, Nietzsche asserted the human being's form-giving will to a future that is distinguished by promise making and the ethicality of a good conscience. The 'new man' of the future would be the product of an overcoming of guilt, shame, and dishonesty (relating to our 'human-all-too-human' nature) who possesses a good conscience. For this reason, ethical thought is very much a part of Nietzsche's thinking about morals and responsibility. Our argument is consistent at this point with Maudemarie Clark's analysis of Nietzsche as an ethical genealogist rather than 'the immoralist' as traditionally misunderstood. The argument that a critique of morality cannot be equated with nihilistic immorality is defensible. That ethics is not synonymous with morals, as Clark[25] shows in her discussion of Bernard Williams and Nietzsche, or morality synonymous with goodness, is an important interpretive shift from previous conceptions (and prejudices) of Nietzsche 'the immoralist'. My point in the argument is that the ethical moment for Nietzsche attends that moment in becoming when freedom has been secured from 'slavish morality'—morality of the herd. It is not a liberation *from* pain, suffering and the human-all-too-human, that is, from reality in order to retreat into an idyllic existence marked by an absence of suffering and conflict.

Such a state will not be distinguished by the obliteration of the tension between 'master and slave' as rank, distance and tension only metamorphose into something new. Improvement, as he showed in *Twilight of the Idols*, is falsified rather than guaranteed by the principle of equality. Nietzsche we can argue sided with ethical responsibility over and above today's 'modern idea' of emancipation through equalization. Yet the pathos of distance in both the soul and city of man does not somehow negate the potential ethical responsibility that is the mark of a man of 'good conscience'. Overcoming, it will be recalled, is a phenomenon strewn across the spectrum of singular (and group) formations, including individuated expressions of resistance. When Nietzsche said that life is appropriation and growth, he was restating the ancient wisdom that the organicity of life is composed of gradations of difference, relation and subordination both in the natural and social worlds. Ethical responsibility or the formation of a good conscience is thereby not presumed a common or easy event. It is perhaps analogous to autonomy: everyone may aspire to it yet some will remain subordinates while others slaves (i.e. degrees of lack and capacity for autonomy). The spectrum constituting the Whole of life is non-teleological in Nietzsche's eyes and therefore it remains relatively indeterminate as to 'who' will forge autonomy and a good conscience out of their existence. The astute realist observation he made vis-à-vis autonomy and responsibility is that the majority of humankind fall prey to their human-all-too-human interest in self-preservation, happiness, obeying the common established (moral) rule, pain reduction, herd-consciousness and masters of Truth. Duty bound modern individuals consequently reflect the order of values of this *reality*—a false appearance that is veiled by a decadent *veritas*. To shatter such a dutiful soul would require the shattering of this reflection and its attendant 'social structure of the soul', making responsibility within autonomy a rather difficult task. Substituting Kantian duties for a responsibility that is the outgrowth of autonomy appears especially difficult now since it also involves overturning the given social order, an order (morality) said to have its origins in Socrates.

Fifthly, yet the present has also served another purpose: by means of morality and its duties and forms of dominance man has become 'calculable, regular, necessary', forging his self-image out of this historical accomplishment. It is in fact a development within humankind, something unknown to the pre-moral human being (ancient ancestors or 'pre-historic' animal natures). The ethical moment of responsibility draws upon this formative accomplishment in a fashion which finds the supermoral stance transvaluating morality itself (moral system). Understanding himself as calculable, regular and necessary significantly alters the human being's orientation to the *Welt* (world). It knows itself to be a *zoon politikon* who is historical—one cultivated by time. Time as becoming and development has left its indelible mark, is manifested in the drive, and will to become autonomous. The developed, cultivated individual now acquires the desire to become something else, to exceed the present of Today by means of a Dionysian drive to forge new promises of the future. For he 'understands' himself—as Kant would say—as the product of his immanent drive and its promise-making capacity. *Zoi* is thereby transvaluated by both the moralization of life and the futurity of promise-making autonomous individuals who seek to transfigure morality with a vital ethical 'table of the good'. Nietzsche reckoned the life of *zoi* to be a far distant thing whom the artist would do well to recognize in the futile attempt to let himself go so as to return to the '"most natural" state'. Although decrying the established "tyranny of capricious laws" of morality, he clearly comes down on the realist side of the divide and declares (against naturalistic idealism) 'in all seriousness, the probability is by no means small that precisely this is "nature" and "natural"—and *not* that *laisser aller* [letting go]' (BGE 188). Further still he concludes in regard to all things noble: 'the curious fact is that all there is or has been on earth of freedom, subtlety, boldness, dance, and masterly sureness'—in culture, ethics, thought and government—'has developed only owing to the "tyranny of such capricious laws"' (BGE 188). The law of duties—'morality' as opposed to ethics—has its teachers and this class of teachers has taught 'hatred of the *laisser aller*' but since we cannot naively return to that 'all-too-great freedom' (of the 'most natural state') we would do better to look at possibilities in *the future*. Such possibilities for growth and extension and the absolving of guilt-shame complexes emerge out of this constellation of the real that importantly possesses the 'metrical compulsion of rhyme and rhythm' (BGE 188).

The 'new man', our 'sovereign individual', shall be steeled by this very tough compulsion 'under which every language so far has achieved strength and freedom'. Nietzsche wanted the bronzed heart and the steeled compulsion of an ethical conscience to characterize the soul of that human being who would respond—not to the innocence of becoming—to the command obeying:

> What is essential "in heaven and earth" seems to be, to say it once more, that there should be *obedience* over a long period of time and in a *single* direction: given that, something always develops, for whose sake it is worth while to live on earth . . . (BGE 188).

Living is made worthwhile by the fact that beautiful or at least profound creations emerge out of steadfast, long and determined commitments and investments in a singular direction. Development—as opposed to repetition or mere circular recurrence—we note becomes possible because of the compulsive 'rhyme and rhythm' that helps to forge new directions, particularly spiritual directions which free the modern soul of its intrepid guilt, envy and slavish impulses. (In another chapter we turn to the 'will to revenge' that Nietzsche believed was a scourge on modern life.) We live on earth for such 'developments' but nevertheless require the discipline, structure, pattern and elevating power of that which also gives languages, he says, their 'strength and freedom' (cited above). Indeed, ethics are similarly formed and grounded: the ethical moment too depends upon the solidity and strength of determined will to found its regime of 'strength and freedom' in time. Ethics require a tenacious, directed force of will, energy and rhythm to take hold in a world of indeterminate, contending forces. In Nietzsche's context, an ethical self-responsibility will need to overcome the prevailing morality of Judaeo-Christian morals which has enjoyed its own long 'metrical compulsion of rhyme and rhythm'. Of course, the argument that ethics can only emerge out of morality—or put differently, autonomy out of slavish decadence—is no longer a threat to Nietzsche's argument since in comparison with received views of Nietzsche (in past decades) we now better understand him. That is to say, it is no longer feasible to assert that Nietzsche could not find anything salvageable in religion or modern culture. He stated rather to the contrary that without the much vaunted 'soul-superstition' of today's world-religions, metaphysics and psychology, we could not shoot for the most goals, i.e. directions. The 'free noble spirits' indeed will be a 'development' of this spirit (soul) heretofore considered problematical because of its affect on man—decline and nihilism. Throughout his writings, we see Nietzsche continuously noting the innovation that was made by those 'decadents'—the priestly caste—and the 'teachers of the meaning of existence'. Without their innovations and attendant types of form-giving (i.e. meaning constructions) the *will* would not have been saved; and if there is no will on earth then there is no meaning or 'worth (value) whileness' to life. The point is what to do with the will; and Nietzsche most decidedly points in the direction of a new ethical language with its own distinctive 'strength and freedom': the language of preparation for an autonomy and responsibility that stems from a rejection of all oppositions or opposite values, i.e. destiny v freedom.

Sixthly, this makes evident (for Nietzsche) one important accomplishment, one further development: 'In order to have this kind of command over the future in advance, man must first have learned to separate the necessary from the accidental occurrence, to think causally, to see and anticipate what is distant as if it were present, to fix with certainty what is end' (GM II: 1). To anticipate the distant 'as if it were present' whilst also having the wherewithal to separate accident from necessary event are important features of capacities which *enable* autonomous beings to bring to fruition 'the possible'. One indeed can commit oneself to the futurity of a contracted promise because she has the faith *in the*

future bearing the ripest of fruits. They are not vicious 'ideals' of one's sentiments. To 'calculate' therefore means the capacity to think causally, to discern
between mere 'accidents' and physics, and most of all to calculate her own limits and commitments because she knows herself as something 'regular' and necessary. The subject, in other words, can traject itself into a future it 'does not
know' yet wills as end with a degree of certainty. Napoleon, for instance, saw
himself as something regular and calculable and thus could see a future Europe
united because he set 'the end' with certainty. Causally speaking, his will was
efficacious in the creation of a future Europe (contra dynastic rule). Like Napoleon, she has in possession her 'standard of value' but is vehemently 'stingy
with [her] trust' even though an unswerving trust in her capacity to uphold
promises gives evidence to a 'mark of distinction'; namely, giving her word 'as
something on which one can rely because [s]he knows [herself] to be strong
enough to uphold it even against accidents, even "against fate"' (GM II: 2
Clarke ed.). Sovereignty is a distinctive feature of such a life because her autonomy allows her to overcome the adversity of 'accident' even 'against fate'.

In short, she can hardly be fated by fate! Instead she anticipates (her) future,
thinks clearly and logically (causally) and is able to commit trust in herself vis-
à-vis the becoming of time because her own genealogy has formed and prepared
her in 'calculable, necessary, regular' terms. She is autonomous not only to
make promises but also is sufficiently predisposed and *capable* of fulfilling her
commitments even if—like Napoleon—adversity of accident and 'fate' may
threaten to derail her. A further argument against fatalism here is the double
proposition that accidents do happen in reality just as the overcoming of 'destiny' is made possible by the 'strength and freedom' of her promise-making
(praxis). As long as it does not sprout from some fanciful 'ideal', her honor is
exonerated by her capacity to keep to her commitment no-matter-what. She can
determine her next future present because she has certainty of what past 'presents' she passed through. Time is a passage for her to pass through rather
than—as with a pessimist—something to fear. She can bind herself to others
without fear of subsumption or distrust through her bond to *kairos* (time), an ally
of her own becoming. In fact through *making* promises she can make herself
futurally, at once binding with others and her own states of strength and regular
causation. To 'come through' at the end of *kairos* with certainty of the actuality
of what one had promised is to demonstrate to the world—as Christ and Napoleon did—one's autonomy as a *compulsion*. Christ was compelled not by his
father's fate but by the compulsion of the task to bind love to the futurity of the
promise to save souls. If Christ were fated then why his need to prepare himself
for the glorious sacrifice? The honor lies elsewhere—in the overcoming of the
human-all-too-human. This might explain why Nietzsche referred to Christ as
the noblest man ever to have lived.

Seventhly, the promise-making animal must gain permission in order to be
honored with the title of 'noble' free spirit. It must first qualify or meet the standard of value that is proper for promise-making activity. In the same passage of
the *Genealogy of Morality* Nietzsche explains the origins of responsibility
through the task of 'breeding an animal that is permitted to promise'—a raising

and cultivation of man the animal into a promise-keeping human being. Without 'breeding' through a 'morality of custom' the long tyranny over man himself to become something more calculable would be of no effect. To be *permitted* to make promises a human being must first be prepared so as to possess 'a true consciousness of power and freedom' that is representative of what Nietzsche finally declared to constitute 'a feeling of the completion of man himself' (GM II: 2). Only a completed *human*-animal can have the psychical and cognitive surety to commit herself to a task in the future that will affect another human being. She knows herself to be capable of onerous great deeds because she possesses the freedom *and* power essential to carrying them without flinching either at their measure of involvement or various obstacles that 'fate' may put in her way. The feeble ones choose to call 'fate' what she otherwise views as her doing, making, promising, calculating and evaluating. Sovereignty is in her eyes while fatalism clouds the crowd's eyes. Through the will to know she can discern the accidental from the necessitated while also having the knowledge that her own acts or deeds are the effect of her aforesaid 'power and freedom'. To become free then is to be completed and one is only complete as a *human* being when one finally has the right (i.e. permission) to give commitment to a promise made. One honors the trust of another person by only making promises that can be realized in their fulfillment, without excuses, e.g., "accident or fate intervened". In doing so one also honors one's own freedom in the power to fulfill the end of a promise made—'they kept their word' signifies a freedom *to be* responsible. I can hardly be responsible if I am fated to complete a designated task or promise. Responsibility, Nietzsche implies, requires a commitment by an individual, one that is situated on the horizon of time and its possibility of fulfillment or completion (in the midst of failures). It cannot be said therefore to exist merely as an epiphenomenon of Destiny whose dictates one mysteriously falls under and pursues. One would be obliged to follow the duty stipulated by Destiny but not know of the *will* to welcome 'hard responsibilities' and to complete promises made. It designates, for the weak and fatalist alike, circumstances master me rather than I overcoming them.

Before examining the question of mastering, it is necessary to draw out the connection to a quantum of freedom that had hitherto been forfeited—a forfeiture owing to the caging process (juridical-political society) and the moralization of forms of life. Nietzsche's genealogy of the 'bad conscience' points to a forfeiture of 'an enormous quantity of freedom' extant in the pre-moral stage of humanity. Its formation owes to the 'instinct for freedom' having been 'forcibly made latent' and 'driven back, suppressed, imprisoned within, and finally discharging and venting itself only on itself' (GM II: 17). With the formation of an ethical conscience, including the confidence in one's ability to 'come through' in the end and fulfill one's promises, this once expended quantity of freedom is returned back to the self. This 'secret self-violation' is reversed by the strength of will necessary to overcome servitude to a bad conscience. A good conscience is made possible because a great quantum of freedom is now diverted, invested, and distributed in her promise-making work and obligations to responsibilities. Against her 'animal old self', she can calculate, think causally, and make necessary her commitments to a responsibility in which autonomy in herself makes possible. Investing the instinct of freedom in her modus operandi affords her a surety of committing to more than empty 'duties'—her compulsion is what sets her free to set out on difficult pathways where great responsibilities are commonplace. Embarking upon these pathways is an act of autonomy because she is not fated toward such directions; rather, the foresaid 'single direction' strengthens her capacity to work autonomously with time's unfolding processes, not fearing the ensuing outcomes but instead taking joyous delight in seeing them as manifestations of her will (power). In necessity she finds things explicable and amenable to her form-giving capacities, including the necessity to be trusted which is itself a sign-language of her having gained permission to make promises. This human being embodies that which is at the end of 'the enormous process' of becoming a complete (i.e. autonomous) human being: 'the ripest fruit on its tree the *sovereign* individual' (GM II: 2). Historical processes of growth (and decay) are for Nietzsche-the-gardener represented by the tree that is 'only the means' for this fruit to grow develop and ripen. She encompasses the totality of processes in nature and culture but once ripened has ends that exceed the mere means. Her consciousness is filled with this important distinction between world-historical means and volitional ends, itself generating a force of power to drive her down this and that particular pathway.

Returning again to mastery we can perhaps better understand why Nietzsche speaks of 'mastery over him [her] self' in the context of an overcoming of customary morality. The completion of 'man' as a once antagonized, estranged and self-violated creature whose tremendous instinct for freedom was forcibly suppressed becomes apparent to Nietzsche as a post-ascetic master of form-giving. Mastery in its ordinary political sense denotes some kind of domination or control akin to the powers of states and rulers. Instead of control, 'mastery' can also mean what Nietzsche time again affirms and reiterates; namely, the capacity to be a 'master over *oneself*'. It is perhaps a dimension that Nietzsche's claimed 'reversal of Platonism' most overlooks. Plato's idea of man as a political animal reflected both the interior and exterior forms of order (justice) prevalent in the polis. Simple oligarchy or aristocracy as ways of making law the basis of civil life would not suffice. Normativity based on the moral 'rule' or 'imperatives' of institutions equally troubled Nietzsche. Hence discussion of her mastery must of necessity also incorporate the earlier insight of expenditure and resistance: she must overcome by means of a resistance to the tenacity of moral rules (morality system) the power of coded duties and 'one's obligations' extant in the system of morals. As such, she is unable to prevail over existing legal-political-moral institutions because 'control' of the Whole of life would be ludicrous and akin to a re-divination of man. She with a good conscience instead better understands, following Goethe's embodiment of the idea, that 'all is redeemed and affirmed in the Whole' (TI 49) even if the present is found wanting. Becoming in the holistic sense will affirm the totality of the Whole and her necessary 'mastery' grasps this fundamental law of development henceforth turning it into an advantage of life. The 'oneself', that is to say, is sublated into the Whole and in doing so; it affirms rather than negates life. Goethe, whose spirit embodied the instinct for freedom, did not 'negate any more' and instead possessed the highest faith of all, the faith that all is redeemed and affirmed in the Whole (TI 49). Being strong enough for such freedom, she, like Goethe, knows how to use to her *advantage* 'even that from which the average nature would perish' (TI 49).

It is not so much the force of inherited physiologies that prevail with such free spirits; it is more a matter of what form-giving powers over herself she is able to marshal in order to appropriate the manifoldness of the Whole— "freedom". Not freedom *from* but freedom *to* is her distinctive mark of sovereignty, a sovereignty that need not assume God's responsibility for the Whole of life. Basking in the multitudinous form of the Whole the noble human being who takes delight in applying herself to diverse tasks and capacities revels in the freedom unfolding herewith. Once again, Goethe is emblematic in this regard: he 'took as much as possible upon himself, over himself, into himself...he disciplined himself to wholeness, he *created* himself' (TI 49). Mastery we can see is inextricably linked to creative form-giving understood as an axiological and praxeological activity which is oriented toward 'wholeness' even though the 'wheel' of life is above him. Most important of all is the tying together of masterful *vita creativa* with the strong disciplined will to take 'as much as possible' upon himself and 'into himself'. Hence, now that she has become an autonomous self-forming legislator, her grand responsibilities appear as phenomena of her steeled 'bronze heart', internalized in a way that her 'self' is defined by them. To be free she now 'must' act according to their immanent articulations, otherwise how could the manifold Whole be 'whole' if responsibilities were subtracted from her vital strength of freedom? Her interiority is indeed fashioned by a good conscience that wills to commit to a relation of trustworthiness—a relation that helps define her permitted privilege of taking responsibility. The law with all its exteriority of 'duty' and 'rules' is supplanted by immanent drives to actively extend and practice a strength of freedom to be responsible for one's life without the injurious presence of the 'bad conscience'. Self-disciplined that she is the lazy feebleness of those who simply want to 'let go' (*laisser aller*) appears to her as both vulgar and irresponsible. Incontinence broadly defined in moral and psychical terms is considered ignoble, 'below her', causing her to frown upon those who shirk from inner states that properly register the force of a good conscience. We can note in passing that it will often illicit resentment and envy from those 'below' because contemptuousness is the weaker will's instinct for revenge (owing to the perceived 'elevation' of her mastery). The burden of resentment and revengefulness confirms their state of servitude while on the other side the nobler free spirit is accused of an avaricious will to power.

Finally, we come to how she is received and receives others as a result of her distinctive autonomy: a mastery over herself that 'necessarily brings with it mastery over circumstances, over nature and all lesser-willed and more unreliable creatures' (GM II: 2). Firstly we note the philological nuance of those lacking autonomy: they are considered 'creatures' rather more so than 'creators'. Due to their unreliability and weakness of will they appear more subject to the forces of nature and fate. Creatures are determined *by* whereas Goethe-like creators have a determined will *to* forge. As she embodies the latter type, her mastery over nature threatens those whose ontology is bound up with the limits of nature. Instead of holding her in reverence—one possibility amongst three—the modern individual or group can be overcome by fear. Nietzsche expresses it more in terms of her awakening a fear in them because the threatened 'creature' cannot understand the creator as Artist but only as Master. Her mastery over nature seems to defy their expectation of who she is because the creature's fatalism dictates that the laws of *zoi* are so profoundly 'imperative' or compelling that a sovereign who represents the completion of the unfinished animal partly because of her 'lord of the *free* will' (in Nietzsche's specific sense) appears counter-intuitive. The fact that she possesses 'a long unbreakable will', conveys 'a mark of distinction' when showing trust, gives her 'word as something on which one can rely' because she knows her strength can withstand not only accidents but work 'even against fate' to fulfill her word (promise) (GM II: 2). It is important to stress at this point in the argument that her own 'direction' against the vicissitudes of circumstance, nature, fate, and 'unreliable creatures' unfolds in the possession of a consciousness of her capacity to overcome and complete. That is to say, to resist what the masses see as 'fate', draw a distinction between reliable and unreliable persons, discern between 'creators' and creatures while also knowing one's own power to keep their word, their promise and their 'extraordinary privilege of responsibility' (GM II: 2).

Indeed, the subjectivity of this state of being privileged is referred to as a 'proud knowledge' in part because she is 'permitted to say "yes" to oneself' and in part as a result of her long unbreakable will in the midst adversity and chance. This noble human being possesses a self-identity that is structured around her proud knowledge of earning and deserving the 'extraordinary privilege of responsibility'—a good conscience is 'good' also according to its own self-knowledge (another of our parallels to Plato). Pride in one's 'standard of value' as it applies to the practical social world (i.e. *bios*) is a distinctive feature of her subjective life, something that is necessarily misunderstood by Them. Yet she remains unswayed by this misunderstanding preferring to exercise her prerogative to judiciously dispense trust and honor to others. Her consciousness is that of a 'ripe fruit', reflecting a long cultivation and fruition of all that which had flowed before through time. This type—a bit of 'rare freedom'—finds those unfree understandably fearful of heavy responsibilities that she admirably welcomes and completes. Nevertheless it should be recognized that she can also illicit a contrary response; namely, a reverence and deep trust of her being. Because her self-consciousness is marked by an internalization of these facets of her will, power and preparedness (becoming) as well as permission to make promises, it may evoke a reverence in those who lack them. Masterfulness is acknowledged by those 'lesser-willed' persons who shy away from heavy responsibilities and the fate of becoming responsible for your promised word. Trust is exchanged instead of punishment, revenge, or guilt in the legal contract of life; they see reliability and preparedness there where others totally lack such precious values. Time and again, she proves her claim to a 'rare freedom' by abiding to her word of commitment that others who lack such reverential qualities could not emulate. Her self-discipline and assured self-knowledge are evident to others, eventually giving her honor provided they can first surmount their own inner fear(s) or contempt. If they are enslaved by their own vicious sentiments including resentment (of power as self-mastery), it is they who commit the treacherous act of self-denial in denying the *possibility* of such a rare freedom. The promise of the future is relinquished in their case whereas through her extraordinary privilege of responsibility she proves her entitlement to the promise of the future. Nietzsche never went on to say quite exactly how this distance between the free sovereign and slave would unfold on the horizon of becoming; and yet it is evident that his previous reference to 'development' is what her futurity embodies. Only one permitted, prepared, and therefore trusted can commit to entrusting humanity's enhancement in a time to come. This is not 'leadership' but it appears to equate with voyagers who can see more distant faint stars in the distance beginning to increase as they become visible one day from the earth. Those lacking the comprehensive eye of the skilled voyager look up in the heavens and fail to see anything; a distant star still remains invisible to their unperceptive eye.

These free spirits of the future are consequently untimely, out of step with the present, as their vital self-consciousness of who they are now intervenes in the wheel of time since futural events are affected by their own tenacious will and good conscience. Forging, forming and pruning as is exemplified in their very mode of life alters the horizon upon which one gazes for the most sublime illuminations. It alters the course of history (i.e. Napoleonic history) of those too fearful to take on the greatest responsibilities of an ethical conscience. This is evident from the impact that Goethe had on European culture and Christ on Semitic civilizations. What eventually will become 'genealogy' was once futural, that is, inventive, creative and 'untimely'. Responsibility we can now see is part of this vital process of becoming (free): one has to be freed from a 'bad conscience'—including guilt, resentment, envy, fear and self-hatred—to form a good conscience. The ethical moment therefore becomes conceivable as something generated out of oneself, one's soul, and one's *Zeitgeist*; it cannot be imposed simply from above as a tyranny of formal abstract Rules or Duties. Nietzsche's fear here is that such categorical rules—thrown into the future by institutional inertia—will stifle and possibly undermine the emergence of such rare spirits of freedom and rigorous responsibility. It is a point frequently missed by analytical thinkers of 'ethics' who lack a genealogical 'historical philosophy' (as explicated in an earlier chapter). Note the historicized language used in the third treatise on ascetic ideals: 'Is there already enough pride, daring, bravery, self-assuredness in existence today, enough will of the spirit, will to responsibility, *freedom of the will* so that henceforth on earth "the philosopher" is truly—*possible?*' (GM III: 10). This question of development and readiness moreover finds 'freedom of the will' (in Nietzsche's sense) and 'will to responsibility' coterminous with each other, a point that makes logical sense after having closely examined Nietzsche's argument.

On Strawson and Nietzsche's Responsibility

Nietzsche's reluctance to sanction the idea of responsibility as conventionally understood has something in common with P.F. Strawson's work on moral responsibility. Specifically, Strawson's argument[26] against the necessity of holding persons responsible on the basis of an objective or external rational justification. Strawson believed conventional models of responsibility were overly intellectualist since they presupposed the ability to found rational grounds for judgment criteria. His attention to reactive attitudes which are responses that derive from our psychological make-up is strangely reminiscent of Nietzsche's own stance. Strawson correctly observed the fundamentally interpersonal nature of our moral life thus enabling him to see the practice of holding others responsible as essentially norm-governed activity rather than something justifiable in aprioristic terms. Unlike his predecessors Strawson repudiated metaphysical freedom preferring instead the non-theoretical dimensions of practices of intersubjective life. Phenomena such as resentment and anger define how we evaluate others' actions because they exhibit a certain psychological attitude towards us as we engage interactively in a mutual relationship of interpretable practices. Someone who for instance acts out of resentment is caught up with reactive forces which in turn impinge upon how I evaluate his conduct towards me. This approach to responsibility helped define the landscape of contemporary discourses on the subject within moral and analytic philosophy. Most continental interpretations of Nietzsche unsurprisingly overlook this connection between two very significant philosophers. However, Galen Strawson—son of the late Peter Strawson—did not fail to identify the intimate connection between Nietzsche's work and modern critiques of free will. In his seminal paper *The Impossibility of Moral Responsibility* (1994), Galen Strawson identifies Nietzsche as a vital thinker of the failures of free will. We shall not reiterate the argument against free will presented in an earlier chapter save to say that Strawson appropriates it to demonstrate the impossibility of true moral responsibility.

This appropriation takes its cue mainly from Nietzsche's critique of the concept *causa sui* citing at length from *Beyond Good and Evil* to endorse the point that it merely concludes in unhelpful (logical) regression. The conventional 'freedom of the will' that is claimed to drive moral choices consequently is illusory because 'free will' depends upon the concept *causa sui* which is itself only substitutive for the hidden God (Being). We simply cannot (and do not) 'pull oneself up into existence by the hair, out of the swamps of nothingness' (Nietzsche cited in Galen Strawson[27]). Nietzsche had repudiated not only the idea of free will but the idea of Being, God, absolute ego and the Will—all faulty ideas or errors which weigh heavily on the human being especially in the form of the burdensome vicious 'bad conscience'. Nietzsche connected this 'bad conscience' with the drive to moralize responsibility—a process not only fundamentally 'plebeian' but one which deadens the fundamentally noble privilege of assuming responsibility in one's life. To demolish 'free will' is not to necessarily disown 'responsibility' though it may require disowning its decadent conventional form, that is, a moralistic conception of the willful self. Demolishing free will and therefore causality will appear to throw us into a nihilistic state where anxiety about the abyss of evil and meaningless existence prevails. Yet if we look closer at Nietzsche's argument, we find on the contrary that because man must now look at himself in the mirror—without the encumbrances of certain errors—the human being faces the perennial challenge of making something noble out of his merely *human-all-too-human* nature.

We have said thus far that it is a 'free spirit', ennobled by its capacity for responsibilities that a philosophy of the future would affirm. To be free of the unnecessary moralization of responsibility by religions and onto-philosophies is itself part of what Nietzsche called the 'great liberation' (HH, *P3*). That is, freedom and responsibility are co-dependent and talk of incompatible versus compatible notions of responsibility are really misguided as Ted Honderich has recently shown.[28] Nietzsche forges a link between responsibility and freedom—as opposed to freedom and determinism—because he overcame the outdated question whether the world is determined or not and whether the human subject is what it is essentially because of its (said) free will. Causation itself is predicated on the notion of a free will that concomitantly draws on the Augustinian concept of Will. Hence, determinism gets it all wrong because it is falsely premised on a non-existent metaphysical Will. We do not therefore have *either* Freedom or Determinism—that is not the object of historical philosophy nor is it what P.F. Strawson set out to problematize either. The flawed *causa sui* argument brings crashing down the efficacy of any free will argument and therefore also any determinist reading of irresponsibility as causally derived (by objective conditions or factors), hence omitting important psychological and reactive forces at play. Indeed, when Strawson discusses our ordinary predilection for holding onto 'true moral responsibility' as an integral part of our legal and moral order, he correctly discerns a commonplace yet fundamental mental-psychological resistance to it. Suggesting a là Nietzsche's critique of the free will that it is nonsensical to speak of a 'true moral responsibility' he recognizes the recalcitrance inherent in its overturning: 'it contradicts a fundamental part of our natural self-conception'.[29] Why is this so?

Galen Strawson answers in a very similar vein to Nietzsche: despite the logical cogency of the argument (against true responsibility), 'Punishments and rewards may seem deeply appropriate or intrinsically "fitting" to us in spite of this argument, and many of the various institutions of punishment and reward in human society appear to be practically indispensable in both their legal and non-legal forms'.[30] It is further augmented as Nietzsche showed and Galen Strawson argues by a 'very powerful' conviction that 'self-conscious awareness of one's situation can be a sufficient foundation of strong free will'.[31] Before we embark on the question of punishment and legal authority in the development of morals, we ought to examine first the origins of this said sufficient foundation of free will. Strawson in fact overlooks an important point Nietzsche first made in *Human All Too Human* (39) concerning the illusory 'intelligible freedom' which Arthur Schopenhauer valiantly defended. Here Nietzsche interrogates the want to 'attribute responsibility' through a history of moral sensations—an itinerary of morality. Identifying three formative phases of moralization the first attributes

good or evil to actions according to their consequences. The second development of sensations judges actions according to the 'good' or 'evil' inherent in
actions themselves owing to a forgetfulness of their origins. Finally, good and
evil are located in the motives behind actions, and then by way of extension to
the 'whole being of a person, from which a motive grows as does a plant from
the soil' (39). Through the process of historical change we 'finally discover that
even this entity cannot be responsible, insofar as it is entirely a necessary consequence, a concretion of the elements and influences of past and present
things'—what is later explicitly referred to as *becoming*.

Against our common conviction and intuitive sense of a free self we therefore confront the reality of an illusion: 'a person cannot be made responsible for
anything, neither for his being, nor his motives, nor his actions, nor therefore
effects' (39). We have become cognizant of an all-pervasive error, that is, the
'error of free will' according to an itinerary of moralities. This genealogical explication of the 'error *of* responsibility', to be sure, pinpoints the basis of the
erroneous idea of responsibility handed down to us by Kant and his concept of
'sufficient reason' as embodied in Schopenhauer's philosophy. The latter expounded the logic that if we know of 'a consciousness of guilt' then 'responsibility must exist' for if the world moved according to necessity guilt would be
unknown to human experience. Schopenhauer therefore instantiates responsibility by proving 'the existence of a freedom that people must have somehow possessed, not in respect of their actions, of course, but in respect to their nature'
(39). The basic error of Schopenhauer is to deduce an ontology of freedom and
responsibility—the *esse*—from the false inference that if experience of uneasiness is a fact then a justification and 'rational authorization for this uneasiness'
can be deduced. Schopenhauer's 'intelligible freedom' built as it is on the *esse*
and its attendant notion of free will (causation) comes to posit 'a person becomes what he *wills* to become, his willing is prior to his existence', thus 'because human beings take themselves to be free, but not because they are free,
they feel regret and pangs of conscience' (39). In effect, on the illusion of an
autonomous will that inheres in man's nature is built the falsehood of "I am free
to act responsibly because I have it in my nature to will it". Yet Nietzsche ac-
cuses Schopenhauer of turning a customary habit and sensibility into an eternal
ontology. Uneasy feelings of guilt associated with irresponsibility are instead
merely 'a habit that we can break' and moreover something 'not present at all in
actions' for many people since it is 'a quite variable thing' dependent upon culture and custom. If customary practices and moralities along with their unexam-
ined presuppositions are demystified, we will no doubt encounter anachronistic
resistance: 'yet here everyone prefers to go back into the shadows and into untruth: from fear of the consequences' (39). This is the fundamental 'strong conviction' that Strawson had recognized at work and the reactive sentiments that P.
F. Strawson had identified before him. Hence although much analytic philosophy is an extension of Kantianism, the critical analyses of free will and moral
responsibility proffered by both Strawsons are actually congruent with this once
ignored German thinker.

The *aporia* we have identified in Galen Strawson's argument concerning the fallacy of true moral responsibility shows that a genealogical account of our taken for granted juridical-moral conscience overcomes some of the difficulties of Strawson simply making a quasi-empirical observation of our claimed 'strong conviction'. Strawson falters on the question of rejecting free will not on account of his idea of our given natures (the way we are) but rather that it lacks a theory of juridical-moral complexes: inter-subjective relations, moral sentiments and customs, reactive forces and moralities of duty unfolding *in time*. These complexes require a dynamic, process-analysis of configurations of meaning and norm-governed morals which themselves flow out of quanta of power and reactive sentiments (unconscious and conscious). To see how this might be exemplified, in his subsequent work *Daybreak* Nietzsche began to identify how moral actions such as duties stem for dynamic interpersonal interactions. (Further elaborations will be given in later works most especially in *On the Genealogy of Morality*.) Here the passage 'On the Natural History of Rights and Duties' properly expounds the critical standpoint we are investigating, a standpoint that takes the inter-subjective moment of interpersonal interactions and evaluations as paramount. 'Our duties—are the rights of others over us. How have they acquired such rights? By taking us to be capable of contracting and of requiting, by positing us as similar and equal to them', argued Nietzsche (D 112). Moral duty then is related to how we are positioned vis-à-vis others within a community of others' expectations and recognition. Luther in contrast to Kant had initiated obedience to a person (God) in sharp contrast to the concept (unconditional imperative) preferred by Kant (D 207). Before the reign of concept-thinking, we obeyed according to the measure and estimates of others in their interaction with us (the 'individual' being a quite late development in human history). The basis of action, Nietzsche argued, is neither intention, or consequence[32] or motive; it is the dialogical nature of existence.

In this regard Nietzsche cannot be said to be a monist as is often thought; social life instead is wherefrom individuality emerges. Hence, to understand duties normally associated with moral responsibility we have to inquire (disclose) into their formation under lived ontological conditions. That is, before the 'dutiful' came under the rule of the concept, one's conduct was anthropologically derived—it was measured and evaluated by others intertwined with our existence. We necessarily act within a matrix of active—reactive sentiments and forces in which power circulates and constitutes. For Nietzsche 'We fulfill our duty—that is to say: we justify the idea of our power on the basis of which all these things were bestowed upon us, we give back in the measure in which we have been given to' (112). In fact Nietzsche conceived of rights as reciprocating from power because power permeates interactions betweens persons; likewise for obligations because 'in doing something for us' others 'have impinged upon our sphere of power' just as we 'impinge upon their power' by requital in performing our 'duty' according to customary protocol (112). In fact our very self-regard is caught up in this requital which in turn bestows to us—through the other—an equality, trust, and therefore 'educating, reproving, supporting us' in the process (112).

The dynamic configuration of action and *inter*-actions in movement is anything but passive and benign for the person. She rather is supported or educated or reproved by her interdependent other—the one whose self-regard depends upon my power to expect things from her, i.e. the will to power to act. If we do not possess the requisite power to perform a duty, the other's 'right' remains hypothetical. More precisely, moral duties are based on a kind of phenomenology of subjectivities: 'only to that which they believe lies within our power, provided it is the same thing we believe lies within our power' (112). Notably, it is the *belief* and not the actual power that counts; moreover the correspondency of beliefs is important for the power to exist, making actions or duties dependent objects of invisible forces that constitute a symbiosis. The symbiosis explains the phenomenon of giving 'back in the measure in which we have been given to' since social relations are seen in terms of an exchange (as opposed to free willing and altruistic sacrifice). After all, for Nietzsche the law has its origins in the economy of retribution, sanctioning and blood expenditure—expenditure forming the basis of *bios* and resistance the essential prerequisite of freedom. Before exploring these origins further, it is significant how morals (duties) are attached to the very way in which we exchange symbols, sentiments, value, unconscious affects, and beliefs in mutual benefits of reciprocity. The error of 'freedom of will' depicts the human being as having a freedom before it enters the society of intercourse with others—an *individuum in abstracto*. In the world of life, action is never *a priori* free since the social gregarious animal is first formed and shaped by his concrete customary practices and sensations. Free will is a logical fallacy which needs to be dispensed with in order to make way for the reality of struggle and tension in our fundamentally interdependent life, a life characterized by blissless states of 'rising and sinking' powers and rights (112).

Already at this stage of development of a genealogy of morality, we find Nietzsche asserting the vital point concerning the capacity to make promises. Within this same passage he continues the line of argument to the point where 'promises' appear possible only as a result of the matrix of power and demands which circumscribe existence as a social phenomenon. The 'feeling of duty depends upon our having the same *belief* in regard to the extent of our power as others have' he argued. If in other words we believe that we cannot reciprocate on the same basis owing to a lack of power, then the *sense* of obligation and responsibility is diminished. It is not enough that the other believes they possess enough power or that even I have sufficient power to fulfill my duty or responsibility. I must have the *belief* that I do otherwise fulfilling my duty might be jeopardized. That would be sufficient for liberalism but with Nietzsche it is the concern with my power to keep promises that is paramount. Beyond preserving one's 'self-regard', as he called it, lies the reciprocal belief in ourselves being 'able to promise certain things and bind ourselves to perform them' (112). Although Nietzsche did not continue with this important thematic in *Daybreak*—a book on the 'prejudices of morality'—he took it up again as we have already observed in subsequent publications. The capacity and therefore willing-power of promise making and keeping is one of those significant strands of self-overcoming (i.e. ethical self-formation) that qualify for singular attention. What is significant here is what distinguishes our aforementioned autonomous individual who is capable of entering into promise-making covenants from ordinary persons who find solace either in fatalism or in mere self-regard. Whilst Nietzsche admits the reality of each of these phenomena in human affairs it is most interesting that his earliest inklings of a transmoral spirit or 'soul' involves the image of a promise-making being.

Man not only requires his self-regard (pride) and mutual recognition within interpersonal exchanges and actions; he also is a creature of (reciprocal) belief structures particularly as they pertain to perceptions of power and, attendantly, power to make promises. It would be tempting perhaps to assign significance of belief to the origins of Nietzsche's own moral conscience vis-à-vis his Lutheran upbringing and acquaintance with the fundamentally Judaic idea of man as a subject of covenants (with God and rabbinic castes). Yet this would need to be tempered with an alternate conception that derives from Renaissance and post-Renaissance societies such as France whose noble figures and idioms were characterized by powers of promise-making. Although this is made clearer in his subsequent *Beyond Good and Evil*, we find the appearance of this most important indicator of ethical commitment central to Nietzsche's first thoroughgoing critical work on morality—customary morals as such. Even though evil and good will recur in seemingly endless cycles of time, Nietzsche commits himself nonetheless to this fundamentally archaic notion of a covenant—that which forms an invisible bond between two human beings. It is all the more fascinating in the face of what he clearly understood to be the essentially 'human-all-too-human': finite *über*-animals with their capacity to deceive themselves and lapse into servitude can nevertheless be trusted to a point. Moreover, they are worthy of entering into contracts and exchanges of various kinds because ultimately we transform our inherently wild, uncivilized nature by doing so. That is to say, we find in relations of reciprocity that the other impinges upon our power as we do upon hers and thus in the process create mutual perceptions and *beliefs*. We hold others responsible because we have esteemed them with our belief and expectation that they are capable of performing their customary 'duty'. Duty here being an effect of demands that action follow on from the right accorded to an other to impinge on our sphere of power.

Yet we are also enhanced and extended morally by what otherwise could appear as shear dominance: 'educating, reproving, supporting us', these others thereby bestow both equality and trust upon us as they intercourse with us in seemingly utilitarian ways. Instead of beginning with the 'right' and 'duty' of the individual here the instantiation of subjective (and inter-subjective) powers is more significant since one's actions are signified or interpreted only within symbolic exchanges occurring between persons (and groups, tribes, nations). Such a moment—of activity, obligations and promise-making—is always dynamic because of the flux of powers and interpretations permeating the experience of (co-)existence. Instead of a monadic self, Nietzsche proclaims the priority of the moment of becoming across the human species—in some ways not dissimilar to both Plato and Hegel's process of Becoming. Importantly, this interstitial moment is marked out by the decisive activity of promise-making. We move from initially giving back 'in the measure in which we have been given to' to a 'feeling of duty' based on 'our having the same *belief* in regard to the extent of our power as others have'; and finally, to our belief that 'we *are able* to promise certain things and bind ourselves to perform them' (112). It is not so much whether we *do* fulfill our promises that is important theoretically here but rather the phenomenology of promising and binding ourselves to a time in which they may be performed. Previously we made the case for enablement and capacity for taking on responsibilities as key dimensions of *becoming* free (i.e. self-overcoming). Yet what was previously missing is now made apparent: the phenomenology of inter-subjective 'contracts' between persons who later come to attribute intrinsic moral worth (values) to quite ordinary interactions and exchanges with others (including conflict, mutuality, self-enhancing work etc.).

The *entre-nous* was left implicit if not even passive; however, now the reciprocity between persons allows the I to become an active promise-making creature—someone who willfully overcomes *zoi* by committing herself to an other moment yet to arrive. A human being sees itself as capable of binding itself to a future time when it will *perform* those promised things. It is a willing creature but uniquely one that understands itself as capable of committing itself to something and therefore by implication to someone *else*. Overcoming now becomes self-overcoming in the sense that oneself commits to another human being by making and indeed contracting a promise with them. The other has a purchase, an indebtedness, on time through the power immanent in my commitment—a commitment that stems from my belief *and* will to commit to time thereby submitting myself to the potential danger of *Chronos*. Time is my and hence the other's futural becoming; it exceeds the present and through binding to this 'other time' I am simultaneously bound to the other through my word. My word must later be followed by the performance of an action that I willed to commit myself to—a promise. To exercise my power to make promises and thus commit to fulfilling them is the very stuff of an autonomous ethical conscience. It is a kind of conscience not beholden to strictures of an historical consciousness since it traverses the temporal limit of a given *Gemeinschaft* (community). For this reason, an ethical conscience requires the kind of freedom that a free spirit knows vis-à-vis customary norms/morals (*Sitten*) because having 'freed himself from tradition' the autonomous individual can transcend its blind stupidity or errors of belief, i.e. 'freedom of will', cause and effect, and unconditional imperatives (HH 225). Thus although moralities emerge out of concrete historical communities, freedom and responsibility transvaluate their temporal delimitations.

Having looked at the decisively important question of promises—a point most often overlooked in analytic moral philosophy—we now turn to the last omission made by Strawson in relation to Nietzsche's critique of free will. Quite apart from omitting the significance of promise capabilities, Strawson failed to draw out the legal and non-legal dimensions of the fallacy of 'freedom of will'. (Fatalism similarly fails to explain why the necessarily concrete social relations of contract between persons should form the basis of normative claims.) The duty to treat others in a particular way is traced back by Nietzsche to a point of becoming before 'bad conscience' had become predominate. The human being *Ab initio* is a pre-moral human being who is enmeshed in reciprocal relations that arise from the demands of preservation, security, eros and (common) belief. To abstract the individual from his world would be an error since it a priori sets apart that being which is concretely enmeshed in the lives of others. For this reason, 'morality' emerges out of the customary norms and practices of an historical community. Strawson while alluding to this fact concerning moral responsibility has however no genealogical theory to account for such phenomena. Evaluations of persons in terms of 'good' and 'bad', argued Nietzsche, emerge out of reciprocal contract relations of punishment, retribution and reward. This is promulgated much earlier than *Beyond Good and Evil* and before *Daybreak*: after Nietzsche had first assimilated the work of his friend Paul Ree in *Human All Too Human*; secondly, through this cathartic work Nietzsche began to identify evidence of conscious work in deriving moral evaluations and standpoints from complex constellations of dependence, duty and reciprocal appropriations of power. Presaging genealogical accounts of later works, Nietzsche in 'On the History of the Moral Sensations' (HH) outlines the basis of moral virtues as deriving from communal enunciations of 'good' and 'bad' conduct (or persons).

Morality is predicated on what members of a historic community understand as constituting 'good' or valuable actions. Genealogies trace the origins, evolution and vicissitudes of moral phenomena to explain their formation in time as opposed to metaphysical concepts of intrinsic (moral) essences. In 1878 we already see his explanation incorporating sociological ideas of 'ruling tribes and castes' determining what belongs to 'good' and conversely 'bad'. For 'a long time, good and bad mean the same as noble and base, master and slave' (HH 45). In terms of our foregoing discussion, the capacity to requite is once again significant: 'Whoever has the power to requite good with good, evil with evil, and who really also engages in requital...is called good' while 'whoever is powerless and cannot engage in requital is considered bad' (45). Why morals feel virtuous or 'good' quite naturally is because one who belongs also 'belongs to the "good", to a community that has a common feeling because all the individuals are entwined with one another by having a sense that requital is due' (45). Bad persons by definition must therefore constitute those who stand outside of the 'common feeling'; whereas one's enemy cannot properly speaking be regarded evil because even one's enemy engages in requital. It is our intersubjective connection and common feeling that conveys to us what is virtuous, right, worthy and not evil. To unravel a moral and intellectual conscience from its interlocking web of interdependencies would be an idealist positing of an intrinsic moral precept. Against Kant, Schelling and Hegel but perhaps closer to Feuerbach, Nietzsche arrives at a social determination of moral consciousness, one that is the product of history (time) and society (space). Obeying here becomes another source of pleasure because the act of affirming the common feeling of belonging to the good takes on the form of a habit. As

> soon as a person has the power to compel others, he exerts it in order to introduce and enforce his *customs*...Likewise, a community of individuals forces every individual to follow the same customs' and this may involve the induce-

ment of pleasure so that one feels good about perpetuating existing customary practices (HH 97).

Pain and suffering are most likely to diminish rather than increase consequently, whereas the individual who acts according to a liberated spirit can expect hardship and even condemnation ('the evil one'). To live dangerously therefore is not about living recklessly but about becoming liberated from the necessity of *Sitten*.

Customs themselves are not the fountainhead of responsibility since an ethical conscience—as we have seen—must stand independent of the hidden *logic* of customary morals. Morality is what jeopardizes ethicality because morals as customs render ethical responsibility most susceptible to its tyrannical logic, whereas the ethical moment of responsibility for the overcoming individual signifies uneasiness with moral life. This uneasiness is further heightened by the fact that norms and established modes of moral life are the effects of slavish values and affects. The paradox here is that communities throughout history have been ruled and maintained by former slave or plebian types who usurped the position of powerful nobles, thereby instituting a table of values that befitted their class or tribe. In effect, to obey meant following the path of particularly slavish ways—obedience to unfreedom. One can add that 'obedience' may even entail obedience to the habit (routine) of *not-caring-at-all*—of habitual irresponsibility. European nihilism represents unfreedom in the guise of this pernicious ethos of irresponsibility even whilst espousing the truth of 'freedom of will' as free will and, concomitantly, true moral responsibility. Contradiction thus pervades the modern individual and yet so many discussions of the primacy of 'freedom' versus 'determinism' will not dissolve this predicament.

Turning a closer eye to the origins of morality we return to previously discussed points about debt and expenditure (in chapter one). Since responsibility is associated with duties as moral actions, and actions themselves are linked to customary morals and duties; and customary norms and morals emerge out of social forms of exchange and intercourse, it is necessary to see how Nietzsche extended this analysis in later arguments. Later writings of Nietzsche display a keener eye for the role, which debt and expenditure in inter-personal exchanges play insofar as ethical life is concerned. We have already seen that expenditure—foregoing as 'cost'—is an integral part of *becoming* free (chapter one). The object here is to demonstrate what was missing from Strawson's critique of true moral responsibility; namely, a genealogical account of the broader legal and non-legal framework of our *Sittlichkeit* (customary morality) which gives rise to the fallacy of absolute (moral) responsibility. This entails an examination of the debt or moral debt incurred through forms of exchange, retribution and even revenge (which is examined further in chapter five). Unlike conventional moral philosophers, Nietzsche deployed his historical philosophy— philosophical anthropology to extract the origins of moral sentiments out of social relations of exchange and cooperation which social theoreticians and anthropologist later would come to appreciate as a *Lebenswelt* (life-world). Hence it is not enough to allude simply to an existing legal or moral order (Strawson;

Williams) as the overdetermining horizon of our 'moral conscience' and its 'psychology of will'—an ideation that ineluctably fails to render the real origins of morality (*Sitte* meaning moral codes and rules rather than ethicality—*Sittlichkeit*). While social philosophers and analysts argue about transcendence of morality or moralities, Nietzsche we have already noted was not averse to acknowledging the need for ethical life to surpass or transcend the confining limits of *Sittlichkeit der Sitte* (morality of mores).[33] This task of difficult freedom is what makes self-overcoming vital; yet paradoxically it is the social dimension of his being that also defines his moral consciousness and world outlook. His ethical conscience recognizes the fundamental jurisprudence underlying all moral actions and to that extent, Nietzsche the so-called 'immoralist' displays in fact an understanding of ethical life as integral to overcoming servitude ('slave morality'). By 'the social' dimension we mean—as did also Ludwig Feuerbach and George Wilhelm Hegel—those deep anthropological forms of intercourse which defined life before established state societies arose. Customary morality we must remember is first communal before it later comes to assume a formal juridical form.

The importance of this subject is shown by Nietzsche having devoted the whole Second Treatise of the *Genealogy* to these dimensions of life. Our examination of debtor-creditor relations, moreover, can be considered as an extension of our previous analysis of 'expenditure' as an important dimension of *becoming* free from slave morality. Before the arrival of the priestly caste and its peculiarly moralized worldview, the stage which Nietzsche considered 'pre-moral' and nobly naturalistic without an overbearing State, human beings are enveloped by complex webs of exchange and contract. The raw 'instinct of freedom' is already sublimated and transmuted into so many forms of requital and interpretation regarding one's belonging to a community of others. Before the complex state emerges, they 'do not know what guilt, what responsibility, what consideration is, these born organizers'; they never the less know communal life, social intercourse and surrender to the deities they hold in esteem (GM II: 17). Coming into 'society' the once half-animal internalizes instincts that it formerly discharged in its wild, adventurous existence, thus developing its 'soul'. Conscience and consciousness now wrestle and mingle with multifarious drives and instincts, though notably without a 'bad conscience'. It at this juncture of human development ('evolution' proving a too problematic term here) that we find a short interval before the onset of a history of nihilism is propelled by a vicious guilt conscience and spirit of resentment. In other words, before Buddhist and Judaeo-Christian ascetic morals (ideals) take their hold on humanity, a brief interval is observable where *Mensch* is in possession of a soul not yet overcome by guilt. In this interval, we find reverberations within man's soul that owe to relations and 'payments' that have yet to become dangerously nihilistic. Danger and error are certainly present as is knowledge and 'artistic plans', but no bad conscience of responsibility yet. In the pre-moral age, man is in intercourse with both his fellow human being and his god.

A kind of contract is entered into on both counts in the form of a 'debtor-creditor' relationship. Eschewing transcendentalist presuppositions of a higher order of Being or Oneness (Schelling's *Absolute*) Nietzsche's wholly secular order of concepts places both mortal and immortal on an equal plane. The creditor, God, enters a covenant with man who thereafter conceives of the Father in terms of indebtedness. Before the onset of the 'most terrible sickness' in man and therefore the whole earth—self-torture of a guilt conscience—there were indeed '*more noble* ways of making use of the fabrication of gods than...self-crucifixion' (GM II: 22-23). The Greeks are one noble case in point. The juridical concept of the debtor who enters into contract with man and God alike however stems further back in basic human activities involving 'purchase, sale, exchange, trade, and commerce' (GM II: 4). In tones very reminiscent of Marx's study of forms of exchange in *Grundrisse der Kritik der politischen Oekonomie* (1857), yet until now quite absent from Nietzsche's *oeuvre*, we find that the material conditions of life are foremost (self-preservation being a shared concept between Marx and Nietzsche). Although at times Nietzsche claims community is the result of a common share in security, reciprocal relations of exchange and payment of some kind or another—material, psychic, spiritual—appear equally significant. Even God is brought into the realm of 'payment', debt, and exchange with redemption (Christ's blood) constituting a payment of kind for Adam's sin.[34] Therefore, although analytic philosophers such as Strawson are right to point out the legal background or presuppositions of 'duty' and moral responsibility, they do not go far enough into this important 'background'. For the very important work of creating memory in the most feeble and temporal creature known as the animal-human is built in fact on the ability to *promise* something in exchange. Promise-making is bound up with, in other words, with the economy of self-preservation and its relations of dominance and reciprocity. The primordial promise, that of a God of deliverance who in taking away our suffering causes us to be eternally indebted to his grace, is a kind of spiritualization of the power to commit to an Other; it is an exchange contract defined by the economy of sacrifice. Leaving to one side the multiple shifts in our mode of sacrifice to idols, we find that an anthropomorphic projection turns the gods' willingness to make compacts with man into an archetypal exchange. We are forever in debt to them and hence a payment is required.

The anthropomorphic is then interrelated with the historical anthropology that finds human beings in commerce and trade both over objects and themselves. Sociability emerges out of this intercourse—a commerce of debt, payment, and repayment, pain-suffering and eventually punishment. Legal subjects are as old as the contractual relationship between 'creditor' and 'debtor', both having derived from the 'basic forms of purchase, sale, exchange, trade, and commerce' (GM II: 4). These most elementary and hence 'primitive' activities are the cornerstone of civilized existence: 'Purchase and sale, together with their psychological accessories, are older than even the beginnings of any societal associations and organizational forms' (GM II: 8). Thus Nietzsche could declare that no 'degree of civilization however low has yet been discovered' in which the 'oldest and most primitive relationship among persons there is, in the relationship between buyer and seller, creditor and debtor' was not present (GM II: 8). Why is it here in *homo economicus* that Nietzsche situates the originary capacity for promise-making? The reason is one must be trusted in order for a (re-) payment to be made hence it is in the *situ* of evaluating that *koinonia* (community) emerges. Out of nearness to others society is formed: 'here for the first time a person stepped up against person, here for the first time a person *measured himself* by another person' (GM II: 8). Thinking itself is associated with thinking about '[m]aking prices, gauging values, thinking out equivalents, exchanging' for in doing so 'man designated himself as the being who measures values, who values and measures as the "appraising animal in itself"' (GM II: 8). Promising, like payment of debt, presupposes an 'appraising animal'—one who measures himself and who knows that measure to be dependent on an other. Man the valuating animal measures his debt and payment needs not because of thought but because he has acquired the capacity to measure debt and recompense toward others. Through exchange and contract, he gauges values not only according to economic price but also according to evaluations of others and his promise to them (e.g. indebtedness).

Reciprocal forms of intercourse in the form of evaluation, gauging, exchanging, juridical recognition and the like are definitive anthropologically of what constitutes a *human* being. Here, Nietzsche argues, 'that oldest acumen was bred, here likewise we may suspect the first beginnings of human pride, man's feeling of pre-eminence with respect to other creatures' (GM II: 8). Next to an indebtedness incurred from the gods we are also held in debt to others as we pay them back for various gains. Having the capacity to measure oneself while also evaluating the other, we are in a position to make promises that will indebt us into the future. It suggests a capacity to will to pay in the future and therefore presupposes a level of trust from a fellow human being. The futural aspect of being in the present we can say henceforth requires an appraising human being who sees himself as fundamentally a promise-making creature able to illicit trust from others. These fellow other 'appraising animals' estimate his value according to this fundamental 'creditor-debtor' contractual relation. It is a communion of sorts that lays the foundation for the 'juridical subject' of law. The measuring subject is however not entirely sovereign over his powers because he is at the same time beholden to the estimation and measuring of others, particularly with regard to one's capacity to keep one's word. One's futurity is bound up with an inter-subjective temporality that lends becoming a high degree of coexistence with others, sometimes manifest in the form of equality (peers, tribe members) and other times in master—servant relations. Becoming is much more a human affair than some Eternal Return interpretations would have it; moreover, it is non-monistic because there is no singular Substance to begin with since Nietzsche eschewed Aristotelian ideas of an *ousia* in things. Responsibility is central to the process of becoming human—or a higher human spirit—because it appropriates and metamorphizes the debtor's promise-making powers to repay their counterpart (stranger, kin, Lord, 'God').

Nietzsche here is closer to Feuerbach (Wagner's philosopher) and Hegel than to Fichte and Novalis. Monism would bode well for the psychology of freedom of will which Kantians and Cartesians alike expounded and propagated through Western metaphysics. Instead Nietzsche's idea of becoming is incorporative of all that which is simultaneously 'inner' and 'outer' of the human-animal. Since there is no free will and bad conscience arises out of historical formations, responsibility can only emerge out of the intercourse and commerce between species-members. We noted above that moral responsibility as conventionally understood was highly problematic because it too adopted a monistic concept of the self—a self that chooses and decides for itself. Nietzsche's critique we may recall targeted the ahistorical nature of philosophic thought and its wont to abstract the individual moral 'self' from its concrete sensuous existence in nature and society. Hence in a sense we have come full circle back to Nietzsche's philosophical anthropology and how it intersects with a non-monistic account of the formation of responsible human (noble) beings. The dyadic relation of exchanges between debtors and creditors, promise-givers and trust-makers, and evaluator and evaluated can now be added to this picture. Against the logicians, an historical anthropology of the economy of human 'expenditure' and cost demonstrates the entwinement of 'the human' in configurations of dyadic relations. To be sure, the intensity and musicality of the individual soul is essentially a *sui generis* phenomenon within a series of psycho-social formations—the configuration of dyadic relations. Formations, argued the grand German genealogist, have their origins and itinerary, and as such can never validate a spurious monism whether of the Cartesian or Aristotelian kind. To this extent, Nietzsche concurred with Darwinism even if he had to invert it.[35]

Of particular importance here is the recognition of oneself as a 'measuring animal' that is equally assessed and evaluated by others who are themselves capable of weighing things up. This is Nietzsche's axiology of responsibility in the broader sense; a sense that finds oneself capable of regularity, necessary calculation, time-keeping, contract-making, exchanging on agreed upon values and compacts. To hold another accountable to contractually agreed upon ends and purposes is to invest one's self-preservation in the promise of an other. Mutual acknowledgement becomes the basis of a communal existence that will in the final instance be defined by forms of power and willing that put distance between individuals and groups. The pathos of distance both regulates and mediates all forms of exchange and commerce even whilst a form of mutual acknowledgment prevails as a kind of prerequisite to general social intercourse. Herd-formation encompasses this type of dyadic life as it both bonds and separates 'types of man' as Nietzsche called it. Those who are not dependent upon herd-morality are autonomous individuals even whilst they are formed from the same contractual mutual acknowledgment that underlies social reality. Hence the reason why Nietzsche also considered himself 'a decadent': to *become* free, to be capable of responsibility, one must first have to belong to civilized society. This is integral to having a 'second nature' once the 'animal self' has undergone the process of taming and caging. The redemption of man cannot take place *ex nihilo* but must emerge from the promise of a philosophy of the future. Being a social animal, the gregarious human being must overcome his nihilistic despair of herd-consciousness in order to aim at more distant goals, the distant star in the navigator's horizon of time.

It is in responsibility that such a noble spirit finds the redemption from decadence an imperative that does not instill fear in him. Holding himself to promises made and the trust that ensues from it he understands himself capable of onerous responsibilities. Intercourse and requital allow this civilized animal a higher sense of humanity than the one presently marked by feebleness and irresponsibility. Although many fear freedom—its abyssal quality—the higher, overcoming individual welcomes its arrival because he strives for it, he wills it without having to suppose an illusory 'freedom of will'. What it requires however is the strength of will not to fear loosening the ties that entwine us or entangle us in contractual relationships. Mutual acknowledgment as equality fails to meet the mark of noble freedom because it merely entices one to take pleasure in belonging. It reduces responsibility to the norms of the herd, morality, rather than setting the goal on an ethical conscience which transvaluates historic norms of conduct (i.e. duty). The basis of such norms—of morality—is the axiology of modes of exchange and contract that require a certain type of human, viz an 'appraising animal' that measures himself 'by another person'. The axiological here refers onto the need for the overcoming individual to appropriate these powers and capabilities immanent within his own soul as a result of having first become 'regular, necessary' through acculturation (sociability). What is 'valuable' is extant in the constellations of power to reciprocate in kind and to contract obligations by means of payment, repayment and debt. Yet the one capable of transcending extant forms of 'duty' or responsibility is the human being who is not restrained by existing social relations of exchange, contract and reciprocal requital. The 'free spirit' is one who emerges out of and surges forth from existing forms of sociability (morality) to strive for heretofore unknown continents of 'becoming', including responsibilities that are devoid of bad conscience and empty abstractions (of Right).

We can see again the saliency of the argument that capacities and enablement are inseparable from the formation of a noble responsible human type. Anti-metaphysically speaking, there is no absolute self, Spirit or Will therefore it follows that the futurity of ethical autonomy cannot be imprisoned by the present—existing concrete relations and moral codes within the State—even though it breaks away from this granite of moral truth. Our 'second nature' in other words is caught between the past and the future, just as it is between nihilistic despair and ecstatic joy, and responsibility and feeble liberty. Freedom and its attendant responsibility (in Nietzsche's sense) cannot be properly secured by the 'civil-law relationship of the debtor and creditor' that antedates and underpins modern society (GM II: 19). The rule of law and its axiology of moral values may not require destruction per se but rather a certain distance to keep the ethical moment from collapsing into decadence, a customary morality that becomes ossified and hardened like clogged arteries. An autonomous person of ethical conscience requires the creative design of a (true) 'artist's plan' to fashion something different out of his 'second nature' (as earlier explained). Although his second nature is a result of the vicissitudes of the taming process of civilized sociability—communal association and contract law—the futural promise of freedom enables him to envision new goals and tableau of values that will further reshape his already acquired 'second nature'. Civility is both constraint and *Bildung* and yet the latter importantly relates to *bios* by making possible growth, extension, renovation and resistance (expenditure). The ossification of *Bildung* would only further stifle the free spirit, preventing the sublimation of impulses from forging grand responsibilities and forms of intercourse transcendent of Today's sickly mob rule. The sickly state we must remember is a condition of guilt prevailing in the deep seat of the soul; hence an overcoming is necessary if our servitude to bad conscience is to be negated by the promise of the future.

Living between the future and the past, the noble free spirit cannot rely on the virtues of morality-as-customary-morality. As creditor, a community may scornfully look upon our sovereign individual as one who appears to be a law unto herself. And she is indeed a 'lawgiver' in Nietzsche's language, someone capable of commanding and legislating onto human nature its new designs or 'plans', each plan having its respective 'table of values'. Breaking away from custom and duty, the 'immoralist' naturally enough incites resentment and ultimately even revenge since the creditor's (society) expected retaliation or retribution is a form of punishment for unpaid 'debt' issuing from receiving all kinds benefits as member of a civil society. Goodness—security, fellow-feeling, moral sentiments, higher culture, spiritualization of instincts, ideals, grand politics, leisurely pleasures and servants—has a cost. You must pay or more precisely *re*pay to society (the naturalized creditor) for advantages it has *promised* you in exchange for dutiful obedience. To disown customary duties is to disown the goodness of that *particular* society and anyone who dares threaten its moral goods (values) is estimated worthy of a creditor's retribution—punishment. You have not exchanged appropriately hence, intentional injury in the form of revenge will ensue just as the gods had punished humanity for its unequal utilization of them (i.e. hubris). Freedom has a cost: you must expend in the form of resistance otherwise, your evaluation of its value is either naïve or cheapened or both. What we have attempted to show is that responsibility is not synonymous with obligations to established customary duties. That would be respecting 'morality' instead of an autonomous ethical conscience that welcomes responsibility because it is open to the future, an ethical conscience that is no longer burdened by the deadweight of guilt—'bad conscience'. To be free of guilt is to be afforded the capacity to exercise a sovereign conscience in relation to one's life and exchanges with others without lapsing necessarily back into a fallacious 'freedom of will' that knows no expenditure. This is Nietzsche's 'lawgiver': one able to command, to assume responsibilities and to make promises she knows she will fulfill.

We can now see the limits of Strawson's critique of moral responsibility based on the fallacious 'freedom of will' concept, a critique that admirably points to an existing juridical milieu ('background') without however providing a *genealogical* account of it. The 'it' or the object in this case shows that such a milieu is a formation that is itself formative of the abstract juridical subject that is supposed to possess a free will—a will to choose what is dutiful. Beyond this analytical deficiency, there lies another flaw in his account: the absence of a notion of *trust* as constitutive of this important juridical 'background' (milieu) from which sprang idealist notions of a *true* moral responsibility. As we have stressed the contractual exchange between persons—calculating price, estimating value and debt, measuring, evaluating and promising repayment—it means that in the inter-subjective *exchange* a type of intercourse is established. Herewith the 'civil-law relationship of the debtor to his creditor' we find showing an inconspicuous reciprocity which often is overlooked in discussions of Nietzsche and his celebrated 'overmen'—solitary, Zarathustra figures who eschew all forms of sociality. This is a fundamental misinterpretation of what Nietzsche understood to be possible in a post-moral age based on the free spirits of future philosophers 'who are coming'. Redemption, in other words, is not a wholly immanent or solitary affair since we know from *Beyond Good and Evil* (188) the aim of Nietzsche's exhortations is nothing less than *humankind* itself. Of course, 'reciprocity' need not imply or necessitate a democratic equality between persons; a projection of 'plebian morality' onto this concept might suggest equality is necessary for reciprocity to take place. Yet this is an error of modern (juridico-political) prejudice: reciprocity antedates both modernity and the State, stemming as far back as when human 'debtors' sacrificed to their gods (creditors) to repay their spiritual debt. Reciprocity, like our aforementioned requital, is anthropologically archaic being an aspect of life that was for millennia defined by the 'pathos of distance' as Nietzsche called it. Our primary concern here rather is the promise-trust nexus found within the economy of communal life as a form of self-preservation. Trust is the other-side of promise-making: it holds the subject-as-promise-maker accountable to a (spiritual) commitment that would be of benefit to the receiver (e.g. creditor). Another human being exchanges something of value with a person who promises to reciprocate value and thereby is trusted for a time in the future.

Nietzsche's commanding legislator, in other words, is dependent upon the trust-giving individual who holds him to his word—to a commitment destined in the time to come. The 'obligation' that this 'promising' human being has is not to mere customary morality but to his fulfillment of a promissory note that was committed to shall be duly paid by actions. Word-giving or giving one's honorable word in the form of a promise is a type of action yet it is suggestive of further action. One's word must be protected, preserved and maintained lest it become 'cheap' and de-valued. That is, one accounts for oneself; one's value is estimated, measured and weighed up vis-à-vis the reckoning of one's worth by others. This is to say, our 'appraising animal' is self-appraising because of the *other*—the other self who reciprocates estimation, evaluation and most importantly valuing. In trusting they accord an axiological significance or worth to the said promise and commitment of action to follow. There is no promise as such until the other recognizes this as a commitment to the becoming moment of time. Hence it is a 'spiritual' commitment because as with all covenants and pacts the present is bound to the future as it is likewise to a past. To receive a promise necessarily implies a giving of trustworthiness to the debtor who wishes to have a purchase on time. In exchange for this purchase the other (creditor, society) must exact a cost for waiting in suspension for something valuable to come forth. Thus trust is linked to an oath: to a pact in which both parties possess a faith in their exchangeable powers to receive—give, promise—trust, and commit—acknowledge. One cannot go without the other; they form a symbiotic relation and at a supra inter-subjective level form the basis of social life in and through communal association. As *Gesellschaft* all kinds of force relations run through its social fabric according to herd-formations and 'master-slave' relations. And yet such phenomena are predicated on the dyadic exchange relation that requires reciprocation between two human beings—beings whose 'second nature' becomes something other than what is because of the economy of this primary 'civil-law relationship' discussed here.

Trust is only reciprocated in the faith that one's promise holds value—a value of truthfulness. The truth lies within time: firstly in its originary form as *promise*; secondly, in the forthcoming action that embodies the *commitment* to keep one's word. To honor one's word is to fulfill it in *futural* time—the time that has not yet come. For the one who awaits and abides in time, trust conjoins them to this *in*visible time that has yet to arrive. They hold onto an oath through entrusting the individual with the power of her word's responsibility—a commitment that is made by her having first become 'regular, necessary,' measured, evaluative, calculative and mnemonic through her promises. An oath such as this manifests a certain spirit, almost a religious spirit because of its *pistis* in the promise of the time to come and a faith in the contract carrying a value that is temporally suspended (in time). Nietzsche's commitment is evident, for instance, in the promise laid out in *Beyond Good and Evil* of a 'philosophy of the future' lying therein. *Becoming* embraces both the trust and promise that marks temporal life just as it holds out a faith in far distant goals: free sovereign individuals who conceive their great responsibilities as a natural outgrowth of a postmoral conscience and *Bildung*. The nexus of promise and trust is incorporated in the 'great promise' of becoming free in the non-present, a moment in which the human being awakens for himself 'an anticipation, a hope', as 'if with him something were announcing itself, something preparing itself' (GM II: 16). It is the fact that man is 'full of future' (GM II: 16) that sees him preparing and announcing a new form of life that is founded on the vigorous capacities to make a promise, hold one's word, commit to action, honor bestowed trust by 'repayment' in kind, and exchange on the basis of acknowledging expenditure as the basis of value-formation. In a key passage on the constitutive power of trust for promise-making activity, Nietzsche identifies two salient features.

First, is the need to prepare or activate the conscience to *become* conscious of obligation or duty. Before the establishment of the moral law in Kant's language, there is a need to create a mnemetic conscience of one's promises to others lest otherwise he remain oblivious to his obligations to repay others (society or creditors). An expendable cost is 'forgotten' by an undisciplined, unprepared conscience. To provide 'a guarantee for the seriousness and the sacredness of his promise, to impress repayment on his conscience as a duty, as an obligation, the debtor—by virtue of a contract—pledges to the creditor' something of value, i.e. his body, wife, freedom or sacrifice (GM II: 5). Without a preparation of this kind no trust can be instilled in the promise to repay someone since dutiful obligation (to reciprocate) appears to lack a firm conscience-substance. Creating a memory for promise-making activity is an essential prerequisite for the formation of an ethical conscience that knows obligation, i.e. responsibility vis-à-vis promises made. In short, without a *mnēmonikos'* conscience the individual loses hold of the value(s) that is exchanged back and forth in either visible or invisible forms, thus forging a third value form: I—not-I sociability (a point we shall return to later). The second salient point concerns the inexorable expenditure involved in being human in the *Bios* sense and, in particular, in living amongst others within complexes of civil order. A promise we must remember is a pledge, a contracted oath that one will pay in return for what one has received from another (a creditor). We saw in a previous chapter that Nietzsche conceived of freedom in these terms of cost and expenditure. In the present analysis, we find that the unfinished animal becomes an 'appraising animal' who measures himself according to others contiguous to him. Each of these important words—measure, appraise debtor, creditor, exchange, repayment, value, cost and price—convey the important significance accorded to the *economy* of the much celebrated yet problematic 'moral conscience'.

Like all economies, this one posits the mutual intercourse between the self and other without necessarily invoking the pejorative term 'herd' feeling and thinking. Before 'the herd' there is already expenditure and value formation between one human being and another—the most primordial association that also forms the basis of the juridical subject of law. To return to the subject of trust once again, it is notable that fellow-feeling as a constitutive element of community cannot exist without trust—the exchange relation of promise—trust giving proves a powerful bonding force between disparate individuals. However, Nietzsche does not trust 'the herd' and its desire to equalize on the basis of trusting others. There seems to be a *sui generis* power to the herd and its peculiar herd-consciousness, one that appalls Nietzsche because the unique moment of promise is overrun by the *demos'* spirit of negation (devaluation). From giving trust to another individual, it turns viciously onto *ressentiment* and its negative force: the other has increased or elevated himself and I find this a threat, an unacceptable breach of the threshold of power (as growth) that must diminish my status. The paradox now reveals itself: the herd cannot be trusted even whilst its very existence owes to the formation of relations built on trusting those who make promises that are in time to be fulfilled. The herd transvaluates what is *sui generis* about the promise—trust keeper relation and perverts it into something ignoble: general conformity. Customary morality poses as the policing agency of this general conformity and what is more, it stifles creative impulses carried within individuals who are actively *becoming* through their various contractual exchanges (broadly conceived)—the economy and axiology of expenditure. Freedom then logically cannot be entrusted to those who merely follow custom and conventional morality. The 'promise' lies in the compact we make with transcendence, a transcendence of present temporality as couched within herd-morality through the higher commitment to a humanity that is to come. Just like the 'one who is to come' in the prophetic tone of redemptive words shared by Zarathustra and the prophets of the Old Testament.

Moses we recall similarly did not trust 'the herd'—idol worshipers—nor did he entrust them with the holy writ of redemption. After having come from 'on high' Moses is nauseated by the mob's collective behavior in quite analogous ways to Zarathustra's nausea with valley-life from atop of his mountain place. Moses cannot trust the 'human-all-too-human' in man just as God cannot either; on the other hand, Moses must be *prepared* to receive God's (creditor's) redemptive value while the creditor himself gives his promise of redemption: the Promised Land. Value, in other words, circulates within the interactions of an exchange but it also requires investment in the 'worth' of a Tomorrow—the future (in Biblical terms, the messianic 'Promised Land'). For this reason it is unsurprising that Nietzsche characterizes the 'second nature' of this once 'animal soul' as enigmatic and 'full of future' even in all its 'contradictory', 'deep', and now regular necessary ontology (GM II: 16). Against repetition, the horizon is open and the supramoral sovereign individual—who no longer believes in the false 'psychology of will'—comes to embody freedom as the *promise* to overcome guilt and the nihilist's fantasy of a subject of free will thereby also negating the specific servitude of the state of morality (as *Sittlichkeit*). Between destruction and the rule of law lies the openness of promise: a promise that one holds immanently (through social intercourse) and transcendentally (through trust in the futurity of *becoming-as-forming*). These polarities of existence are similar to the aforementioned poles of past and future that give tension to the *present* moment.

We have finally stumbled upon, quite naturally in a circular fashion, Nietzsche's much celebrated idea of the 'tension of the bow', Apollo's bow. The tension is *itself* very important: between past-future, immanence-transcendence, servitude-freedom, customary-novel values, juridical precepts-ethical preparedness and so and so forth. To think *contra*-dualisms is most important for Nietzsche when eschewing traditional metaphysics and therefore the last dualism of all must similarly be overcome (negated): necessity-freedom. This chapter has concerned itself with demonstrating the possibility of responsibility *not* stemming essentially from either of these (false) polarities—polarities that were said to define the very essence of human existence. What is penultimate here is the one who is 'permitted to promise' to use Nietzsche's exact phrase (GM II: 2). This permission, we have now seen, emanates neither from 'God', or the State or one's Master and nor from one's guilt-ridden conscience: permission instead derives from one's formative ability to vouch for oneself owing to a well-honed preparation and distinct 'standard of value' as evidenced by their manifest will to responsibility. Those who are not 'permitted' clearly lack these capacities as a sign of their manifest feeble will: the lack of power to assume responsibility and sovereignty over oneself and one's intercourse with others. They cannot muster the necessary trust and noble authority which is required to call oneself 'a legislator', a law-giving 'commander' of a new table of values that reflects the *Sich-wiedererzeugen* of a 'free spirit' (self-regeneration) rather than *der Herdentrieb* (herd instinct) of a slavish conformist. The latter in particular lacks a conscience imbued with what eventually will form as a dominant instinct: the 'consciousness of this rare freedom' which Nietzsche notably equated (in the same passage) with 'this power over oneself and fate'—one determined to become master of himself (GM II: 2). This is the 'ripest fruit' of historical becoming—*physus* and *bios* brought together: that free spirit who has the 'proud knowledge of the extraordinary privilege of *responsibility*' (GM II: 2). Hence only the ripest noble union of *physus* and *bios* can be said to properly constitute the measure of any higher 'standard of value' for the following highly apposite reason: through 'his range and multiplicity' the sovereign ethical individual 'would even determine value and rank in accordance with how much and how many things one could bear and take upon himself, how *far* one could extend his responsibility' (BGE 212).

Notes

1. E. Levinas 'Substitution', *The Levinas Reader*. Edited by Sean Hand. Oxford: Blackwell Publishers, 1989, 113.

2. The most cogent theoretical analysis of the interaction(s) between sociocultural and physiological logics is given by Richard Schacht in 'Nietzschean Normativity', *Nietzsche's Postmoralism: Essays on Nietzsche's Prelude to Philosophy's Future*. Cambridge: Cambridge University Press, 2001. In arguing against 'naturalism' our discussion in this chapter confirms the highly nuanced treatment of Nietzsche's thought in this essay.

3. For a fatalist reading of Nietzsche see Brian Leiter *Nietzsche On Morality*. London: Routledge, 2002.

4. R. Schacht *Nietzsche*. London: Routledge, 1983. Nietzsche's sporadic use of Lamarckian explanations is justifiably identified therein as problematic.

5. *Züchtende* refers to a selective 'cultivating influence, always destructive as well as creative and form-giving...is always multiple and different according to the sort of human beings who are placed under its spell and protection' (BGE 61).

6. See note 3 above. An earlier statement of the argument is found in his 'The Paradox of Fatalism and Self-Creation in Nietzsche', *Nietzsche*. Edited by John Richardson and Brian Leiter. Oxford: Oxford University Press, 2001.

7. 'Why has nature been so stingy with human beings that it did not allow them to shine' asked Nietzsche (GS 336). The object of the next 'book' (Part V), written after *Zarathustra* and *Beyond Good and Evil*, is to work out 'the beautiful' in form-giving, in cultivating and in education. It is captured in the most decisive book-section of the *Gay Science* (IV) thus: 'I want to learn more and more to see as beautiful what is necessary in things' (276). It is necessary, arguably, that as creators we *overcome* nature's stinginess by adding to and *re*forming 'the creature' in man.

8. Maudemarie Clark and David Dudrick 'Nietzsche's Post-Positivism', *European Journal of Philosophy* 12:3 2004: 369-385.

9. In his correspondence of July 30, 1881 to Overbeck Nietzsche mentions Spinoza as a 'precursor' whose 'over-all tendency' was similar and thus in five main doctrinal points could recognize himself. See also Richard Schacht's *Making Sense of Nietzsche: Reflections Timely and Untimely*. Urbana: University of Illinois Press, 1995, ch 9.

10. Increasingly Nietzsche referred to the predominate force in the cosmos as the *will to life* rather than the 'will to power'. Although often used interchangeably the former concept he later realized encompasses wider aspects of experience and history than

'power' does, a view consistent with Spinoza's *conatus* (that exerting impulse which endeavours to persist in its very being).

11. Contra romantic-liberal voluntarism, Nietzsche argued in *Twilight of the Idols* (6, 8) 'One is necessary, one is a piece of fatefulness, one belongs to the whole, one is in the whole'; and this statement fully accords with our discussion of *comprehensive* knowledge in an earlier chapter.

12. See Walter Kaufmann's treatment of the *Dionysian* in Nietzsche's latter work as incorporating both polarities of Greek *mythos-logos*, *Nietzsche: Philosopher, Psychologist, Antichrist*. Fourth Edition, Princeton: Princeton University Press, 1974.

13. It follows logically that if Kant's attempt to find a 'faculty' of reason is falsified then the abstract determination of a standard of freedom—'absolute' freedom—is similarly falsified. History rather evidences an instinct for freedom in the struggle of human existence.

14. Robert C. Solomon, for instance, defends such an interpretive stance against Leiter's fatalist reading of Nietzsche along 'essentialist' lines ('Nietzsche on Fatalism and "Free Will"', *Journal of Nietzsche Studies*, 23, 2002: 63-87). Solomon's point is plausible except for the fact that he overinterprets existential motifs in Nietzsche's philosophy.

15. At this point I caution against any existentialist concept such as 'self-mastery' to describe this development since Nietzsche's love of fate, *amor fati*, precludes any highly voluntaristic notions of subjective and unconscious mastery. Of course this does not negate subjectivity per se; it merely denies a mastery of life in its Whole sense and, concomitantly, our experience of it through enculturation. For this reason, it arguably is more correct to speak of 'self-overcoming' in the unfolding of human natures (Becoming).

16. This ambiguous dimension of Nietzsche's argument often leads to the charge of aristocratic elitism, especially with respect to its political implications (cf. Ruth Abbey *Nietzsche's Middle Period*. Oxford; New York: Oxford University Press, 2000).

17. The problem with a deterministic reading of Nietzsche's *future* is that no 'destining' to become this-or-that-person can exist *if the condition* is not first met for overcoming to be possible. Part of a 'fate' (in non-deterministic language) is the necessity of conditions being available for the preparation and 'education' of *potential* noble souls to overcome necessarily difficult limits of being human in 'a higher sense'. Solomon's reading of 'destiny' in the abovementioned article (note 14) rightly allows for a non-deterministic rendering of destiny à là Fatalism properly defined.

18. In this respect, modern democracies are increasingly socialistic, according to Nietzsche, and unsurprisingly even less capable of a spiritual transfiguration of the soul, i.e. high spiritedness.

19. Giorgio Agamben, for instance, shows how the 'eschaton' is not synonymous with messianic time but rather succeeds it in the *kairos* of the world ('The Time That Is Left', *Epoché* (1) Vol. 7, Fall 2002; 3-4).

20. Rüdiger Safranski correctly rejects the claim that 'love of one's own fate' takes precedence in Nietzsche's overall philosophy in *Nietzsche: A Philosophical Biography* trans. by Shelley Frisch (London: Granta Books, 2003) (cf. note 15 above). In describing the young Nietzsche and his wrestling with the problem of freedom, Safranski articulates the fate-freedom relation helpfully thus: 'Only freedom can experience fate as a compelling power, and only the experience of fate can prod "free will" into liveliness and enhancement. Unity lies in dissonance' (37).

21. The concept of 'potentiality' is discussed at length in the chapter above 'Being Human, Nature and the Possibility of Overcoming'.

22. Walter Kaufmann *Nietzsche: Philosopher, Psychologist, Antichrist.* New Jersey: Princeton University Press, 1974, Ch 10.

23. Eugen Fink *Nietzsche's Philosophy.* London: Continuum, 2003.

24. Interpretations that privilege a naturalistic reading of Nietzsche do not explicitly circumvent this problem: in the absence of any supreme omniscient Being, or alternatively, blind Fate of forces what definitively eliminates the possibility of self-mastery? Can naturalism, in other words, sufficiently distinguish between forces of self-formation and those of self-mastery without re-introducing essentially organic categories? Our analysis allows for the former but rejects the latter for its overly confident position against destiny or the destining of time in 'becoming who you are'. Nietzsche's freedom denies the possibility of *mastering* myriad living forces and conflicts; it harnesses what the Greeks similarly understood as freedom vis-à-vis human destiny on earth.

25. Maudemarie Clark 'On the Rejection of Morality: Bernard Williams's Debt to Nietzsche' in Richard Schacht (ed.) *Nietzsche's Postmoralism: Essays on Nietzsche's Prelude to Philosophy's Future.* Cambridge: Cambridge University Press, 2001:100-122.

26. Strawson, P. F. 'Freedom and Resentment.' *Proceedings of the British Academy* 48 (1962):1-25.

27. Galen Strawson 'The Impossibility of Moral Responsibility', *Philosophical Studies* 75:5-24, 1994 (15).

28. Ted Honderich 'After Compatibilism and Incompatibilism', *Freedom and Determinsim.* Edited by Joseph K. Campbell, Michael O'Rourke and David Shier. London: MIT press, 2004.

29. Strawson, 'The Impossibility of Moral Responsibility', 16.

30. Strawson, 'The Impossibility of Moral Responsibility', 15.

31. Strawson, 'The Impossibility of Moral Responsibility', 22.

32. The definitive statement against the *non-sequitor* of consequentalist arguments is given in *Daybreak* 129. Here Nietzsche posits that if we most often 'torment ourselves on account of the great difficulty of divining what the consequences will be, of seeing all their implications, and of being certain we have included them all without omission'; what is more, 'all these consequences so hard to determine individually, now have to be weighed against one another on the *same* scales' even though we lack the means for a perfect determination (imperfect value-estimates).

33. See further the extensive useful explanatory note of Maudemarie Clark (36:18 on page 140) in *On the Genealogy of Morality.* Translated (with Notes) by Maudemarie Clark and Alan J. Swensen. Indianapolis: Hackett Publishing, 1998.

34. More precisely, Nietzsche inverts the common (mis)understanding: 'God sacrificing himself for the guilt of man, God himself exacting payment of himself, God as the only one who can redeem from man what has become irredeemable for man himself—the creditor sacrificing himself for his debtor, out of love (is that credible?-), out of love for his debtor!' (GM II: 21).

35. What distances Nietzsche from Darwin (amongst other things) is evident from the following explanation of formations: 'But all purposes, all utilities, are only *signs* that a will to power has become lord over something less powerful and has stamped its own functional meaning onto it...the entire history of a "thing", an organ, a practice can be a continuous sign-chain of ever new interpretations and arrangements, whose causes need not be connected even among themselves...The form is fluid but the "meaning" even more so...' (GM II: 12). For our purposes then the individual organism cannot be a sovereign atomism because it simply lacks total control of highly fluid meanings that keep it buoyant.

CHAPTER FIVE

Revenge of Modernity: the Unfreedom of Revengefulness

The following discussion examines a perverse side of conventional responsibility that is incorporated in the 'morality of custom' but is manifested as irresponsibility. To reiterate, irresponsibility emerging from the morality of customary morals and not as an *ethical* conscience. Such an irresponsibility—the antithesis of autonomous individuals' responsibility—issues from what Nietzsche called the 'instinct of revenge', an instinct that negatively pursues 'a cause' for a harm or injury done to oneself to attribute 'responsibility' to someone (enemy) or something (gods). Hence the causalist notion of responsibility—predicated on the fallacy of a free will behind every action or event—unwittingly gives rise to a politics of vengefulness against all those who cannot be trusted—who do not share the pleasure of fellow-feeling on the basis of contractual reciprocity. In our previous discussion of Nietzsche's economy of values in the modes of exchange human beings engage in (Ch.3), the idea that promise, trust and requital give rise to a certain sociality based on 'contract' relations was adumbrated. This argument counters the oft-stated view that Nietzsche lacked a dialogical conception of human society—that human sociality was somehow an anathema to his deep-seated monist position. While certain passages do in fact incline towards this dark interpretation of social intercourse, it can be argued to the contrary that his 'tamed animal' undergoes its completion not through *physus* but through configured relations of sociability and power. The civilizing process tames the animalic self, transfigures her formerly spontaneous impulses into new metamorphic drives of will, power, and hence 'will to life'. Similarly, that discussion showed the importance of the moralization of a pre-moral world particularly with respect to the formation of 'bad conscience' and its illusory 'subject of (free) will' that choices its moral duties. Once again rather than being under-socialized, our claimed 'natural animal'—under the sway of a pernicious moralization of the instincts—acquires over a very long period of time a conscience of duty that is continually reproduced and reinforced by the 'morality of custom'. Every 'interesting animal' becomes human by inculcating and reproducing the customary norms (of duty, guilt and indebtedness) by which it was tamed and instinctually weakened. Spiritualization, we might add, of such physiological states is an integral part of this taming process, a process that is amplified by the emergence of a juridical subject with its attendant contractual forms of intercourse and moral requital. We therefore arrive at a critical question concerning what might thwart the development of human beings who embody a

'promise of the future': is a lack of trust and (proper) requital a function of irresponsibility? That is to say, is modern freedom thwarted by a will to revenge
that is fundamentally irresponsible? This is the question now worth posing after
having examined the relation between freedom and responsibility in chapter 4.

Revenge and Resentment

The foregoing analysis indicated the conditions under which the 'ripest fruit'
can emerge to exercise freely its power to promise, hold to one's commitments
and therefore assume the 'greatest responsibilities'. It demonstrated the need for
a human being to be prepared for the task, a preparation that requires both overcoming and the promise—trust exchanges of ordinary socio-legal intercourse.
What remains to be examined, however, is an apparent absence of 'trust' in the
face of a culture of revenge—modernity's unacknowledged blight. For
Nietzsche, freedom cannot be realized under the sickly condition of one being
overwrought by an instinct of vengefulness. Revenge or the 'will to revenge', to
be more precise, is particularly manifest in the kind of 'herd-morality' that prevails within modern democracies; indeed, it constitutes part of the 'morality of
custom' due to the various constitutive conventions by which herds are formed
and maintained. To be free from guilt and abstract concepts of imperative
('duty') is not sufficient: the free spirit that wills to be responsible also acts as a
counter-force to sickly revengefulness. Yet the happiness that is the mark of an
affirmative spirit is instead supplanted by the inferior instinct of fear that rules
the weak-willed slavish spirits—revenge is their venting of self-hatred. 'Overcoming' therefore now requires not merely the overcoming of 'morality' per se
but rather that which obstructs trust and (contractual) requital in the formation of
an ethical conscience—an autonomy that is set apart from a dangerous and pernicious ethos of resentment and vengefulness. Nihilists—modern decadents—
fail to exercise control over their feeble venting of anger, fear and resentment
onto others outside the herd. This type of human nature is highly poisonous to
the rest of humankind, a sick form of existence that has not turned out well because revenge infects the depths of its soul, thus turning potentially noble souls
into something grotesque and inhuman. This concern with the dark, destructive
force of will as becoming—the 'will to revenge' (GS 359)—appears as early as
The Wanderer and His Shadow. It is given further elaboration by way of acute
analyses of resentment, self-hatred and a poisonous spirit of contempt 'for man'
himself in the later *On the Genealogy of Morality*. In the former work, Nietzsche
takes up an important aspect of inter-human exchanges and modes of intercourse
that seems particularly pertinent in the early twenty-first century. That is, the
phenomenon of exacting revenge upon others when the creative plan of the 'true
artist' and the 'seeker of knowledge' (the experimenter) are subordinated by a
potent willing-force that is essentially negative (rather than affirmative and joyful).

Revenge we must remember is often associated with the vile politics of resentment; a vicious politics of those Nietzsche called 'slaves' who resent the

superior will of their masters, their 'freedom' in other words. They feel emasculated and allow the affects of resentment to override their entwinement with others in forms of exchange and requital (economy of value-formation). Not merely their social status but their being in the deepest phenomenological sense poses a hindrance to freedom. They are slaves to their destructive affects; a free reign of combating impulses usurp the master and his 'table of values', leaving the soul in a tormentful disarray. Unfreedom is thus not only social, political, economic and legal in dimension; it is fundamentally unconscious, affective and 'spiritual' to the extent that poisonous souls find it nigh impossible to overcome their own toxic states. Responsibility remains at some distance for them because the politics of usurpation makes impure or poisons an otherwise healthy and vital soul. No intercourse predicated on revenge, which issues from affects such as envy or hatred, gives rise to an ethical responsibility. Why? Because an autonomous conscience would require the absence, indeed the overcoming, of malice, envy and resentment. 'Reciprocation' defined by the negative feelings and impulses of these 'all too human' aspects, what Nietzsche (GS 351) called 'the filth of the soul', would simply be slavish; that is, lacking freedom. To resist such sickly impulses is to overcome the force which morality attempts to shroud under its holiest virtues and duties of renunciation. We recall here an earlier argument (in Ch.1) that freedom entails a cost, an expenditure of drive and power, in overcoming resistance. To rid oneself of bad conscience is a significant mark of becoming free, free from guilt and the 'revenge against the spirit' known as ascetic 'moralization' (GS 359). Now the imperative has become to be free from the destructive willing power that is manifest in a determinate *revenge* against the spirit. The abovesaid 'filth of the soul' is what the self-disciplined and self-denying priests of asceticism attempted to arrest by way of a meditative, quiet, hygiene of soul and body. In a post-moral development of the spirit, the challenge is to find a new health—a joyous affirmation of life—that issues forth from the self-overcoming of vengeful resentment. We can express this in political language even while Nietzsche appeared to prefer the 'psychologist's' language: a slave is enslaved by his own affects of resentment, self-hatred and envy—each a disease (of the soul) that plagues the human spirit until the very end. Hence overcoming 'bad conscience' also requires a mastery of these slavish affects: the feeble sentiments and politics encompassed by those still subject to the forces of resentment and envy (while malice remains septic in those souls that failed usurping the superior position of their master).

It entails the power to abjure and transvaluate the self that has become full of poison: the human being 'who has turned out badly' and is unable to enjoy life because he despises himself is a human being 'who has become poisoned through and through...eventually ends up in a state of habitual revenge, will to revenge' (GS 359). His revenge against high, free spirits is Morality itself (though not ethical autonomy as we have already seen). To command, to be a 'lawgiver' of one's life, and to make promises in *Kairos* (time) one must first have overcome such weaknesses (and poisons of the spirit): to despise another— person, tribe, being—is to despise oneself. The noble spirit, by contrast, has overcome himself while at the same time being capable of vouching for oneself with pride, strength, and substantive responsibility. In short, it is difficult to conceive of freedom without also assuming responsibility for the ugliest side of human nature—revenge against the spirit that affirms life in its 'dual descent' (EH 1:1). Freedom and responsibility, in other words, are co-extensive with what Nietzsche defined as the centerpiece of his philosophy: the *dual descent*, viz one's 'destining' according to 'the highest and lowest rung on the ladder of life, at the same time a *decadent* and a *beginning*—this, if anything, explains that neutrality, that freedom from all partiality in relation to the total problem of life, that perhaps distinguishes me' (EH 1:1). Everywhere throughout Nietzsche's corpus, this philosophic motif looms large in discussions of things both natural and 'spiritual'. The 'dual descent' is Nietzsche's pathway to the Whole and, concomitantly, a comprehensive perspective onto life. Here good conscience lies between destruction and creation, past and future, and pessimism and joyous affirmation. It develops *out of* immanent forms grounded in social reality—civilizational forms in other words. There is no revolution or massive rupture, only the 'anarchists' and socialists (i.e. herd-decadents) seek revenge against the order of reality.

It is necessary to take a closer look at revenge as an encumbrance upon becoming free. In modernity, we see revenge has not only returned with a vengeance, but that it mars responsibility in an age of greater civilizational confluences. Beginning with the forementioned earliest work that discourses on revenge, *The Wanderer and His Shadow*, Nietzsche shows how revenge is inextricably bound with identity—one's self-evaluation. Speaking of the causes of retaliatory action, 'one has fundamentally been thinking, not of the person who caused the injury, but only of oneself'—for self-preservation reasons (WS 33). In the same passage, he argues revenge of a certain kind is resorted to when it is felt that one's opponent has harmed our *honor*: 'restitutional revenge'. Restitutional revenge, different from the cause of self-preservation, does not care for 'what the opponent will do' nor fears the opponent; rather, it aims at restoring one's honor which has suffered as result of the opponent's blow. By 'revenging ourself on him, we prove that we do not fear him either: it is in this that the compensation, the restitution lies'. These statements help us to elaborate reasons why 'slaves' in the modern world succumb to the temptations of revenge in their desire to usurp the power of their master-lords, i.e. imperial masters. Perhaps the more interesting dimension to Nietzsche's early conception of the will to revenge is the phenomenological treatment of measuring oneself against others, i.e. intersubjectivity. Nietzsche nuances his account of restitutional revenge by calling attention to the mutual interdependence of foe and enemy and thus self and other. Beyond reciprocal exchanges of violent acts, he announces the importance of *seeing* the harm, the diminution, of one's honor in the eyes of others. For instance: 'An essential element in this is whether he sees his honor as having been injured in the eyes of others (the world) or only in the eyes of him who injured it' (WS 33).

Perceptual reciprocity between the self and an other self is one extant form; the other level of interdependence is with our *cosmos*—the ordered world beyond this single antagonism. The 'feeling of honor', moreover, must exist if revenge is to occur. The extent to which this *feeling* inheres in the subject is paramount in determining quite how incensed or not he is by the injury. Nietzsche gives one important statement to his phenomenological explication of this affect-phenomenon: depending on 'how deeply or weakly he can think his way into the soul of the perpetrator and the witnesses of his injury' (WS 33). Most notably without this imaginary power ('thought'), there is no feeling and therefore no retaliatory revenge as well. Figures on two sides, the President of the United States and the (terroristic) leader of al-Qa'ida, must of necessity be capable of thinking their 'way into the soul of the perpetrator'—each, in other words, is beholden to the forces immanent in the other's soul. One's own affects, indeed, are dependent upon perceptions from without (of oneself) being *dis*honored by an opponent. We are not sovereign over our moral identity or over affect-structures that are symbiotically linked to affects of the other's soul.

To bring society further into the picture, Nietzsche adds that our phenomenology of the injury suffered is further dependent upon any 'witnesses of his injury'. Quite separate to the perceptions of our foe then is the existence of other conscious beings who deem that your honor has indeed suffered an injury, a decline. One's feeling of a loss of honor then is caught up with so many wider forms of exchange and contract at the thought-psyche level of intercourse. Witnesses in this case, not fear or guilt, instigate a course of revenge in the attempt to salvage one's honor *in the eyes of others*. Hence, it seems reasonable to say at this point that Nietzsche eschewed 'liberty' because of its naïve idealism—a romantic moral stance that lacks any realism about 'this world' and its socially constituted reality.[1] The phenomenological disclosure of an injury incurred only further reinforces the dialogical nature of intercourse and exchange between members of the species. Revenge it could be said is a retaliatory modality of that which lies *entre nous* between self—other self (or tribe/nation). Reality is fundamentally configurational just as the power-quanta of forces are in the physical world. It is the configured reality, not atomistic 'liberty', that demands responsibility from those capable of holding themselves into account by some *measure*. The 'measurer', as we saw in the previous chapter, knows how to measure him or herself according to the other person (i.e. configurations of meaning and requital). Measuring is a kind of valuating, a measuring of *axia* (worth) or relative value, that occurs via evaluation and estimation; and all this activity of the 'assessing animal' is inextricably inter-subjective and hence social in nature since no animal exists outside of (or without) its herd. But here mutuality is transmuted by a pernicious will to revenge that is fundamentally at odds with *this world*, a rage against the spirit of the world and its natural beings (as distinct from the 'untimely philosopher's' rebuttal of herd-morality).

Instead of joyous affirmation, the will becomes ill, thereby directing its willing-force against the world since it can no longer restore the loss or the time it values.[2] It rages against the future (of others) as the 'spirit of revenge' instead of 'the liberator' because its impotence in restoring its own sacrosanct virtues in time *necessitates* revenge against happier spirits (Z On Redemption). To hate oneself, to not love man, and to bring about his ruination naturally concludes in poisoning the will: the will enslaved in the revenged will. The 'human being who has turned out badly'—'weak characters without power over themselves that *hate* the constraint of style' and adore nature—cannot attain satisfaction with himself, consequently abjuring their (human) nature (GS 359, 290). This ugly type of the human embodies the will to revenge: 'Whoever is dissatisfied with himself is continually ready for revenge, and we others will be his victims' partly as a result of turning gloomy after having to endure 'his ugly sight' (GS 290). Self-denial as self-hatred logically entails a projection of negative 'ugly' *willing* drive onto human beings whose spirit has not turned out badly but instead nobly. Resentment of strong, noble, autonomous, patient, honest, disciplined and quiet spirits turns the soul poisonous; and such a soul is toxic for the rest of mankind, an ugly modicum of humanity that symbolizes what has 'turned out badly' in the errors of human history.

Acts of revenge are commonplace for Nietzsche with slaves whose insidious resentment of injury and loss suffered causes them to deny suffering, the *pathos* of life, while artificially projecting animosity toward their Master—those who appear in command of their sensations and sentiments. Just as Plato had earlier stated, the ruler must be capable of exercising self-discipline in order for commanding—autonomous lawgiving—to be just. Similarly those who are overtaken by the sentiment of resentment (or envy) remain slavish to its forceful dictates: resentment (like guilt) rules over the individual and its *Dasein* instead of the inverse. Their life is ignoble and ugly, marked by excess and servitude to '*free* nature: wild, arbitrary, fantastic, disorderly, and surprising' human nature (GA 290). Constraint is hated and resented because 'they feel that if this bitter and evil constraint were imposed upon them they would be demeaned' (GS 290). Between constraint and masterly autonomy lies the evil forces of resentment and envy; both affects registering the effects of suffering and pain but turning the (weakly) spirit into a diminished form of *Mensch*, an ugly piece of the granite of *homo natura* from which spirit develops and transmutes itself. They desire the overthrow of the regime that causes them such strong pain—injury and loss that cannot be reclaimed because the moment (time) has passed. Weakly souls or slavish souls—who dislike their own self-image—seek to attain the *feeling* of power that appears diminished within them by taking revenge against the *future*[3] of noble spirits, those who exercise mastery instead of servitude to the excesses of the said 'free nature'. Not being able to demur at giving free reign to excess and poisonous resentfulness, slavish souls succumb to—if not 'bad conscience'—the power of suffering constraint as a form of demeaning the self. Pathos is all they know, but only negatively. To displace this negative will is to (supposedly) affirm the power to project the responsibility for their anguish to (their) masters doing, the masterly will that 'caused' them their injury, their loss, i.e. diminution of self as 'I am demeaned' because of you! Hence, the outcry of necessity must appear cloaked in the deceptive robes of 'right-of-equality': freedom from inequality will relieve us of our sufferance.

Nietzsche continually rallied against the vile resentment that underlies the destructive impulse to equalize all kinds of social relations that naturally produce differences and distances. The socialist and democrat's attempt to level inequality in the name of justice is merely another exercise of power—a will of self-preservation cloaked in the virtues of Christianized Platonism. Freedom, he argued, does not lie in the utopian's false sameness where all cows appear indiscernibly grey in the dark of night of modern republican values. To equalize is to tyrannize; it is a mirror-reversal of their master's 'tyranny' only under the guise of justice it lays claim to freedom. To escape the tyranny of their master they poison the will by turning it into a tyrannical will of revenge that declares evil or 'illegitimate' any existence which appears to either stand-out or stand above 'the herd'. Freedom is transfigured into general conformity; and general conformity carries with it the virtue of diminished pain and injury: life no longer needs to be painful or harmful just as it need not be unjust, i.e. unequal. The solution to hardship is ensuring the law of the commons (herd morality) is not abrogated by any one individual since 'height' or elevation or enhancement would pose a threat to the security of the herd. Each of these would only subvert the 'happiness' which the herd feel they are deserving of because life after all should not be a struggle, painful existence or subservient to anything outside the herd's *Welt* (world). Greatness—which Nietzsche thought was dying on the vine of modern life—is reduced to predictable preservation, commonly ways of belonging and morals that demand of the individual a firm belief in the freedom of will and, conversely, the superiority of *Sitten* (customs) for herd membership. One ought to, that is, believe in the illusory 'free will' while at the same time subscribing to the morals of 'the many', as Aristotle once called them, as the measure of good conscience. But how does one set out to equalize a plenteous world while simultaneously affirming the right of a free will to decide upon particular matters, that is highly specific and nuanced matters pertaining to one sole individual? Nihilism then is not only the sense that God has abandoned you, but that in a world bereft of meaning (and greatness) the human being at once is stretched across the chasm of reactionary nihilism (guilt and resentment) and active nihilism (overthrowing noble values). Between singularity and collective herd-thinking, the modern self is formally promised "sovereignty" even whilst being torn asunder between two incommensurable polarities of being. Nietzsche finds the modern individual in fact lacking freedom: she needs to *become* free from the schism of individual v herd freedom. In order to do so, however, she must first recognize the perverse logic that simultaneously binds her to a) the fallacy of free will and b) the cage of morality perpetuated by herd animals and values. Resentment and bad conscience (as we saw in the previous chapter) fail to be displaced and overcome by the customary modality of what Nietzsche calls 'morality' as opposed to ethical responsibility. Resentfulness as an affect of weak will and self-castigation consequently simply festers at the interstices of idealist consciousness and herd moral codes.

Besides the weight of bad conscience and ossified moral duties, the spirit is also overwhelmed by a deadly fiery 'will to revenge' in the sentiment of resentment against those she finds 'responsible' for her plight. The 'tyrannomania of impotence' clamors for equality because 'aggrieved conceit, repressed envy...erupt from you as a flame and as the frenzy of revenge' said Zarathustra (Z, On the Tarantulas). As victim, the slave embodies what Nietzsche calls 'the tyrannic will of one who suffers deeply, who struggles, is tormented, and would like to turn what is most personal, singular, and narrow…into a binding law and compulsion' (GS 370). Responsibility as cause-of-suffering (law) is attributed by psychical projection to those with more power, determination and masterly will who forge a plan and impose it onto nature. As causation, responsibility becomes external—something outside the subject—rather than *my* responsibility for wishing to take revenge and feeling animosity toward others dissimilar to me with whom I wish to vent my revenge-taking. Since resentment is outwardly manifested so too responsibility is objectified into a problem from without; and our argument here is that Nietzsche wants the human being to take responsibility for his or her *own* reactive sentiments, and the compulsion to project negative affects apropos a diminished self-image onto others who are estimated to be the *cause* of their misery or injury. If as the Old Testament God declared, 'Vengeance is mine', then responsibility lies foremost with the self and revenge (archaic *dike*) with a higher transcendent authority. To deny ownership of one's affairs and affects is to be both ignoble and 'ugly'—a human being who has turned out bad and shames the image of man. Nietzsche's philosophical anthropology, we noted in a previous discussion, seeks to redeem humanity from a self-induced renunciation and diminution, hence the importance of his rebuttal of the 'ugly', poisonous spirit that diminishes the self-image of man. Only a slave to their *weak* will projects his or her destructive impulses onto others without being cognizant of the need to take responsibility for pernicious sensations (affects and drives) that swirl inexorably within the depths of its soul and spirit.

What can be inferred from Nietzsche's plentiful criticisms of resentment arguably is that it acts as a block to responsibility (in Nietzsche's sense a là our previous chapter). The resentful type cannot act responsibly if it lacks consciousness of its own inner state, its own reactive *polemos* (civil war). To be in turmoil or conflicted by competing drive-affects is reasonably comprehensible; but to languish under the dire negative affects of the will to revenge and its peculiar *ressentiment* is an altogether slavish fate. And one is fated, by numerous accounts in Nietzsche's corpus, to the slavish attitude of rendering punishment as justice; the penchant for punishment is the logical end of the man of *ressentiment*.[4] It is succinctly captured by Zarathustra's enunciation: preachers of equality 'wish to hurt those who now have power' because in the name of eternal justice they 'shall wreak vengeance and abuse on all whose equals we are not'; and this vengeance will take the form of punishment 'For "punishment" is what revenge calls itself' (Z On the Tarantulas, On Redemption). A complete discourse on punishment vis-à-vis revenge and resentment (and self-torture) cannot be entered into here; however, we can note Nietzsche's total repudiation of the vile man of punishment—one of the ugliest and poisonous 'types' that historical willing has produced. It is reasonable to say moreover that destroyers of modern life—anarchists, socialists, democrats—are vengeful of life *as it is* and necessarily so: 'it can also be the hatred of the ill-constituted, disinherited, and underprivileged, who destroy, *must* destroy, because what exists, indeed all existence, all being, outrages and provokes them' (GS 370). As reactive nihilists, they must destroy that reality which outrages them, an unequal, slavish mode of life that engenders resentment, envy and destructive will to power (destruction). This rage within their outrage is expressed as revenge for that fundamental 'freedom of will' that is emasculated by a superior will, a Cause that sits high above them but appearing as inertia to their subjectivity (refer to Figure 1, in chapter one). What the diagram illustrates is the construal of 'resistance' as externally given by weak-willed individuals who are unable to grasp the power of the Thought Command (specific only to the overcoming, autonomous human being). The Cause of inequality, in other words, commands their affect-structures and drives their impulses according to the determinants of resentment, envy and vengeful desire. Subjugated subjects who on the one hand believe in the doctrine of free will determination are never the less in reality ruled by the concept: Cause determines responsibility. If 'they'—the noble ones—are the 'cause' of my misery then *they* are 'responsible' for my suffering and unhappiness. Since I am in possession of a free will but cannot properly exercise it owing to these restraints from without, then the *non-sequitur* follows 'I must lack will-power in not being able to overcome these outward forces'. Thus between a false externalism and an illusion of subjective will is the fundamental contradiction within which the modern subject is located.

Nietzsche's desire is to break-up this fundamental schism in order to allow the proper articulation of 'abundant' drives and powers immanent in the human being and its futurity. The fundamental basis of our unfree existence is the double-helix contradiction that finds the human being (of this kind) inexorably fixated on this double-sided (false) reality. She or he cannot afford—due to fear and the rule of Concepts—to easily and willingly shatter the underlying presuppositions of both a false externalism and illusory subjective will. The implication from Nietzsche's ongoing attack of the despiteful 'will to revenge' a là the resentment of bad conscience is that we mortals are in fact prone to taking revenge out on others because of the vicious circle of this fundamental contradiction. Between 'being—becoming' and 'fatalism—free will' there exists yet another possibly more dangerous, ugly, and sickly dimension to the moralistic man: he is neither free according to a Kantian Will nor is he able to untangle himself from the conceptual web of causal thinking, i.e. cause—effect reasoning a là scientific positivism. The outrageousness of revenge is now embodied in the *ad hominem* principle that some concrete Him, Her or They must be responsible for my misery—a misery stemming seemingly from without (i.e. politics, industrialism, law) while in fact derived immanently from one's essential contradictory existence. To not rage against God as a Job would is to obey the rule of the concept, Cause, while contrarily pointing the finger at concrete human beings whose (superior) will is considered responsible for your underprivileged existence. "I am commanded by the higher type's reality and therefore must overthrow this order if I am to equal them; I envy their position because they are free of constraints and thus can exercise their free will while I, on the contrary, am constrained by their commanding will", so says the slave-spirit. What is more, moralistic man is further burdened by the weight of bad conscience; and between the fundamental contradiction described here and his perennial 'bad conscience', Nietzsche finds modern society is bereft of high noble spirits who could transcend (overcome) the reality of what he called European nihilism. For our purposes, it is most important to see then that revenge-taking is not an activity peculiar to extremists or ideological fundamentalists but rather a constant drive-affect impulse within the modern unconscious. To dislodge revenge from modern life would require more than a 'liberal education' or tolerance within the rule of law on this count; neither the state, religion or Christian metaphysics would suffice in dissolving the dangerous will to revenge that explicably marks, indelibly, the spirit of modern man.

Dual Logic—Inner and Outer Realities

To return to the theme of *Bildung* and the dysfunction of modern institutions discussed earlier in a previous chapter we could state—even though Nietzsche does not draw explicit links—that the failure of a proper educative culture reinforces the plight of those weighed down by European nihilism. Consider for example the possibility of rupturing the nexus of this fundamental contradiction that is held out by vigorous education and cultivation, and proper philological *arête*—what we have called *bios* thus far. The spirit of modernity, Nietzsche declared, partly derives from what his historical sociology explains as the juridical-institutional configuration of impoverishment of the soul. Education and the 'teachers of meaning' in diverse institutions have failed to question the metaphysics of Free Will and its concomitant 'psychology of the will' in accounts of moral responsibility. The foresaid fundamental contradiction reigns over the ontology of the human precisely because philosophers-as-mental-laborers have forgotten their duty to think anew the existence of man. They are, largely, ahistorical laborers of the present who simply cannot understand what a 'philosophy of the future' holds out for mankind. Revenge is sustained indirectly by institutions that fail to challenge the supremacy of the metaphysics of will promulgated by the common belief in 'freedom of will to choose' and on the other hand, the reign of abstract concepts of Cause and 'responsibility' embedded in the herd's institutions of morality. This is true at the material, social-historical level of institutional life but revenge is also sustained by modernity in its embodiment of bad conscience in the sinews of educational practices and the 'morality of custom' that binds atomistic persons together in a collective conscience. Emile Durkheim, shortly after Nietzsche's death, went on to expound a similar account of the latter phenomenon after having observed the deleterious effects of nihilism in Europe in the form of what he called *anomie*.[5] The impoverishment of the spirit and physiology of man was not for Nietzsche simply a matter of what is in the 'mind' but instead a phenomenon produced by a whole complex of juridical, moral, intellectual and social institutions and sensibilities—real forces that envelop the self and its unconscious. One cannot simply 'will' themselves out of this reality 'by the bootstraps' given all its attendant structures and meaning-rationales; you do not get to eschew 'herd-morality' and 'herd-thinking' that simply.

Perhaps ahistorical thinkers or Kantian autonomous beings would naively believe so but Nietzsche's idea of recurrence prohibits such idealist thinking, suggesting recurrence rather than sudden total breaks from "the people's" traditions, i.e. customary morals and values. 'Overcoming' therefore must also entail an overcoming of the malaise of decadent institutions and modern *Bildung*. Already in his time Nietzsche lamented the spirit and operations of faculties in his own University of Basel and the way Loeb and other pious philological technicians had come to replace the *paideia* of Voltaire, Leibniz, Spinoza and the medieval quadrivium. Subjects of 'modern society' with their 'modern ideas' cannot but fail to see the decadence of their own institutional culture, edified as it is by the errors of 'cause—effect' thinking and the customary morality that upholds the illusion of an *a priori* will that moves all agents into the distinct directions of 'good' and 'evil'. Their unfreedom is situated in their very *modus operandi* and cogitation since the institutions that promulgate both of these errors also perpetuate the corrosive 'bad conscience' that we analyzed earlier (in our discussion of responsibility). Hence, unfreedom is externally sanctioned and internally inscribed so that one's servitude is objectified in the conditions of existence. Logically, it appears before the subject as a reified Cause and Responsibility (of a concrete other person/herd) simultaneously since causation at the same time deems some 'other' willful agent as responsible, as 'the cause' of their injustice and suffering or injury. My fellow human being is now accessed via the Concept: he or she, the stranger as They, become the object of my projection of resentment that a thing—object or force—is moved by their exercise of an autonomous will (causality).

The mechanics of cause and resentment now become entwined: each is interrelated since resentment is *felt* as moving Will and causation (of a suffering) and causation is *experienced* as the force(s) from without. It appears as immanence of the self yet assumes the form of a Gordian knot; it appears inexplicable to the self yet paradoxically is constituted by this same binary contradiction. The modern subject is riveted by such a two-sided tension that finds forces trajected in opposite directions. The revenge-taking activity of a weak soul is logically explicable action that seeks to destroy objectively existing objects or forces (i.e. master enemies) that are blamed for its suffering predicament. Projection is immanence but now directed outwards so that it hits an external object to itself; it seeks to objectify the 'cause' of its misery in the concrete embodiment of the flesh and bones of another human being. The impulses, destructive or creative, are unhappy to remain constrained by the Gordian knot's amorphous form: they struggle to get out, to be vented and to become actualized in a reality that the Gordian knot denies them. To blame someone else *is all-too-human* as it reassures us that it is the vile world—the external cause—that is to blame for *my* lack of freedom since my free will exists without any question. If what is immanent in my being a free willed agent is not the cause of my slavish existence then *it must follow* (by logic) that the *cause* of it stands from without. Having first objectivated the Will and consequently turned immanence away from the contestation of conflicting drives, immanence now incorporates the Will as a free will within my consciousness. Someone I blame for the injustice in the world, understandably, is thought to have also acted on 'their free will' in subordinating my existence and I know this through resistance I encounter when attempting to exercise 'my (willing) power', says the modern individual to itself. The blockage (to freedom) is affective yet it assumes the form of outward resistance—as my diagram shows—objectified in the institutions of 'injustice and inequality'.

For Nietzsche, it is never accidental that a revengeful self takes aim at venting his anger and hatred at others who are considered to be superior or different to themselves—either horizontally (tribes) or vertically (classes/distinctions)—because the forces of 'self-hatred' are decidedly rational and hence explicable. Instead of incorporating what he called the 'pathos of distance', more feeble characters and nihilistic spirits are overwhelmed by their own despondent state (and affective states too) so much so that they seek to overturn the table of values in order to make distance and distinction highly problematical in moral terms. That is, 'inequality' becomes the evil that causes me to suffer the conditions of inequality and to become envious of the freedom embodied in the lives of those higher than me. "I lust after the kind of freedom they possess but resent the fact it derives from my subjugation—an 'unnecessary' subjugation since the democratic rule of law warrants that I freely choose to act upon my own free will". Conventional statements and moral claims such as this is what philosophers as moralists have unconsciously avowed, in part because of their own unthinking thinking—an ahistorical method of philosophizing. They too must free themselves from the 'moralist's' tyranny which has prevailed over humankind ever since human beings were riddled with a poisonous 'bad conscience'. Nietzsche often denounces thinkers and jurists who come under the tyrannical spell of the psychology of will; it is 'the foulest of all theologians' artifices' that makes mankind 'depend upon them' because in making persons "responsible" 'in their sense' it also thereby makes them dependent on moralists and punishment-minded state officials. In seeking to make manifest the 'psychology of all "making responsible"' Nietzsche shows the critical task of philosophy to be that of revealing, genealogically, the deep-seated psychology underlying the operations of modern institutions under the reign of the celebrated 'free will'. Responsibility is now extended to the class of teachers of meaning and jurists of moral responsibility as a need to rupture the said dependence that confines the everyday man and woman; a confinement that is sealed by the pangs of guilt and self-torture that naturally ensue in a sickened soul riven with so many contradictory tendencies. Nietzsche recognized from the example of two proper philosophers—Voltaire and Goethe—that *Bildung* is highly significant in the formation of freer or unfree souls, responsible or irresponsible vengeful characters. Hence, 'responsibility' is inextricably tied to the institutions of modernity because decadence is objectively sanctioned as well as intrinsically or immanently validated. To change, that is, to overcome the 'will to revenge' means to have to also transform decadent 'modern' institutions into more noble institutions; that is, institutions that no longer perpetuate the illusion and psychology of the (free) will, a will that is fundamentally unfree because it creates unhealthy chains of dependence.

We could say consequently the 'will to life' is explicitly linked ontologically with 'a way of life'; if the latter remains preserved it expresses a particular constellation of reality that appears before the self as 'will to life'. Yet such a reality is in fact a negation of good health, of natural life without the dead weight of moralistic concepts, and therefore a negation of those instincts that keep free spirits vital, life affirming and light on their feet.[6] Vengefulness as a 'way of life', a negative will *against* life, is an unhealthy condition expressive of an embittered soul—the smell of revenge is what Nietzsche's nose could pick up, a nose for stench and toxic souls which he liked to believe enhanced his capabilities as an astute analyst of civilizational forms. Hence the analyst of diverse civilizational forms—Jewish, Christian, Buddhist, humanist and modern—can declare this toxic form of morality—'herd animal morality'—to be only one *form* of morals 'after which many other types, above all *higher* moralities, are, or ought to be, possible' (BGE 202). To be emancipated from the impoverished, 'sickened' soul of the man of resentment, anger and projective hostility will therefore require the overcoming of revenge itself—the very antithesis of promise-making. Here is not the place to discuss the logic and dynamic process of promise-making and keeping since they were examined in the previous chapter. Suffice to say, Europe's morality being that of a decadent herd-morality acts as a resistance to the futural potential of promisor—promisee exchange relations where, it will be recalled, a certain faith and trust are instantiated by the exchange relation of she who promises and he who trusts in waiting. But he who is overcome by the vitriolic sentiments of revengeful hostility and hatred can never possess rightly the self-image of a promise-maker nor would his spirit convince potential trustworthy persons of his powers to *keep* promises.

The avenger is merely committed to himself, to his self-despising energy that, due to its excess, overflows his being to find itself directed at some other human being outside one's herd-morality. This predominant herd form of morality which produces the morals of revenge and guilt argued Nietzsche, 'resists such a "possibility," such an "ought" with all its power' (BGE 202). The overcoming autonomous human being must therefore be capable, *able*, to resist the tenacity of its hold and declare to the world 'there are, as have always been, other moralities'. 'The (true) philosopher', as Nietzsche (BGE 205) calls such a person, consequently 'feels the burden and the duty of a hundred attempts and temptations of life—he risks *himself* constantly, he plays the wicked game' of posing alternate values to the established order of morals in order for the stranglehold of decadence (feeble projective power) to less loose. A true philosopher, as opposed to a mere mental laborer, acts freely only to be (mis)construed as an immoralist—he lives dangerously because his ethical stance is transcendent of the herd's customary morality. Free thinkers in this sense can act as critics rather than skeptics in ridiculing the 'morality' of revenge-takers. Leveling critiques at liberal moral duties is not the end itself however since the philosopher, as moral legislator, places a keen eye on the horizon of possibilities coming even if 'morality' (as extant system) seemingly obscures their appearance. The (free) legislator is one whose will to institute an ethical conscience is not obstructed by the power-ploys of guilt-ridden, resentful moralists who shout from on high: morality is ethics itself. To criticize, to negate, is not sufficient; true philosophers, as lawgivers, must also possess an ethical conscience that transcends vengefulness and bad conscience in order to *inscribe* a new table of values in time—one that has transvaluated morality's sickly spirit of revenge (and fear of the 'neighbor').

Power of Revenge As Negation—The Other Side

It is important not to dismiss the power of revengefulness as merely an 'error' or 'weakness' of human beings owing to their 'human all too human' nature. We want to recall the penultimate significance of Nietzsche's primary conception of the 'dual decent': the fact the world *becomes* what it is by means of a tenacious tension between opposing elements or forces. In this particular case the tension between 'good' and 'evil' is surpassed by the tension between 'noble' and 'slave' groups, tribes and individuals. Action or activity more precisely is never one-sided. Though Nietzsche poured scorn on dialectics, the method—a rationalistic *phantasia*—much of his elaborate, mature thinking unfolds in a dialectical way even though it does not utilize 'dialectics' per se. His account of the 'natural history of morals' for instance, indicates a tremendous tussle between decadents or 'slaves' and nobles or 'free spirits'—a tussle situated in time and space, and between positions of commanding and obeying. Those who come to 'obey' (or command) do so for reasons which only *becoming*—as a dual descent—shows as a human effort to contain and mobilize exuberant forces, energies, and instincts that seek growth through their predominance. Because of nature's exuberance, growth as extension ensues and manifests itself as excess—the desire to extend the living form over and above other organisms or forms (in culture). Contestation and struggle therefore are to be expected and this often leads to conflict, domination, opposition and distance as well as decline, destruction, decadence if not greatness, elevation and noble enhancement (i.e. freedom). It is indeterminate what exactly will emerge from becoming even if the classic trope of 'destiny' may imply otherwise—*willing* as struggle and overcoming is what ultimately 'determines' one's destiny. Hence, one's destiny as that person inclined to obey rather than command is never accidental or causally explainable. It is the outcome of so many battles both within and without the individual (or group), occurring in social-historical time where a configuration of tension fields finds 'noble' and 'plebeian' elements vying for predominance. The reality of such a configuration constitutes a 'necessary' facet of one's existence and Nietzsche oftentimes implores us to acknowledge and cede this necessity as a welcomed component of our individual formation.

Amor fati expresses a love of life that does not deny how one is 'fated' historically by specific configurations of tension and contestation—including psychical contestation—that arise amongst and between 'herds' and individuals. Now resentment plays a significant part in the formative processes of human beings and herds (castes, classes, tribes) and in particular those 'unprivileged' persons whom Nietzsche found representative of a 'herd man' (BGE 199). The main explanation for this becomes evident after Nietzsche had completed *Zarathustra* and consciously articulated thus:

> Wandering through the many subtler and coarser moralities which have so far been prevalent on earth, or still are prevalent, I found that certain features recurred regularly together and were closely associated—until I finally discovered two basic types and one basic difference (BGE 260).

Referring to 'master morality' and 'slave morality' as well as a third mediative type interposed between them, he argues these two types of morality and their basic difference is what universally forms human natures into moral natures—high or low, or a synthesis of them. Slave morality emerges triumphant, according to Nietzsche, when the Jewish people 'mark the beginning of the slave rebellion in morals' (BGE 195).

However in every great overturning it is the slaves' usurpation of the noble class—of noble values more importantly—that is most definitive for understanding Nietzsche's highest concern: the moralization of man and his 'force of the will'. By moralization, we refer to the development of customs and norms of 'goodness' versus wicked evil, but more importantly a psychical orientation that is characterized by 'bad conscience'. When the high priests of Judaism—the ascetics of a moral Divine order—overwhelmed the ancient world with their otherworldly values, they inaugurated a moralistic world-outlook which swept the common people and nobles into a singular illusion: this world is decadent and only God represents an immutable justice in the universe. With cunning, a plebeian 'commoner's' will to overcome, the priesthood usurped the prerogative of noble kings and states-craftsmen to arrange the affairs of both subjects and nature according to what Nietzsche called an 'artistic plan'. Instead of simply finding an extant strong Will presiding within the souls of these priests, Nietzsche correctly identifies the psychical nature underlying their social-historical location in time. Before the rule of bad conscience, noble values reflected the predominance of a nobility of mind and soul that was materially anchored in a preponderant nobility. Noble spirits did not as yet understand the language of guilt nor of formal abstract duties; theirs was a world of commitment, loyalty, tyrannical will, honor and the strength of courage to command—a freedom of spirit before the keepers of the holy of hollies moralized the mundane world. Yet holding their position within a field of tension, nobles also produced resentment in the souls of their subjugates through their superior form of life, an existence marked by freedom or a will to power as a psychological force marshaled to exploit, make regular and evaluate life itself. This power within was simply conflated to their social position: the nobles' official juridico-symbolic sovereignty as commanders of society. Unhappy individuals who resented the embittered condition of their own existence—an unprivileged life marked by revengefulness—sought relief from their self-incurred suffering and pain that they denied all responsibility for. Responsibility for 'their pain', injury and harm therefore becomes integral to the morality which demands 'justice' for such exploitation and, on the other hand, clears the way for 'the people' to over-

turn noble rule—standards, valuations and estimations which appear too sublime and lofty for 'the commoner'.

Nietzsche the historical sociologist then couples this analysis to a necessary
depth-psychological perspective that enunciates the operative affects[7] of this
particular constellation of forces and social relations. Nietzsche the psychologist
discerns the specific psychical forms that attend a particular social order: the
love of hatred for those responsible for my misery and subjugation is an affect
of *ressentiment*. This affective structure of the human being is linked to slavery:
man's servitude under predominate destructive affects of being envious and
hateful toward those who do not suffer equally from life's tribulations owing to
their superior mode of life. The caste of ascetics which Nietzsche would eventually call 'the most evil enemies' (GM I: 7), the priests, transfigure this will to
revenge by spiritualizing it thus transforming the face of the earth by making all
things terrestrial exceedingly more dangerous. By negating the natural world—
the vital joyous drives and instincts—the priests embodied the spirit of revenge
against cruel nature in religious ascetic ideals, offering in the most cunning of
ways an escape from the dreadful suffering of earthly life—the Fall. In other
words, a release from the bitterness of finitude and its dread in the form of
higher ideals, removal of self and the renunciation of this-worldly values of the
noble ideal. In effect, they shattered the existing world of noble heroic and virile
strength in order to meditate on the world thereafter and the redemption from a
decadent life such as this. To take revenge means to have a *spirit* of revenge and
these masters of 'the spirit', according to Nietzsche, were the creators of an unhealthy, embittered soul that fundamentally rejected the natural world. Salvation
invoked a hostile attitude—one not dissimilar to that of our enemies—toward
the mundane world, including the necessary injustices that accompany the fallen
state such as the politics of domination and social hierarchy. Therefore,
Nietzsche's genealogical explanation is simultaneously social-historical, psychological and theologico-philosophical. Vengefulness is pre-modern; it has
origins, vicissitudes, spurts of development and intensification that span very
long processes of formation; and it has a religio-metaphysical dimension which
science fails to explain. One's enmity toward foreigners and hostile strangers in
the social-historical world is only one dimension of the spirit of revenge; and
just as we found the creditor-debtor exchange relation to have existed between
God and man so here too the spiritual world of the priests lets loose a 'spirit of
revenge' that plagues the earth for millennia.

The 'will to revenge' is *spiritualized* into a pernicious 'secret black art of a
truly *great* politics of revenge' (GM I: 8), an overturning of the table of values
that inaugurates the rule of unselfishness, humility, self-denial, pity, forgive-
ness, abstinence and subservience to holy authorities (and officials). This secret
black art challenged the virtues of Roman noble life and later again those of the
'knightly-aristocratic' rule in Europe, finally finding favor in so-called Christianized Platonism and its launching of the modern scientific revolution(s). The
only way that a priestly people could in the end usurp 'the noble', 'the mighty',
'the lords', 'the power-holders' and overcome their Egyptian bondage was
through this 'act of spiritual revenge' (GM I: 7). Were the Jewish people to

blame for this? Not quite, since Nietzsche lays the charge constant with his social theory of power and elites (oligarchs), viz 'the people of the most suppressed priestly desire for revenge' (GM I: 7). As spiritual oligarchs the priests
reign supremely over 'the people' by sublimating their 'priestly desire' into so
many forms of *spiritual revenge*. And the conquest of her enemies—different
gentiles and heathens—was effectively achieved by means of this kind of revenge—a spiritualization of the will (desire) for revenge. Why the Book of Job
was particularly instructive for (priestly) ascetics is because it showed that only
God was in possession of a might to ridicule the Jews' will to revenge against
their own impoverished state. What, in other words, applied to their enemies
could not apply equally to their Lawgiver and so God could not be overcome
like Israel's enemies because spiritualized revenge only led, logically, to hatred
and God demonstrated to Job what the fruits of (self-)hatred are. To take revenge against the Father is to take revenge against life itself since He is the
Creator and life itself. Hence, hate as the seat of revenge is a negation of life,
not a joyous celebration of life as God has bequeathed it to mankind. In contradiction to the 'chosen people of Israel', Nietzsche thought Jewish hatred in fact
abrogated the righteous act of God in giving life to the human race since they
irresponsibly eschewed the Lawgiver's command to man himself—poor,
wretched man(kind). By inverting the 'aristocratic value equation
(good=noble=powerful=beautiful=happy=beloved of God)', the Jews' slave
revolt represented the most triumphal 'unfathomable hate' of powerlessness
(GM I: 7). Why? Because the 'most evil enemies'—priests, the most 'ingenious
haters'—'are the most powerless'; and, importantly, Nietzsche observed 'Out of
their powerlessness their hate grows into something enormous and uncanny,
into *something most spiritual and most poisonous*' (GM I: 7, my emphasis).

Most evidently, a depth-psychological account is used here to intertwine the
sociological, political and theological aspects of this spurious 'secret black art'
of spiritualizing the desire for revenge and sublimating into religious virtues and
customary values. The artistry of the priesthood and the artistry of state-building
are now interlocked; for the language Nietzsche uses here, if we pay closer attention, is that of a 'black art of a truly *great* politics of revenge' (GM I: 8). The
evil priests hate life not because they are Jewish but rather because as ascetics
they will to renunciate that which their own Lord had bestowed upon all human
beings: finite being. *Esse*, however, is now revaluated as the misery of powerless unprivileged existence; thus, freedom escapes them only to give rise to a
will to spiritualize their deep-seated desire to revenge that which is responsible
for their own self-hatred. The object of Job's torment was to overcome; yet
spiritualizing a hatred for one's mortal life only results in servitude to the bitter,
poisonous affects of Egyptian slavery. To deny life is to deny man; thus to deny
overcoming is to deny becoming free. Disdain for power-holders, enemies, and
personal injury are all symptomatic of the cunning ideal of ascetic removal from
the world and its sins. In order to overcome one's bondage to Egyptian slavery
it is necessary to deny the ascetic's truth-value by affirming the power of freedom to experience joy in *this* world and no other. Religious vengefulness is uncanny—it cannot be trusted because 'the most evil enemies' subtly seek power

through an overcoming that amounts to a radical 'revaluation of all (good) values'. The slave revolts against its master and installs its own 'slave morality'
where noble master morality once reigned. Hence, usurpation of the master's
sovereign position only renders a slavish life even if formally speaking 'the
people' now rule. Formal juridico-political power does not eliminate either the
desire or the spirit of revenge, a vengeful spirit that emerges out of resentment,
envy and above all self-hatred. Statecraft can harness and mobilize such negative affect-impulses into some kind of 'black art' but it can never substitute for
them in some eliminative way. For Nietzsche what is more, to democratize the
state only further compounds the errors of the first great slave revolt against
noble freedom—the mob now think they are *free* under the tyranny of their own
plebian moral values. The rule of law can only obfuscate or at best sublimate
what Nietzsche found to be the root 'cause' of revengefulness—'a vehement
attack of fever'—consequently, 'To desire to revenge and then to carry out revenge means to be the victim of a vehement attack of fever' whether with the
force of the state or without it (HH 60). The might of the first slave revolt—the
spirit of Jewish hatred—resides in the fact that the intensity of this fever was
diffused by priestly statecraft: 'but to desire to revenge without possessing the
strength and courage to carry out revenge means to carry about a chronic illness,
a poisoning of body and soul' (HH 60). And similarly applies for Christianity
and its Redeemer—it succeeded in preventing a poisoning of the body and soul
by realizing the will to revenge in its most sublime spiritual form. Spiritualization of the force of vengefulness is what conquered the Roman Empire, not
arms, prejudice, or doctrinal truths from the Septuagint. Nietzsche interwove
this dimension of human creativity with the ascetics' ideal of self-control
through self-mastery in the sense that this intense 'fever' had to be tempered,
marshaled and finally harnessed for 'higher purposes'. Disgust in contemporary
society over the harm and dangers of revenge-taking arguably stem from such
long-entrenched techniques of self-discipline and spiritual mastery and their
attendant valuations (essentially pacific in nature). Quite logically, revulsion
thresholds are higher than in pre-Roman antiquity since disgust associated with
allowing a free reign of affects issuing from a 'vehement attack of fever' is far
more intense now.

These important emotions and drives of modern life are further linked to the
illusion of an ego in possession of free will. 'The evil act at which we are now
most indignant rest on the error that he who perpetrates them against us possesses free will, that is to say, that he could have *chosen* not to cause us this
harm', argued Nietzsche (HH 99). This is a modern prejudice—to elevate
choice above all other possible elements of human necessity. Morality as perhaps Jewish lawgivers well appreciated is 'preceded by *compulsion*' just as customary morals are 'good' only because the 'collective individuality' of state-
society demands adherence to them out of compulsion (HH 99). Forgetfulness is
what divides the modern soul from its originary compulsive force, a force that
first forged 'good' (member) and 'evil' (stranger) cleavages. When today's
stranger (alien) takes revenge and causes us injury we mistakenly attribute the
wrongdoing *ad absurdum* to identity and its voluntary will to choose. Both are

ahistorical interpretations of the real. A genealogy of revenge reveals the ahistoricity of these accounts and therefore their paucity in explaining why vengefulness is associated with a destructive soul that is a beneficiary of the spiritualization of the instinct of revenge. By means of a decisive moralization of the natural world, religion has transformed the whole face of the earth, turning everything of the individual human being and its society into something far more dangerous and therefore something exceedingly more interesting. After all, the best German book remained the Bible; in particular, Luther's Bible outshone all other books (BGE 247). Consonant with Nietzsche's well acknowledged contesting of anti-Semitism, this great Book and Jewish priestly ascetics contributed to the spiritualization of man (kind). What does 'spiritualization' mean here? Many things but one key feature is summed up well by the following statement: 'Religion and religious significance spread the splendor of the sun over such ever-toiling human beings and make their own sight tolerable to them' (BGE 61). The 'slave rebellion of the Jews' is therefore not a cultural slur of some kind but a recognition of the enormity of their spiritual overturning of mundane life. What is more, what *prima facie* appears to be a complete denunciation of religious life is transmuted into a dialectical observation of its operations in earthly life. Countervailing the 'opposite values' of conventional philosophers—not to mention Deleuzian interpretations of such phenomena— Nietzsche declares 'religion also gives to some of the ruled the instruction and opportunity to prepare themselves for future ruling and obeying' (BGE 61). The redemptive power of religiosity of spirit is at once the 'splendor of the sun' glistening over everyday pessimism and the preparation of human beings for *future* 'ruling and obeying'.

The so-called 'Jewish revolt' is therefore characteristically a 'dual descent' of the Whole (as we have argued all along) since it condemns man to a spiritualized existence that is unhappy with the pessimism of life while also acting to give certain powers of overcoming to the herd animal man that once roamed the earth with its original animal-spirit. Arguably Nietzsche sees the instinct of revenge as incorporated in our animal-human natures, that is, before the priestly metaphysical revolution transformed human societies; yet once the latter took hold in human history the *spirit* of revenge developed a distinctive *sui generis* form, living out a life in the 'soul' of men and women which could not have previously been known or experienced before asceticism succeeded in overturning appearances on their head. Religion more than merely a 'slave revolt' against secular masters actually harbors the quintessential force or power for overcoming—preparatory education and cultivation towards heights (future goals). For instance, 'Asceticism and Puritanism are almost indispensable means for educating and ennobling a race that wishes to become master over its origins among the rabble and that works its way up toward future rule' (BGE 61). Hence it is plausible to argue that the masters of 'spiritualization'— decadent ascetics—bring about an overcoming through a double magnification of the 'will to nothingness', the ascetic's original nihilistic will that put natural existence into high relief (GM II: 24). The first is the sublimation of hatred (revenge) of organic finitude—putrid decay, injury and pain, and human suffering owing to bodily sensations of weakness. As physicians of the soul, the high priests inaugurate techniques and spiritual practices that equip the mortal for a transmogrification of this-worldly existence, instilling high beliefs of an elevated higher plane of being that evades the strictures of organic constitutions. These ascetic forms of self-discipline and renunciation establish 'silence and solitude' in the soul of those future masters who are still to come—noble exemplars of self-mastery who will emerge out of the 'educating and ennobling' means of religion (BGE 61). Overcoming sovereign individuals, in other words, will be *spiritually* adept in the arts of transfiguration and transvaluation but not 'despite religiosity'; they will instead have developed the necessary art or 'gay science' to overcome the *resistance* of religious piety and moral rectitude, and this resistance as we recall from chapter one is a key element of Nietzsche's conception of freedom.

The second is a two-sided phenomenon: the creation of a supposed 'metaphysical need' in *Mensch* that was attended by the illusory Soul, what Nietzsche called the 'soul—superstition' (BGE *P*). The primordial animal-human previously lacked the *agon* set into place by ascetic spiritual self-mastery (and knowledge in the case of Buddhism and Judaism). In 'denying the world', they assisted in engendering types which would affirm the world. 'With the strength of his spiritual eye and insight grows distance and, as it were, the space around man: his world becomes more profound; ever new stars, ever new riddles and images become visible for him', argued Nietzsche (BGE 57). It is precisely here that we glimpse more clearly Nietzsche the non-naturalist, a thinker who is no longer content with (quasi) Darwinian conceptions of man. If 'Darwin forgot the mind' then Schopenhauer remembered the Indic redemptive will of 'the spirit' and Nietzsche's work on asceticism clearly testifies to the great influence that his mentor, Schopenhauer, had until the very end.[8] Spiritual exercises in annulling the finitude of being and the pain of human suffering were inexorably bound up with forms of learning, classifying, regulating, dividing, measuring, evaluating and assessing, training, disciplining and therefore educating. Without these innovations the 'will to truth' could not have culminated in a scientific, naturalistic outlook on life—an impartial, 'objective' account of power-quanta and force-quanta that remains decidedly godless. The godless viewpoint needed the religious overturning of the natural world for its own instantiation.

Spirit of State, State of Spirit(uality)

We could add here a 'third' dimension without committing any interpretive violence to his published writings. This extra dimension owes more to a Wagnerian-Goethean influence that any so-called naturalistic interpretation. Mention was made earlier of a grand politics—the black art of resentment—and Nietzsche often referred to the ways in which originary state-builders were grand artists of a kind: creative tyrannical wills (types) that are capable of forging something new out of the wild nature of pre-state human beings and creatures. The conceptual parallel is evident in at least two ways, but we should first

note the important precedent ground on which formation occurs since some reductive naturalistic treatments (e.g. Leiter and Clark, 1997) overlook strong
Goethean analytic themes in Nietzsche's thought. As early as *Human All Too
Human* Nietzsche observed the lawgiving nature of priestly guardians. Even 'at
very low stages of culture man does not stand towards nature as its impotent
slave', hence the 'believer in magic and miracles reflects on how to *impose a
law on nature*' since the 'meaning of the religious cult is to determine and con-
strain nature for the benefit of mankind' (111). Religious or spiritual administrators are akin to primary state-builders: they must 'impress upon it [nature] a
regularity and rule of law which it does not at first possess'; and the cult is a
society presupposing 'relations of sympathy between man and man' just as
state-societies or civilizations do. It was not the Jews who overturned some idyllic pre-moral existence but rather the lawgivers of religious cults already extant
in 'religiously productive primitive cultures' (111). Turning now to the aforementioned dual ways in which a conceptual parallel becomes apparent we can
see that with the occult and religious sects of non-monotheistic religions the
civilizing principle (imperative) is already at work: viz, 'it is we who are the
more or less secure and calculable; man is the *rule*, nature is *irregularity*' (111).
State-formation is an imposition—what Nietzsche called a 'tyranny' or tyrannical will—of regularity onto the natural (primitive) world, an imposing will that
projects man's rule onto an inchoate, unruly, arbitrary sphere of physical forces.
The first state-builders were lawgivers in this specific sense because they had
imposed regular law-like patterns on an otherwise inchoate external natural
world. They built as grand architects upon the fertile ground of religious cults
whose spiritual 'regularity' of invisible forces and elements in the form of sac-
raments and ascetic practices were formative for centralizing powers of ancient
states and poleis. The greatness of such complex states lies not in taming human
beings but in the willing power underlying creative but *necessary* laws of social
integration. The state and monotheistic states in particular, is a compulsory unit
of social cooperation in which fellow-feeling (belonging) is reinforced by the
customary morality of the master class. Forging, artistic creative forging, requires a strong will that can muster chaotic forces or elements into a new (ju-
ridico-religious) polity that functions unlike nature. A polity embodies necessary regularity and this is why Nietzsche declares the 'ground for any kind of
morality can then be prepared only when a greater individual or a collective
individuality...subjugates all other individuals' thus '[m]orality is preceded by
compulsion' (HH 99). The artist-statesmen or *tyrannos* in Greek is closer to this
ethos than our own: 'Thus does the man of violence, of power, the original
founder of states, act when he subjugates the weaker' (HH 99). To the man of
resentment, the true artist who creates organized social structures from the religious ascetic laws of regularity and necessity is one whose own genealogy is
indebted to the spiritual administrators of religious cults and communities.
Spiritual drives are akin to state progenitors: they must transcend the chaos of
physus and *koinonia* to impose a higher *nomos* that integrates disparate peoples
into a regular identity (i.e. *citoyen libre*, believer, faithful subject). Each type of

revolt against the indifference and irregularity of *physus* is a manifestation of the will as it transfigures and propels human (social) life.

What is peculiar to this world-historical rupture is the transmutation of the creature's original cruelty toward other creatures into that which every known 'higher culture' has incorporated: the 'spiritualization of cruelty' (BGE 229). Thus when states act out of resentment or revenge they express a deep-seated 'spiritual' strata of their own founding origins, since states—as both Spinoza and Kant had observed—can emulate the kind of violent cruelty that once was the preserve of natural creatures. Cruelty in civilized, tamed societies is thereby not actually eliminated but sublimated by powerful impulses of the 'spirit' that render cruelty into a form of grand politics that embodies the custom or moral of seeking revenge against those seen responsible (choosing) for our injury and suffering. Violent vengefulness is anything but vanquished in the modern world; it merely is elevated to a higher plane of technical unfreedom. It looks wholly technological while in fact being predicated on a will to spiritualize what first manifested itself in religious cults and sorcery. What Nietzsche first touted as forms of cruelty in *Human All Too Human* and *The Dawn* increasingly appears in later writings as the custom and politics of revenge (resentment).[9] Yet political approaches to these phenomena are mostly too crude to realize the moral psychology behind different historical social forms of being that simultaneously evince a theologico-religious dimension. Analytically Nietzsche committed himself to a comprehensive perspective of the Whole and this required, he assiduously observed, a transdisciplinary synoptic framework.[10] Perhaps now we are in a position to appreciate the enormity of the following statement: 'compared with the spirit of priestly revenge all the rest of spirit taken together hardly merits consideration' (GM I: 7). Priestly revenge, more than animalic cruelty, lays the foundation for centralized, palatial-temple state-societies that are distinctly marked by social distance and classes of 'slaves' and masters. High religious officials are proto-type nihilists—masters of alienation and sublimation who invent the 'dangerous' but most interesting animal-human type. They induce a form of ascetic self-mastery which states (civilized societies) later will harness and mobilize to prevent malicious vengefulness to pervade and thus permeate every sinew of civil society. The spiritualization of revenge is purposive and useful for state-artists since hatred and self-torture are diffused and tamed by the spiritual directors of state-religion(s) and customary morality (system as opposed to ethics).

Moreover, the outward projection of revengefulness onto one's enemies serves to vent energetic force which the tame, civilized man otherwise keeps pent-up in himself. As an object of vengeance, the enemy substitutes for what one cannot otherwise perform upon oneself or a fellow citizen: the act of requital in psychical terms. The deep fundamental connection between religion and state is also apparent in how Nietzsche conceptualized Justice vis-à-vis the caged existence within states. Lowly spirits that are prone to malice against 'those overflowing with the wealth and privileges of the spirit' seek revenge by means of fighting for the 'equality of all men before God' which he claims is symptomatic of malice but appears to themselves as a form of 'high spirituality' that 'is the spiritualization of justice' (BGE 219). Malice shown toward 'master-types' both within and without state-sovereignties is only perfectly consistent with the grand principle of *becoming*: the 'order of rank in the world, among things themselves—and not only among men' as he says within the same passage. Feebly spirited souls deny the principle—distance between identities—and seek recompense for the metaphysical constitution of the world thus; they deny and negate whereas higher, noble spirits acknowledge and affirm the world thus. Creative or true artists organize state complexes that evince the latter rather than the former, recognizing that claims to Justice are often interested and one-sided in the sense that they reflect resentment, malice and hatred toward those considered 'overflowing with the wealth and privileges' of freedom and noble responsibility. Attacking in other words is a substitutive form of will to power that exacts its own illusion on 'the herd': seek recompense for injury done unto oneself by those who have the *free* will to exercise it over you—an innocent if nevertheless malicious interpretation of life itself.

By contrast, a nobly spirited statesman would take responsibility for the lack of greatness that his (or her) state-society embodies due to the presence of malice and resentment in the social strata of its religio-juridical soul. The foresaid Justice that undoubtedly would seek to restrain the poisonous spirit of resentment and revenge (malice) is in fact another (further) development of the originary drive to '*impose a law on nature*' through the believer's belief in magic and miracles (HH 111). Natural law and civil law were parallel as was testified to by the status of Pharonic and other ancient rulers whose authority traversed several interlocking domains of life or Being. Hence Nietzsche's anthropological-philosophical claim that morality was only a later invention of ascetic priestly ideals rests on this argumentative point that '[m]orality is preceded by *compulsion*' (HH 99) and therefore when it comes to predominate it do so also as 'compulsion'—the necessity of the so-called 'moral law'. Those original designers and creators of complex states understood the law of necessity and built their kingdoms and empires on the dual basis of law-as-necessity: natural law and civil-religion were governed by a moral compulsion to submit to the higher, transcendent authority of the Almighty (King, Ruler or God). This point is perspicaciously given not in the later study of *beyond* good and evil (1886) but rather in a cool and moderate work of an earlier period, *Human All Too Human* (472) wherein he observed: 'Without the assistance of the priests even now no power can become "legitimate"'. So if are to take responsibility as free spirits—the major theme of this work—we must first recognize the interlacing of 'secular and sacred' within a very long genealogical lineage that spans much wider than the onset of a) nihilism and b) the dominance of the moral will. The roots of the politics of revenge lie very deeply in pre-moral religious beliefs and compulsive, necessary laws of social integration and order of rank (e.g. priestly caste).

What often goes overlooked in such matters is that although this constitutes part of the 'taming' of the human-animal spirit, it is at the same time a form of estrangement that elevates the human being above the indifference of nature and her naturalistic arbitrariness. When Nietzsche declared he did not advocate a

return to nature a la Rousseau, it was because he consciously interpolated creativity or 'artistry' between *natura* and *Mensch*. Reversals are impossible and
undesirable; and besides there is no freedom to be found in anything that lacks
the distinct regular nature of spirited human beings. Nietzsche's objection is not
against religion or morality per se as each of these he states quite clearly are 'a
bit of tyranny against "nature"' 'but this in itself is no objection' (BGE 188)
since the object of any master lawgiver is to tyrannize through his/her powerful
will to create something new or different. The state is an inorganic body and
here we arrive at our second observation regarding the creative impulse: behind
every artistic plan to forge a polity of coexistence thus putting a critical distance
between 'nature' and ourselves, the 'eternal joy of becoming' becomes concrete
in and through ascetic religious ideals of the Good and Justice. The system of
morality, codified ethical norms and practices, preserves traces not only of tenacious religious beliefs but the main fundamental element of all artistic creation:
'how strictly and subtly he obeys thousandfold laws' which on 'account of their
hardness and determination' defy the solipsistic prejudice of artists' freedom
laisser aller (letting go) (BGE 188). The proper artist not only knows that his
immediate nature is in the long past but also that she must transvaluate it
through the valuations of spiritualization and political man. In all probability, it
is the 'tyranny of such capricious laws' that actually constitute this 'nature' and
'natural' which naïve or romantic artists confuse with the myth of *laisser aller*.
In terms of freedom the implications of Nietzsche's complex reading is not a
problematic return to some pre-state, pre-religion existence; the process of human development with all its variegation and vicissitudes has heightened and
elevated the human being by means of the very travails and challenges (to the
will) which creation *and* taming have produced. What is most critical *contra*
romanticism and idealism is the 'metrical compulsion of rhyme and rhythm' in
the *long duree* of religions and moralities since what is 'essential and inestima-
ble in every morality is that it constitutes a long compulsion' (BGE 188).

   Through the necessity of the latter all phenomena can acquire strength and
freedom, but without the compulsive laws of great artists (state-makers) there
can be no 'strength and freedom' in newly generated forms of spirit and creativity. What is essential in the 'beyond' of good and evil is not the moral goodness
of a thing but the duration or tenacious hold which any form has over time.
Goodness emanates out of the high regard or honor with which subjects of a
given form behold it. Only metaphysically can one speak of an *a priori* good
inhering in the object or the substance, a viewpoint clearly eschewed by
Nietzsche throughout his works. Hence it can be argued religious spirits are also
beyond good and evil in the sense that though they may pose metaphysical postulates their value lies in acting as a force for the extension, regulation and
deepening of the soul of man (kind), an agent or class that alters the face of the
earth by its numerous longstanding cult practices, beliefs and rituals that appear
as 'law' and spiritual necessity (compulsion). As creators priests both as nihilists and 'lawgivers' give enduring substance(s) to the temporal finitude of the
animal-spirit and its feeble consciousness[11] and thereby establish the soul-
hypothesis as enduring gift of high learning and discipline. Their ascetic ideals

aid the savage animal to 'forget' the 'state of nature' from which it emerged and to look to the future of its own existence as a desirable non-present presence in the fundamental void of chaos. The repetition and non-repetition of cosmic processes—between being and becoming—as the *fatum* of eternity (recurrence) is one important immaterial heritage of their world-historical overturning (rupture). Through their 'revenge' against the material visible world, the human world consequently remains inexorably transformed—permanently redeemable. Nature could not have taught humankind redemption because there is only ever generation, excess and innocent death. Once estranged from nature by these artists of the spirit, men and women begin to search for beautiful unity in artifacts of *Bildung* and *paideia*, with nature embodied in the body itself. The state is only one substance which lays claim to embodying such a unity, a splendid or attractive unity of disparate individuals (and tribes) which knows the 'good' and in time stands to represent it before every challenge to the rest of mankind. The Divine Good and the King (or Emperor) thus most often appear synonymous to 'the people' throughout history. The cruel realism of Nietzsche's analysis at this point appears in his claim that behind this splendid beauty of the Good there lays an insidious instinct of cruelty—the basis of revengefulness. Every religion possesses a form of self-torture as its basis, a cruelty against man himself that drives the economy of sacrifice and punishment in diverse religions—the basic sub-theme of the *Genealogy of Morality*. Yet the theme of cruelty and violence recurs prominently in Nietzsche's account of state-formation. In this work, consistent with previous pronouncements in *Human All Too Human*, the tyranny of 'formation' is explained: 'the oldest "state" accordingly made its appearance as a terrible tyranny, as a crushing and ruthless machinery, and continued to work until finally such a raw material of people and half-animals was not only thoroughly kneaded and pliable but also *formed*' (II: 17).

Essential here is the key concept of 'formed' emphatically stated in the original text. In the same passage, he refers to these half-animals as superior in number but 'still formless, still roaming about'. State-religion complexes are crucial in forming something out of the 'raw material of people'—clearly an artistic, sculptor's metaphor for creation, a kind of juridico-military-religious will exercised over inchoate nature[12] to forge a spirit (*Geist*) of a kind. To sculpt, to form, is man's *fatum*; his spirit necessitates expressive form-giving so much so that freedom and necessity are no longer antithetical but complimentary aspects of 'becoming human', i.e. of having a human form. Spirit compels a human being to do just what state founders were required to do artistically: 'to impress upon it regularity and rule of law that it does not at first possess' (HH 111). Regularity necessarily 'forms'; it gives structure, goal, end, purpose, measure, ideal and above all value as to why human life is worth more than mere existence, more than mere endurance of suffering. Necessity and spirit-formation compliment the 'tyrannical'[13] will of the 'true artist' who understands the necessity of compulsion to create out of *un*-regular *physus* something worthy of elevated (human) natures. Here the *macro* and *micro* conjoin: design, plan or *schema* (in Greek) suggest 'forming' through a kind of necessary one-sided steeling of raw materials; as with the state, in ascetic spiritual matters too 'certain men feel so great a need to exercise their strength and lust for power...they at last hit upon the idea of tyrannizing over certain parts of their own nature, over, as it were, segments or stages of themselves. Power to form— whether materially or spiritually—necessarily means subordinating and mar- shalling elements which would otherwise remain simply numerous but formless. The spirit (or psyche) and the polity in short are homologous. As with morality (customary official) so too with 'every ascetic morality man worships a part of himself as God and for that he needs to diabolize the other part' (HH 137). After *Human All Too Human* Nietzsche will redress his insufficient recognition of this diabolizing as the work of revenge and its sibling, 'bad conscience'. The state- society of civilized man diabolizes the non-herd member just as the soul of bad conscience diabolizes the ugly poisonous part as its revengeful will.

Nietzsche's correction or possibly elaboration of a somewhat cruder propo- sition, will uncannily lead him to that noble vision expounded by Plato regard- ing the homology of the polis and soul. Nietzsche—by his own word—being a 'stranger to ourselves' of course did not recognize this form of Platonism as consonant with his own critique of modernity as the rule of 'the mob' (*demos*). Minus decadent Socraticism, as Nietzsche thought of it, Platonism shares with Nietzsche a conception of the interrelation between spirit and the *bios* of a po- litical community. By the time of '"Guilt," Bad Conscience, and Related Mat- ters', an appreciation of this interrelation has come to the fore as has the creative inventiveness of those (artist-rulers) who come like lightning, 'like fate, without basis, reason, consideration, pretext' whose 'work is an instinctive creating of forms, impressing of forms' (GM II: 17). Denying the fanciful 'contract' view of Hobbes and company, state-formation—like spiritual, religious cult forma- tion—is the work of 'whoever is "lord" by nature', 'whoever can give orders' and steps 'forth violently, in deed and gesture,' whom one does not reckon with (GM II:17). What does Nietzsche call these special figures of forms? These 'born organizers' who know not guilt or responsibility, who are ruled neverthe- less by 'that terrible artists' egoism' and responsible for the banishment of 'an enormous quantity of freedom' by means of the 'blows of their hammers, of their artist's violence' (GM II: 17). Born organizers with hammers of an artist's violence 'forcibly made latent' the extant 'instinct for freedom' which pre-state peoples (without a 'bad conscience') possessed, now subdued by their terrible artistry of power which fixes 'a gaze like bronze...that knows itself already jus- tified to all eternity in its "work"' (GM II: 17). Hence although these ferocious, talented creative 'organizers' were 'not the ones among whom "bad conscience" grew', the 'ugly growth' of bad conscience 'would not have grown *without them*' since they helped to suppress and make latent that 'instinct for freedom' which the human-animal lived by (GM II: 17). The spirit of the state and the state of the spirit were now conjointly manifested in the human nature that is caged by its 'discharging and venting itself only on itself'—this is revenge it- self. To be responsible therefore requires recognition of this subtle wedding of forces since the idealist moralistic penchant of demanding 'Just stop the re- vengefulness' falls short of such a reality. Neither a so-called 'attitude' or 'duty' *apropos* liberalism will applicably remove the danger of revenge, especially a spiritualization of the instinct of revenge embedded in state bodies and the metaphysics of free will underlying their claim to freedom.

This makes for a *difficult freedom* since the twin 'ugly growths' of bad conscience and spiritualized revengefulness are intricately unraveled into each other and into state-religion complexes that have very long genealogies. Ascetic ideals we can say have not only overturned the world but, importantly, have inexorably transformed the face of the earth, leaving the pure state (instinct) of freedom suspended in the far reaches of human forgetfulness. We cannot simply 'know' freedom nor can one somehow 'remember it' just as it is impossible to institute formally freedom in the structures of the modern state. The tamed, civilized human rather has an ethos and pathos that is imbued with valuations from this dominant matrix and hence its *Wesen* (being, essence) is wholly tied up with its reality (*Wirklichkeit*). Nietzsche the phenomenological meta-psychologist can grasp the tenacious hold—'tyranny'—which such historic 'forms' have on the soul of man (kind). *Difficult* freedom testifies to this reality; it posits, against Free Will, that a veracious struggle with social-historical constellations of power (forms) is integral to the actual process of *becoming* free—it is a process, not an *a priori* condition represented best by the phantasm of the Free Will. For the present discussion the problem lies not so much with the recurrence of things in eternity but the necessity inherent in the compulsion of everyday 'rhyme and rhythm'. Slave morality sees this compulsion as shear obstacle, a menacing inertia and a deadening weight on Free Will. Master morality values necessity and resistance by reclaiming what is extant in world-historical time while at the same time overcoming its limited 'form' through energy and power already invested in existing (axiological) forms, thus sublimating them into valuations which at first only appear as remote distant stars (futurity). One must affirm life, that is, adopt a Yes-saying attitude without however ceding to its base and decadent forms of life.

By 'affirmation' Nietzsche means a non-denial of 'errors' and reversals which moralists and sickly 'herds' have performed: eternity will recur with error, reversal of sorts and the debasement of man (or life) and therefore such pain—the pangs of birth and creation—is to be celebrated along with the joyous delight that life otherwise brings. The human being is not free *from* errors (reversals) but free *to* learn from errors and rapturous reversals. Humankind is free to appropriate the once reactive will to power of the ascetics in order to overcome its own self-limits while retaining the explosive concept of the hypostatized 'soul' and its attendant forms of esoteric mysticism. Every ascetic reversal—revenge against nature—merely signifies pliable dangerous conditions from which genuine 'free spirits' emerge sovereign and strong; that is, opposite to the reactive psychology of soul of ascetics these conditions do not pose constraints but rather dangerous 'opposite conditions' from which the ennoblement of the spirit grows. The opposite of 'modern men' are those 'free spirits' who see how 'the plant "man" has so far grown more vigorously' 'under the opposite conditions, that to this end the dangerousness of his situation must first grow to the point of enormity' (BGE 44). This arduous process, a process of endurance and birthing, is explained in terms of enhancement: 'his life-will had to be en-hanced into an unconditional power-will' (BGE 44). But by what means?

Structures of Soul—Responsibility

In the same passage Nietzsche states 'his power of invention and simulation (his "spirit") had to develop under prolonged pressure and constraint into refinement and audacity'. Because life is dangerous, as nature itself is, reversals, errors and negations of vital life all accumulate into 'prolong pressure and constraint' which are not to be considered obstacles but the resistance which 'commanding thought' is oblivious too (see chapter 1, Figure 2). As was shown in that chapter, resistance according to the False Reality schema is something objective and ex-ternal to the human subject. Whereas under the Pure Concept (Figure 2) the process from 'commanding' to 'affect of command' is described in terms of self-overcoming because in this instance a noble spirit understands itself as overcoming an immanent force instead of merely a force from without (what reactive spirits do). The twin interrelated illusions of 'cause—effect relations' and 'free will' are the actual impediment whereas the (standard) misinterpreta-tion has it that restraints pose the real obstacle to overcoming revengefulness as a type of unfreedom. She who masters their immanent drives and willing-power can command and expend the requisite drive-energy to overcome without feel-ing depleted or restrained into (nihilistic) servitude. In other words, historical formations are not an impediment as such; they are the dangerous grounds from which prepared, able and stronger spirits emerge to command creative designs or 'tables of value' over temporal presences. Such an elevated view, the view-point from above herd-morality, defies the conventional wisdom of restraint as a negative power over the individual. Historicality of present forms is what the overcoming human being in fact embraces because it sees the human-all-too-human manifest itself within the reactive slave's psychology who necessarily misunderstands resistance as constraint. As artist-commander—akin to state-builders—pain, suffering and spiritual revenge are the human raw material with which new forms, new valuations and futural goals are established from such claimed 'constraints'. Only the weak-willed or 'feeble man' as Nietzsche calls him finds constraint as an evil resistance (in Figure 1) that intervenes and pre-vents one's free will from taking its 'natural' course.

Moreover, such a type of human being fails to accept the necessary expendi-ture or cost involved in overcoming; they conserve energy through fear and angst, withdrawing inward whereas its counterpart knows expenditure to be part of the physics of life and thus also the economy of value-tableau creation. In-stead of denying the 'cost' of freedom—labor and power invested in each over-coming of unfreedom—commanding masters of the spirit possess the requisite self-knowledge of physics to understand that an expenditure of energy (psychi-cal power) is necessary proportionate to 'the resistance which has to be over-come, by the effort it costs to stay *aloft*' (TI ix: 38). Denial of such a psycho-physiological expenditure is symptomatic of slavish spirits and their feeble-power vis-à-vis the will to transcend limits of one's own finitude. Our concern here principally is precisely with the 'effort is costs to stay aloft' rather Nietzsche's own claimed political and 'moral perfectionism'.[14] It is the general economy of expenditure and resistance-overcoming which is most instructive for understanding Nietzsche's new conception of freedom (and responsibility). At this point, we diverge therefore from a commonplace view that Nietzsche's (own) overcoming is the exemplar *par excellence* for overcoming extant types of unfreedom. There is an unwarranted conflation here if we suppose that one man's overcoming of suffering and nihilism can be extended to overcoming more generally in the future. If Nietzsche consciously struggled to 'get over oneself', then are we not also responsible enough to get over Nietzsche's limitations? And to at least dispense with conflations of this kind? *Überwindung* (overcoming) is a dynamic, processual concept that cannot render static or fixed some exemplification of struggle, expenditure, suffering and staying 'aloft': it always exceeds the social-historical form of its own germination thus making it necessary to recognize the limits of one particular expression of it.

To be responsible thinkers we must be free to overcome or exceed the finite limits in which Nietzsche conceptualized the hold of decadence. It is not enough simply to draw a parallel between the concept of 'overcoming' and a person's life *of* overcoming and to overlay a spurious linkage with a speculative gesture that it can possess sufficient generalizability properties to warrant pan-cosmic status. Overcoming is irreducible to a single person's life-event whether that is Nietzsche himself, Napoleon, Goethe or a democrat-Christian. Herd-thinking promulgates the reductionist idea that the author of a critique of modern decadence stands as the emblem *for us* of overcoming Today's spirit of resentment and vengefulness. Independence of mind and will is after all what we saw earlier (in the previous chapter) as the mark of the sovereign individual. Subject-centered accounts, i.e. Nietzsche the man, moreover conform to the humanist's penchant to look for 'idols' wherever difficulty, complexity and above all necessity appear in historical time. So at this point we may disagree with the viewpoint expressed by analysts of 'the political' who argue 'Nietzsche resists the idols of modernity not in order to vanquish his decadence...but in order to transform himself into a more resilient type of decadent'.[15] Firstly, Nietzsche himself is not the focal-point of overcoming and its future. Secondly, it falls short of our analytic criteria that interpretation of existence apropos responsibility and freedom surpasses the need to be simply 'a more resilient type of decadent'. The two compound each other only to diminish the import of futural becoming as a process of becoming free by means of welcoming the 'greatest responsibilities'. Decadents of any ilk, resilient or otherwise, cannot understand let alone incorporate and live-out those enormous responsibilities that mark a noble life. We know Nietzsche to be an historical man—possessing the *human-all-too-human*—and this is precisely why he abjured the want to turn himself into some sort of centerpiece of philosophical idealism or fetishism. We are obliged to carry and swing 'the hammer' wherever 'the people' may be in search of a new Idol. It is undoubtedly true that Nietzsche is a figure, a figuration perhaps, of the overcoming moment like many other figures whom Nietzsche himself drew inspiration from in order to overcome cultural pessimism, e.g. Voltaire, Goethe, and Florentine nobles. A figure, nevertheless, is not and ought not to be an idol; otherwise we regress from one moment of unfreedom to another. The point of course is not to take revenge against Nietzsche in order to negate him and thus surpass him (or his limits). To become free from revengefulness and idolatry is the crucial difference but quite naturally, he expected to be misunderstood on this most fundamental of points as well.

While we have already discussed at some length the importance of the *human-all-too-human*, it behooves us to remember that the Fallen condition of decadence (feebleness) propels us of necessity toward such one-sided accounts and perspectives. That is to say, if we cannot adore and idealize Nietzsche the Idol then we 'must' at least be able to vent our revengeful will *against* him. This slavish attitude only reproduces and then manifests itself in that fundamental error of the metaphysicians: 'the faith in opposite values' (BGE 20), that is, either *in* Nietzsche or in *attacking* Nietzsche himself. To deny this duality is simultaneously to eschew Nietzsche-the-harbinger of man's redemption (Idol) and the revenge against one who seems to have so much 'promise' and yet 'fails us'. Neither position is justifiable, at least not from the standpoint of eschewing slavery and general herd-consciousness (conformity). A higher, elevated interpretive stance demands that the analyst adopt an incisive yet charitable interpretation (as per Donald Davidson's principle). A 'charitable' interpretation entails a magnanimous yet rigorous spirit of intellectual interrogation that is not given over to affective susceptibility or emotional hubris; on the other hand, a certain independence is maintained by way of a critical distance between interpreter and 'figure' (mentioned above) creating a productive tension of distance. To conclude on this point, the present discussion eschews analyses that unduly focus on Nietzsche himself as exemplar or his personal efforts in capturing, once and for all, the essence of overcoming (for the purpose of evidencing freedom in real time).

Returning to servitude in various forms of revenge, what appears superordinate in Nietzsche's analyses is the phenomenon characteristic of all higher cultures: the transfiguration of cruelty. Since cruel vengefulness is one aspect of modernity in the twentieth and twenty-first century, we can now turn more explicitly to the 'artist and transfigurer of cruelty' (BGE 229). Why? Because the spiritualization of cruelty—just as with the spiritualization of resentment-based revenge previously—raises cruelty to a more profound level. Profound cruelty underlies Today's revengeful spirit and its various expressions within and between states of spiritualized revenge (i.e. its institutional form). These states are at once intra-subjective (self), inter-subjective (herd, nation) and inter-human since as we have already seen religiosity of spirit and complex societies are intertwined genealogically. The earth has in fact been transformed by these twin universal developments: morality (ascetic ideals) and civilized taming (irreversible sociality). These overriding logics of formation notably are examined mostly without (explicit) reference to 'will to power' since, as Clark and Leiter correctly argue, this important concept does not continually suffuse all of Nietzsche's published writings and examinations.[16] This significant development in world-history—unlike repetition derived arguments concerning Recurrence—marks a difference in the process of becoming human, one which enravels 'spirit' and ethico-political systems. Here is the point where Nietzsche the political philosopher emerges and not rather, the claimed *aristos* of his select philosophers or the abovesaid 'perfectionism' of his sublime vision. What is political in this sense is the embodiment of strong instincts in spiritual transfigurations of existence that are founded on compulsive forms of cooperation. These forms however are themselves underscored by the contradiction that man's search for joy occurs within a kind of sociality that is demarcated by 'laws' of necessity—the *nomos* of every *poleitia*. But we now know that one's *poleitia* (polity) necessarily encompasses the particular state of the soul (spirit) from which its origins stem. Its 'politics' involves necessity but now it is the necessity of the artist's art, that is to say, the art of the 'transfigurer of cruelty' (cited above). The tamed soul (spirit) like the tamed city of man is anything but tame (passive, negative); in fact, it is an amplified and deepened soul (and *eo ipso* city) that has reconfigured the spiritual will to revenge into so many kinds of individuation and ascetic-derived disciplines of order (distance). Freedom in not being immune to such developments of *becoming* must similarly reflect their amplification, extension and deepening; it is always defined and reconfigured by this three-level process of becoming: intra-subjective, inter-subjective and inter-human. There is no eternally fixed notion of freedom as a result which fittingly is wholly consistent with the cognate argument that there is no eternally fixed being, atom, ego, Will or 'God'.

We should conceive of freedom instead as that which is integral to the underlying creative force behind such world-changing developments since freedom cannot *a priori* rule out errors and their consequences. Erring on any one of these three fundamental 'levels' of social being can never be eliminated since becoming presupposes a will to truth that continually sifts through reality to negate errors. It follows then—given our *contra* antitheses posture—that freedom coexisting amongst historical unfreedoms is analogous to truths mingling amongst a sea of errors. Reality is impure whereas the faith of the metaphysicians holds onto the illusion that life and personal freedom can somehow be free of contamination (impurity). If we think in terms of the complimentary copula *and/with* rather than the troublesome *either/or* then we can manage to escape the plebian weakly grasp of (un)reality. The transcendent '*beyond*' good and evil so often invoked by Nietzsche is indicative of such a 'beyond' pure freedom and unfreedom, truth and untruth. The will to eliminate the impure (badness in goodness) is arguably a form of revenge against reality, against the chaos of existence and its attendant feeling of void (*nihilo*). For us Nietzsche's Yes-saying must recognize this fundamental drive to extirpate the ugly, poisonous or 'evil' element within every moment of *becoming* is a manifestation of man's spirit of revenge. As opposed to the affirmative (noble) spirit, a reactive psychology finds it necessary to deny this reality to the soul, wishing it could once and for all eliminate the bad or evil from the face of the earth. Reactive human beings enjoy negation for negation's sake; their *raison d'etre* is bound up with containing hostilities from without since a reactive soul is essentially outward looking and projective (of its own fears, anxiety and hatred). Others, or the world itself, are always seen as an impediment to one's personal freedom: 'if only I could be freed from this and that constraint I'd be happy; but I'm unhappy simply because others impede my free will or else they burden me with all these responsibilities'. Hence, institutional figurations of social life ipso facto appear as merely the embodiment of evil, badness or nihilistic despair— they are the historic 'error' that the reactive soul despairs over because its own spiritual pessimism precludes it from affirming life in all its complexity. Yet it is unfree essentially; in other words, within the scales of its own soul, constantly wishing to blame a seemingly hostile world that it thinks it has no control over despite believing strongly in the power of its own 'free will' (another illusion of false reality). It is for this reason that terrorists or hatred-avengers dissolve themselves of the responsibility of life when it is the life of (their) Others— those whom they despise or blame for their own misery and injury. Spiteful spirits, those that are replenished by vengefulness and abjection of creative impulses, vent forces lying immanent within their destructive, negative souls. Every effort to avenge a lost life in turn breeds further resentment of him or her who represents so-called 'master' values: power and values are conflated into a uniform repulsive identity.

This conflation eases the tension within their soul that ordinarily increases each time the adversary commits another destructive deed. Weak-willed individuals require this projective venting: as they cannot master their impulses and fail to realize their creative energy in *bios*, the power overcoming them is too great to withstand—they must release it in order to be free of its pain (force). What is 'pain' for the feeble decadent is 'force' or power for the nobly free spirit. We should recall at this point that is also why the former type cannot withstand the weight of great responsibilities. Burdensome weight is too much to bear if you already feel weak, vulnerable or impotent due to a superior power. The will to attack appears on the surface to be quite the opposite of feebleness: it might suggest 'will to power' and aggressive self-assertion. However, I wish to question this specious interpretation because it is merely a surface appearance of what wanting eyes and 'seeing' are otherwise easily beguiled by. Adversaries in the so-called 'war on terror' are caught up in this illusion; each side prefers to deny the inextricability of revenge and power as an axis upon which their very existence turns; and each side erroneously perceives the other to be of superior might or aggressive self-assertion (i.e. Islamic radicalism) which may in due course overwhelm them. Now whilst conflict and even war are not denied their place within this realist conception of the three fundamental levels of social being, nevertheless we can point to the absence of one vital element that defines sovereign autonomy (a free noble spirit in other words). To destroy and to overwhelm as barbarians have done for centuries is not per se problematic. What Nietzsche by contrast considered highly problematic, that is, plebian and therefore the mark of inferiority of spirit is the *mentalité* that defines the struggle—the perspective of life. The 'sign of strong, full natures' is not resentment or envy of predominance but rather the presence of 'an excess of formative, reconstructive, healing power'; and most importantly, that power which 'makes one forget' (GM I: 10) instead of simmering to the point of perpetual decline (i.e. embittered affective-states). Without this vital capacity to 'shake off with a single shrug a collection of worms' that otherwise will fester and dig itself further into the wretched soul of the poisonous one, there can be no reverence for one's enemy (GM I: 10). As against the 'human being of *ressentiment*' who conceives of his enemy with contempt, '[w]hat great reverence for his enemies a noble human being has', one which is without contempt and devoid of identifications such '*the evil one*' and 'the evil enemy' (GM I: 10).

The nobler figure, who knows the pathos of freedom, is free from this vile contemptuousness and insipid idealization of itself as the virtuous one, what Nietzsche calls the 'good one', that is the counterpart of the 'evil one'. Freedom being *beyond* the false antithesis of 'good' and 'evil' cannot be realized whilst one party or other conceives of itself as righteous, virtuous and knowing absolutely the Good. To transcend this two-sided illusion—vile contemptuousness and illusory idealization—is necessary if either party is to honor their enemy with reverence and see them 'as his distinction' (GM I:10). For the said surface appearance of reality this distinction holds as the divide between the forces of evil versus the forces of good (virtuosity). Antithetical reactive psychologies thus reign and imprison each other in a *mentalité* that simply juxtaposes one civilization (or tribe) against another, one political ideology (secular democracy) against another (theocratic democracy). Antithetical souls, those that hold fastly onto pure ideals and histories, are intoxicated with the power of resentment: 'they have brought this onto us and therefore they'll pay'! shout both sides, both ideological decadents. Morality is of course on 'their side'; that is an indisputable fact because both decadents—of purity and reactive-negation—cloak their struggle to survive in the necessary language of customary morality (system).

Histories are deployed to evoke the virtuosity of their respective moralities so that the will to revenge one's lost citizens inevitably leads to grand words, since 'grand politics' at the close of one millennium and beginning of another requires grand words: preservation of 'civilization' in the case of the United States and the infallible holy command for (parts of) political Islamism. Grand politics, grand words, grand ends and thus grand wars—all built on a surface appearance which has underlying it an ugly belly of falsehoods such as inalienable 'free will'. Perhaps this is a tragic comedy of the new millennium: 'for even war is a comedy and conceals, just as every means conceals the end' (BGE 273). Does the war on terror or the war against Americanization camouflage reality and allow the means to take over reality? Strategic means usurp the original appeal of the ideological commitment to 'American civilization' and 'holy Islam'. For this reason we can dismiss the claim that *ressentiment* essentially occurs when 'men do not exteriorize their affect into action' or 'when the affect does not *necessarily* lead to action' since actualization through war disproves this proposition.[17] More salient is the point of argument concerning the restlessness of these antagonists: the 'will to power characteristic of *ressentiment* assimilates experience into the person (makes it his past) in such a way that the man of *ressentiment* is always driven forward, unable to rest with the present'.[18] The present is contestation for both agents of revenge as experience inexorably drives them forward to a time when they shall be free of 'radical

Islamists' and 'American imperialists'. Unlike the Buddhist's moment in the present, each of these civilizational protagonists drain the promise of the future by ironically drawing on their respective civilizational heritages to challenge the 'evil one' only to then cut away the significance of assimilated experience (*historie*)—the nihilist must look forward only to save himself from the valuelessness of the present. This present is tainted by a deep resentment of a threatening power that *appears* to decouple existence from one's historic life (genealogical lineage). The desire for freedom is projected onto a particular forward-looking horizon since the present is now colonized by the impurity of the 'evil one' and its morality. In the absence of reverence for one's enemy (moral) impurity is imputed onto one's experience of historical identity and delusion consequently sets in. Futural experience of that once considered pure moral identity—liberal man versus 'true Islam'—provides much needed release (and relief) from the anxiety of losing one's own rich customary norms of life and morals. To live in the present, to dwell on the moment, is too painful because it is too nihilistic whereas the futurity of consciousness provides a way-out from the dreaded malaise of 'masterly' negation of precious values and morals (civilizational reality). What appears as a defense of the present is in fact a flight into unreality, an illusory hopeful future which religious discourse crowns as 'redemption'. Fear of valuelessness due to the sovereign powers of negation—nihilistic despair— drive each side of the enmity line toward the future without a requisite reverence for the other that would enable an upholding of one's responsibilities. The flight or more precisely projection into the future is essentially irresponsible.

As such, each side is recreating the basis of its own unfreedom 'in the future'. There is no promise *of* the future preserved as denial of one's genealogy combined with a deep nihilistic despair regarding penultimate valuations only results in a phantasmatic reality of wish fulfillment. Lacking responsibility, the perspective is characteristically illusory; 'seeing' forward ahead in time gives relief to the present chaos, a chaos that is related to multiplicity and its profusion of seemingly chaotic forces. The realm of unfreedom is contiguously marked by so many forms of irresponsibility within and between each one of these intermingling forces. By contrast, futurity of time evokes a homogeneity of calm and peaceableness where blood shall fill the veins of 'our brothers' rather than the streets of Bagdad, London, New York or Istanbul. This is reactive politics, the grand politics of resentment and hatred played out in the souls and 'cities' of modern human beings who pervert time (by claiming it for their redemptive purposes and) by abandoning the promise immanent within the present *for* the future of humanity. The other reason it is reactive and not noble (free) is the herd-nature of this expropriation and perversion of time: the 'tribe' however large and ubiquitous, with its distinctive herd-consciousness abrogates the 'promise' which species-development holds preciously within its breast. Civilizational complexes which (mis)understand themselves as organic whole entities—liberal western states v Islamic legitimacy—forget that these volatile forces of multiplicity constitute *processes* (becoming) and not organic whole entities. The noble free spirit sees time as an unfolding process; time encompasses the present in all its historicality and its *be-coming* whereas the perversion enacted by slave morality eschews the present event while hypocritically claiming the Past to have privileged status. Slaves purchase time through their destructive forward-looking release from the present while at the same time claiming legitimacy for violent deeds through the authority of customary knowledge (morality, tables of values). The latter quite naturally is better suited to the falsehood of a real organic entity in time whereas the noble human being is better suited to the reality of underlying and surface-level *processes* unfolding in time (i.e. past-present-future as intertwined in each moment of becoming).

To overcome the politics of revenge necessitates therefore a redemption of time as that manifold, dynamic and seemingly 'chaotic' becoming that life encompasses—an encompassment that knows no holiness or 'holier than thou' morality. This is no cause for pessimism since every 'present' is dually marked by the manifoldness of becoming—its origins, existents and traces of untimely[19] existence. If the slave revolt of the will to revenge was of historic importance then the will to overcome can also be seen to reside within that very innovation, that spurt to growth and extension in the soul and city of man that the spirit of the state and the state of the religious spirit each helped to forge. Unlike some political interpretations, we do not need to posit a transitory *schema* or matrix of principles that will show 'the way' out of modern decadence. Degeneration certainly suggests regeneration but we have already cautioned against a faith in fundamental antitheses and opposite values. The so-called problem of regeneration (out of decadence) emerges out of commonplace antithetical thinking: future versus history, resistance versus conformity, and most of all being versus becoming. The illusory 'problem' drops away once we dispense with the heavyweight thinking of antitheses and thus find being to be integral to becoming. It requires the same conceptual shift in logic as the once formidable antithesis: freedom (from) versus responsibility (to). Each of these conceptual shifts is in fact necessary to grasp the nature of Nietzsche's radical redefinition of freedom vis-à-vis the will to revenge. Revengefulness as *Wesen* (being, essence) is only representative of a particular form or type of human nature—the reactive, vengeful weakly kind—which constantly recurs in the species' history yet is at the same time transfigured and overcome by morphologies of the human that have transcended its strong reactive appeal.

This is the fundamental perspective of *Werden* (becoming); it sees revengefulness in all its reality but assigns it a contingent power or status; however, the resentful 'powerless type' misreads this reality as something permanent, a *Wesen*, instead of a corrupted attempt at *Überwindung* (overcoming) which becomes unfreedom because of its own inherent slavish, reactive psychology. Our standpoint adds another dimension to this argument: the slavish reactive psychology of particular human natures is further bolstered by both the state and the spirit of the state which now embody a transfiguration of the original 'instinct of revenge' vented more freely before the coming of civilized existence (see chapter on civilization). It is critical to state as much because a purely monist or liberal individualist view of the modernity of revenge would tend to privilege the individual as either some *super*man or bourgeois 'last man'. For Nietzsche, the institutions of *Bildung* and *bios* across the horizon of European

modernity—humanity one could say—are themselves definitive in this important regard. That is to say, contra romanticism Nietzsche can be understood as a
theorist and analyst of civilization(s) rather than of culture. Overcoming cannot
simply occur within the realm of culture (whatever that is meant to mean today);
it must take place—consistent with the logic of our previous analysis—through
preparation, enablement, and cultivation which are all *long duree* processes (of
becoming something else). The reactive soul of the mediocre 'last man' must
not be seen to be overcome by essentially a great *über*-person (individual). After
all, Nietzsche consistently refers in his genealogies to classes and castes of
'types'—nobles, aristocrats, slaves—of human nature that are essentially of
noble or ignoble cultivation ('breeding') or otherwise some admixture of each
(the third, meditative form). The sovereign individual, like the great artist-
philosopher, takes so many epochs and generations to cultivate and reach fulsome ripeness. Like excellent, beautiful fruits of the tree autonomous responsible human beings only reach their manifest maturity after very long processes of
preparation and extension, which themselves are fraught with dangerous errors
and possibilities of elimination. No single individual can embody the promise of
the earth—a Dionysian divine vision—that is why Zarathustra knows he must
descend from the mount and socialize with others: the message, the higher state
of overcoming, must leave the solitude of the One and disseminate amongst
ordinary humankind. No form of overcoming mediocrity and decadence can
simply take place in one's self-consciousness; unless it is objectified, the will to
life remains caged within the confines of a solipsistic consciousness which
Leibniz had already corrected two centuries ahead of his time.[20] While a noble-
man or Zarathustra knows that revenge is a scourge of valley-like existence, this
'knowledge' has no value if it simply remains in the head of a solitous ascetic
who breathes alone nature's cold mountain air. In our language, *physus* is not
bios: and value only has meaning within the *welt* of human beings.

A further dimension aids the tenacity of such an appearance of the real: 'romantic pessimism'. Nietzsche describes one of the major consequences of the
state of spiritual transfiguration as that perverse vengeance which is embodied
by two penultimate influences upon the modern soul: Schopenhauerian philosophy and Wagnerian music. Together they form the 'last *great* event in the fate
of our culture', he argued (GS 370). Nietzsche himself had to overcome this
romantic pessimism as he had misunderstood Wagner and Schopenhauer in his
youthful days; the mature Nietzsche realizes that one who suffers from the 'impoverishment of life' seeks redemption through art. Romanticism is made the
substitute for realism. Within the terms of realism, romantic pessimism possesses one corrupting, decadent flaw: namely, as 'a remedy and an aid in the
service of growing and struggling life' this 'last great event' is built upon the
necessity to 'turn what is most personal, singular and narrow…into a binding
law and compulsion' (GS 370). What is the precise nature of this 'binding law'?
In the same passage, Nietzsche explains 'one who, as it were, revenges himself
on all things by forcing his own image, the image of his torture, on them, branding them with it'. Is this the condition of unfreedom in late modernity, the condition prevalent in the first decades of the new twenty-first century? That is, the

forcing of one's own image, one's tortured *imago*, 'on them'—their fellow believers as well as their adversary. Branding our enemy with this callous image of tortured life which must be repaid by returning it to the one who has instigated this act of violence (power) and who is responsible for *our* injury, is this not harmful to good health (growth)? The harm caused by such a weakly projection of one's inner damage, a returning or repaying of injury and pain, further denigrates one's life into ignobility: "If I suffer then others must suffer too" is the cry not of the noble one(s) but of those who 'suffer from the *impoverishment of life*' (GS 370). How can one side or tribe lay claim to representing freedom, goodness, or holiness if they seek to incur injury blindly through spiteful or hateful revenge? The injurer is slavish to the impulses of his or her impoverishment of life—an impotence with respect to the said 'formative, reconstructive, healing power' of more flourishing healthy souls. This impotence is greatly shrouded by acts of revenge that *prima facie* appear to the contrary as courageous acts of powerful force or will. This appearance or *visage* of power is referred to as 'the tyrannical will of one who suffers deeply' (GS 370). The one who suffers deeply, that is to say, is himself tyrannized by the force of an embittered, poisonous state of spirit (affective economy). Objectification of his own pain will cause others pain too yet he is oblivious to the perpetuation of suffering because responsibility appears too weighty, too burdensome, for such a weakly 'type'. The object for him is to dispense with the state of suffering from within by taking revenge on others in order to alleviate the sense of injustice perpetrated against him.

Politics of Revenge and Transfiguration

As was argued earlier, the reactive (nihilistic) psychology of slave morality conceives of the external world as fundamentally opposed to him, as a hostile place that constantly erects impediments and resistance against his own 'free will'. What eludes 'slave' consciousness is the tragic moment of recurring violent revenge in which he is caught and is *responsible* for at the same time. When 'romantic pessimism' is not as pervasive in slave consciousness Nietzsche finds the wastage of grand politics fills the void of modern nihilism. Here both patriotic nationalism and devotion to the state's war-machine sicken the spiritual body of those whose preparation and growth has been siphoned by the business of war. The 'sum total of all these sacrifices and costs in individual energy and work is so tremendous that the political emergence of a people almost necessarily draws after it a spiritual impoverishment and enfeeblement', argues Nietzsche (HH1: 481). Given Nietzsche's view of war as a vitalizing element of stagnate civilized existence, this is a strong statement against the blind faith invested in committing vital 'spiritual' growth and stocks to pathetic political causes, i.e. warring based on mutual revenge. Suicidal revenge and state-terrorist acts of war exact an enormous cost on the promise of the future within a single *Bildung*: 'more spiritual plants and growths in which its soil was previously so rich have to be sacrificed to this coarse and gaudy flower of the nation' (HH1: 481). As opposed to the moralist's disgust, Nietzsche 'the immoralist'—in the particular sense given in the previous chapter—wages war not against war itself but the profound stupidity involved when 'every efficient, industrious, intelligent, energetic man belonging to such a people lusting after political laurels is dominated by this lust and no longer belongs wholly to his own domain, as he formerly did' (HH1: 481). A human being cannot be free as long as they remain slavish to lusting after such 'political laurels'—the mass ideologies of divergent political 'ideals' and idols. The wastage of spiritual capital is increased whenever individuals come under the sway of 'grand politics'; as soon as they no longer belong wholly to their 'own domain' human beings get caught up in the vortex of a state-religious faith (in the new ideal) and spiritual revenge. Becoming spiritually depleted, individuals caught in such a vortex find refuge and meaning in the drive to exact revenge of a spiritual kind (symbolic, moral and axiological) against the so-called evil one. The evil one, paradoxically, thus becomes a source of 'spiritual' nourishment, of spiritual regeneration and extension, because the will to power it must mobilize to exact revenge against it enhances its own wayward, feeble state of the soul (e.g. the 'American psyche' or 'Islamist psyche' as commonly understood).

Out of this profound stupidity of wasting and depleting one's own spiritual stock—an 'error' as Nietzsche called such things—an advantage of the spirit will emerge in the form of a revitalization of one's own customary morality with its attendant distances of the soul. The lesson to be drawn from this might be that the claimed 'war on terror' and 'struggle against American imperialism' in the twenty-first century will only help to revivify the spiritual ideals of contending faiths with common metaphysical roots. Namely, on the side of 'the West' a faith in the idea of progress expressed in scientific-secular terms and on the side of radical (extremist) Islamists the faith in a recoverable original spiritual truth (customary morality) before its corruption by western modernity. Conflict with all its challenge-and-response ebbs and flows in the end may bring out contradictions immanent within modernity and its kernel: the 'death of God' event. In *Beyond Good and Evil* (53) Nietzsche drew attention to an important facet of the nihilistic condition often overlooked by the crude 'death of God' thesis: 'the religious instinct is indeed in the process of growing powerfully'. Just as Nietzsche had foreseen the rise of Russian self-assertion and a future European identity, the drive to re-divinize the modern world by means of faith was integral to his philosophic outlook. The West's will to completion—a seemingly secular completion of eschatological ideals to overcome evil—and the said religious faith in a pre-modern Koranic purity of truth exhibit a common fundamental faith: a 'faith of the metaphysicians' in the atemporal ideal, a realization of that elusive transmundane goodness devoid of moral errancy (evil). This underlying universal behind the façade of an invidious world-conflict is rendered explicable by Nietzsche's emphasis on the significance of *faith*.[21] A parallel exists here between the explication of the 'modern world' without a God and the Christian nihilist's invention of modern science. Science evolved out of the metaphysics of Being and the *causa sui* (as we saw in previous chapters) and yet still encompasses the fundamental faith embedded in the 'will to truth' of (neo-) Platonism. As a non-theistic tradition, scientific thinking nonetheless exudes a positive faith in the power of reason to disclose the inner workings of nature. The West's will to completion (of modernity) is analogous to the secular form of scientific faith in the modern world. Conversely, Islamic fundamental revivalist politics assumes theistic language in its revolt against the nihilistic decadence of 'contemporary America', evincing a faith in the spiritual power of morality and customary tradition against 'western decadence'. The instinct of revenge manifested on both sides of the battle for supremacy is thereby linked to two distinctive types of faith even if they should *appear* to be secularist on one side and theistic on the other. If deeds or 'works' are secondary to faith, as Nietzsche maintains, then faith in a this-worldly completion of liberal freedom and, conversely, faith in an otherworldly glory based on sacrifice in this world demonstrates an extension and not a dissolution of metaphysical faith, viz. that which transcends immanence.

The problem with the standard 'death of God' thesis is that it presumed the rise of an atheistic naturalism, a world in which 'the divine' and the spirituality of the self would no longer loom large because of the decapitation of the Godhead. A reductive interpretation of nihilism would incline to represent the world in this fashion; a non-reductive treatment by contrast understands that the drive to re-divinize the world after scientific positivism by means of faith is itself an expression of the *spiritualization* of the will to power, that is, the will to life. Forms of spiritualization manifested in different faith-structures—religious, moral, rational-scientific and juridico-political—are thus responsible for the operations of modern states as well as individuals and 'tribes' or herds in their broadest possible sense. A non-reductive argument concerning active and (so-called) 'reactive' forms of nihilism need not therefore claim an absence of Godly dimensions in modernity when it finds instead a prevailing transfiguration of the 'old God' in and through the 'metaphysical need' of 'the people'—a need to maintain faith in something transcendent of modern meaninglessness while also sustaining the faith kernel of secular scientific reason. The civil-religion of contemporary America evinces precisely this two-sided valuation of life: secularist nihilism (scientific materialism) and a Christian 'metaphysical need' of the people. Rather than to will nothingness we see modern individuals and different 'tribes' preferring to appropriate for themselves the piety of a redemptive power of faith (religious or scientific)—a faith which aids in overcoming hardship and suffering related to their felt powerlessness.[22] Redemption as the transfiguration of the slave revolt in morality is most useful here because it exemplifies the reactive soul's desire to *create value* out of the morass of plebian impotence. It arguably echoes the following point on resentment: 'The slave revolt in morality begins when *ressentiment* itself becomes creative and gives birth to values: the *ressentiment* of beings denied the true reaction, that of the deed, who recover their losses only through an imaginary revenge' (GM I: 10). Modernity now confronts its imaginary revenge in both the spirit of the state and the state of the (human) spirit.

This is clearly the essence of several observations made after *Zarathustra* regarding the horizon of the spirit of man in confronting its own 'imaginary revenge'. First, the naturalistic drive in the sciences to disclose a real world is underscored by an incessant 'metaphysical faith' that is actualized in the forementioned will to completion. Discourses on so-called 'rogue' or 'recalcitrant' political societies exemplify resistance to this form of will. Second, talk of asceticism or ascetic ideals as *the explanandum* of religious phenomena is, at best, limited; for the *form* which imaginary revenge has come to assume requires explanation, namely accounting for the vicissitudes of revenge through its numerous transmutations into specific 'forms'. Third, the limited discourse concerning Nietzsche's claimed 'fatalism'[23] forgets the centrality of faith in affirming the pathos of time and the promise immanent in man's becoming. In *Twilight of the Idols* (ix: 49) Nietzsche says: 'Such a spirit who has *become free* stands amid the cosmos with a joyous and trusting fatalism, in the *faith* that only the particular is loathsome, and that all is redeemed and affirmed in the whole...Such a faith, however, is the highest of all possible faiths: I have baptized it with the name *Dionysus*' (original italics). Put simply: there is no 'fate' as such without the higher importance of faith (and its order of faiths) and, in particular, its standing or apprehension of the Whole. Fatalism is thus a contingent proposition: it alone, isolated from the *Whole* and detached from *faith*, would simply amount to yet another metaphysical truth. To understand one's 'fate' or destining in the world—as the above quotation indicates—further requires that one above all 'becomes free' and thus able to see the cosmos in joyous and trustful ways, and thereby affirm one's standing *in relation* to the (necessary) Whole. This point counters the flawed claim that Nietzsche's 'affirmation' is too vague and therefore should instead be considered a strong proposition for 'good health'. Our proposition by contradistinction posits the centrality of spirit, becoming, *faith* in goals we aim and set for, preparation and enablement of higher types (partly through the 'slave revolt in morality' itself), and the overcoming of poisonous states present in virulent objectifications of others as the 'evil one'. It confirms the 'necessity' of such a world while also holding onto the possibility inherent in the 'promise of the future' which inextricably is linked to Nietzsche's Dual Descent and its 'politics of revenge' on one side, and its overcoming through a transfiguration of reactive states of the soul on the other. Nor is ascetic discipline considered enough either because the dance of the joyous spirit of a 'gay science' eludes the claimed closure of asceticism.

Fourth, imaginary revenge in actuality is confronted in the realization of those powers and capacities that paradoxically stem from the struggle intrinsic to the 'impoverishment of life'. That is, when the avenging moralists seek to overturn the world of high values to pursue their particular (ascetic) 'idols'— theistic, secularist or an admixture of both—they inadvertently give impetus to the *requirements* for overcoming. The 'long spiritual will to interpret all events' according to a religious or moral schema 'has shown itself to be the means through which the European spirit has been *trained* to strength, ruthless curiosity, and subtle mobility' (BGE 188, emphasis added). The cost being historical significant, an important impetus is gained in the preparation, cultivation and hence growth of the human being and its spirit—its height, depth and breadth of scope. Thanks to the moralist and his avenger cousin, everything becomes more dangerous, interesting, holier, compulsive and intensely agonic regarding the state of one's soul and its governance. Nature or *laisser aller* (letting go) is simply no longer obtainable in all its proclaimed immediacy—she has been pushed back and made more remote by the taming process of civilization. Through religious and philosophic metaphysics, we develop so many superstructures about the soul and human natures that the said immediacy and simplicity of *laisser aller* can no longer be trusted. In this context, the instinct of revenge has gone through so many permutations and contortions that its sublimation in the taming of the human-animal through the state and state-religions renders the naturalistic condition almost mythical, that is, remote. Spiritualization, as Nietzsche calls this paradoxical logic, does not actually annul revenge since its manifestation as 'imaginary revenge' makes the attack on life (in this world) one between two types of spirit, two types of soul and hence two adversaries of the 'true and good' life—the honorable or virtues life, i.e. of the devout democrat and theocrat. Rivalrous tribes of the twenty-first century exemplify both the heightened and extended distances between master-slave dimensions of their own 'souls' and tribes. Monotheistic religions and their concomitant 'soul-hypothesis' have inexorably transformed the spirit of man and its *bios* not merely by way of spurious 'ascetic ideals' but through a long-term 'tyranny'. Nietzsche explained its positive value in the following succinct way: 'this tyranny, this caprice, this rigorous and grandiose stupidity has *educated* the spirit' (BGE 188). Doctrinal truth aside, what the moralization of the world and its incorporation in state-civilizations shows is the indispensable benefit it provides for 'spiritual discipline and cultivation'—a point that is made throughout Nietzsche's work from *Schopenhauer as Educator* onwards. What is of penultimate importance here is the resistance which (spiritual) freedom must come up against in order to become *phenomenal* in this world. Without tension, a 'tension of the bow', the spirit becomes lax and the human being merely lapses into the myth of escaping from the necessary suffering of earthly existence. Similar to Plato's *gymnasia*, there is no life beyond mere *zoi* without a training of the mind and body of man to levels that reach the *arête* of man himself. Nietzsche's idea of greatness, for instance, requires the cultivation precisely of this kind of *arête*.

Here the scourge of revenge is what endangers the realization of such a subtle noble greatness and yet defines the conditions of a pathos from which the education of the spirit springs. The long, historical task of preparing—of being 'trained' as Nietzsche says—the human spirit to transvaluate *ressentiment* requires more than subjectivity or a single generation. The asceticism and moralism of the 'slave revolt' in values in fact plays an affirming and creative role despite its devaluation of the corporeal self because it sustains the necessary tension that is vital for the spirit to deepen, widen and regenerate the *Bildung* that envelops it. Only the tension of a bow will allow one to shoot for the most distant stars (BGE *P*). In the contemporary scene this could translate into the reactive psychology of the vengeful type posing as a resistance to an overcoming of a perverse form of irresponsibility at the level of 'grand politics'. The impetus lies therein, in the conflict itself, where two kinds of faith seek to dissolve resistance to their (particular) 'freedom of will'—a liberal capitalist and an Islamic extremist will. Recurrence of revenge-taking, as the perpetual seeker of knowledge understands, will not however eliminate the power of the commanding thought to overcome the temporal resistance posed by such poisonous natures; for the 'commanding thought' (as discussed in Chap.1) is continually sustained by the tension intrinsic to such phenomena and their re-production of it (i.e. recurrence of tension producing dynamics). Nietzsche's diagnosis of the age reinforces the essential element of preparedness for overcoming: 'For this age shall prepare the way for one yet higher, and it shall gather the strength that this higher age will require some day' (GS 283).

The present acts as the ground upon which the future unfolds in particular directions: it will 'prepare the way for one yet higher' despite the overemphasis which Deleuze and others mistakenly placed on the logic of 'repetition' vis-à-vis time's eternity. In the same passage of *Gay Science* Nietzsche further observes—consistent with our entire thesis—'To this end we now need many preparatory courageous human beings who cannot very well leap out of nothing'. The reason Nietzsche never renounced warfare itself—even though he was most critical of resentment politics—was that the drives, instincts and affects mobilized in waging wars were interpreted as vital parts of the Whole and therefore of the tension in man himself. His realism ill affords a cutting away of one side (the violent, destructive side of human nature) of the Dual Descent pertaining to the Whole; his 'gay science' we must recall enunciates the justice of the Whole and its interdependent poles (of Apollo's bow) in order for us to be able to unreservedly affirm life in all its anguish, pain, and suffering. Only nobler, resentment-free souls can affirm such a life in the face of cycles of 'imaginary revenge' and the grand politics of revenge played out by both religious 'tribes' and scientific-technological civilizations.

Finally and fifthly, we may ask the question whether to 'live dangerously' a century and a quarter later is a responsible normative proposition? Nietzsche's declared realism—his resolute anti-romanticism and anti-idealism—would seem to point to the necessity of life being lived in such a manner for without dangerousness there may be no 'harvesting' of the 'greatest fruitfulness and the greatest enjoyment' from existence (GS 283). Moreover, the joyful dance of his *gaya scienza* which grasps the Dual Descent in all things may be endangered if it is robbed of this vital component. Why? Because chance, the wanderer's venture, willing, the religious impetus to transfiguration, and the 'blood' in human cultivation ('breeding') may be precluded from social life itself. Is it not reasonable to suppose that a more pacific ethos would be more ethical? To eschew the dangers of violence and everyday conflict would surely be more civilized; that is, more moral. There are two distinct problems with this line of argument. First, it is the illusion of a rationalist moralist that life in all its complex chaos can be pacified and tamed so it is rid of every conceivable danger. In fact, to attempt to rid the world of all forms of danger—as modern utilitarian neo-liberalism appears inclined toward—is to dangerously court fate with the possibility that you may in fact amplify or distort further what it is you wish to eradicate. The danger lies therefore in the rationalistic ideal to live *un*dangerously by forcing others to renounce dangerous life that is inherently dangerous, explosive and unpredictable. This fundamental moral shortcoming is not groundless but rather grounded in the moralist's psycho-social investment in the tamed human-animal (which we examined in 'Nietzsche as Civilization Analyst'). Being a product of the cage that socialized the animal spirit into a tamed 'civilized' creature, the moralist-rationalist as philosopher begins to believe—that is, have faith in—in the power of the will to eliminate all undesirable facets of existence, with the help of the spirit of the state. To use the instrument of the state and/or religious piety under the guise of redemption to take revenge against the cruelty of life is yet another form of sublimated revenge. Engineering life (*bios*) to purify it of evil and its dangers is another kind of politics of revenge—it retaliates against the one-sided ugliness of life in order to fulfill a redemptive will to completion that is the *raison d'etre* of modernity. Spreading 'democracy' throughout the world has parallels with the old colonialist *noblesse oblige*.

The second problem with the argument (of the rationalist-moralist) is the arrogance of its *aprioristic* claim on eternity, on futural time. It wildly assumes, for instance, the consequences of our no longer having to live with danger(s) are both knowable and entirely desirable, that is, without fault and wholly consistent with the Good. An inherent danger resides paradoxically in the desire to eradicate evil from the face of the earth on the basis of a metaphysics slanted toward a partial, this-sided perspective on the *totality*[24] of life. The challenge of the joyful *Wissenshaft* is in fact to recognize the necessity of all dimensions of human existence and their recurrence on earth while still being prepared to affirm life regardless of human suffering and danger. To eschew the totality of life is to delude ourself of the 'capricious laws' of nature (and society); it is to lapse into the unfreedom of romantic-idealism and its concomitant feeble (reactive) soul. Second, to suppose the elimination of violence, evil and danger from the world must be 'positive' is to usurp the divine position of 'God' as it claims to know with foresight that formative developments of the spirit of man—issuing from recurrence of suffering and danger—will not be endangered by this severe truncation. It is to destine into futural time a determined image of man that is comprised on one side by the will to knowledge's predictive power to control *natura* while on the other side a certain Augustinian-Kantian prejudice against the ugly, poisonous side of human nature leads to its metaphysical decapitation. The abovementioned 'will to completion' is consequently supported by a positivist science and a metaphysical truncation of the evil half of the Whole; and this double tyranny upon the conditions of existence restricts the possibilities of futural becoming because the revenge of the present perpetuates evil even whilst it seeks to negate it by means of both metaphysics and scientific determinism. Hence although western powers may scornfully look upon some Arabs as trying to reinvent God in the 'proper place' of politics, it can be argued that the spirit of revenge and the state of the spirit (American Christianity and Muslim theocracy) are mutually entwined on both sides.

What is more, a second level of intertwinement exists between the two opposing 'spirits of revenge' and their attendant state-religions, i.e. political sublimation. *Zusammensein* (being together) is only perversely manifested here because as nihilists engaged in the politics of revenge, neither side can be with or live alongside 'the evil one'; yet the activity of warring pulls them into a reactive (negative) form of *Zusammensein* simply because of their intertwinement. For Nietzsche what is of uppermost importance is the generative tension which binds such opposites into a struggle for mastery. On each side broods the spirit of revenge, sublimated in the politics of faith and the will to avenge a form of injustice, while each tribe claims Justice requires retribution and punishment. As we have already seen, Nietzsche conceived of punishment as the product of a) a weak, sickened spirit and b) as an outgrowth of a pernicious will to revenge that is otherwise cloaked as moral rectitude. Thus acts of retribution in the contemporary world in the form of suicide bombings, mass bombing, extreme or severe punishment, torture of an enemy, and declarations such as 'You are either with us or against us' (President George W. Bush) signify feebleness and servitude to one's instincts for revenge.

This is entirely counterfactual to the realm of appearance: both sides appear strong and determined (willed) to realize their ideals and yet the reality is quite the contrary. The claimed 'noble' cause of defending civilization and freedom for the modern world is another illusion in the hall of mirrors which also shatters the false image portrayed by radical Islamicist leaders who pronounce the abovesaid acts as 'holy' (*jihad*). Ignobility is the mark of such souls and states (tribes) despite appearances of holiness and sacral authorization from 'God' or more precisely one's *Sitten* (customs, mores). Against both God and nature, this highly dangerous existence owes to a political sublimation of a once primordial instinct of revenge, its metamorphosis into what I call the 'spirit of the state-religion'; and finally its transmogrification into an 'imaginary revenge' associated with the spiritualization of the world through the 'metaphysician's faith' we have examined here. Tension and dangerousness therefore go together in life, as Nietzsche sought to show; however, it contradicts—as it rightly should—the metaphysics of the idyllic vision of a 'free will' reigning over this-worldly matters and its *human-all-too-human* aspects. 'Freedom of will' in reality proves highly dangerous and explosive without the noble ethos of responsibility, particularly once it is attached to the politics of revenge and its necessary construction of an 'evil one'. Hence, although modern liberal philosophy rejects the idea of living dangerously in existential-ethical terms, it ironically and perhaps tragically reproduces danger in the modern world. To complete the project of annihilating forms of danger and illiberal 'extremism' it inadvertently reproduces the conditions of its own nihilistic idealization. When Nietzsche wrote of the German's 'romantic pessimism' he had not (as yet) envisaged its transplantation onto the world stage: can we say now that romantic pessimism (apropos Schopenhauer and Wagner) is better identified in the desire of those great powers to bring a completion to the end of tyranny through egalitarian democratic values, i.e. a generalized 'slave revolt' as ending history? Yet this raises the alloyed question of whether the democratic slave as Master will only incite a countervailing 'slave revolt' from those who possess a counter *faith* in values antipodal to the Master's. That is, can the tension presently evincible in the politics of faith and the politics of revenge on the world stage produce yet another overturning which finds 'master' democratic (western) values toppled by heretofore 'slave values'?

Given that political sublimation necessarily involved a spiritualization of the will to revenge in the form of the 'spirit of the state', the definitive tension of our *zeitgeist* may in fact see a contestation occur on the basis of the politics of faiths, not between the 'sacred and the profane' as commonly thought but their synthesis in two divergent types vying for mastery. Instead of ethical autonomy coming forth the world stage may see a recurrence of 'evil' against 'good' whereby both faith-structured political 'tribes' shall seek to claim the moral Good for their expressed will. In the guise of nobility, moralists from either side of this world conflict may well overshadow those of ethical conscience who uncoincidentally go (again) misrecognized. The will to err and to self-deception—being aspects of human nature and the Whole itself—appear integral to the conditions of a 'freedom of the will' and the very tension that sustains it in time. To know this as does the 'knower' of joyful wisdom is to eschew idealism in the realm of the *human-all-too-human* and to understand that 'becoming' necessarily is fraught with tension, growth and the agonistic struggle for freedom in so many master-slave *re*valuations of life. "Let us transcend nonetheless," says calmly the noble one. Transposing and, more importantly, surpassing the finitude of being human is the active part of *faith*—that element which is expressly found in the affirmative *amor fati* of life but is also discerned in those who experience the pathos of (everyday) life and can therefore make and see the promises of the future. Nietzsche's Platonic counter to Christian faith leaves its trace: man is caught between past and future, finitude and eternity, and the *pistis* of the soul and power of *physus*. Like Pythagorean Platonism, Nietzsche finds religion not an antithesis to refined cultivation but a further spiritual catalyst: the philosopher as free spirits understand him is one who, having the 'conscience for the over-all development of man' makes 'use of religions for his project of cultivation and education' because he is a 'man of the most comprehensive responsibility' (BGE 61). Can the mass carnage of innocent lives be understood as a sign of such noble 'comprehensive responsibility'? What Nietzsche's quasi-Christian Platonic faith acknowledges here is that the 'selective and cultivating influence' exerted 'with the help of religions, is always multiple and different according to the *sort of human beings* who are placed under its spell and protection' (BGE 61; emphasis added). That is, decadents and masters respond differently and this entails the possibility that only some may be afforded the capacity for the most 'comprehensive responsibility'. Finitude in human nature form-giving will undoubtedly restrict some, stunting their soul-amplification and thus impeding the art of governing their own lives. Like Plato, Nietzsche seems to agree that she or he who is unable to practice the art of government over oneself[25] cannot legitimately lay claim to governing others' lives—at least not *responsibly*.

Self-cultivation and *bios* are then inextricably bound together in the city of man. However, what is the status of 'faith' in this constellation in which man finds itself between past and future, decadence and redemption, and faith and science? If Nietzsche signifies the make-up of Yes-sayers, as against nihilists, that is those embarking on new seas by virtue of being 'compelled to do this by...*faith*' no less, then what is meant by the proposition (in an earlier passage) that 'Faith is always coveted most and needed most urgently where will is lacking' (GS 377 & 347)? What is critical here is to discern *whose* faith and hence a faith in *what*. This is consistent with the abovementioned reference to the 'sort of human beings' placed under the spell of religious cultivation. In the latter passage of *Gay Science* Nietzsche clearly is referring to those weakly human natures that require a prop of some kind, just as the 'demand for certainty' is the unique metaphysical prop of positivistic science. Both science and religion in searching for complete certitude and promising purity of knowledge share one essential ignoble characteristic: 'that *instinct of weakness*' (GS 347). Nietzsche moves on to say that fanaticism is also caught up in the 'metaphysical need' of 'the people' and succeeds in its soteriological promise because when the will has become exhausted ascetic religion offered people support. Fanatical faith in an otherworldly condition besides provides 'a new possibility of willing, some delight in willing' (GS 347) thereby reconstituting a diseased spirit and giving futural hope to an emancipation from one's helplessness. Since will 'is the decisive sign of sovereignty and strength', they lack the 'affect of command' which is will. In lacking will they desire it; they desire the affect of command in order to gain sovereignty. Hence sovereignty is conflated with that which returns will(ing) to exhausted human natures, namely the pious faith that is offered up as release from impermanent world. Faith is eternal yet man's condition is finite, fleeting and injurious owing to force—the power and will of their master. Nietzsche appears to grasp the powerful 'spiritual' saliency of faith in sustaining and cultivating future noble spirits who are free in *this* world. And it is this aspect of Nietzsche's conception of the soul and eternal time that arguably is different to the ancients, the pagans of theism: it is a Nietzschean quasi-Christian free-spiritedness.

Just as Nietzsche paid honor to Platonism by attempting to overthrow it, his revaluation of Christianity's moralism unwittingly sublimates key Christian mystical motifs and values. The overcoming of nihilism—instigated by religious metaphysics—returns to him the necessity of his own spiritual growth, cultivation and self-overcoming[26]: a Protestant critical faith in a self that reconstitutes its world. Overcoming necessitates a 'pruning' of that which grew out of the soil of his native spiritual *Grund*; and when Nietzsche pruned the branches of Platonic metaphysics he preserved the *faith* of Christian spiritualism in opposition to the finitude of Being and the custom of morality. This kind of 'faith', as opposed to faith as a 'sort of hypnotism of the whole system of the senses and the intellect for the benefit of an excessive nourishment (hypertrophy) of a single point of view and feeling that henceforth becomes dominant', does not issue forth from 'a tremendous collapse' and '*disease of the will*' (GS 347). Nor does it obtain in a desperate 'delight in willing' owing to a precursory enfeeblement of man and its attendant weakness of spirit, the latter sustaining the commanding position of spiritual directors[27] and hence unfreedom. So what *is* Nietzsche's 'faith'? What is different or distinctive about it (just as his 'responsibility' can be distinguished from conventional liberal notions of it)? Nietzsche does not shirk the question, but instead posits a counter faith that is wholly consistent with his Dual Descent approach. Namely, a 'pleasure and power of self-determination, such a *freedom* of the will that the spirit would take leave of all [such] faith and every wish for certainty, being practiced in maintaining himself on insubstantial ropes and possibilities and dancing even near the abysses' (GS 347). This counter "liberated" faith which eschews certitude and yet embraces man's dangerous traversals of the abyssal is only found in that specially cultivated, pruned and prepared human being: 'Such a spirit would be the *free* spirit par excellence' (GS 347). A free spirit in Nietzsche's sense is not one which is free *from* something but that which possesses a noble soul. And what is decisive in the noble soul 'is the *faith*' that determines the 'order of rank' and not 'works' or actions; that is, the *archē* of valuations and drives in accordance with 'an ancient religious formula in a new and profound sense' [faith]: the 'fundamental certainty that a noble soul has about itself' because the '*noble soul has reverence for itself*' (BGE 287).[28]

Notes

1. Often Nietzsche is accused of maintaining an overly monistic conception of life, one that celebrates solitude, the uncommitted 'wanderer', and a Protestant idea of human subjectivity. Yet we should recall Nietzsche's important statements about the 'tamed animal' of civil-contract relationships and, equally, the status of consciousness vis-à-vis *Dasein*: "My idea is, as you see, that consciousness does not really belong to man's individual existence but rather to his social or herd nature'; and 'It was only as a social animal that man acquired self-consciousness' (GS 354). Moreover, as soon as uniquely individual actions are translated 'into consciousness *they no longer seem to be*' (354).

2. In 'On Redemption' (of *Zarathustra*) Nietzsche describes the metamorphosis of the will into a 'great folly' that is now a 'curse for everything human' since it now has 'acquired spirit': 'Thus the will, the liberator, took to hurting; and on all who can suffer he wreaks revenge for his inability to go backwards. This, indeed this alone, is what *revenge* is: the will's ill will against time and its 'it was''. This passage sheds light on the imperative, stated at various times, to take hold of what is necessary ("that which is necessary in life") and assimilate into one's 'fate'. Destiny is composed of the necessary 'past' and the promise of futural time, but importantly it is imperative not to become alienated or embittered by forces constitutive of your 'it was', one's origins and genealogy. Once again, this appears very close to naturalistic fatalism while in fact—as we have argued all along—it is wholly consistent with the growth-cultivating language (and metaphors) of Nietzsche the gardener-philosopher whose ideal was the affirmation of life.

3. An excellent account of the problem of time expressed in terms of the 'past' and 'future' of revenge-taking is given by Joan Stambaugh in *The Problem of Time in Nietzsche*. Translated by John F. Humphrey. London/Toronto: Bucknell University Press, 1987, Ch 3.

4. The *Übermensch* (overman) is the very antithesis of the man of *ressentiment*—an underprivileged figure who languishes under the weight of resentment and its attendant revengeful politics. Thus Nietzsche linked the drive to equality to a form of self-hatred that saw the politics of envy underlying every democratic push to equilibrate social relations as particularly evil and lowly. To eschew the commanding power of an overcoming

spirit is not to obey oneself; but to obey is ultimately easier 'than to command because commanding requires responsibilities which in turn presuppose a freedom to obey oneself. C.f. Walter Kaufmann's useful statement on revenge in *Nietzsche: Philosopher, Psychologist, Antichrist* (Fourth Edition: 372): 'To have claws and not use them, and above all to be above any *ressentiment* or desire for vengeance, that is, according to Nietzsche, the sign of true power'.

5. C.f. Emile Durkheim *The Division of Labor in Society*. Translated by W. D. Halls. New York: Free Press, 1984.

6. Throughout his writings, Nietzsche used the metaphor of light and heavy spirits— a pathos that is either weighed down or lifted high above the nihilistic despair and pessimism of existence. Noble spirits are most decidedly high, light spirits who elevate themselves above the average 'everydayness' of self-preservation. Instead of lapsing into the dire *human-all-too-human* condition as he described it in a book of the same title, such spirits of the kind *Mensch* dance on the earth with light, joyous yet skillful, intelligent feet. Joyful wisdom is thwarted by the negative affects of resentment, guilt and envy; therefore, knowing becomes important for the noble spirit who can transcend the false reality of *this* 'will to life'.

7. As early as HH, Nietzsche's unwavering meta-psychological view of contending vital forces that direct human conduct becomes manifest: '…it is in *his* affects that he is most moral; higher excitation presents him with quite novel motivations which, in his more usual cold and sober state, he would perhaps not even believe himself capable of. How does this come about? Probably through the proximity to one another of all great and highly exciting things' (I: 138).

8. For a discussion of the important theoretical links between Nietzsche and Schopenhauer, see further *Willing and Nothingness: Schopenhauer as Nietzsche's Educator*. Edited by Christopher Janaway. Oxford/New York: Clarendon Press, 1998.

9. In BGE (109) 'necessity' and grand politics are logically intertwined: 'The time for petty politics is over: the very next century will bring the fight for the dominion of the earth—the *compulsion* to large-scale politics'.

10. Consistent with the Second Part of HH, Nietzsche declares in the essay on "Good and Evil," "Good and Bad" (GM I:8): 'You don't have eyes for something that has taken two thousand years to achieve victory? . . . . There is nothing to wonder at in this: all *lengthy* things are difficult to see, to see in their entirety'.

11. Nietzsche agreed with Gottfried Leibniz's assessment of consciousness as a relatively limited and weak component of the universe and its operations. He saw Leibniz indeed as an untimely thinker whose insightful intelligence would take another 200 years to be fully realized and absorbed.

12. We have already examined Nietzsche's view of nature in an earlier chapter, noting that he found her 'indifferent' and stingy to enormous degree. This counters the commonplace naturalistic view of him and not merely its poor cousin, viz materialism. Nietzsche's Spinozian naturalism is countervailed by his deep-seated artistic conception of the will and drive, and therefore distinctly human possibility for growth (gardener's cultivation).

13. *Tyrannos* in Greek stands for the commanding lawgiver, leader or ruler who knows how to exercise governance over the Hellenic body-politic. A ruler, for example Pericles or Solon, was the *megalos* (great) *arche* (origin, authority) of the city-state whose *Bios* (life) depended on the wilful drive of its ruler. And Nietzsche the philologist appropriated this Greek concept in part to distance his conception from that of the *Reich*'s 'grand politics'.

14. Daniel W. Conway *Nietzsche and the Political*. London: Routledge, 1997, ch 3.

15. Conway, *Nietzsche and the Political*, 77.

16. C.f Leiter *Nietzsche On Morality,* 142. Conspicuous in this otherwise incisive treatment is the pivotal role of the divine, mystical or spiritual dimension of life which Nietzsche's thinking consistently evinces.

17. Tracy B. Strong *Friedrich Nietzsche and the Politics of Transfiguration*. Expanded edition. Berkeley: University of California Press, 1988, 246.

18. Strong, *Friedrich Nietzsche and the Politics of Transfiguration*.

19. 'Untimely' refers here to that which has arrived 'before its time', that is, before it has become assimilated by 'the people' and usually requires a gestalt-switch of some kind.

20. In contradistinction to neo-Kantians, Nietzsche saw a beacon of light in the scientific-philosophical propositions of Leibniz who considered consciousness to be of far lesser importance in the constitution and fundamental operations of the universe. Nietzsche thought it would take at least another two centuries before educated minds could grasp the depth of Leibniz's insight.

21. In many studies an overdetermination of (will to) power, eternal recurrence, language, and the murder of God obscures or ignores the critical role of 'faith' in his exegesis of the human being and spirit (i.e. non-ascetic forms). For instance, in discussing 'what is noble' and the identification of nobler human beings under the heavy 'overcast sky of the beginning rule of the plebs that makes everything opaque and leaden', Nietzsche refers the reader not to actions or 'works' but instead to faith in the determination of 'order of rank'. 'It is not the works, it is the *faith* that is decisive here, that determines the order of rank' vis-à-vis 'some fundamental certainty that a noble soul has about itself' (BGE 287). Both Jaspers (1961) and Roberts (1998) are notable exceptions yet differ in both their aim and departure-point from the present study.

22. As argued above, acts of revenge not only vent feelings of anger and resentment but also give purpose and symbolic meaning to the source of one's suffering. Against British physiology, Nietzsche maintained that suffering is not itself repudiated—as evidenced by the will to self-torture—but rather the value or meaning associated with it. Taking revenge is thus fuelled by the *sense* of an injustice carried out against 'us' and the will to find an object which can be made 'accountable' (responsible).

23. Its foremost exponent is Brian Leiter (as discussed in previous chapters), c.f. *Nietzsche On Morality*. Routledge: London, 2002.

24. As early as *Human All Too Human* (1878) we find the anti-Romantic Nietzsche an exponent of 'the most universal knowledge' and the 'evaluation of the totality of existence' (436).

25. Before *Beyond Good and Evil* in book IV of *Gay Science* (300), Nietzsche had already observed: 'one might ask—would man ever have learned without the benefit of such a religious training and pre-history to experience a hunger and thirst for *himself*, and to find satisfaction and fullness in *himself*?' This is consonant with Plato's Pythagoreanism.

26. In the Preface to the second volume of *Human All Too Human* (1-2) Nietzsche refers to his work as speaking '*only* of my overcomings' as a 'continuation and redoubling of a spiritual cure'; and finally, for the anti-romantic purposes of 'good health' to 'teach their precepts more powerfully and clearly...to the more spiritual natures of the generation just coming up as a *disciplina voluntatis*'.

27. For a discussion of the concept of spiritual directors, c.f. John Mandalios *Civilization and the Human Subject*, Lanham: Rowman & Littlefied, 1999.

28. When trust breaks down between opposing herd-members and requital and exchange are vanquished, Nietzsche leaves us not with power-quanta or vital drive excesses but rather with the mystic's phenomenology of *Geist-wissenschaft* 'in a new and more profound sense'. This further challenges a purely naturalistic or empirical outlook on our worldly *pathos*. Nietzsche's 'faith' it could be said rests partly in that which constitutes freedom (a là neo-Kantians Schelling and Hegel): 'freedom here understood as facility in *self-direction*' (WP 705).

Bibliography

Agamben, Giorgio. 2002. 'The Time That Is Left'. *Epoché* 1, 7 (Fall):1-14.

Abbey, Ruth. 2000. *Nietzsche's Middle Period*. New York: Oxford University Press.

Adorno, Theodore and Horkheimer, Max. 1979. *Dialectic of Enlightenment*. Trans. John Cumming. London: Verso.

Arendt, Hannah. 1978. *The Life of the Mind*. Volume Two. *Willing*. New York: Harcourt Brace Jovanovich.

Badiou, Alain. 1999. *Manifestations of Philosophy*. Trans. Norman Madarasz. Albany: State University of New York.

Bauer, Karin. 2004. 'Nietzsche, Enlightenment, and the Incomplete Project of Modernity' in *Habermas, Nietzsche, and Critical Theory*, ed. Babette E. Babich. New York: Humanity Books: 105-122.

Boscovich, Roger J. 1966. *A Theory of Natural Philosophy*. Trans. James M. Child. Cambridge: MIT Press.

Boyle, Nicholas. 2000. *Goethe: The Past and the Age*. Volume Two. *Revolution and Renunciation*. Oxford: Clarendon Press.

Clark, Maudemarie. 1990. *Nietzsche on Truth and Philosophy*. Cambridge: Cambridge University Press.

———. 1994. 'Nietzsche's Immoralism and the Concept of Morality' in *Nietzsche, Genealogy, Morality: Essays on Nietzsche's Genealogy of Morals*, ed. Richard Schacht. Berkeley: University of California Press.

———. 2000 'Nietzsche's Doctrine of the Will to Power: Neither Ontological Nor Biological'. *International Studies in Philosophy* 32: 119–136.

———. 2001. 'On the Rejection of Morality: Bernard Williams's Debt to Nietzsche' in *Nietzsche's Postmoralism: Essays on Nietzsche's Prelude to Philosophy's Future*, ed. Richard Schacht. Cambridge: Cambridge University Press: 100-122.

Clark, Maudemarie and Leiter, Brian. 1997. 'Introduction', in *Daybreak: Thoughts on the Prejudices of Morality*. Trans. R. J. Hollingdale. Ed. Maudemarie Clark and Brian Leiter. Cambridge: Cambridge University Press.

Clark, Maudemarie and Dudrick, David. 2004. 'Nietzsche's Post-Positivism'. *European Journal of Philosophy* 12 (3): 369-385.

Conway, Daniel. W. 1997. *Nietzsche and the Political*. London: Routledge.

Deleuze, Gilles. 1983. *Nietzsche and Philosophy*. Trans. Hugh Tomlinson. New York: Columbia University Press.

Dennett, Daniel. 1995. *Darwin's Dangerous Idea: Evolution and the Meanings of Life*, Ringwood: Penguin Books.

Durkheim, Emile. 1984. *The Division of Labor in Society*. Trans. W. D. Halls. New York: Free Press.

Eisenstadt, Shmuel. N. 1987. *European Civilization in a Comparative Perspective*. Oslo: Norwegian.

Elias, Norbert. 1983. *The Court Society*. Trans. Edmund Jephcott. Oxford: Basil Blackwell .

———. 1982. *The Civilizing Process*. Two Volumes. Trans. Edmund Jephcott. Oxford: Basil Blackwell.

Fink, Eugen. 2003. *Nietzsche's Philosophy*. Trans. Goetz Richter. London: Continuum.

Frank, Manfred. 1989. *What is Neo-Structuralism*? Trans. Sabine Wilke and Richard Gray. Minneapolis: University of Minnesota Press.

Haar, Michel. 1996. *Nietzsche and Metaphysics*. Trans. and ed. Michael Gendre. Albany: State University of New York Press.

Habermas, Jurgen. 1982. 'The Entwinement of Myth and Enlightenment: Re-Reading the Dialectic of Enlightenment'. *New German Critique* 26: 13-30.

———. 1987. 'The Entry in Postmodernity: Nietzsche as Turning Point', *The Philosophical Discourse of Modernity*. Trans. Frederick Laurence. Cambridge, Mass.: MIT Press.

———. 1987. *The Philosophical Discourse of Modernity*. Trans. Frederick Laurence. Cambridge, Mass.: MIT Press.

Heidegger, Martin. 1962. *Being and Time*. Trans. John Macquaries and Edward Robinson. Oxford: Blackwell.

———. 1991. *Nietzsche*. Volumes One-Four. Trans variously: David F. Krell (1-2); Joan Stambaugh, David F. Krell and Frank A. Capuzzi (3); Frank A. Capuzzi (4). Ed. David F. Krell. New York: HarperCollins.

———. 1993. 'The End of Philosophy and the Task of Thinking', *Basic Writings*. Revised and expanded edition. Ed. David F. Krell. London: Routledge.

———. 1993. *Basic Writings*. Revised and expanded edition. Ed. David F. Krell. London: Routledge.

Honderich, Ted. 2004. 'After Compatibilism and Incompatibilism', in *Freedom and Determinism*, ed. Joseph K. Campbell, Michael O'Rourke and David Shier. London: MIT Press.

Honneth, Axel. 1995. *The Struggle For Recognition: The Moral Grammar of Social Conflicts*. Trans. Joel Anderson. Cambridge, Mass.: Polity Press.

Hutter, Horst. 2006. *Shaping the Future: Nietzsche's New Regime of the Soul and Its Ascetic Practices*. Lanham: Lexington Books.

Jaeger, Werner. 1943. *Paideia: the Ideals of Greek Culture*. Volume Two. *In Search of the Divine Centre*. Trans. Gilbert Highet. New York: Oxford University Press.

Janaway, Christopher, ed. 1998. *Willing and Nothingness: Schopenhauer as Nietzsche's Educator*. Oxford/NewYork: Clarendon Press.

Jaspers, Karl. 1961. *Nietzsche: an Introduction to the Understanding of His Philosophical Activity*. Trans. Charles F. Wallraff and Frederick J. Schmitz. South Bend: Gate way.

Kant, Immanuel. 1933. *Critique of Pure Reason*. Trans. Norman Kemp Smith. Second edition. London/Basingstoke: Macmillan.

———. 1997. *Groundwork of the Metaphysics of Morals*. Trans. and ed. Mary Gregor. Cambridge: Cambridge University Press.

Kaufmann, Walter. 1974. *Nietzsche: Philosopher, Psychologist, Anti-Christ*. Fourth Ed. Princeton: Princeton University Press.

———. 1976. *The Portable Nietzsche*. Trans and selected, with an introduction,Walter Kaufmann. London: Penguin.

Kirk, Geoffrey S. and Raven, John E, eds. 1983. *The Presocratic Philosophers*. Second edition. Cambridge: Cambridge University Press.

Klossowski, Pierre. 2005. *Nietzsche and the Vicious Circle*. Trans. Daniel W. Smith. London: Continuum.

Leiter, Brian. 2002. *Nietzsche On Morality*. London: Routledge.

———. 2001. 'The Paradox of Fatalism and Self-Creation in Nietzsche', in *Nietzsche*, ed. John Richardson and Brian Leiter. Oxford: Oxford University Press.

Levinas, Emmanuel. 1969. *Totality and Infinity: An Essay on Exteriority*. Trans. Alphonso Lingis. Pittsburgh: Duquesne University Press.

———. 1989. *The Levinas Reader*. Ed. Sean Hand. Oxford: Blackwell Publishers.

Löwith, Karl. 1997. *Nietzsche's Philosophy of the Eternal Recurrence of the Same*. Trans. J. Harvey Lomax. Berkeley: University of California Press.

Mandalios, John. 1999. *Civilization and the Human Subject*. Lanham/Oxford: Rowman and Littlefield.

McIntyre, Alex. 1997. *The Sovereignty of Joy: Nietzsche's Vision of Grand Politics*. Toronto: University of Toronto Press.

Müller-Lauter, Wolfgang. 1999. *Nietzsche: His Philosophy of Contradictions and the Contradictions of His Philosophy*. Trans. David J. Parent. Urbana: University of Illinois Press.

Nehamas, Alexander. 1985. *Nietzsche: Life as Literature*. Cambridge, Mass.: Harvard University Press.

Nelson, Benjamin. 1969. *The Idea of Usury: From Tribal Brotherhood to Universal Otherhood*. Second edition. Chicago: University of Chicago Press.

Nietzsche, Friedrich. 1989. *Beyond Good and Evil*. Trans. Walter Kaufmann. New York: Vintage Books.

———. 1997. *Daybreak: Thoughts on the Prejudices of Morality*. Trans. R. J. Hollingdale. Ed. Maudemarie Clark and Brian Leiter. Cambridge: Cambridge University Press.

———. 1996. *Human, All Too Human One & Two*. Trans. R. J. Hollingdale. Cambridge: Cambridge University Press.

———. 1967. *The Birth of Tragedy*. Trans. with commentary, Walter Kaufmann. New York: Vintage Books.

———. 1962. *Philosophy in the Tragic Age of the Greeks*. Trans. Marianne Cowen. Washington DC.: Regenary Publishing.

———. 1968. *The Anti-Christ*. Trans. R. J. Hollingdale. Harmondsworth: Penguin.

———. 1974. *The Gay Science*. Trans. Walter Kaufmann. New York: Vintage Books.

———. 1968. *The Will to Power*. Trans. Walter Kaufmann and R. J. Hollingdale. Ed. Walter Kaufmann. New York: Vintage Books.

———. 1967. *Ecce Homo*. Trans. Walter Kaufmann. New York: Vintage.

———. 1968. *Twilight of the Idols*. Trans. R. J. Hollingdale. Harmondsworth: Penguin.

———. 1976. *Twilight of the Idols*. Trans. Walter Kaufmann. *The Portable Nietzsche*. Trans. and selected Walter Kaufmann. London: Penguin.

———. 1995. *Unfashionable Observations*. Trans. Richard T. Gray. Stanford: Stanford University Press.

——— 1998. *On the Genealogy of Morality*. Trans. with Introduction and Notes Maudemarie Clark and Alan J. Swensen. Indianapolis: Hackett Publishing.

———. 1978. *Thus Spoke Zarathustra: A Book for All and None*. Trans. Walter Kaufmann. New York: Penguin Books.

———. 1995. *Human All Too Human, I*. Trans. Gary Handwerk. Stanford: Stanford University Press.

————. 1990. *Philosophy and Truth: Selections from Nietzsche's Notebooks of the Early 1870s*. Ed. and trans. Daniel Breazeale. New Jersey/London: Humanities Press.

————. 1995. *Unpublished Writings: from the period of Unfashionable Observations*. Trans. R.T. Gray. Stanford: Stanford University Press.

————. 2001. *The Pre-Platonic Philosophers*. Trans. Greg Whitlock. Urbana: University of Illinois Press.

Reginster, Bernard. 2006. *The Affirmation of Life: Nietzsche on Overcoming Nihilism*. Cambridge, Mass.: Harvard University Press.

Richardson, John. 1996. *Nietzsche's System*. Oxford: Oxford University Press.

Roberts, Tyler T. 1998. *Contesting Spirit*. Princeton: Princeton University Press.

Safranski, Rüdiger. 2003. *Nietzsche: A Philosophical Biography*. Trans. Shelley Frisch. London: Granta Books.

Schacht, Richard.1983. *Nietzsche* London: Routledge.

————. 1990. 'Philosophical Anthropology: What, Why and How'. *Philosophy and Phenomenological Research* 50 Fall: 155-176.

————. 1994. 'Of Morals and *Menschen*', in *Nietzsche, Genealogy, Morality: Essays on Nietzsche's Genealogy of Morals*, ed. Richard Schacht. Berkeley: University of California Press.

————. ed. 1994. *Nietzsche, Genealogy, Morality: Essays on Nietzsche's Genealogy of Morals*. Berkeley: University of California Press.

————. 1995. *Making Sense of Nietzsche: Reflections Timely and Untimely*. Chicago: University of Illinois Press.

————. 2001. 'Nietzschean Normativity', in *Nietzsche's Postmoralism: Essays on Nietzsche's Prelude to Philosophy's Future*, ed. Richard Schacht. Cambridge: Cambridge University Press.

————. ed. 2001. *Nietzsche's Postmoralism: Essays on Nietzsche's Prelude to Philosophy's Future*. Cambridge: Cambridge University Press.

Schelling, Friedrich W. J. 2002. *Philosophical Investigations Into the Nature of Human Freedom*. Revised translation. James Gutman. London: Living Time Press.

Schopenhaeur, Arthur. 1970. 'On the Indestructibility of Our Essential Being By Death', *Essays and Aphorisms*. Trans. R. J. Hollingdale. London: Penguin.

————. 1966. *The World as Will and Representation*. Two Volumes. Trans. E. F. Payne. New York: Dover Publications.

Simmel, Georg. 1991. *Schopenhauer and Nietzsche*. Trans. Helmut Loiskandl, Deena Weinstein and Michael Weinstein. Urbana: University of Illinois Press.

Small, Robin. 2001. *Nietzsche in Context*. Aldershot/Sydney: Ashgate.

————. 2001. 'Zarathustra's Four Ways: Structures of Becoming in Nietzsche's Thought'. *British Journal for the History of Philosophy* 9 (1): 83-107.

Snell, Bruno. 1982. *The Discovery of the Mind in Greek Philosophy and Literature*. Trans. T. G. Rosenmeyer. New York: Dover Publications.

Solomon, Robert. 2002. 'Nietzsche on Fatalism and "Free Will"'. *Journal of Nietzsche Studies* 23: 63-87.

Stambaugh, Joan. 1987. *The Problem of Time in Nietzsche*. Trans. John F. Humphrey. London/Toronto: Bucknell University Press.

Strong, Tracy B. 1988. *Friedrich Nietzsche and the Politics of Transfiguration*. Expanded edition. Berkeley: University of California Press.

Strawson, Galen. 1994. 'The Impossibility of Moral Responsibility'. *Philosophical Studies* 75: 5-24.

Strawson, Peter F. 1962. 'Freedom and Resentment'. *Proceedings of the British Academy* 48:1-25.

Stauth, George and Turner, Bryan S. 1988. *Nietzsche's Dance*. Oxford: Basil Blackwell.

Urpeth, Jim and Lippitt, John, eds. 2000. *Nietzsche and the Divine*. Manchester: Clinamen Press.

White, Richard. 1994. 'Zarathustra and the Progress of Sovereignty: From the Overman to the Eternal Recurrence', *International Studies in Philosophy* 26 (3): 107-115.

Wiggershaus, Rolf. 2001. 'The Frankfurt School's "Nietzschean Moment"', *Constellations* 8 (1): 144-147.

INDEX

a priori, 38-39, 115, 124, 128, 132, 156, 159, 185, 198, 201, 205

Adorno, Theodore, 3, 4, 16

Aeschylus, 67, 75, 84

affect, 6, 9, 11, 22, 45, 61, 85, 89, 112, 116, 117, 119, 124, 127, 132, 140, 156, 160, 177, 179, 181, 182, 183, 184, 186, 190, 192, 202, 204, 207, 211, 216, 220, 222nn6-7

Agamben, Giorgio, 172n19

agon, 25, 41, 54, 56, 60, 65, 75, 76, 95, 104, 110, 117, 118, 119, 120, 194, 215, 219

Ανάγκη φύσιος, 109, 138

Anaxagoras, 70, 90

Anaximander, 62

anthropologic (-al), 17, 34-36, 40, 42-43, 45, 49, 50, 55-56, 63, 66, 68, 73-74, 76, 86, 87, 104, 125, 126, 128, 130, 155, 161, 163, 167, 182, 197

Apollo (-nian), 20, 58, 70, 73, 91-93, 110-11, 120, 127, 170, 216

apparent world, 115

appraising animal, 163, 165, 167, 169

arete, 52, 184, 215

Aristotle, 22, 40, 52, 61, 83, 84, 92, 105, 108, 113, 129

artist's plan, 22, 57, 106, 107, 109, 111, 139, 140, 161, 165, 189

atomon, 83

Badiou, Alain, 71

beauty (the beautiful), 24, 73, 75-76, 79n35, 87, 107, 111, 120, 121, 145, 171n7, 191, 199

becoming, xiii, 21, 26, 36, 45, 49, 54, 58, 63, 66-67, 69, 81, 82, 83, 84, 86, 89, 99, 103, 104, 107, 108, 109, 111, 113, 114, 116, 117, 118, 119, 124, 125, 126, 127, 129, 130, 131, 132, 133, 136, 138, 139, 140, 143, 144, 146, 148, 150, 151, 154, 157, 158, 159, 160, 163, 165, 167, 168, 169, 170, 171, 176, 183, 188, 197, 198, 199, 203, 205, 208, 209, 210, 214, 217, 219

Being, 3, 24, 33, 36, 45, 58, 62, 70, 72, 81, 84, 87, 89, 107, 124, 136, 152, 162, 173n24, 197, 212, 220

Bildung, 21, 34, 72, 82, 87-88, 98, 101n12, 106, 115, 118, 123, 133, 142, 166, 168, 184-86, 199, 209, 211, 215

bios, 15, 21, 34, 36, 39, 44, 51, 55, 65-66, 72, 76, 85, 106-7, 115, 118, 123-24, 132, 139-40, 150, 156, 166, 169, 171, 184, 200, 206, 209-10, 215, 217, 219, 222n13

black art, 190, 191, 192, 194

Boscovich, Roger, 55, 91

burden. *See* weight

Burkhardt, Jacob, 81, 109

caged (en-), 39, 50-51, 53, 55, 60, 64-65, 142, 181, 196, 210, 217

causa sui, 20, 23, 114, 121, 141-42, 152-53, 212

cause (and effect), 7-8, 10, 23, 30n22, 55, 78n29, 158, 183, 184, 185

chaos, 9, 74, 85, 106, 111-12, 118, 130, 195, 199, 205, 208, 216

Christ, xiv, 104, 146, 151

231

About the Author

John Mandalios is senior lecturer in philosophy at Griffith University, Australia. His research work and interests lie in German and Greek philosophy, and European philosophy including multidisciplinary modes of thought. He is the author of *Civilization and the Human Subject* (Rowman & Littlefield) and a contributor to *The Blackwell Companion to Social Theory* (Blackwell).